DEVELOPING

MANAGEMENT ABILITY

600 Questions and Answers

EARL G. PLANTY

Professor of Management, University of Illinois
Formerly Executive Counselor, Johnson & Johnson

J. THOMAS FREESTON

Personnel Director, Ethicon, Inc.

THE RONALD PRESS COMPANY

NEW YORK

Library of Congress Catalog Card Number: 54-7651

PRINTED IN THE UNITED STATES OF AMERICA

To Our Families

FOR THEIR ENCOURAGEMENT AND UNDERSTANDING

FOREWORD

As one travels across the length and breadth of this country, he cannot help but be impressed with its ever-expanding commercial and industrial enterprise. Beautiful new plants and entirely new industrial cities dot the landscape. We have the greatest productive capacity of any nation in the world, and a greater productive capacity than any previous civilization. However, as we look at these plants and offices and the communities that house them, we realize that it is not the buildings—the brick and mortar—that count, but the effort, ability and creativeness of the people inside them. These people, from the janitor to the chairman of the board, are responsible for the ever-improving standard of living for America and the world in general.

Our fabulous growth is, by and large, the result of the dynamic leadership of the industrial community—a leadership that has come to express itself in efforts to improve people at all levels of our business operations. Most good managements strive to improve continually their own performance and the performance of all who work with them. Today it is recognized that growth of the individual members of an organization leads to company progress and prosperity.

However, there are many problems in this process of growth and improvement. Questions are asked and must be answered. Messrs. Planty and Freeston have, from their own experience and the experiences of others, collected and answered many of those questions. In this book they give the answers which have proved highly successful in training and management development in Johnson & Johnson and its affiliated companies.

As long as American managers continue to grow in breadth and willingness to explore the path to better management techniques, we need have no fear for the future. This book promotes that growth.

PHILIP B. HOFMANN
Vice Chairman of the Board
Johnson & Johnson

New Brunswick, New Jersey
January 1, 1954

v

PREFACE

This book is a direct outgrowth of several thousand questions on training and management development which we have been asked over the past four years. Some were asked us when we lectured at training and management conferences in many parts of the country. Other questions came in by mail and by telephone, and many were the result of personal visits to New Brunswick by business executives and their associates. Some of our questioners were managers and executives interested in establishing or improving development facilities in their companies. Others sought help in developing themselves or their subordinates. Still others were concerned with industry-wide programs, with the program of a division of industry, or with the administration or teaching in an established program.

It soon became obvious to us that many questions kept recurring, that the majority of them had to do with specific problems, and that these problems affected all sorts of business enterprises. What we have done here is to make a careful selection of these repeatedly asked questions and provide practical-minded, self-help answers that embody both the ideas and practices most common among successful training men today, plus the working techniques we have evolved from our experiences in Johnson & Johnson and its affiliated companies. Except for occasional grammatical or structural improvement of the questions, they are given just as they were asked us. We have added about fifty to bridge gaps and provide continuity to the content.

We have organized this book so that it will be of equal usefulness to the reader who wants to progress from chapter to chapter and to the reader who will repeatedly take it off the shelf for help on specific problems. The questions in each chapter have a continuity which binds them together, yet each question and its answer is self-contained. The Bibliography groups together many references which our readers will find helpful as background material. Those who are interested in the more theoretical background to the many interesting problems of training and management development are especially referred to *Training Employees and Managers*, by Earl G. Planty, William S. McCord, and Carlos A. Efferson.

Readers of this book will quickly sense that we are not timid or uncertain about our position or methods. We have been factual and positive in tone but, because we welcome and respect different points of view, we cannot and do not make any arbitrary claim of finality for our methods and viewpoints.

We are indebted to many executives of Johnson & Johnson and its affiliated companies for the opportunity to use, here, some of the established and some of the experimental development activities carried on within their firms. We are also indebted to the training and personnel men within our family of companies who have helped to build training and development into a useful, practical adjunct of business administration.

We appreciate the assistance of the American Management Association in granting permission to quote from their publications, and are grateful for the contributions of many individuals to this book and to our philosophy regarding development and training. In particular, we wish to thank Lawrence A. Appley, American Management Association; E. Wight Bakke, Yale University; C. Kenneth Beach, Arabian American Oil Company; Thornton F. Bradshaw, Harvard University; Earl Brooks, Cornell University; Robert K. Burns, University of Chicago; William A. Borrie, Kaiser Aluminum & Chemical Corporation; Richard P. Calhoon, University of North Carolina; George B. Corless, Standard Oil Company of New Jersey; Robert R. Crow, Continental Oil Company; Peter F. Drucker, Management Consultant; Dean George R. Esterly, Rutgers University; Carlos A. Efferson, Kaiser Aluminum & Chemical Corporation; Frederick H. Harbison, University of Chicago; Ralph M. Hower, Harvard University; Schuyler D. Hoslett, Columbia University; Everett W. Jones, Technical Advisor, *The Modern Hospital;* William H. Kushnick, American Management Association; Louis W. Lerda, Esso Standard Oil Company; Myles L. Mace, Harvard University; John F. Mee, University of Indiana; Russell F. Moberly, Marquette University; Bernard Muller-Thym, McKinsey & Company; Charles A. Myers, Massachusetts Institute of Technology; Thomas G. Newton, Armstrong Cork Company; John M. Pfiffner, University of Southern California; Paul Pigors, Massachusetts Institute of Technology; John W. Riegel, University of Michigan; Virgil K. Rowland, Detroit Edison Company; William R. Spriegel, University of Texas; Robert Tannenbaum, University of California; Charles A. Waters, Prudential Insurance Company; and Dale Yoder, University of Minnesota.

EARL G. PLANTY
J. THOMAS FREESTON

New Brunswick
March, 1954

CONTENTS

PART I

Introduction to Development

CHAPTER | PAGE
1 DEFINITIONS AND VALUES 3
2 LEARNING AND TEACHING 13
3 LEADERSHIP 25

PART II

Methods of Development

4 THE MANAGEMENT AUDIT 37
5 THE GUIDED EXPERIENCE METHOD 54
6 THE CONFERENCE METHOD 63
7 JOB ROTATION 77
8 MULTIPLE MANAGEMENT 94
9 ROLE PLAYING 99
10 THE CASE STUDY METHOD 109
11 STAFF MEETINGS FOR DEVELOPMENT 125
12 MISCELLANEOUS DEVELOPMENT METHODS AND PROGRAMS . 137

PART III

Types of Development

13 EXECUTIVE DEVELOPMENT 167
14 SUPERVISORY DEVELOPMENT 200
15 MANAGEMENT TRAINEE PROGRAMS 229
16 GENERAL EDUCATION 249
17 ORIENTATION TRAINING 257
18 TRAINING FOR BREADTH AND CHANGE 279

CHAPTER		PAGE
19	SKILL TRAINING	283
20	DEVELOPMENT FOR RESEARCH, SCIENTIFIC, AND TECHNICAL PERSONNEL	303
21	PROMOTING SELF-DEVELOPMENT	309
22	HUMAN RELATIONS DEVELOPMENT	315

PART IV

Organizing and Operating Development

23	ORGANIZATION OF TRAINING OR DEVELOPMENT	337
24	DETERMINING NEEDS FOR DEVELOPMENT	348
25	SECURING ACCEPTANCE FOR TRAINING OR DEVELOPMENT	353
26	GETTING TRAINING OR DEVELOPMENT UNDER WAY	360
27	DUTIES AND RESPONSIBILITIES OF THE DIRECTOR OF TRAINING OR DEVELOPMENT	365
28	PREPARING THE FULL-TIME DIRECTOR OF TRAINING OR DEVELOPMENT AND HIS ASSOCIATES	374
29	TRAINING AND USING LINE AND STAFF OPERATING MEN IN THE PROGRAM	380
30	MECHANICS OF TRAINING	386

PART V

Evaluation

31	EVALUATING DEVELOPMENT ACTIVITIES	409
	BIBLIOGRAPHY	429
	INDEX	435

PART I

INTRODUCTION TO DEVELOPMENT

Chapter 1

DEFINITIONS AND VALUES

---

1   What Is the Distinction Between "Industrial Training" and "Development"?

The term "industrial training" has long been used to designate the learning activities of all levels of employees and of managers in business organizations. In recent years, however, use of the word "training" has more and more been restricted to activities of wage earners and operators, and "development" has been increasingly applied to the training of professional people, supervisors, and executives. This distinction is based upon levels served.

Now and then one meets a different attempt to distinguish between training and development. Here the difference is one of method. "Training" is considered to be formal, classroom, group activities and "development" is thought of as an individual and on-the-job approach.

Although these distinctions between "training" and "development" have some merit, we shall not follow them rigidly in this book. Development and training overlap. Both are practical phases of adult education. We therefore shall use these terms interchangeably when it suits our purpose to do so.

2   I Am Confused About What Is Meant by a Training or Development Program. Can You Help Me?

The words "training program" are used in at least four different senses:

1. A *training program* may refer to one specific course or series of meetings devoted to a particular problem or subject, such as communications, public speaking, business economics, machine

3

maintenance and repair, conference leadership, public relations, and product training. Each of these and many others are commonly referred to as training programs.

2. The term *training program* also may be comprehensive in meaning, denoting an organized curriculum made up of units like those described above and designed to meet the needs of particular groups of employees—secretaries, supervisors, engineers, and so on. Some of these are continuing programs covering a year or more, as the example shows:

Supervisor Training Program	*Secretarial Training Program*	*Personnel Interviewer Training Program*
(1) Human Relations	(1) Speed Typing	(1) The Employment Process
(2) Business Economics	(2) Advanced Dictation	(2) Recruitment
(3) Scientific Management	(3) Letter Writing	(3) The Patterned Interview
(4) Leadership	(4) Filing Refresher	(4) Reference Checks
(5) Industrial Engineering or Office Methods	(5) Public Relations	(5) Psychological Tests
(6) Public Speaking	(6) Office Management	(6) Personnel Administration
	(7) Telephone Technique	

3. A *training program* may be something much more informal than either of the preceding. It may involve no classes or lectures, or conferences, and no written teaching aids. Training and development activities may be conducted on the job, where they are carried on directly by the superior and his subordinates. In such a plan, training may be accomplished through guided experience, coaching, counseling, job rotation, committee assignments, just plain telling and demonstrating, setting good examples, etc. Informal as these activities are, they constitute a program as long as they are planned and carried out according to some established policy.

4. The term *training program* frequently denotes a combination of the preceding plans or programs with others, such as use of in-plant libraries, tuition refund plans for college and university studies, visits to other plants, staff meetings, multiple-management, understudy systems, magazine racks, and so on.

Part of the confusion that has existed about training programs and what they are comes from applying the words to a composite of all activities as in definition 4 and to its specific parts, as in definition 1, 2, and 3.

3   What Are the Different Types of Training?

Training (or development) may be classified in several ways, as shown by the following examples:

1. Classification by level in the company:
   a. Employee Training
   b. Management or Supervisory Training
   c. Technical or Professional Training
   d. Executive Development
2. Classification by broad traditional functions within the business:
   a. Sales Training
   b. Foremanship Training
   c. Public Relations Training
   d. Engineering Training
   e. Secretarial or Office Training
3. Classification by special functions, the titles indicating the specific work to be done:
   a. Filing
   b. Making Decisions
   c. Carton Sealing
   d. Policy Making
   e. Reprimanding
   f. Typing
   g. Office Management
   h. Job Instructor Training
   i. Motor Vehicle Repair
4. Classification as in schools and universities, with titles that indicate the course content or subjects:
   a. Human Relations
   b. Industrial Psychology
   c. Shop Mathematics
   d. Speech and Diction
   e. English Literature
   f. Accounting
   g. Business Economics
   h. Banking
   i. Business Organization
   j. Advanced Electronics

None of these classifications is better than the rest, and none is all-inclusive. It is regrettable that there is no good logical or psychological method for adequately classifying the kinds and types of training.

4   In Our Company Training or Development Stops with Skill Training of Production Operators. What Else Is There?

There are as many possibilities for training and development as there are facets of the human personality, or differences in work performed. In the past, management has regarded skill training as the type most urgently needed. During recent years, however, a broader and more realistic view of training needs has begun to prevail. As a result, courses as varied as those listed below have become commonplace in most progressive organizations. These exact titles are taken from the catalogs of a half-dozen businesses and industries, selected at random from the many that issue such publications.

Handling Grievances
American Values
Job Relations Training
Conference Leadership
Employment Interviewing
Job Instruction Training
Report Writing
Communications
Principles of Supervision
Job Methods Training
Laws of Learning
Counseling
Human Relations
Human Motivation
Production Scheduling
Quality Control
Cost Control
Time Budgeting
Safety and Fire Prevention
Company Organization
Standard Hour Incentive Plan
Suggestion Systems
Orientation to the Company
Budget Controls
Top Policy Formation
Financial Management
Business Cycles
Structure of the Economy

Flow Charts
Government Regulations
Safety
Merit Rating and Evaluations
Company Plans and Policies
Time Study
Discipline
Nuclear Physics
Listening
Cooperation and Teamwork
Employee Selection and Induction
Applied Psychology
Union Contract Interpretation
Interpretation of Annual Report
Blueprint Reading
Basic Economics
Job Evaluation
Case Studies on Business Policy
Forecasting
Retirement Plans
How a Business Operates
Good Housekeeping
Effective Use of Time
Productivity Measurements
Role Playing in Advanced
    Management
Capital Budgeting
Pricing
Dynamics of Organization

5   For Whom Is Training Intended?

It is intended for everybody, at all levels and in all functions of the enterprise. Training, once used only for skilled tradesmen and machine operators, is used by today's managers, who have learned to recognize their own deficiencies, face them frankly, and seek help in correcting them. Training, in its broad sense, is provided by management for four essential purposes:

1. To motivate ALL PEOPLE in the organization, from president to receptionist, so they will do their best.
2. To enable EVERYBODY IN THE COMPANY to pass on to their followers, with as little loss as possible, the skills and know-how that already exist within the organization.
3. To bring into the organization, FOR EVERY EMPLOYEE AT EVERY LEVEL, appropriate skills and ideas that are known and applied successfully outside the business, but do not yet prevail within it.
4. To help ALL EMPLOYEES keep pace with work methods, scientific discoveries, innovations in management, and new attitudes and points of view as they are developed in the years to come. Only thus can the best of the new thinking and practices be given a fair appraisal, a fair trial, and a meaningful application in commerce and industry.

6   Why Train?

We should train employees—and here the term includes managers and executives at all levels and in all branches of our operations—for two reasons: to help them perform better the work which they are doing and to prepare some of them for other and perhaps more responsible positions.

The reasons why we train—whether through guided experience or formal training in schools or classes outside the organization, whether for production workers or top executives—are the same:

A. To increase knowledge and skill.
B. To develop wholesome attitudes, satisfying to the individual, to his superiors, to his subordinates if he has any, and to the company in order to:
    1. improve each person's operating effectiveness and his feeling of worth and dignity in the organization.
    2. reduce costs.
    3. maintain and improve the competitive standing of the organization.

7   What Methods Are Most Often Used in Industrial Training or Development?

No one method is best for all areas and types of learning. Every available training method should be at the disposal of the industrial training department. In the early days of training the lecture method with limited discussion probably was used more extensively than any other. Then came a decade or two of over-reliance upon the conference method. Today the industrial training man, faced with the task of building broad attitudes and understandings as well as developing limited skills, must understand and be able to use a variety of training methods. Rotation, conference leadership, the syndicate system, workshops, lectures, role playing, the case-study method, staff meetings, vestibule training, guided experience and counseling probably are the most familiar methods, but they do not exhaust the list.

8   Isn't Experience the Best Teacher?

"Experience is the best teacher" is a phrase sometimes used to deprecate training. The facts are that *unguided* experience is costly and can be completely fruitless in improving men or operations. This is because individuals don't automatically and inevitably learn better ways from experience. They must be guided and assisted in choosing, utilizing, and evaluating their experiences. This guidance is provided by training. Unguided experience is as likely to teach bad habits as good ones. After a few years of experience, it may cease to teach anything at all. There is nothing more discouraging than to find a man who has spent five or ten years as an assistant foreman, for example, but who stopped learning from experience after his first year or two in the job. Training is needed to keep this man growing after his experience has ceased to serve him as a stimulus.

9   Why All the Present-Day Interest in Development?

There are a good many reasons for this. Some are:

1. The rapidity of change; the frequency with which old hands must learn new ways. This involves learning to live with each specific change as it comes along. More difficult than that, however, is learning to live happily in a social climate where change is more constant than stability.

2. The constant demand for increased productivity. This involves better and more work. It means—where physical labor is involved—better ideas and more efficient application of them where mental processes are more important in the work than physical skills. It means a clearer understanding of complex operations, or specializations, and of one's own part in the creation of a whole product or service. This leads to increased cooperation, teamwork, and respect for others and their needs.
3. The expense of raw materials and the cost of the partly finished article upon which any new operator works. Errors that are common in trial-and-error learning are more costly today than formerly because the product, whether it is a single item or an assembly of costly parts, has so high a value that training which will reduce loss through scrap, waste, and rejects is an economic necessity.
4. Social changes—unionization, legislation, higher educational standards—have stimulated interest in leadership training. Workers demand and expect more humanized treatment.

10 We Have Psychological Tests, the Patterned Interview and Careful Placement of New Employees to Help Guarantee That They Are Qualified and Successful. Our Employees Are Already Trained for Their Jobs When We Hire Them. Why Do We Need More?

This question is well answered in *Public Personnel Administration*,[1] where the authors list the following facts to justify training even under the conditions outlined in the question.

1. People are recruited largely for broad categories of jobs, not for each specific job, and therefore require orientation in the work of a particular agency or unit.
2. Programs rarely remain static, and the quickest way to adjust a going concern to such changes is through conscious, orderly training of its employees.
3. Training often accounts for the differences between organizations in such matters as knowledge of employees about the activities and rules of their total organization as well as their own jobs, courtesy and attitude of employees toward the public, interest of employees in their work, skill and speed in performing a service.
4. Occupational fields usually evolve. Neither medicine, nor engineering, nor accounting, nor even stenography remains quite the same.

[1] William E. Mosher, J. Donald Kingsley, and O. Glenn Stahl, *Public Personnel Administration* (New York: Harper & Bros., 1950), p. 389.

Training is the process through which specialists can keep abreast of their specialty as well as avoid the limitations of the expert.

5. It is more efficient to improve the skills of existing employees to a maximum than to rely solely on initial recruitment to provide a hypothetical supply of the highest-skilled available.

6. It is important, in order to achieve cohesiveness and coordination in a company, for employees to understand the aims and functions of the rest of the organization, not by chance or in fragments, but by an orderly presentation of policies and programs that builds mutual respect and confidence.

7. Films, talks, interesting reading materials, systematic tutoring, planned staff conferences, manuals, or other training devices go much further in creating enthusiasm for one's work than does "turning a man loose."

8. In most situations training of some kind necessarily takes place anyway; it is largely a question of its being systematic or haphazard, efficient or wasteful, effective or useless.

9. If it were not profitable for organizations to carry on systematic in-service training, private industry would not have engaged in it so extensively.

10. There are now sufficient illustrations of the success of systematic staff development to prove the case for adequate provision for it from a budgetary standpoint.

11   What Are the Beginnings of Training in Industry?

The authors asked Allen B. Gates, of Eastman Kodak, one of the earliest men in the training field, to handle this question. His reply follows:

About the turn of the century a number of industrial managements realized that something should be done in the training field and naturally turned to the educators, who specialized in the art of imparting information.

As a result there came into being schools, such as those conducted by Westinghouse, later Hawthorne Works of Western Electric and many others. They provided training and related subjects with which the worker should be familiar, such as drawing, blueprint reading, shop math, etc. Later there was added to these programs a complete high school curriculum. This did not solve the problem, and, in the period from the middle teens and into the early 20's, there developed a recognition that industrial training was a specialty which deserved more consideration on the part of management. Better job training methods grew rapidly as a result of the work in World War I, and formal programs in supervisory training appeared during and following the war period.

Charles Allen, as a result of the work during World War I, brought out a book on *The Instructor, the Man, and the Job,* in which he developed all of the principles which were later simplified and put into effective use through Training Within Industry during World War II. Allen intended his book for use by educators, both in the vocational schools and in industry. Although very helpful to many people, his suggested analysis was so complicated that the principles were not accepted fully until the streamlined version of Job Instructor Training was brought out in World War II. Many companies had used these principles in developing job training and perfecting their apprentice training long before the World War II period.

12   Is Development Solely a Management Tool, As Some Labor Unions Think?

No. Development through group discussions, meetings and conferences, vestibule schools, and on-the-job training serves both employees and employer.

Development helps individuals, through improving their skills, to become more secure and satisfied in their jobs and prepares them for advancement. More than half of the time spent in supervisory development in American business and industry today deals with human relations, with strong emphasis on supervising so as to satisfy employee needs.

For the welfare of both management and employee, development programs help discover and eliminate management's weaknesses and employee limitations.

13   Why Has Interest in Supervisory Development Increased Greatly in Recent Years?

Because the working force has changed, making supervisory training necessary. A generation ago, most workers had grade school education or less. They were glad to have jobs—any jobs— and were willing to be bossed at their work. They also accepted inefficiency, limited rewards in both wages and satisfactions and lifelong insecurity.

Today's worker is better educated, more ambitious, and more demanding than his predecessors. Usually, he has a high school education, in which he has gained varied interests, an understanding of democracy, some ability to express himself, and experience in understanding problems. Laws and unions, plus long-continued scarcity of labor have convinced him that he has rights and has the power to get them, while technologic progress and scientific management have made him unwilling to accept inefficiency on the part of his employer.

Modern workers want employment security (jobs), good pay (financial rewards) and personal satisfaction (nonfinancial rewards). Personal satisfaction, in turn, involves pride in workmanship, opportunity for growth, participation in decisions and freedom to improvise, adapting assigned processes or methods to individual peculiarities.

The old-time boss who "knew the job" but whose idea of managing people was to give orders, bawl out those who made mistakes, and punish failures cannot deal with such workers. Today's supervisor is a leader who must satisfy the needs of his organization at the same time that he satisfies the social and psychological needs of his employees.

Since men with these abilities do not come ready-made from trade schools or the production line, they must be produced by training. Since needs constantly change, the supervisor must be retrained to meet the new requirements. For this reason, Management development is essential. It can never stop.

14   What Is the Future of Development?

Development or training is becoming more and more widely accepted as a vital necessity for industry. Today there are twice as many members of the American Society of Training Directors as there were a few years ago. Over forty schools and universities now offer credit-earning courses in industrial training, in contrast to the situation in 1950, when only two schools were known to offer such a course. Both the Ninth and Tenth International Management Conferences included training and development as one of seven management areas to be reported upon and discussed. Other areas were distribution, control, human relations, policy making, etc.

The extent to which this trend will continue depends upon the quality of the job done by training men. Since that quality evidently is improving, all signs indicate that organized development work will become a basic part of the management structure in America.

Chapter 2

LEARNING AND TEACHING

15   Do Adults Accept the Idea of Continuing Education?

As of today, many do not; that is why training men must use great tact and persistence in selling their intellectual wares. But acceptance is growing rapidly. Many factors are responsible for this change: One is the growing complexity of life, with its demands for new skills, new knowledge, and new insights. Experience with adult education in the armed forces has helped, as have G.I. educational support after discharge, the T.W.I. programs in plants and offices, and a wider realization that adults can learn with ease as well as with pleasure and profit. Old dogs *can* learn new tricks, and they often get pleasure as well as stimulation out of doing so.

Essert has estimated that 30 million adults in the United States now engage in some kind of organized educational activity each year.[1] Of this number, twenty million are actually reported in figures for enrollment in private correspondence schools, armed forces educational programs, public school evening adult courses, Farm and Home Bureau courses, etc. The remaining ten million are estimated figures. They cover enrollments in courses offered in business and industry and in other adult activities.

**16   What Is the Primary Educational Problem
        in Development or Training?**

Earl Kelley states the problem succinctly: "getting new knowings past the outer defenses of the individual and into his inner being so that they become functioning parts of him."[2] Too many

[1] Paul L. Essert, *Creative Leadership of Adult Education* (New York: Prentice-Hall, Inc., 1951) p. 37.
[2] Earl C. Kelley, *The Workshop Way of Learning* (New York: Harper & Bros., 1951), p. 74.

teachers are content to expose the learner to new knowledge, new skills, new attitudes, but this is not enough. The learner must not only meet the subject matter; he must assimilate it into his thoughts and action, with consequent change in behavior. Teaching has not taken place until this process of "internalization" occurs. Recently this has been called "gut learning."

17   What Are Some of the Newly Discovered Fundamentals of Training or Development?

Training or development has been described as the continuous, systematic development, among employees at all levels, of the knowledge, skills, and attitudes which contribute to their own welfare and to that of the company that employs them. By implication, the objectives of training are increased productivity, greater effectiveness in the present job, and for some employees, readiness to fill a better position.

This definition indicates the new and broader outlook which has come to training in recent years. Business and industry have given belated recognition to a few fundamental truths of long standing. These are:

1. Learning is a process which continues throughout the life of every person.

2. Guidance and direction must also be continuous if we are to have willing, rapid, and permanent learning.

3. New problems, techniques, and information arise constantly at every rung of the organizational ladder. Training therefore must be broad enough to meet the developmental needs of everyone from the youngest apprentice to the chairman of the board of directors.

4. Left to take its own course, this continuous process of learning on all levels is slow, fumbling, and often fails to achieve satisfactory results. To attain full and early possession of skills, knowledge, and attitudes necessary to both the individual and his company, training must be planned, systematized, and organized in accordance with well-known principles of learning and teaching.

5. An employee is a psychologically complex being in a complex world. His developmental needs are various and often confusing. Training must deal with this whole person in the social and industrial environment in which he lives and works; it must provide a flexible program that adapts itself to the individual rather than a rigid pattern to which he is forced to conform.

6. In conjunction with Point 5, training must recognize the essential role of attitudes and understandings in the application of skills and information. The employee who knows but does not care is a liability to himself and his company. The plumber who comes to the job with all his plumbing skills but with no desire to do a good job has left his most important tool at home. On the other hand, the employee who takes the right attitude toward his job and his company will put his best effort into his work because he wants to learn and to succeed, is eager to qualify for higher jobs, and is willing to cooperate in his department's and company's efforts for the progress of the business and society at large.

7. Finally—and perhaps this is the most important single concept in the whole business of training—teaching means establishing situations that call for and encourage learning. Men grow intellectually and spiritually in one climate but are stunted in others. Training, whether it utilizes classes, conferences, or individual daily counseling, will succeed only in an industrial atmosphere that encourages growth and places a premium upon it. Wages, promotional practices, status symbols, the words, actions, and attitudes of those who manage a concern—all these, like the signs of the ancient astrologers, must be propitious before the kind of development described in this book can take place. Unless this favorable climate exists, the most elaborate plans, the finest curricula, the most imposing array of teaching aids will fail. Training must devote its first attention to creating this atmosphere.

18   How Does One Break Down the Personal Defenses of Learners—Defenses Which Resist New Ideas, Group Participation, Two-way Communication, and Learning?

This requires an easy, friendly approach which builds up the learner's confidence and establishes him as a respected and needed member of the group.

There are many devices for this—golf, card games, tea dances, theater parties, after-class bull sessions, nonsense and horseplay, opening and graduation ceremonies, name cards, frequent introductions, mimeographed lists of conferees' names and titles, singing, coffee hours and coke breaks, use of first names, rooming and eating together; week-end visits to libraries, parks or industries, return of graduates at various times in the course, and so on.

Even the authors are surprised at the frequency with which business executives in the well-known university development programs attend Sunday morning church services together, ask permission to read the class a serious poem or editorial, and on more than one occasion introduce a prayer. Here the men are finding integration and spiritual motive on a high level indeed. Once achieved the group can work together and learn together with great success.

Development directors must check those impatient, ultrapractical souls who consider these activities a waste of time and who want to "get down to work" and stay at it continuously. Unifying activities which sometimes look like play *are* work—the work of preparing men for free communication, for understanding, and for consideration of new ideas on their merits without personal blocks and biases.

19   What Do You Think of Quiz Programs, Humorous Skits, and Other Light Approaches in Development and Training?

They are excellent, especially in programs that continue for several days or more. As we said before, informal changes of pace prevent monotony, relax the trainees so that learning improves, and build group spirit. These devices also serve as escape valves for strong emotions sure to develop when active, mature adults return to concentrated study. Coffee and cocktail hours, golf, tours, cards, theater parties, swimming, fishing, dancing, and trips to ball games, operas, race tracks, mountains or the shore all contribute immensely when training is to be worked at continuously.

20   How Can We Get People to Take an Interest in Learning?

Provide freedom for the learner to choose his goals, his reading materials, and his associates in bull sessions. Let him make his own interpretations, develop his own solutions to problems, and set his own pace in learning. This is the way of workshops, the case studies, role playing, syndicates, and other nondirective methods of teaching which encourage learner participation.

Trainees who seem to be lazy or disinterested in learning generally are not so at all. They may be bored with other people's purposes, other people's goals, and other people's values and methods. Businessmen and women who in their school and university days willingly meet the goals set by textbook writers, teachers and state departments of education should be forgiven if their maturity and independence make them less eager to meet your expectations. For a change, try getting them to state their own goals and then help them to achieve them.

21   There's an Old Adage That "Attitudes Are Caught More Often Than Taught." How Do You Feel That Attitude Teaching Ties In with It?

Attitudes are not "caught" like the germs of disease. Nor can they be implanted by sound argument or the best of emotionalized lectures.

Attitudes grow out of experience. Pleasant experiences, satisfying experiences, experiences in which one participates in the making of decisions and then finds himself reasonably free to carry them out in his own preferred manner—these help to build constructive, wholesome, and cooperative attitudes. Some social scientists say that attitudes grow so clearly out of actions that business and industry have only to give attention to their deeds, if they wish to establish wholesome, constructive feelings. If deeds are reasonable and consistent with a clearly expressed philosophy, attitudes take care of themselves. Though this implies that attitudes are always reasonably related to facts—a dubious assumption—still there is much value in the thought. Certain it is that no amount of words or artificial attitude building activities overcome the effects of ruthless or even thoughtless actions taken by management in regard to its people or to society in general. An organization which wants its members to develop "good" or "sound" attitudes must provide a basis in the form of intelligent, socially responsible action.

22   What Limitations Do High Executives Place upon Teachers and Teaching Methods?

Only highly able and successful men can influence the behavior of major executives. This means men of reputation and acknowledged ability in their fields who also have professional skill in presenting their subjects to others. Executives are justifiably critical of mediocrity in teaching.

Most executives think easily in terms of generalities within the fields of their experience, even though it is not detailed. Excessive detail almost always bores them. However, they accept, almost too well, the direct approach. They accept good lectures or good telling, but are likely to regard equally good case studies, workshops, role playing, or other nondirective group approaches as a waste of time. This attitude presents difficulty, since some of the gravest needs for individual development can be met only by nondirective approaches.

In general, executives are unwilling to participate as freely as middle management. They are more reserved, less free with opinions in group situations. Enjoying high status, they are unwilling to do anything that may endanger it, in their own eyes if not in the eyes of others. Since pride in position is justifiable, the wise training man will respect it and will help to preserve it in areas where trainees are likely to be sensitive.

23   What Psychological Preliminaries Must a Training Man Undertake Before Learning Becomes Possible for His Trainees?

Men must be made ready for learning. Preferably before the training starts, they should be led to realize that it will meet their own needs and serve their own interests. This is accomplished most easily by getting trainees or their representatives to participate in planning the training. It can also be done by pointing out how the new knowledge, skill, and attitude will be useful to the learners, and by getting the trainees themselves to point out the values of the training to them.

Another means of developing readiness to learn is to organize the program so that trainees select problems to be solved, roles to be played, readings and research to be undertaken, avenues to be explored in any case study, and the meaning and weight that will be assigned to "facts" in each case. Men who help to choose their avenues to learning are eager to follow them.

Readiness for learning also comes when blocks and barriers are removed. A plant superintendent who leaves his office during a busy day for an hour or two of role playing or case studies is so preoccupied with the burden of his operations that he can give little real attention to learning. For best results, he should be taken far away from his job and its urgent problems. If training can be concentrated into two or three days, or even a week, it probably will pay to hold the meetings in some quiet resort hotel that is not too far away.

Learning cannot take place efficiently if trainees feel unsure of themselves, anxious about what is to happen, insecure because they lack formal training, or afraid they will be shown up or embarrassed. These obstacles must be overcome by devices outlined in the answers to Questions 17, 18, 19 and 24, in this chapter.

Another common block is the preconceived idea that training

will be so theoretical and academic that it cannot help practical-minded operating men. This misconception must be corrected by seeing that the practical day-to-day needs felt by trainees are met, that learners have a part in planning their own development, and that the methods of teaching used allow for full, meaningful participation. For this the workshops, the case study, and the group dynamics approach is best.

The professionally trained specialist in management development knows these barriers and is prepared to remove them. He is not annoyed that they exist nor is he perplexed over what to do about them, as might be the engineer, accountant, or chemist who found himself compelled to solve these problems, in which men seem to resist, unreasonably, steps that will lead to their own progress.

24   What Can We Do to Establish the Desired Atmosphere for Learning?

Teach executives that men grow and develop in some climates and become sluggish or negative in others. Teach them that their leadership may determine which course a man takes. Teach them how to lead so as to get the optimum growth from each follower.

Create a feeling of self-respect and confidence in the learner, so that he can face up to new and disturbing things that may threaten his opinion of himself. Direct his attention from a preoccupation with himself and his problems to group needs or, at least, to the fact that other people share his problems and need his collaboration if they are to be solved.

Help the learner to set or perceive a clear purpose for his training. Build the training so that the learner's own objective can be reached, and show him that your purpose coincides with his own desires.

Provide time for learning. Barriers to new ideas, to different ways of thinking and acting, are often firmly established. If such barriers have grown out of years of experience they cannot be reduced or removed in a hurry.

Provide a physical setting that is comfortable, relaxing and without distracting elements. This means comfortable seating, a cool meeting place in summer and an adequately heated one in winter, and freedom from constant interruptions.

25   Can Training Aids Help Motivate Learning?

Yes, Professor Lynn Emerson[3] tells how in the following paragraph:

It is not easy to provide motivation of the trainee through instructional materials in written form, but certain things can be done toward this end. If the material is attractive, with orderly arrangement of items, good typography, and carefully chosen words and illustrations, it may stimulate the trainee to want to study. Information may be included which shows the trainee the values that will accrue from such study. Instructional units may be so designed and arranged that they challenge the ability of the student, permit him to see progress from one unit to the next, and thus motivate him to further learning.

26   Do Adults Learn as Easily as Younger People?

Professor John Carr Diff, after consultation with leading authorities on gerontology, has answered this question for us as follows:

There is no clinical or experimental evidence in support of the popular misapprehension that adults, including those in the older age brackets, are slower at learning than they may have been at an earlier age. It was the opinion of the group that in all adult learning, as in all learning situations involving younger persons, interest is primary. It is obvious that it is somewhat more difficult to secure and maintain the interest of adults if the matter offered to them for learning purposes represents a demand upon them which is in some degree in conflict with their already established interests. However, when the adult is highly motivated by some personal desire to know and to understand some factual information it seems likely that he can accomplish the learning involved as readily and as satisfactorily as could a person of fewer years. It seems obvious also that the person who has had much experience and has derived from this experience some understanding of general principles must have a greater apperceptive background for learning than is the case with a young learner. Since almost all learning is accomplished by association, it stands to reason that the older person, having more associations—more hooks on which to hang new ideas—is capable of making associations more readily than a person of less experience.

27   What Are the Differences Between Industrial Training and Instruction in Schools and Colleges?

Training in industry becomes ancillary to production and is necessarily irregular and uncertain. It calls for great originality

[3] Lynn A. Emerson, *How to Prepare Training Manuals* (Albany: The New York State Education Department), 1952.

of method and very often must be designed for immediate application. There is, of course, no problem of discipline. The teacher,
however, must be able to hold his class, whose attendance is
voluntary, and must not expect unquestioned acceptance of his
teachings.

College instruction, on the other hand, is provided for those
who seek it voluntarily and pay for its privilege. They are not
likely to abandon their training so quickly as might the more
independent industrial worker. Moreover, college instruction is
provided for those whose primary or whole objective at the time
is learning.

28   Why Is Participation So Much Stressed in Modern Training and Development?

It is stressed because participation is probably the best method
to make sure that training will take the direction most useful to
the adult learner. Through participation he helps determine what
the content of training shall be, how it shall be organized, and the
manner of presentation.

Participation also makes the trainee receptive to other people's
ideas. By getting his own ideas and problems off his mind and
into the general hopper, he takes the first step toward hearing
other points of view. As Professor Joe Bailey of Harvard says,
"Good listening makes good listeners." If the class and the instructor show a willingness to hear a trainee express himself frankly,
he is likely to listen to his instructor and his associates in earnest.

Participation builds the trainee's stature in his own eyes. As he
presents his own ideas he feels important; he acquires stature by
being heard and perhaps listened carefully to. Thereafter he lets
himself go. His real personality comes out and the group has
opportunity to react to him and affect him as he really is—not as
the cautious, timid, or reserved person he would seem to be if the
communication were all from the instructor to him.

Participation also may enable the learner to see himself a little
better than he otherwise would, and to learn how other people
actually react to him when they are freed from the restraints of
everyday authority and organization.

Active participation—physical, mental and emotional—seems to
release and direct energy. Man can release motive power which
makes him persistent, diligent, enthusiastic, creative, and productive. He can be these things in whatever degrees of intensity he
chooses.

If one of us is to teach another, something must pass between us. It may be only the meaning conveyed by words—but if this were all that went from most teachers to learners, then books and lectures would suffice for teaching. Especially in the workaday business world, more than words are necessary if the rich and often subtle experience of one executive or one employee is to be transmitted and made useful to another. Transfer of knowledge or understanding from one person to another seems to take place best when there is group participation, a common attack upon a problem. Members of the group search, together, for enlightenment, and share in analyzing a problem, describing its facets and ramifications, investigating causes, and proposing and criticizing solutions. From these activities, new attitudes and habits of thought and action seem to get deeper into the consciousness than words alone can carry them.

Participation involves people, usually several people. It gets away from individual study—library research, term papers, reports on books read, etc. To the degree that participation involves group activity, learning becomes easier for "it is a widely held dogma in social science that it is easier to change the attitudes of a whole group of people than to change the attitudes of one person within the group."[4]

29   When Is Teaching Completed?

For training which involves knowledge or skill, training is completed (a) when the learner *understands* what has been taught, (b) when he *accepts* what has been taught, and finally (c) when he translates understanding and acceptance into *action*. Action may take the form of overt behavior—the operation of a machine, the filling of forms, a decision upon a sales or production problem. It also may appear in patterns of thought, such as attitudes toward labor, efficiency, government, or self-improvement. It may appear in deeper insight, more systematic thinking, and more open-mindedness toward facts that once were discounted, denied, or resisted. In any event, action is the culmination and completion of the teaching process.

Successful attitude training may require the acceptance of a particular point of view, but it is more likely to have as its objective the open-minded review of conflicting opinions. In such training, the learner is free to express his own convictions, and the

4 Lloyd Allen Cook (ed.), *Toward Better Human Relations* (Detroit: Wayne University Press, 1952), p. 54.

teaching is truly "nondirective." It is completed when the trainee establishes analytical, independent, unemotional habits of thinking and applies these habits in his work.

30   Do Line and Staff Executives Make Good Teachers?

Yes—and no. The business world must guard against the assumption, still made in many universities, that the man who knows a subject surely is able to teach it. On the other hand, business must not assume—as it sometimes does—that the "practical" man has neither the ability nor the desire to teach.

Actually, many high-level executives who know their work "backwards and forwards" have little aptitude for teaching and no sympathy with its techniques. Others, no more able as executives, possess the ability to impart information, encourage initiative, and guide associates or subordinates. These men should and will do as much development work as their other responsibilities permit.

One other fallacy has greatly impeded executive development. Some highly successful top-level executives believe that it is enough to let subordinates watch them in action or work beside them without counsel. In this they are like the old-time foreman who said, "Watch me do it a couple of times," and then expected a new employee to do an effective job. People learn something by watching, but not very much—and that holds for junior executives as well as for assembly-line operators. Every man needs a chance to think the job out for himself under the guidance of someone who knows it much better than he does. If a high-level executive cannot provide that guidance, with essential counsel, he should learn how to do it or assign the task to someone who can. This someone may be another executive, a member of the training department, a professional consultant, or a specialist from some university or technical school.

31   Do Men Improve at a Consistent and Regular Rate or Are There Periods When No Growth Takes Place?

Development does not take place at a uniform rate. Some men who attract attention by the speed of their growth and improvement seem to level out after a few years. The executive responsible for the development of such people should not be surprised. The learners are assimilating their learning, and taking a view of what's ahead. A good many of them come on again after two or three years of what may appear to be marking time.

32   Are the Outcomes of Nondirective Techniques Different from the Outcomes of Lectures, Readings, Telling Followed by Questions and Answers and Directed Conferences?

Yes. The results of role playing, counseling, case studies, workshops, and other nondirective methods are quite different from the outcomes of directed teaching. Professor Ralph Hower of the Harvard Graduate School of Business describes[5] the results of the case study method. The same or similar outcomes result from other nondirective methods.

The fruits of case study discussion emerge not as an unwieldy collection of facts and opinions but rather as new insight and improved administrative skills. Most participants improve their ability to perceive interrelationships between human, technical, and economic factors; to distinguish between relevant and immaterial data; to discern unstated assumptions and implicit issues; and to grasp administrative situations in their complex entirety. Equally important men develop skill in listening, understanding other points of view, communicating ideas, logical thinking, constructive imagination, formulating useful courses of action, and envisioning the probable consequences of these actions.

Directive methods convey information, knowledge, subject matter. The outcomes are facts, sometimes inert and unrelated to each other or to meaningful experience. Where knowledge for its own sake is the goal, or where it is safe to assume that the learner can organize and use the data without help or practice, directive teaching is adequate.

[5] Ralph M. Hower, in "Management and Executive Development in the United States," one of a group of papers written for the International Management Congress, São Paulo, Brazil, 1954. Compiled and edited by Earl G. Planty.

Chapter 3

LEADERSHIP

33 What Is Leadership?

Although there are hundreds of useful definitions, the one given by Ordway Tead is so practical and so frequently quoted that we shall repeat it here. In Tead's opinion, "leadership is the activity of influencing people to cooperate toward some goal which they come to find desirable."[1]

This definition has two elements: a goal which people "come to find desirable" and someone who has the ability to make it appear desirable to a number of complex human beings. To be effective, that goal must be shared, which means that, if it comes from above, its acceptance is worked out cooperatively, and thus gains the acceptance and approval of the entire group. However, good as Tead's definition is, it avoids saying clearly whose goal it is that the leader seeks to achieve.

Another statement of leadership makes clear whose goals are to be reached: leadership is a process which achieves the needs and purposes of the organization it serves, and at the same time satisfies the fundamental human needs of the people within the organization. No organization can exist for long if its leadership accomplishes only one of these objectives. This definition is most important. It is the premise from which leadership training is approached in this book.

34 What Has Research Revealed About the Qualities of Leadership?

Leadership—especially political and military leadership—has long seemed a mystical quality, an inspired method of getting

[1] Ordway Tead, *The Art of Leadership* (New York: McGraw-Hill Book Co., Inc., 1935), p. 20.

results. Much about the subject still is unknown, but research has done much to reduce mysteries to usable facts. Our present knowledge has been summarized by Cecil E. Goode:[2]

1. The leader is somewhat more intelligent than the average of his followers. However, he is not so superior that he cannot be readily understood by those who work with him.
2. The leader is a well-rounded individual from the standpoint of interests and aptitudes. He tends toward interests, aptitudes, and knowledge with respect to a wide variety of fields.
3. The leader has an unusual facility with language. He speaks and writes simply, persuasively and understandably.
4. The leader is mentally and emotionally mature. He has come of age mentally and emotionally as well as physically.
5. The leader has a powerful inner drive or motivation which impels him to strive for accomplishment.
6. The leader is fully aware of the importance of cooperative effort in getting things done, and therefore understands and practices very effectively the so-called social skills.
7. The leader relies on his administrative skills to a much greater extent than he does on any of the technical skills which may be associated directly with his work.

35   What Are Some Traits of Leadership?

Professors W. E. Henry and B. B. Gardner of the University of Chicago believe that successful executives have all the following traits, though in varying degrees. They came to the following conclusions after giving the Thematic Apperception Test to hundreds of executives.

1. *Achievement Desires:* The leader is motivated by sheer accomplishment of the work itself. He must achieve and move upward to be happy.
2. *Strong Mobility Drives:* These drives dictate the kinds of work and positions that will be of interest to him. The most successful executives have drives ranked in this order: (a) Achievement, (b) Material Rewards, and (c) Prestige.
3. *The Idea of Authority:* He willingly cooperates with his superiors. He regards them as helpful.
4. *Organizational Ability:* He plans, systematizes and follows up well.
5. *Decisiveness:* The leader has a nonstereotyped ability to select one of several courses of action.

[2] Cecil E. Goode, "Significant Research on Leadership," *Personnel*, March, 1951.

6. *Firmness of Conviction:* He feels he knows what he is, what he wants, and knows how to get it.

7. *Activity and Assertiveness:* He has a constant drive to be moving and doing. He is mentally and emotionally active. He is usually in constant physical motion either outwardly or internally. This internal motion may result in stomach troubles or similar psychosomatic symptoms. This perpetual motion type is unable to enjoy a leisurely vacation.

8. *The Need to Overcome a Sense of Frustration:* He has a pervasive fear of failure.

9. *Realism:* He is interested in the practical and the direct approach. He is more interested in what the facts are and have been than in what they will be. When reality (i.e., progress) is too slow for his drives, frustration and restlessness result and may disrupt his personal relationships.

10. *Relations with Others:* He identifies himself with and is responsive to his superiors, who symbolize his goals. He has no real interest in his subordinates, whom he looks upon as "work doers."

11. *Attitude Toward Parents:* He is psychologically free to make his own decisions. He has cut his strong emotional ties to his mother without resentment. He continues to consider his father or some father representative (e.g., an uncle) as helpful and unrestraining.

36　　What Makes for Unsuccessful Leaders?

Professors W. E. Henry and B. B. Gardner believe that the following traits are found in unsuccessful executives who are lacking in leadership:

1. *Inability to See the Over-all Situation:* The true leader and successful executive must be able to grasp the broad problems in order to see alternative courses of action.

2. *Failure to Carry Responsibilities:* Responsibilities multiply as one goes higher in executive levels. In these positions concrete goals may be undetermined. Timing must be planned. There are more alternatives present, and more reliance is placed on initiative.

3. *Unconscious Desire to Do Something Else:* Where motivations other than achievement are primary, a man will not be sufficiently interested in his job to turn out his best performance.

4. *Unconscious Desire to Be Someone Else:* When a man plays a role which he desires to achieve but for which he is unfit, his

self-referring goal is foreign to that of his company and job.

5. *A Yen for Express Trains:* He is too ambitious for broad executive power and success to do a good job on the intermediate, routine tasks.

6. *Inability to Make Room for Other People:* He is unable to accept criticism or to cooperate with associates.

7. *Resistance to Authority:* The unsuccessful leader's mind follows one of two channels: (a) He thinks he should have the jobs of the authority figures (father, boss, board chairman, etc.) or (b) he thinks that they are determined to keep him down; that they are prohibitive and destructive.

8. *Arrogance with Subordinates:* His real attitude toward people will emerge with subordinates rather than with superiors.

9. *Prejudices Which Interfere with Judgment:* He has fixed ideas about himself and others and acts upon them rather than facts.

10. *Overemphasis on Work:* When he regards his family and personal life as expendable he becomes too sensitive to any job frustrations. This is an exhausting situation as well as an unstable one.

11. *Gravitation Toward Self-Destruction:* He feels inadequate. When his big chance comes, he proves his inadequacy by failing.

12. *Mental Ailments:* These are often not apparent. They are usually deep and abiding depressions springing from his feeling of inadequacy. He may push this feeling to the point that he never can succeed.

37   How Important Are Qualities of Leadership in Obtaining High Productivity and Employee Satisfaction?

Personal qualities help to determine whether a leader stimulates or discourages profitable group activity. Recent research shows that there appear to be people who depress and people who facilitate the normal level of performance of the other members of the group. There are, however, other very important elements which help determine whether or not a man can lead other people to cooperate toward organization goals with pleasure and profit to themselves. One of these elements is the situation in which the leader operates, including the task to be performed, the tools, the method, the business philosophy of the company, the pay, and other elements of the environment. Of equal importance are subordinates—their age, experience, education and personal characteristics.

In the past we have overemphasized the leader and his behavior and have ignored the effect which his situation and followers have upon his leadership. We must remember that leadership is a process—a dynamic process. How a leader acts and reacts in response to others and how they behave toward him may be as important as any personal qualities he possesses.

38 How Useful Are Check Lists and Rating Scales in Determining Potential for Leadership?

As dependable measures of over-all executive talent, they have limitations. A leader is more than a static list of traits and qualities, even where these can be appraised objectively. He is a man operating in a give-and-take relationship with other men, in an environment that sometimes calls out the best in him, and at other times provokes the worst. He does not act uniformly from situation to situation, according to his traits. A man who is usually honest, dependable or loyal probably has some set characteristics predisposing him to be so in most circumstances. Still, situations may exist in which he is disloyal, undependable, or less than completely honest.

Every leader plays many roles and some of them are shaped as much by the situations in which he finds himself as by his personal qualities. This is why men succeed in some departments or climates, under some leaders, and with certain associates and subordinates, but fail dismally when they are transferred to other jobs.

Another objection to the use of check lists and rating scales is the lack of satisfactory definitions. Under some definitions, ambition or imagination are desirable traits in any degree. When other concepts of ambition and imagination are applied, the man who has them to an excessive degree becomes either a selfish climber or a visionary liar.

Evaluation by traits, however, is a widely used tool and has certain merits. We will probably continue to use it until more scientific tools prove their worth and become available for general industrial use.

Probably the greatest value of check lists of traits and qualities is in the fact that they force superiors to give detailed attention to their subordinates, their behavior, and the personal traits that may be responsible for it. When a superior uses a check list to evaluate a subordinate he is forced, perhaps for the first time, to review the man's job performance objectively in order to find evidence that will give or justify a rating. Many an executive weakness has been uncovered by check lists, thus enabling corrective training to be undertaken. Lists probably do more good in this way than by providing total or composite pictures of executive potential.

39   Are Certain General Abilities and Skills of Leadership Useful in All Kinds and Levels of Administration?

Yes. One of these is the ability to communicate, to pass on and receive information, to get common acceptance of goals and to get individual participation in setting them. Part of the ability to do this involves fluency and word knowledge, and skill in choosing and presenting information clearly and persuasively. Another part is the skill involved in stimulating participation so that groups share in making decisions and accept them as their own.

These are important general skills, but general attitudes and qualities of mind are also involved. First of these is willingness to consult with one's subordinates and to be influenced by their ideas and needs. Another is a realization that people need to be informed, to know what is happening and why.

These and many other general abilities and skills are needed in all kinds of democratic leadership, regardless of the levels of people to be led or the special functions of the organizations in which leadership is exercised.

40   Does the Nature of American Business, or the Attitudes of Its Leaders, Require a Man to Possess Any Particular Traits or Abilities?

Some students of business leadership say "yes" to this. They claim that American business leaders reward authoritarianism and aggressiveness to a degree not justified by their value in achieving executive success. Those who hold this view believe that leaders who are high in authoritarianism will in general be accepted by their superiors, but rejected by their subordinates.

This can be true only in old-fashioned authoritarian organizations. Some of these still exist, but they are changing rapidly under the impact of education, the power and opposition of unions, and inefficiencies growing out of the frustration, turnover, indifference, and lack of responsibility which this attitude provokes in middle management and employees. Public condemnation has also been a factor in compelling authoritarian companies to mend their ways.

41　What Is the Most Important Attribute to Look for in Appraising an Individual's Qualifications for Leadership?

Unless one knows in what situation a leader is to function, one cannot judge the qualifications required or list them in order of importance. The requirements of successful leadership depend largely upon the characteristics of the people being led, their previous history of success or failure, the conditions in which they now find themselves, and the nature of the operations to be performed. Since these factors vary according to time and place, leaders must also vary. Lincoln, for example, was the right man to lead the United States from 1861-65, but some of his qualities, important though they were at that time, would have been useless in World War II. Similarly, it is doubtful whether the qualities that made Carnegie and Frick successful would have the same result today.

There also are great individual variations. One leader may achieve success with one set of traits; another leader lacking in those characteristics may also be highly successful. Sometimes an abundance of one trait seems to make up for deficiency in another. It is, for example, possible to have enough drive and enthusiasm to offset shortcomings in tact and courtesy, creative ability, or analytical skill. We do not, however, know how much plus credit one must have on any one trait to balance weakness in some other.

42　What Characteristics or Traits Are Absolutely Essential to Executive Success?

As we have already said, no specific trait or traits can be called essential. We know of no way to put exact values upon the various traits that are popularly thought to contribute to executive success. Various executives and writers, however, have favored traits which they think rank above others as prerequisites to success. Ordway Tead places physical and nervous energy at the top of his list of ten qualities. He then has this to say about it:[3]

> Almost every study of the secret of the successful leader has agreed that the possession of a generous and unusual endowment of physical and nervous energy is essential to personal ascendancy. Those who rise in any marked way above the mass of men have conspicuously more drive, more sheer endurance, greater vigor of body and mind than the average person. The leader's effectiveness is in the first instance dependent upon his basic constitutional strength and robustness.

[3] Tead, *op. cit.*, p. 83.

43   In What Light Do the Group Dynamics People Conceive Leadership?

This question was analyzed at a workshop conducted at Arden House by Professor Robert Livingston of Columbia. The workshop was attended by executives from the public utility field. As part of a larger project, one group of workshop members investigated this question and answered it as follows:[4]

According to the Theory of Group Dynamics, Leadership cannot be regarded as the characteristics of behavior of one individual, a "leader," but instead involves the interrelation of three things:

1. The Leader
2. The Followers
3. The Situation

The requirements of leadership vary from one group of people to another and from one situation to another. A person who can effectively lead one group of people in one situation may be completely unable to perform leadership functions in other groups in other situations or for the same group in other situations.

Leadership is defined as follows: *A leader is that person in a given situation whose behavior and characteristics most closely approximate the norms of the group.* This means that a group of people will not follow (with the maximum degree of effectiveness) anyone who does not measure up to their idea of what a good leader should be. Clearly, the idea of what constitutes a good leader is not the same for all groups.

Therefore, two types of leadership situations can be described:

1. Leadership which is freely evolved by the group from within.
2. Leadership which is imposed upon the group from without.

Type (1) is the most effective from the standpoint of efficiency, but type (2) is the most common. When drastic means of imposing leadership are used, such as by force, efficiency is characteristically high in the short run, but suffers severely in the long run.

44   Do Attitudes Toward One's Leadership Roles Influence One's Behavior as a Leader?

Yes. Robert Burns, drawing upon an unpublished Ph.D. dissertation by Charles Nilson at the University of Chicago, outlined them as follows:

[4] *The Utility Executive: His Job and His Training* (Department of Industrial Engineering, Columbia University, 1953), p. 32.

LEADERSHIP TYPES AND CHARACTERISTICS[5]

LEADERSHIP ATTITUDES	BUREAUCRATIC-REGULATIVE "Bureaucrat"	AUTOCRATIC-DIRECTIVE "Autocrat"	IDIOCRATIC-MANIPULATIVE "Diplomat"	DEMOCRATIC-INTEGRATIVE "Quarterback"
1. FRAME OF REFERENCE	"They"	"I"	"You"	"We"
2. ORIENTATION	Rule-centered	Self-centered	Individual-centered	Group-centered
3. MOTIVATION	Personal security	Power and prestige	Personal recognition	Recognition—self and group
4. OBJECTIVES	Develop a system	Develop self	Develop individual	Develop group
5. CONTROLS USED	Formal	Technical	Psychological	Social
6. SOURCE OF AUTHORITY	Rules	Self	Individual	Group
7. CONCEPT OF LEARNING	Trial and error	Repetition	Rewards and punishments	Ego-involvement
8. DEMANDS ON EMPLOYEE	Loyalty	Obedience	Ambition	Cooperation
9. CONTACT WITH EMPLOYEES	Infrequent and impersonal	Detailed and critical	Informal	Informal, close and frequent
10. COMMUNICATION WITH EMPLOYEES	Avoids	One-way	Superficial two-way	Sincere two-way
11. EMPLOYEE IDENTIFICATION	None	Negative	Employee self-interest	Leader and company
12. EMPLOYEE RELATIONSHIP	Official	Authoritarian	Manipulative	Integrative
13. EMPLOYEE MORALE	Apathy	Antagonism	Competition	Teamwork

[5] From Robert Burn's contribution to "Management and Executive Development in the U. S.," a paper compiled by Earl Planty, for the International Management Congress, São Paulo, Brazil, 1954.

PART II

METHODS OF DEVELOPMENT

Chapter 4

THE MANAGEMENT AUDIT

45 What Is a Management Audit?

It is a systematic analysis of the executive, supervisory, and technical manpower within a company. It includes a study of the men's potentials and their training and personal needs. It also includes a full study of the jobs in the organization. This is followed by predictions, telling who is likely to fill management positions in the future.

46 Who Makes a Management Audit?

The staff individual charged with executive development usually becomes responsible for the management audit, although members of management actually make it.

All executives prepare or assemble up-to-date job descriptions and man specifications for the positions they supervise. They appraise their subordinates, plan and execute management development activities for them, estimate future management needs, and name replacements. The individual in charge of management development assists executives in these tasks and usually combines departmental audits into one for the entire organization.

47 What Are the Values of a Management Audit?

A formal audit of management has the following values:

1. It directs the attention of operating executives to present and future personnel needs in their divisions.
2. By helping to have adequate reserves and understudies avail-

able it aids in making management changes with dispatch while maintaining continuous, harmonious operations.

3. It reveals the training needs of management.
4. It stimulates training and development activities for members of management.
5. It forces executives to take corrective action concerning inefficient subordinates.
6. It leads executives to analyze the organizational structure of their departments and to make plans for the future.
7. It helps to raise the standards of performance for all executives and thus for the organization as a whole.
8. It places executive selection and development on an objective, and therefore on a fair basis. This improves both the morale and the efficiency of the management group.

48   How Do You Make a Management Audit?

The management audit varies in complexity from company to company. A recommended step-by-step procedure[1] would include all the actions outlined below:

1. Preparation of an organization chart for each department and statement of the principal duties of all executives.
2. Preparation of man specifications for each position. Determination of what training, experience, knowledge, and skills are required by the position.
3. Accumulation of all available data regarding each executive, such as personnel evaluations, merit ratings if they are available, health records, and personnel records.
4. Evaluation of each man as to performance in his present job, in order to discover his general effectiveness as well as his specific strengths and weaknesses.
5. Evaluation of the individual's promotability. An over-all appraisal of each man is made which defines his worth in his present job and his potential.
6. Planning the additional experience, formal education, and on-the-job training required by each man.
7. Counseling each individual on his performance in his present job, with advice as to how he can prepare himself either to do his present job better or to advance to a higher job when the opportunity occurs.

[1] John F. Mee (ed.), *Personnel Handbook* (New York: The Ronald Press Co., 1951), p. 1017.

8. Preparation of a replacement chart showing:
   a. Positions now inadequately filled and those to be vacated through retirement, transfer, expansion, separation, etc., in the near future.
   b. Men in the organization considered capable to fill these positions as they become vacant.

49   Should There Be a Review of Organizational Structure Before a Management Audit Can Be Accomplished?

As indicated in the previous answer, the first step of management audit is the preparation of organizational charts. The usual method of constructing such charts is to show the senior executive at the top with subordinate levels pyramided below. The names and titles of the executives are included. Such a chart gives a graphic portrayal of the formal relationships between positions and departments in the organization and helps management evaluate existing organizational arrangements. In order to make this study of organizational structure as effective as possible, job descriptions and man specifications for all management positions should be prepared or reviewed if they already exist.

A job description is a definition of the duties assigned to a particular position. It should be prepared by the incumbent, and reviewed and approved by his superior. The usual format for a management job description contains the following major sections: Function, Responsibilities, Authorities, Relationships. From a study of the job description, management determines the qualifications of the individual who will fill each position. These qualifications may include education, experience, health, and personal traits such as character, decisiveness, imagination, tolerance, drive, persuasiveness, initiative, etc. Since no one knows for sure what makes a successful executive, each man specification must be tailored to meet the particular requirements of the job, and should be prepared after careful study of the job description and discussion with experienced senior executives.

50   How Often Should a Management Audit Be Made?

The frequency of management audits will depend primarily on the size of the organization and its rate of growth, the rate of management turnover, and the development needs of the management group. In many companies a comprehensive audit of all key personnel is conducted annually.

51   What Are the Chief Limitations of Plans and Practices in Management Audits?

Business conditions too often influence the amount of attention given to management audits. They should be essential elements in planning, not luxuries to be used when the economic sun is shining and put on the shelf when the sky is dark and manpower needs appear less urgent.

Some companies feel they have a management audit and development program when they actually have prepared only management appraisals. They fail to realize that the appraisal is the base upon which development and replacement plans should grow.

Some companies fail to realize that a management audit is temporary, providing a picture of conditions at a particular time. Since conditions change, the audit must be repeated often enough to provide an up-to-date summary of the executive strength of the organization. Men change—sometimes quickly. What is written in the audit may be out of date when the charts and papers are committed.

Audits must be kept in strict confidence. If this is not done, men may be hurt by general revelation of management's opinions of certain supervisors, executives, or technical men.

Sometimes the opinions about men are inaccurate and the audits provide no check upon men who are poor at judging others. If such men are high up in the organization, the audit merely records their errors and misconceptions. Serious harm and injustice may result if these faulty elements are accepted by other executives.

52   What Is a Replacement Chart?

A replacement chart is a color-coded organizational chart which shows the quality of performance of executives on their present jobs and their potential for advancement. The chart, therefore, gives an over-all picture of the effectiveness of the management manpower of the organization and its probable ability to meet future requirements.

53   Can You Illustrate a Replacement Chart?

Replacement charts can be simple or elaborate, depending upon the amount of information desired on them. Usually, only the quality of present performance of executives and their probable potential are coded on the chart. When preparing a replacement chart, choose a code which is easily read. The following illustrates such a system.

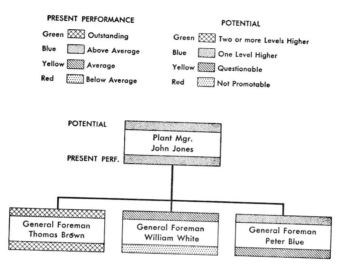

54   What Is a Replacement Table? Will You Illustrate One?

A replacement table is a list of the key positions in a department or an organization accompanied by the names of the incumbents and the first and second replacements for each position. Information concerning age, seniority, quality of present performance and potential of these individuals is usually included.

An illustrative replacement table is shown below.

COMPANY _____ XYZ _____   DEPARTMENT _____ Cotton Mfg. _____   DATE _____

Position Title	Incumbent	Age	Service	Present Perf.	Today's Potential	Replacement #1	Present Title	Age	Replacement #2	Present Title	Age
General Foreman	William Jones	42	8 yrs.	Above Average	One Level Higher	James Gordon	Asst. Gen. Foreman	34	Paul Burns	Ind. Engineer	32
Asst. Gen. Foreman	James Gordon	34	8 yrs.	Outstanding	Two Levels Higher	Paul Burns	Ind. Engineer	32	John Williams	Finishing Foreman	36
Process. Foreman	Peter Lewis	55	12 yrs.	Average	Not Promotable	Harry Boyd	Assistant Foreman	33	Fred Morris	Assistant Foreman	30
Finishing Foreman	John Williams	36	9 yrs.	Outstanding	Two Levels Higher	Fred Morris	Assistant Foreman	30	Tom. Brown	Assistant Foreman	31

55   **How Does One Determine the Number of
          Future Executives His Organization Will Need?**

No formula can be used, but answers to the following questions will help make reasonably accurate forecasts of the probable vacancies at each executive level.

1. How many executives will be eligible to retire within the next year, next three years, next five years?
2. What departments will be expanding or contracting next year, in three years, or five years?
3. How many executives are performing less than adequately in their present jobs? How many of them may not be improved by your development activities?
4. What has been your management turnover in the past at various levels?

After the answers to these questions have been found and analyzed, a forecast of management needs can be made, preferably for the next five years. This forecast should be reviewed and revised annually, and more often if unplanned organizational and personnel changes occur.

56   **What Is an Executive Inventory?**

An executive inventory is a list of every key job, with the names of men who could fill each one. John W. Riegel, who surveyed executive development plans in fifty American companies,[2] found this type of record used only in large companies and defines it as ". . . a classified list of candidates for each key position. Such a list is more comprehensive than the replacement table. The classified list includes the names of all individuals who were mentioned as possible candidates for the stated job when their capacity for advancement was considered. The listing does not establish their competence; it merely serves to call them to the attention of the executives who are responsible for seeing that a sufficient number of reservists are in preparation for the job."

57   **How Do You Prepare a Man Specification?**

A man specification is a statement of the human qualities necessary for adequate performance of a job. Usually the person who

[2] John W. Riegel, *Executive Development, Common Policies and Selected Practices in Fifty American Corporations,* Report No. 5, Bureau of Industrial Relations, University of Michigan, 1952.

supervises a job prepares the man specification with the assistance of the present incumbent and the staff personnel specialist who will be involved in the selection of a man to fill the position when it becomes vacant. A man specification usually answers the following questions:

What are the desirable personality traits for this particular position?
(Initiative, intelligence, social skills, etc.)
What are the physical requirements?
(Age, size, general appearance, physical condition, etc.)
What are the educational requirements?
(Amount of formal schooling or special courses.)
What are the experience requirements?
(The kind, variety, and extent of experience desired.)

A man specification is illustrated on page 44.

58   What Is an Executive Appraisal?

An executive appraisal usually is identical with an executive evaluation or executive rating. It is a written judgment of an executive's present and potential usefulness to an organization. This appraisal may be made jointly by several people who are in a position to judge an executive's performance. It also may be made by the executive's immediate superior, who sometimes secures assistance from the director of personnel or development. Usually some type of rating scale or form is used which lists important factors in the executive's performance.

59   What Are Executive Evaluations Used For?

There are a number of uses for executive evaluations. Most important, they are employed to determine:

1. Each executive's over-all job performance.
2. The potential of each executive.
3. The training needs of executives, in order to improve present job performance and to prepare them for higher positions.
4. Equitable salary adjustments.
5. Appropriate transfers, promotions, demotions, and terminations.
6. The validity of selection tests.
7. The quality of management in the organization at any specific time.

MAN SPECIFICATION

POSITION: General Foreman
DATE: May, 1954
DEPARTMENT: Process Department-Manufacturing
PREPARED BY: John Jones, Superintendent

PERSONALITY REQUIREMENTS

Initiative:	Works independently with little or no technical guidance or assistance from supervisor except under unusual conditions. Exercises independent judgment in making decisions of considerable consequence.
Mental Ability:	Superior intelligence. Errors may result in production delays of considerable consequence due to poor coordination between various sections and units supervised. Faulty decisions may have important effects on labor relations or improper coordination of areas supervised.
Social Skills:	Numerous contacts with other departments and with individuals in administrative or executive positions, consulting on problems and presenting information, recommendations or suggestions; requires tact and judgment in presentation in order to obtain cooperation or approval of action to be taken. Important contacts with subordinates as required in advanced supervisory jobs. Must possess ability for leadership.

PHYSICAL REQUIREMENTS

Sound emotional, mental and physical health. Energetic.

Age: 32 to 45

EDUCATION

1. College graduate. Degree in business administration or engineering preferred. Broad management courses, especially those in psychology, business administration, and industrial engineering.

2. Equivalent. High school graduate, who through experience, outside study, correspondence schools, has the equivalent of the above.

EXPERIENCE

1. Essential: three to five years of applicable experience in addition to education requirement. This must include three years of direct supervisory experience.

2. Desirable: at least one or two years' experience in a staff position within a manufacturing department.

60   Why Is a Formal Appraisal Necessary?

Some top executives may feel that the time-consuming formal appraisal is not necessary. They know their men, their organization, and the needs that exist or are likely to arise. True, they often do, yet four reasons still make the formal appraisal necessary:

1. The top man who knows his organization backwards and forwards seldom has time to put that knowledge into the clear, concise form he rightly demands in reports and programs from such fields as sales, production, and finance. Yet the need for precise information on management personnel is even more essential than it is in these other fields.

2. Development is not a one-man function, to be carried out only by the top executive. Other people must take part, and they must have access to facts which only a formal appraisal can provide.

3. As has been said, each member of management has his own development needs, and his program must be tailored to fit them. This requires the information provided by an appraisal.

4. The executive making the appraisal learns a lot from doing it.

61   What Is the Group-Appraisal Method?

In the group-appraisal method of evaluation an executive meets with two or more members of management to evaluate his subordinates. Usually, the immediate superior of the man to be evaluated chooses the group to assist him. It is most frequently composed of the immediate superior of the men appraised, the member of management in charge of executive development, and one or two other high-level executives who have adequate knowledge of the men's performance. A rating form may or may not be used to assist the group in making its evaluations.

62   What Are the Advantages and Disadvantages of the Group Appraisal Method?

E. A. Mesics, Director of Training for the Otis Elevator Company, offers the following advantages for group appraisal of executives:

1. Judgment is pooled.
2. There are several sources of information.
3. Personal likes or dislikes are minimized.
4. Appropriate facts are developed by discussion.
5. Ratings are correlated between departments.
6. Appraisal is based on recollections of long-term performance rather than on recent events.
7. Appraisal is based on over-all performance rather than on performance in one field, such as service or sales.

8. The process is accepted by the men appraised, who consider it fair and adequate.
9. The supervisor acts as the employee's representative, rather than as a single and isolated judge.
10. The raters have an opportunity to learn more about each employee whom they rate.

On the other hand, group appraisal has the following weaknesses:

1. Some group members dominate the appraisal meeting. Even though their knowledge may be limited, their positiveness, assertiveness, or their status leads others to agree with them.
2. Because some superiors have a few outstanding men in their departments there is a tendency to infer that all are outstanding.
3. Busy executives find it difficult to appraise executives in their own departments without serving on committees that review the performance of men in other departments.
4. The responsibility for counseling an executive, following appraisal, rests with the man's superior. Conclusions on a man's weaknesses may be reached in the group appraisal which the man's superior does not wholeheartedly accept and he is therefore not able to counsel the man effectively on them. Instead of developing high morale and improved performance in the executive group, this may contribute to feelings of frustration, dissatisfaction, and bitterness in the men appraised.

63   Should a Man's Immediate Superior Appraise Him?

Yes. He knows the man better than anyone else. He is responsible for his actions and must accept responsibility for improving him. He may receive assistance from the staff specialist in development, from his own superior, or from a group of fellow executives, yet he is bound to play the most active part in appraising any subordinate and should be responsible for doing the job.

64   Isn't Appraisal a Line Responsibility, from Which the Personnel Director or the Director of Development Should Be Excluded?

Appraisal of an executive is a line responsibility, but this does not mean that the appraiser should not use the assistance of a staff specialist. The personnel director or the director of development has usually had broad experience and intensive study in the areas of appraisal and developmental activities and is able to offer the line executive valuable counsel. When a research, engineering, accounting, or advertising problem confronts a line executive he readily turns to a specialist in the field for assistance and counsel. He should do the same when confronted by problems of appraisal and development.

65 How Much Time Should a Man Spend In Evaluating a Subordinate?

Evaluation is a continuous process; executives judge the performance of their subordinates every day. However, there has to be a summing up of these judgments, and that is usually done once a year. If notes of both good and poor performance have been kept, this summing up can be done with dispatch and thoroughness. The responsible executive should study these notes carefully to determine each subordinate's weaknesses and strengths, to summarize them into general statements of performance, to determine the causes for the men's failures, and to outline a program of development.

The evaluation of executives is too important to be done in an off-hand, unplanned, or routine manner. There must be adequate time for a sound, conscientious, complete, fair, and meaningful appraisal that will insure the developing of a competent management team. This process may take anywhere from an hour to ten hours of hard thinking.

66 What Role Should the Staff Man Play When He Sits with an Executive Who Is Appraising His Men?

His primary purpose is to assist the executive to make accurate, objective, constructive appraisals of his subordinates. The staff man does not evaluate; he acts as adviser and counselor who:

1. Encourages the executive to use a logical, systematic approach to the appraisal. This means that the staff man helps the executive to decide what he is looking for and to choose a rating form or develop some other device for recording evaluations. The staff man helps the executive determine the order in which he should evaluate his men and establish a timetable for completing all the evaluations.
2. Advises the executive on the use of employment and merit rating records.
3. Questions the executive doing the evaluations to help him dis-

cover concrete evidence on which to make his judgments. For example, an executive may be making a judgment on a subordinate's "decisiveness." The staff man may ask for specific, recent examples of good or bad performance of the man on this characteristic. Further, he may, through questioning, help an executive to determine whether the examples are descriptive of behavior that relates to decisiveness and really measure the subordinate's performance on this trait.

4. Cites examples of actions that may be significant in measuring a man's performance. These examples show the executive what to look for in order to determine the subordinate's effectiveness with regard to specified behavior. Thus the staff man can point out that "decisiveness" is measured by observing a man's reluctance to give an answer. (Is he reluctant only in situations other than routine? Does he give one answer and then change to another? Does he avoid making decisions?) Specific illustrations drawn from the man's field will make these questions more meaningful.

5. Assists in applying uniform performance standards. Since the staff man sits in on many evaluations he can reflect experience he has had with other executives and assist those who are evaluating to spread their judgments over the full scale.

6. After a man has been evaluated on a variety of performances, the staff man encourages the executive to weigh all characteristics and determine those that have the greatest bearing on success in this position. Following this, the executive can arrive at a sound and impartial summary evaluation.

7. Assists the leader in determining specific developmental activities for the man. Also guides the leader in how to draw from the subordinate suggestions for his development.

In short, in a very informal, friendly, and realistic manner, the staff man is training the executive in evaluating men and planning their development needs.

67   What Are Some Precautions to Be Observed by Executives When They Evaluate Their Men?

Some common errors in evaluation can be overcome by observing the following precautions:

1. Understand thoroughly the duties and requirements of the positions held by the employees who are to be evaluated, and determine the desired standards of performance. It will be help-

ful to review an employee's job description before evaluating him.

2. Do not confuse level of responsibility with work performance. A junior clerk may very well be meeting the requirements of his position more effectively than the senior clerk. Judge each against standards for his own position.

3. Recognize your own personal bias and take this into account as you evaluate.

4. Constantly observe and analyze employees to be evaluated. Keep a record of your observations.

5. If you do not have evidence on a man's performance, get it before you judge him.

6. Base your judgment on *demonstrated* performance and observed characteristics, not on anticipations or assumptions.

7. Evaluate employees on their performance during the entire evaluation period. Do not judge exclusively on single accomplishments or failures or upon recent performance.

8. Guard against the common tendency to evaluate too high and against the less common tendency to evaluate too low.

9. Do not allow a man's performance in one instance or on one type of assignment to prejudice you in your evaluation of him on different assignments.

10. When the evaluators are inexperienced in the rating procedure, or when the men to be judged are new to the organization or their jobs, make formal evaluations at least once a year and preferably more often.

11. Discuss an employee's evaluation with him as soon as possible after it is made.

68   Are Superiors Really Willing to Go on Record with Good or Bad Comments on Their Men?

They usually are. However, whether they are willing to or not depends to a large degree on how the information is going to be used by their superiors or others in the organization who may have access to it. If a written statement of a man's performance is treated as a positive characterization of his present and future performance, and if he is pegged from that point on as good or bad, superiors will be reluctant to express themselves in writing. On the other hand, when such comments are looked upon as snapshots of the man's performance in a given job at a given time, and are subject to change as the man or the situation varies, superiors seldom hesitate to write comments.

69   Isn't Appraisal a Day-to-Day Operation?

Certainly. Every interaction with subordinates is used by a superior as a basis for making judgments. As a result he corrects or commends men daily. However, in no one day does a subordinate display all his strengths and weaknesses. Therefore, in order to get him in proper focus it is necessary for the superior to make periodic reviews of these daily, independent judgments, weigh them, and determine their "long-haul" meaning. When he does this he is making a formal appraisal of the man.

70   What Should the Individual Know About His Appraisal? Who Should Tell Him?

The primary purpose of an executive appraisal is the improvement of the executive. Therefore, an executive must know the degree of success he is obtaining—his strengths so that he may utilize them fully, and his weaknesses so that he may overcome them. The immediate superior of the executive should give him this information.

Just how directly the subordinate should be told or led to see (a) the over-all quality of his performance, and (b) his specific strengths and weaknesses, depends upon his personal traits, his degree of success or failure on his job, the counselor's objective, etc. Improvement, however, is most rapid when counseling teaches each man to understand himself, and when he himself makes judgments about his abilities. The skillful superior leads each subordinate to improve his self-evaluations. It is what a man sees for himself and accepts that really motivates improvement.

71   What Danger Is There in Stating a Man's Potential for Development or for Promotion?

There is little danger in stating it for organizational planning purposes, provided it is kept in confidence, but there is considerable danger in stating it to the man. At best, evaluations of a man's performance and potential represent the considered judgment of other executives, who are human and may err. No one can predict a person's future with certainty, since organizational conditions, job requirements, and the man all change. Therefore, he should be encouraged and helped to improve himself in his present job and, when he has accomplished this, to prepare himself for a better position in the area of his ability and interest. He should not be promised any specific position or advancement to any particular level.

Usually there is less danger in talking with a man who has unlimited potential about his future than with a man who has probably reached his level and can go no higher in the organization. When a man seems to have reached his potential, he need not be told this directly. The skillful executive leads such a subordinate to realistic evaluation of himself. Failure to do this, or blunt statement that "you can go no higher" may turn an executive who is performing his job well into a dissatisfied low producer who loses interest in doing his present job to the best of his ability. This is the greatest danger in telling a man what his potential is. The majority of our executives are not going any higher. But the morale and productivity of this group must be maintained; it is corporate suicide to destroy their loyalty, interest and incentive by abruptly telling them they have reached their potential. Besides, who can be *sure* they have?

72   What Do You Think of Using Rating Forms When Evaluating Supervisors?

Rating forms are a valuable device when properly developed and used. They serve as a guide and a tool for the evaluator, helping him to be objective and providing a standard against which supervisors are judged. Rating charts increase the accuracy of appraisal; they don't insure it. They are most effective when the executives who use the forms and those who are to be evaluated have been instrumental in developing them.

73   Would You Recommend a Particular Evaluation Form That Can Be Used to Help Evaluate Executives?

There is no one best form that can be recommended. In some organizations a standard rating form which lists traits with descriptive phrases to indicate degrees of proficiency is used. In others a series of questions which are designed to lead executives to evaluate the actual performance of men on their jobs without any reference to traits or qualities is used. This latter type appears to be more successful since it places emphasis on the subordinate's behavior on the job—rather than on traits or qualities that may appear to be too general or easily misunderstood. One such questionnaire[3] has seventy-five questions, of which fifteen are reproduced below.

1. Where possible does he invite his men to propose changes and improvements?
2. Do his subordinates come to him first with their work problems?
3. Does he have a plan for orienting and inducting new employees? Does he follow it?
4. Does he counsel with subordinates about their strength and weaknesses.
5. Does he give responsibility to his subordinates? Does he see that authority is clearly delegated and understood?
6. Does he act decisively and promptly when conditions require it?
7. Is he creative and resourceful?
8. Is he usually alert to improve work methods and procedures?
9. Does he distribute his time effectively among his various duties?
10. Is he stable when under pressure? Is he easily upset?
11. Does he meet time schedules?
12. Is he constructive in his thinking? Is he more interested in ways to accomplish difficult projects than in finding reasons why he can't undertake them?
13. Does he welcome and act promptly on suggestions for improvement of his performance? Will he accept criticism graciously?
14. Is he taking steps to prepare himself for advancement and to meet the growing challenges of his present job?
15. In what way has he grown since his previous appraisal?

The full list of questions is distributed to executives before they evaluate their men. The sheet is suggestive only. In some evaluating sessions the Industrial Relations Director who sits in on the evaluation may never refer to it. Now and then he may ask an executive a question or two from the list to open new lines of thinking or to sharpen some generality.

74   Once the Methods and Forms for Evaluation Are Complete What Else Is There to Do?

The program must be explained to the individuals who will be evaluated, and raters must be trained to evaluate. Researchers have found that one of the major factors which contribute to the failure of evaluation plans in industry is the lack of adequate training in rating for the evaluators.

Since an evaluation scale is only an instrument in the hands of

[3] Used in Personal Products Corporation, Milltown, N. J.

the executive who uses it, its effectiveness depends on his skill. Although well constructed forms and a carefully thought-out procedure for evaluation are essential parts of a sound evaluation program, the application of principles of rating and the proper use of forms are critically important. To obtain best results from an evaluation plan, teach your executives how to rate.

75   Is the Counseling That Follows Evaluation Part of Training?

The primary purposes of counseling following evaluation are: (a) to let a man know where he stands, and (b) to help him lay plans to overcome his weaknesses and utilize his strengths. When viewed in this light, counseling following evaluation is a training activity. The employee is made aware of the standards of performance that are expected, the degree to which he meets them, what improvement is possible, and how it can be obtained. This type of counseling will encourage his growth and development.

Chapter 5

THE GUIDED EXPERIENCE METHOD

76 **What Is the Method of Development
Known as Guided Experience?**

The Guided Experience Method, abbreviated as G.E.M., is
planned and organized development given *on the job* by a man's
superior. It is specific in that it attacks weaknesses one by one and
does not scatter its attention. It relies heavily upon experience in
the form of work assignments which are made, carefully arranged
in order of difficulty, to overcome or remove the basic causes of
specific failures.

The guided experience may take the form of day-to-day work
contacts, special project assignments or problems to be solved,
participation on committees, task forces, junior boards, visitations,
research work, reports to write, investigations to make, controls to
establish, etc. No matter what the assignments are, they are preceded by and accompanied by frequent observation of the learner
and counseling with him.

Quite as important as the right choice of experience is analysis
of the individual to determine the cause of each weakness that is
to be overcome. G.E.M. places great emphasis upon discovering
why the employee behaves as he does. Only when the reason for
a particular type of conduct becomes clear is the superior in position to determine what experience and guidance will eliminate the
cause of the failing and therefore the failing itself.

Guided experience systematizes a method which already enjoys
wide use and practically universal approval in American industry.
Many students of management have claimed for years that training and development are the responsibility of line men. G.E.M.
provides a systematic method by which they can meet this responsibility. It provides the help which the line man needs to meet the
training responsibility so widely assigned to him and sometimes
ignored or inadequately handled.

77 What Are the Steps to Be Followed in Applying the Guided Experience Method?

There are four steps in the G.E.M.:

1. Decide upon a major weakness to be corrected in a particular man.
2. Review its full effects.
3. Decide what causes the weakness.
4. Plan remedial experiences and guide the learner into them.

In the first step an executive or a supervisor examines the audits or evaluations of his subordinate. He also reviews his own daily experience with his subordinate to find the major weakness that requires immediate attention. The subordinate may have several faults—all men do—but his superior, influenced of course by the subordinate's opinions and feelings in the matter, selects the fault that is most serious to the man and the company and offers the best chance for correction.

Once a weakness has been selected for treatment, the second step is to determine its effects. This shows how serious the fault is now, and indicates its potential for future harm. Equipped with this information, the superior is able to arrange development assignments and to counsel or guide the man on a factual basis.

The third step is more difficult, for in it the executive determines the causes of the weakness to be corrected. Here he closes his door, shuts off the phone, and settles down to some difficult thinking. The superior must list *all* possible reasons why the man does the thing that reduces his effectiveness, costs the company money, and limits his own future. The superior then reviews his list, throws out those reasons that do not fit, and accepts only those for which there is good evidence. This calls for deep insight and skill in analyzing people, which most executives must develop through practice. The determination of causes is very important for, if the executive is to lead the subordinate, he must clearly understand the reasons for failure.

In Step Four, the executive builds a program of experience to remedy the defect by getting the subordinate to see and overcome its cause. At this point, or in Step Three, the boss may wish to call for help from training experts or those rare men who seem to be born with an understanding of people. Alone or with help, the executive works out a plan of assignments, conferences, and informal talks which will help the man discover his fault, give him experience to overcome it, and provide guidance when he needs it.

78   How Are the Four Steps in G.E.M. Worked Out?

This question is best answered by an example, in the form of planning notes and work sheets developed by a president for work with an assistant. His chief failure was that he too often jumped to conclusions, making some of his decisions more on insight or hunch than on full investigation and deliberate judgment.

GUIDED EXPERIENCE PLANS FOR:
John Palmer, Assistant to the President

1. MAJOR WEAKNESS (STEP ONE):

Both audits and careful observation show that he makes too many snap judgments based on guesses or preconceived opinions, not on facts.

2. EFFECTS (STEP TWO):

a. Costs the company money through poor decisions as in his recommendation to build a new warehouse. Example: He estimated savings of $250,000 yearly over previous rental costs. No savings resulted.

b. Loses confidence of associates, since he is often wrong. Associates recognize that he sometimes acts on insufficient evidence or without considering facts.

3. CAUSES (STEP THREE):

a. Doesn't know that some of his snap decisions have caused trouble in the past. Doesn't investigate his results and no one tells him of his failures.

b. Too much a man of action for top policy making, too little a man of thought. Likes action; dislikes disciplined, careful thinking.

c. Doesn't know how to secure the facts needed for considered decisions.

d. Thinks the mark of a good executive is to have an immediate and definite answer to any question that arises. Does not realize that the good executive also explores problems as fully as time and evidence permit before making a decision.

e. Knows well the specialty through which he rose to his present position and is able to make quick and able decisions in that field, but does not realize his ignorance of some other areas now under his supervision.

f. Hurries too much—work is often piled high, and so hastens through it.

g. Doesn't realize that his present high position requires better judgment than was needed in lower positions where he had less responsibility.

4. REMEDIAL ACTIONS (STEP FOUR):

All these causes seem to apply in John's case, though "a" and "d" are most important. In view of this, I may ask him to make a report summarizing the major projects I undertook on his recommendation this year and their results. Or put him on a review and evaluation committee where men from other divisions join him in examining and evaluating our annual progress report, which includes John's contributions. This may lead him to question some of the results he has been so confident about, and some of the fast judgments responsible for poor results.

I will have him work closely with me on the problem of our proposed plant in Oregon. I will ask him to help me in deciding whether to build now. When he brings in his recommendations, I will ask him whether he has:

a. Projected the cash position of the present business somewhat beyond the estimated date of completion of the new plant.
b. Estimated the additional working capital needed to finance the higher volume which will be produced by the new factory.
c. Determined whether present resources are sufficient to pay for the new factory or whether additional financing is necessary.
d. Studied the availability and cost of labor, both to build and operate in the new location.
e. Reviewed and brought up to date the most recent estimates of building costs.

These and other questions I will drop one or two at a time hoping, if he has not prepared himself thoroughly, that he may get the idea of thorough study and recognize his own inadequacy without my telling him. When he reports on any factor, I will question further to learn whether his conclusion is based on objective evidence, carefully weighed and interpreted. I will arrange to work with him while he goes over some part of his proposal, like the availability of labor. Thus I can learn what sources he uses, how he uses them, and perhaps suggest other approaches. In this manner I will work through a few major aspects of this problem with him.

After I have worked with Palmer through one major problem, I will assign him several specific problems to handle by himself, asking for his final report and recommendations. If there are any evidences that he has not done a thorough job, when he returns with his decision, I will question him until *he* sees the problem as broadly as it must be seen, and until his decision can be supported by facts. When, for example, he makes a quick judgment not to alter our retirement plan and says, "Everybody is satisfied with it as it is and, anyway, we don't have enough old people now to be concerned with it," I will ask:

a. What the figures are on the various age groupings.
b. How our retirement plan compares, in detail, with plans of our competitors and those in force in our local area.
c. What evidence we have, or can get, as to what people actually think of the present plan.
d. The specific costs of various possible revisions of the plan.
e. The probable effects of revisions on worker morale.

Sometimes when he comes in to report his recommendations, I will deliberately arrange to have present other executives well informed on the subject and who generally hold different opinions from Palmer. Their questions of him and their own carefully supported arguments may convince him of the need for adequate evidence and careful deliberation.

After Palmer has had a little experience in studying problems, collecting data, and thinking about his decisions, I will now and then test his progress and give him further experience by telling him I need a survey or preliminary study made on some problem of my own. I will ask him to collect preliminary data and brief me on his findings.

As these things are going on I will find opportunity to make some skillful and appropriately favorable comments on one of our senior executives—on his deliberate, thoughtful, careful approach, pointing out how much a man at the top is one of judgment and reflection rather than precipitous action.

After working with Palmer like this for some months, I shall review his progress, plan any further experiences that may be needed, and arrange to use his newly developed skills.

79   What Are the Strengths of G.E.M.?

Some advantages of the method are as follows:

1. It is a simple, organized approach. Practical people understand it and like the ease with which it can be used.
2. In terms of actual dollars spent and dividends returned, this is the least expensive way to develop a man.
3. Guided experience is always timely, always real, and always related to actual conduct of the business. It is learning by doing, in accord with the first law of the psychology of learning.
4. As in other business activities, successes pay while errors are costly. Beyond the first few projects, the trainee's acts and decisions take effect. This leads to responsibility, while close scrutiny from a superior guarantees rewards for success and penalties for continued failure. Both are incentives to progress.
5. The trainee develops in areas where his superior believes development is needed, not where some outside faculty proposes.
6. All training is to the purpose, since assignments are made only in fields where weakness has been demonstrated. The trainee does not sit through classes or programs important to others but not to him.
7. Closely related to the above is the fact that G.E.M. learning is specific. The learner is not confused by attempting too many things at once; his chance of success therefore increases, and the satisfaction of one success motivates further learning. Evalu-

ation also is simplified when weaknesses are attacked one at a time.

8. Most executive habits of the kind we are trying to change are deeply entrenched behavior, not shaken by such flimsy weapons as words, be the words the telling of another or even our own "intellectual" acceptance of a fault within ourselves. Good habits must be built by continual and cumulative action in doing things the right way. Knowledge of a weakness and acceptance of it helps set the stage for one's improvement, but change comes only after practicing the good habit over a long period of time. Guided experience provides opportunity to practice and fix habits, not to talk about them.

80   What Are the Limitations of the G.E.M. Method?

At the outset, many high executives lack the skills needed for guiding the experience of learners, and a few develop these skills very slowly. Some lack the understanding and vision needed to analyze causes for failure. They also find it difficult to draw suggestions of remedies from their subordinates or to suggest them tactfully.

Many executives feel that they cannot spare the time for this work. They prefer to delegate it to training departments, universities, or consultants, or they take no action at all.

Most trainees grow slowly. High-level executives and some supervisors are likely to be impatient, an attitude that delays learning more than in other methods, where the training is done by professional educators who are patient with learners.

While it is generally true that a superior may develop a good subordinate to a point where he is better than the superior himself, some traits or habits still cannot be developed in the subordinate unless the boss himself has them. This is especially true in the field of human relations and in patterns of thinking and feeling. For example, a superior biased against industrial research or company participation in community activities is not likely to develop a dispassionate feeling about these things in his subordinate.

81   What Help Do Line Executives Need
   to Conduct Guided Experience?

They need to be trained in the method. This will probably require one or two conferences, including considerable practice in applying the method. The first half hour will be devoted to a description and illustration of the method. Thereafter the conference leader will draw case illustrations from the group and will get trainees to apply the four steps, recording analyses on the blackboard as each step proceeds. These analyses are then mimeographed and distributed to the trainees for reference.

Group practice sessions usually must be followed by one or two visits of the training man to the line executive's office, where he reviews the cases where G.E.M. has been used, or help to get the method applied if the line executive has not tried it.

82   Do Groups Respond Well to Training in How to Use G.E.M.?

Yes. One group recently considered the problem of an executive who was delinquent in reporting to his chief. This man's written reports usually came late, and sometimes never arrived. After clearly stating the problem, the trainees reviewed in Step Two the costs of this weakness and then, in Step Three, listed on the conference room blackboard the following possible reasons for the failure.

a. Too busy—has too much work, too many outside interests, too little help.

b. May also use his time ineffectively, making too few plans or schedules for his work and appointments.

c. Is too practical to be interested in reporting. He is preoccupied with immediate problems, likes to discover problems and solve them but loses interest thereafter. Gets less satisfaction from reporting on results than he does in achieving them.

d. Doesn't recognize need for upward communications which should keep his superior informed.

e. Has a disregard for punctuality and time. Sometimes comes late to appointments and handles other aspects of his job in the same manner. Does not know the schedules his superior must maintain for reports nor does he care to find out.

f. Has some fundamental resistance to authority in general; independent and egocentric. Not primarily a team-man where the team involves upper levels of management from which he must accept guidance and direction.

g. May not himself be able to get information on time due to production schedules, closing of books, or failures in his own operations.

h. Doesn't require his subordinates to be prompt in submitting facts for his report. Is too lenient with them, excusing their tardiness. Fails to instruct them in advance of his requirement for facts at a particular time.

i. May fear that facts in his report will be used to evaluate or control his operation. He may have been dealt with too severely at previous times for what he has written in his reports.

After compiling this list, the group chose several causes which they thought were compelling and then spelled out guided experiences to correct them. The executive who posed the problem reported, six months later, that he had secured improvement in his subordinate by applying the suggestions made by the group.

83 Guided Experience Seems to Require a Large Amount of Time. Have You Been Successful in Persuading Managers to Devote Their Time to This Activity?

Not always. Men who see their responsibility to develop their subordinates, who accept this responsibility, and who willingly undertake development, do not seem to object to the time—probably because the results are more certain with G.E.M. than with other approaches. However, those who object to role playing, to case studies, to conference programs and to development in general also resist this method.

84 What Psychological Supports Are There for the Guided Experience Method?

Guided Experience rests upon four accepted facts:

1. The best way to learn is by doing.

2. Development is most effective when it takes place under the guidance of an able and sympathetic superior. Besides knowing what is needed, such a person is in a position to provide the opportunity to learn. He can determine what work assignments, committee placements or job rotations will strengthen a particular weakness, and he has the authority to make the assignments. He also is uniquely placed to motivate learning, to advise, and to reward. Since he often needs men to share his responsibilities and lighten his load, he also has a strong incentive to secure results.

3. Learning is most efficient when the learner sees his goal

clearly, as he does in G.E.M., concentrating upon improvement in a single skill, attitude, or understanding at a time.

4. Studying the cause or reason for any inadequacy. (Step Three) and planning training to remove that cause brings rapid and substantial improvement.

Chapter 6

THE CONFERENCE METHOD

85 What Is the Conference Method of Teaching and How Is It to Be Used in Training?

The conference method of teaching is very old, and is the plan by which over fifty per cent of the industrial training in America is accomplished. As a method of teaching, it is a device for exchanging ideas and for obtaining democratic participation, thereby getting the greatest degree of acceptance for what is taught.

In its oldest and probably purest form, the conference method of teaching was wholly devoted to problem solving. Men were called together when costs, waste, or absenteeism became too great, or when other problems faced the operating head of a department or business. Solutions were asked for and one usually was agreed upon—more or less democratically, depending upon the permissiveness of the leader, the character of the group, and the problem itself. There are some who think this sort of meeting is not training at all but is administrative action carried out through group meetings. Whether it was one or the other probably depended upon the purpose of the conference and the method by which it operated. If the leader consciously emphasized growth and development and used the problem to facilitate learning, he certainly carried on training.

After long use in problem solving, the conference method has been modified into what is called the directed conference. This is used to present information and knowledge, and even to build attitudes. Its success in these areas is, of course, much more limited than in problem solving largely because few skilled leaders are available. In problem-solving conferences, knowledge of the subject and good judgment are the essential qualifications of a good leader. In directed conferences, on the other hand, the leader needs not only a good grasp of the subject but skill in leading the group to sound and generally accepted principles or conclusions. For this he must question, illustrate, adroitly adapt the comments of conferees, and encourage them to think broadly and deeply concerning the subject. In the directed conference the leader endeavors to draw from the learners that which he intends to present. If by questions, challenges and good thinking he can draw the desired ideas from the group, he merely supports, illustrates or reinforces them. If not, he presents them indirectly, with as little telling as possible.

86   What Is the Conference Method of Organizing and Carrying Out a Training Program?

The term "conference method" has two meanings. One denotes a system of organizing or administering training; the other designates a method of teaching. In the former sense, the conference method means that a series of training conferences is planned to deal with eight or ten topics such as reduction of waste and errors, routing of forms, telephone technique, how to use an executive secretary, systems and methods improvement, and so on. Teaching materials, lesson plans, tests, etc., are assembled and each session of the full course is prepared. After some practice runs, a master presentation is then given, usually by the training coordinator, to ten or a dozen line executives. They attend the conferences, study the subject matter, and finally teach the same material to their supervisors. In turn, these supervisors pass the material downward in similar meetings.

By this method a program given once to ten or a dozen men at the top eventually reaches the bottom. This is the method relied upon almost wholly where there are central training staffs in the home office who prepare programs to be presented by line executives in operating plants and branches.

The advantage of this method is obvious: it seems to get a lot done, rapidly and cheaply. When results are measured, however, this seldom proves to be true. There is too much dilution of teaching as it goes down the line. There is poor teaching, too, and indifference at levels far from the top. In fact, some programs which are supposed to interest men in growth and development are so badly taught that men go away resentful of further learning or training. Finally there is danger that the instruction will not fit the needs in some of the departments. When that happens, training is doomed to fail and negative attitudes can develop toward all types of development.

87 What Is a Typical Conference Program for Supervisors?

The following outline summarizes a conference program conducted for a group of first-level supervisors. This program is distributed to conferees at the first meeting of the course:

SCHEDULE OF CONFERENCES IN
SUPERVISOR TRAINING

June 30–September 8

June 30	A Supervisor's Duties and Responsibilities
July 7	Principles of Organization and
	The J & J Organizational Structure
July 14	Labor Laws, Unionization
July 21	Building Production Incentives
July 28	Company Rules, History, Services, Policies
August 4	Introducing the New Worker to His Job
August 11	Cost Consciousness, Waste Control
August 18	Giving Orders and Directions
August 25	Supervising Women in Industry
September 1	Safety and Industrial Hygiene
	Housekeeping
September 8	Developing Understudies, Building Confidence and
	Leadership and Self-Improvement
Conference Leaders:	V. F. Brown, J. T. Freeston, V. Smith, W. S. McCord,
	F. E. Fischer, Sally Quinlan, E. G. Planty
Conference Hours:	9:00 a.m. to 11:30 a.m.

88 Is the Conference Method as Used in Supervisor Training a Pooling of Experience?

It is more than that. Pooling of experience implies that all members of the conference group have had experiences from which to draw and are willing to express themselves. It also implies that majority opinion determines the conclusions of the group; each member is confident that the combined experience of all will reveal the practice which all should follow. This, however, is not true. Some supervisors fail to learn from experience; others lack adequate experience from which to draw principles or determine sound practices of supervision. Finally, the majority opinion of a group may not be sound, especially if the members of the group do not effectively interpret and apply the ideas learned from experience.

To obtain the best results from the conference method, the experiences of the conferees must be used to gain acceptance for concepts or practices of supervision that are considered sound and generally acceptable. The group will not be left free and unguided to determine what sound practices are or to relate experiences that support them. The leader will have determined beforehand the essential material which the group is to be taught, will skillfully integrate the ideas of all members, and will lead to group acceptance of this material. This is much more than pooling experience.

89   How Should We Determine the Makeup of a Conference Group for Training Purposes? When Should We Use Horizontal Groupings of Management Levels—and When Vertical Groupings?

Each type of grouping has its advantages and limitations, depending upon the size of the organization, who is doing the training, the experience of the conferees, and the subject and aims of training.

The following analysis may help to get good results from either vertical or horizontal groupings:

Use Vertical Groupings:

1. Where the organization is small and total number of supervisors is forty or less.
2. When the subject matter can be discussed intelligently by men who do not have long experience and fairly high rank in the organization.
3. When the attitude of high-level supervisors is favorable toward individuals who are learning; when leaders show patience and understanding with learners, and exercise democratic leadership.
4. When no more than two levels are to be included in one group. When more than two levels are represented, teaching strain is sure to result. The teaching also is relatively ineffective, since the material must be presented so that the interest of all is maintained, in spite of the wide range in experience and ability presented by more than two levels of trainees.

5. When the subject of the conference must be understood, accepted, and acted upon in uniform manner by all levels of supervision in a department or small company.
6. When it is desirable for the upper level supervisors to learn how lower levels think and vice versa.

The Specific Values of Vertical Grouping Are These:

1. Information contributed by experienced and high-level supervisors give authority and reality to the subjects discussed.
2. Specific problems of a whole department can be solved.
3. Upward communications may be encouraged. The big bosses have a chance to learn how their subordinates think and feel.
4. Bosses at all levels learn to work together, since in the mixed groups status may vanish as a barrier to exchange and cooperation.

Use Horizontal Groupings:

1. In large organizations, where the number of supervisors to be trained is more than forty.
2. When the subject matter concerns only supervisors of a single level—for example, conferences in basic supervision prepared for beginning supervisors.
3. When trainees are so alert, competent and able that they can explore subject matter effectively without the experience, vision and leadership of superiors.
4. When full participation of all members of the group is expected or required. (When interests are common, discussion usually comes most easily.)
5. In large companies where whole programs are sometimes developed for particular levels. For example, the content, method, and administration of a program of economic education for Ph.D. research specialists will be quite different from that of a similar program for office supervisors.

The Specific Values of Horizontal Grouping Are:

1. Discussion is easily controlled since the interests of conferees are virtually uniform, and the conference leader is not concerned with problems of status.
2. Conferees feel free to participate when superiors are not present. Many men are unwilling to say what they really think or reveal their problems when the boss is listening.

3. Improved relationships between departments result when more than one department has representatives of comparable standing at the conference.

90   Who Should Lead Management Training Conferences?

In the first place, we all agree that not everyone can be an effective conference leader. However, most supervisors can be trained to lead problem-solving and information-giving conferences with good results. When broad concepts of supervision and administration are being taught and attitude building is a major objective, more skillful leaders are necessary. Knowledge of teaching techniques, full understanding of the conference method, knowledge of individual and group psychology, and broad experience in leading discussion groups are some of the basic qualifications of the skilled leader.

Untrained supervisors generally fail as conference leaders. They do too much talking and not enough listening. They want to pour out a certain amount of subject matter without waiting to make sure that it is understood, is being accepted, and will be acted upon. They do not realize that they can best achieve their purpose by drawing ideas from the group and controlling their own desire to express themselves.

91   How Does One Select Conference Leaders?

Here are some of the questions to be answered, in this order, when a conference leader is selected:

1. Is he interested in training activities? Does he believe that training is worth while? Does he support training programs? Does he sincerely like to help people?
2. Does he know the subject matter? Is there some part of a supervisor's job that he does exceptionally well or in which he specializes?
3. Does he have real ability to lead conferences? Has he taken a course in conference leadership or has he shown exceptional native ability to stimulate group discussion and group participation in training or problem solving? Does he realize the value of participation by conferees? Will he welcome your assistance in planning his presentation?
4. Does he have time to prepare for and lead the conference?

92 When the Conference Method Is Used, Should the Conference Leader Be an Authority on the Subject Being Discussed?

No. He need not be an *authority*, but he should have a better-than-average knowledge of the subject and probably should be better informed than any member of the group. Acquiring this knowledge is part of the preparation the leader must make before the conference. Though the precise amount of knowledge needed by a leader can hardly be specified, this example may be helpful:

In one plant, a conference on "Supervising the Woman Worker" was led by a practical supervisor who had no special knowledge of the subject and had made only routine preparation. Members of the group were about equal in their opinions as to whether or not women should be used as supervisors, whether they were more gifted than men in any fields, and whether they were too emotionally unstable for jobs in industry. Many arguments were advanced, and opinions were pooled so freely that on points where the majority was right, some good was accomplished. Unfortunately, where the majority was evidently wrong, there was no one to guide it away from error, since the conference leader had no special knowledge of the subject and did not believe in injecting himself into the discussion. Toward the end of the conference, one supervisor asked, "What about dysmenorrhea?" No one else knew the meaning of the word, yet dysmenorrhea almost totally incapacitates from ten to twenty per cent of all working women every month for periods that range from a few hours to a day or more. Here was an area of vital importance which the unprepared leader had overlooked, and which he could not handle when the conference encountered it.

93 When Should the Conference Method Be Used?

The conference method has proved a valuable training method for supervisors and employees. It is one of the most successful group teaching methods for giving adults information and attitudes that will improve their job performance. It succeeds because it gives trainees a chance to take an active part in the learning process and to shape the teaching to their own needs. It can be used most effectively when:

1. Participation on the part of conferees is desired.
2. The group to be trained is small (ten to twenty) or can be divided into small groups.

3. There are instructors available who have been trained to use the conference method of teaching, as it is defined in the answer to Question 1 in this section.
4. Time is available for group analysis and discussion.
5. The subject matter relates directly to the conferees' experience or knowledge.
6. The experience of the conferees is varied but of comparable extent.

94 What Are the Advantages and Limitations of the Conference Method?

ADVANTAGES	LIMITATIONS
1. This is a relatively active way of learning with ample chance for participation by each member of every group. For this reason it appeals to people and secures ready cooperation.	1. Conferences can be dominated easily, but sometimes not discernibly, by the highest-level executive or most positive person present.
2. It appeals to practical men and to those of long experience who wish to talk about their experiences.	2. At least some of the conferees must be well informed about each subject. Otherwise the group is likely to exchange ignorance or prejudice rather than knowledge and logic.
3. It has the traditional approval of training men of long standing.	3. Conferences sometimes are used to present information where lecturing or other means would be more appropriate.
	4. Unless ably conducted, the conference may become a brush-over, never coming to grips with fundamentals or giving them adequate discussion.

95 When the Conference Method Is Used with First- and Second-Level Supervisors, the Leader Usually Hears Unfavorable Criticism of the Conference Members' Superiors. How Does the Leader Use This Information?

In order to run effective conferences with supervisors, you must assure them by word and act that their comments will not go beyond the training class—unless they give their consent. Your objective is to get them to express themselves freely in an objective way without, however, encouraging discussion of "personalities."

When criticisms show conclusively that a man is erring or failing in some respect, the conference leader should take action. In some cases—not many—he may bring the critic and his superior together and let them discuss the latter's mistakes. More frequently, the conference leader will tactfully discuss the superior's shortcomings with him, emphasizing opportunities for future progress rather than past failures. With or without such preliminary discussion, the man may be guided into the next supervisor training class, or may be asked to lead conferences in which he realizes and begins to correct his faults. Finally, trainees should be convinced that it is their duty to guide, counsel, and stimulate improvement in their superiors. They can do this by discussing ideas and information secured in training classes in order to obtain the understanding and support of the men under whom they work.

It is human to perceive faults in other people yet fail to recognize them in ourselves. While conferees apply principles of supervision to their superiors, the leader will help them apply those principles to their own conduct. Many will realize for the first time that their subordinates may perceive their faults, just as they perceive the lapses of their own superiors.

96   In Training Conferences, How Should the Following Be Handled by the Conference Leader: (A) the Silent Group, (B) the Man Who Won't Talk, or Who Declines to Express an Opinion, (C) the Wise Guy?

A. *The Silent Group.* Try to find out why the group is silent. Are its members inexperienced or afraid to reveal their shortcomings? Are you presenting the ideas for discussion properly? Were the men forced into the training?—and so on. In general, the most common causes are inexperience on the part of the leader or the participants, fear of showing ignorance or of being rebuffed, lack of interest in the subject, and hostility to the leader or to the training idea itself. The use of practical illustrations and examples as thought-provoking devices is one successful way of stimulating groups to talk. Call on conferees to comment. Go around the group asking for expressions of opinion. Give everyone a chance to talk, and don't show embarrassment at silence.

B. *The Man Who Won't Talk.*

1. Ask him to describe certain techniques or practices of supervision with which he has had experience.
2. Build up his answers. Give him credit for a little more than he actually said.
3. Draw comments from him when you are sure he can provide the right answer.
4. Find out why he won't talk; adapt your approach accordingly.

C. *The Wise Guy.* Don't attempt to outsmart him. Overlook his cracks and if the group doesn't control him, speak to him after the conference about his attitude. Make it clear to the group that the discussion is a serious affair, calling for careful thought. Still, meetings don't have to be somber; there are times when the wise guy can inject fun that forms a welcome and helpful relief. Properly used, he may be as much of an asset as a liability.

97   What Is Conference Leadership Training and What Are Its Values?

Conference leadership training is a training program designed to prepare supervisors or others in management to act as conference leaders. The values from such training are:

1. It develops the conference leader's skill in obtaining creative ideas through analysis of problems and group discussion. Every leader needs to obtain the best performance from his subordinates. One of the more important ways of obtaining this best performance is through skill in encouraging subordinates to express ideas, plus skill in listening to them and helping them to make the ideas meaningful and practical. Conference leadership is a workshop where this skill be can developed, practiced, and refined.

2. It stimulates the participants to take an active part in helping their superior with the problems he faces. When supervisors are trained in the skill of obtaining and discussing ideas of others, the barrier to communications that exists between superior and subordinate which restricts cooperative activity and team play will be reduced. The more effectively the leader can demonstrate his willingness to accept ideas from others, the more likely he is to receive them. A trained conference leader must be competent in stimulating participants to actively express and explore ideas that relate to their problems.

3. It assists the leader in developing skill in changing attitudes of others. Habits and attitudes of adults are not changed by telling and lecturing. To change a man's pattern of thought or action, he must be motivated to want to make the change; he must feel the need to make it. Through conferences where the participants are allowed to express their ideas, explore these ideas and the ideas of others, and where they are active in the teaching process, motives are easier to establish and learning or change will be more effectively achieved.

4. It reduces waste of time in conferences since the training in conference leadership assists the leader to plan specific objectives for the meeting and how these will be obtained; recognize and control irrelevant discussion; limit those who monopolize discussions; determine when discussion has been adequate; develop skill in getting others to reach agreement; and to conclude the meeting.

5. It develops tolerance and understanding of others. Since the conference method demands obtaining ideas from others, the successful leader must encourage participation and tolerance of opinions. If participation is to be encouraged, the leader must protect the contributor from ridicule, embarrassment and feeling of insecurity. He will do this by his own example of tolerance and by finding plausible ways to use each man's contribution.

6. It assists the leader in being a better conference member himself since he understands the role of leader, he will express himself more freely, listen more attentively to what is said and assist the leader in keeping the conference on the beam and generally obtain more from the discussion than other participants.

7. It develops ability to verbalize and express one's ideas and to reflect the ideas of others. Supervisors and managers live in a climate of ideas, and the ability to express themselves clearly and effectively is most important to their success.

8. Finally, conference leadership training improves ability to develop and train subordinates. Conference leadership training is really a form of teacher training. It prepares a supervisor to lead his own staff meetings where some small amount of training is always accomplished and where much can be done with the proper approach. It also prepares him to lead conferences in his own department or for the training director that are primarily training in nature—conferences such as the handling of grievances, duties and responsibilities of supervisors, cost control, good housekeeping, etc.

98   What Is the Best Way to Sell Conference Leadership Training to Top Management?

The job of selling conference leadership training to top management does not differ from that of selling any other training program. Top management must be convinced that the need for such a program exists and is urgent, that the proposed program will meet the need effectively, and that it can be carried out with competence and dispatch. There is, however, no one best way to present a program to top management and persuade them to participate in it. One method which has proved effective is this:

Sit down with the highest executive who can be reached, describe the program, outline its values, ask his support for a trial course to be made optional for persons who may need and want it. Prepare a memo for the executive's signature, describing the course and the need for it, and inviting those who are interested to attend. Distribute this to all executives who report to this man and give the course to those—no matter how few—who are willing to attend. Indulge in no forthright campaign, but prompt satisfied participants to recommend the course to others. After a few months repeat the offer. Keep at it until at least a majority high-level executives have been trained.

Sometimes the only way one can entice top management to take training in leading conferences is to suggest they take a condensed course, shortened by reducing the number of practice sessions. In the authors' opinion this should be a last resort, since condensation reduces the value of any course, and participants may realize that they are learning less than they should be. On the other hand, some members of top management are able to learn or crystallize sound concepts of conference leading with a minimum of exposure to class training. The good that can be done for them must be balanced against possible failure with men who are hampered by lack of adequate skills and by firmly fixed habits. Such men need full exposure to training before they can get rid of their anxieties and fears of change, and can develop conference skills of leadership.

99   What Should a Course in Conference Leadership Include?

Conferences enable supervisors to utilize the knowledges and abilities of employees, and at the same time allow employees to participate in making decisions that will affect them. In order to become effective conference leaders, supervisors must develop

certain attitudes and master certain essential methods. Specifically, they must:

1. Learn how to make proper preparation before conferences are
   begun. In making such preparation the supervisor will list the
   objectives of the conference, study and outline the subject matter, and assemble all teaching materials in readiness for each
   conference. Last but not least, he will analyze the group and its
   needs.
2. Learn how to stimulate discussion by means of illustrations,
   questions, demonstrations, and even silences.
3. Learn how to guide the discussion through the use of direct
   questions, summaries, and other devices.
4. Learn how to conclude discussion by means of a summary based
   upon blackboard or other notes.

As supervisors work to master these essentials, they must be
taught specific attitudes and understandings which supplement
the techniques of conference leading. Some of these attitudes are:

1. Willingness to listen to what the conferees have to say.
2. Realization that leading conferences is an integral part of the
   supervisor's job; that it enables him to teach his subordinates to
   do their job effectively.
3. Respect for conferees' contributions.
4. Desire (not reluctance or mere willingness) to make proper
   preparation.
5. A feeling of obligation or duty to use the conference method
   effectively.
6. Confidence in his own skill as a conference leader.

We suggest teaching these essentials and attitudes through the
use of the conference method with considerable time devoted to
the leading of practice conferences which would be analyzed by
the group.

100   **How Frequently Should Conferences for Supervisors Be
           Held and How Long Should They Last to Be Most
           Effective?**

Supervisor training conferences of an hour to an hour and a
half in length held once a week for a period of from five to ten
weeks per course are generally considered to be most effective.
There are a number of reasons for these limitations:

1. Supervisors are primarily hired to direct the work of others and to get out production—not to attend training classes. They usually cannot be spared from their jobs more frequently.

2. If supervisors are under pressure to get back to their jobs and to get production out, their minds are not on the training. People learn best when they are motivated to learn, their interest is sustained, and they can apply themselves completely to the subject matter.

3. Learning is a process of change. Between instruction periods, there should be enough time to enable the student to apply what he has learned so that the change can become permanent. Instruction which takes place weekly allows time for practice and application between the meetings.

Chapter 7

JOB ROTATION

101   What Is the Method of Development Known as Rotation?

Rotation is the planned movement of men from one job to another for the purpose of developing their skills and understandings. It is different from transfer, since transfer usually contemplates no more than one change for each person and is made to meet specific needs other than development. Rotation usually contemplates several changes and its purpose is the development of men.

In the narrowest sense, rotation may mean the movement of trainees from one department to another for the mere purpose of orienting them to the operations of each department. However, the term usually implies much more: the movement of men to positions of line or staff responsibilities where they must perform effectively and "carry their own weight," like any permanent incumbent. Sometimes the purposes are to broaden men for better service at the level where they currently work, but more often the ultimate objective is to prepare the men for advancement.

102   Where Is Rotation Most Often Practiced?

Rotation is most common in railroads with their great number of stations, freight yards, and rail centers; in mail order houses with retail outlets; in chain operations of all kinds—groceries, men's or women's wear, auto accessories, drugs, novelties; and in multi-unit manufacturing companies. Furthermore, insurance firms and banks with branch offices find rotation a useful method of training men, filling vacancies, and introducing new ideas and practices. It is, of course, practiced within shops and offices, regardless of size, where managers are alert to use every opportunity for development within the organization itself.

103   **What Are the Advantages and Limitations of Job Rotation?**

ADVANTAGES	LIMITATIONS
1. Rotation broadens an individual by exposing him to different problems, functions, and people. It tests men by letting them prove themselves in varied circumstances	1. Rotations upset established plans and operations. Rare is the executive who willingly endangers daily operations by transferring one successful man and trying another.
2. It brings new challenges and new interests to men who may have gotten into a routine pattern of action.	2. Men are bored by change as well as stability if the former comes too often and without careful planning. Rotations should be limited.
3. It improves jobs by putting them in the hands of new men, with new ideas and abilities. Some experts say that any man has given his job his best creative attention during his first five years at it; thereafter it neither grows nor improves, but just gets done.	3. Top management must make sure each man understands that rotation is a compliment to his past work and an investment in his future. Without preparation, some men interpret rotation to mean that they have not done well enough on their old jobs.
4. Rotation meets the needs of keen and able people who are ready or almost ready for promotion at times when no appropriate vacancies exist. New experiences hold their interest and provide much the same challenge that would come in a promotion.	4. Employees suffer some insecurity when a new boss comes to them via rotation. If supervisors are changed too frequently, this loss of stable leadership is a serious one for the worker. Careful explanation of the reasons for the rotation helps to reduce employee anxiety.
5. Rotation permits men to find the field in which they do best. This prevents two costly errors—the assumption that a man who does poorly in one position cannot perform well elsewhere, and the equally dangerous assumption that a man who makes good under one executive will do as well at any other job.	

104   **What Is the Easiest Kind of Job Rotation?**

The kind that shifts people from old jobs to new ones in which the work is similar or closely comparable. Industrial engineers, for example, may be shifted from one department to another without significant increase or decrease in responsibility. Foremen may be moved within departments or plants; salesmen may be shifted from one territory to another.

Such rotations provide changes of supervisors and opportunities to work with different groups of subordinates and associates. Rotations like this also provide a variety of departmental, company, or geographic climate, as well as different work standards and philosophies of operation. They keep each man alert and growing while they test his adaptability.

105   What Are Some of the More Complex Job Rotations?

Exchanging one specialty for another within a functional unit is a little more complex than the rotations described in the answer to Question 104. An example is the rotation of buyers in a purchasing department, so that the man who bought trucks and passenger cars trades places with the one who handled office equipment, stationery, or raw materials such as steel and cotton. On the same plane, an employment interviewer may exchange with the man handling job evaluation or merit rating, both being in the personnel department. In this same category comes the rotation of a lawyer from patents to trade-marks, or to labor law.

Still more difficult is the movement of men from staff to line work and vice versa. Probably the most difficult movement is that of rotating men from one technical specialty to another because specialists like chemists, physicists, and bacteriologists are the product of years of intensive specialization. Still, it is possible to turn the plant medical director into a research worker, or a chemist in an explosives plant into a safety director. The person who directs rotation also will find that some shifts are easier than others. The step from personnel to public relations or from engineering to production may not be so difficult as one from research to finance or from advertising to quality control.

Once a man has moved through several rotations and has gotten into general management, where he coordinates many different kinds of work, the one or two moves that may be needed to complete his development cause little difficulty. Thus it is relatively easy to shift the competent, previously rotated manager of a paper products mill to a textile plant. After one has experienced a few rotations, he can shift readily yet still derive profit from work that presents new problems and responsibilities.

106   Should Rotation Start with Junior or Senior Men?

Good programs of rotation start with the easy, simple move-ments and work toward the more difficult ones needed by mature top executives. It is unwise to begin with extensive rotation of top-level men and go down the scale. Start with juniors and when they grow in experience rotation will be easy for them.

107   Doesn't Job Rotation Free Management from Much Plan-ning and Stimulating of Trainees, Leaving Them, as They Should Be, on Their Own to Sink or Swim?

It could do this. Whether or not it does depends upon its pur-pose. If the rotation is primarily a testing process, then the man will receive very little guidance and will be faced with challenges that test and measure his ability and resourcefulness. On the other hand, if learning and growth are the primary objectives the trainee will be given careful guidance and constant supervision, especially in his early days on the job. Learning, even where it is so closely related to experience as it is in job rotation, is most efficient when it is planned, motivated, and supervised. This takes time on the part of superiors, but this type of rotation is a device for training promising people, not one designed to free superiors from hard work in developing understudies. By combining careful counsel and coaching with job experience, however, it does make learning fast as well as efficient.

108   Who Should Be Rotated?

Rotation should be accorded those people who learn well from experience, who are strong in theory but lacking in practical ex-perience, and whose particular developmental needs can be met by a particular rotation. More care should be used in picking a man for rotation than in selecting one to attend an executive de-velopment course in the plant or at a university. Both men may fail to learn, and the one in class may be a burden to his teachers and associates. Still, his failures do not slow up or disrupt daily operations, as do those who fail in job rotation.

Whether or not a man will participate in rotation depends upon his training need. If, for example, he needs to broaden his knowl-edge of the operations performed in his company, and if one or more positions can be opened for him in different departments, he is a candidate for rotation. On the other hand, if he needs skills or attitudes too complex to be developed easily from experience, or if they are not possessed by any company supervisor under whom he could serve a period of rotation, then other training devices must be used.

109   Who Plans Rotations?

When they take place within a department, the department head usually plans them after consulting both his superior and his subordinates. The person in charge of executive audits, training, or executive development, may assist the department head. Such assistance may include critical analysis of rotation plans, selecting specific training activities for the men being rotated, or working out future rotations.

When rotations are made from one functional unit to another, a plant-wide committee is usually helpful. Committee members work closely with a coordinator who may be either a personnel or training specialist or a high-level line executive.

Sometimes rotations are planned by a very able personnel director or his training man instead of by a committee. This man collaborates with individual department heads in planning exchanges and rotations. This arrangement has several advantages. The personnel director is the officer chiefly responsible for effective use of human resources. He has time, special training, and aptitude for the job, and is likely to know over-all organizational strengths, weaknesses, and needs.

110   Must Rotations Be Planned in Advance, or Can They Be Made Whenever Opportunity Arises?

For best results rotations should be planned in advance. They should be set up to meet learning needs revealed by a man's executive audit, and long-range planning makes sure that men will be rotated into positions where they will have a chance to overcome their own particular weaknesses. Then a man who is weak at control and follow-up will be rotated to a supervisor who is strong on these aspects of management, while one who is headstrong and positive will go to a superior who is tolerant and moderate. However, management's resistance to what its members may consider "overplanning," can compel unplanned rotation. Even if a series of particular moves cannot be planned well in advance, there must be planning before a specific move takes place, however suddenly it is decided upon.

Where long-range plans cannot be made, alert personnel men, training directors, and line executives can make successful rotations by taking advantage of opportunities as they arise.

111   How Do You Start Rotation?

1. Use periodic evaluations to locate men who need the development or challenge that is best provided by rotation.

2. Prepare your department or organization for rotation. In your staff meetings, tell them what it is and why it's important to them and the company. Invite suggestions as to how it can be carried out.

3. Locate and designate positions where men may obtain the development they need. Some positions useful for development will be so important in company operations that they cannot be used. Proper development of executives and improved staffing should eventually reduce the number of these positions to a minimum.

4. Prepare the man to be rotated for his opportunity. Tell him why he is chosen, what is expected of him, and to whom he should take his problems.

5. Watch for or develop vacancies through retirements, quits, discharges, promotions, transfers, or rotations of incumbents. Move men who need development into the vacant positions.

6. Learn how to handle rotation problems by beginning with one or two men, increasing the number as you gain skill.

7. Keep an eye on the men who are being rotated. Help them and encourage others to do so. Above all, do not cast them loose to provide for themselves at a time when they are in need of stable personal relationships.

112   Is It Good Practice to Identify Certain Positions as Training Spots and Rotate Men into Them Regularly?

Yes. The advantage is that spots can be picked which will provide adequate training and still not upset work needlessly. Frequently such positions are indicated by the words "assistant" or "assistant to" with responsibility for handling special assignments.

Such positions, earmarked for men who are being rotated, provide for broadened experience as well as training in cooperation and coordination. Sometimes, however, they carry too little responsibility, so that the learner does not profit from the rewards and penalties that accompany *full* responsibility for work of some department or section. If certain jobs are to be reserved for men being rotated, most of them should allow occupants to carry full responsibility and authority for whatever they are assigned. A man does not learn to be fully responsible by carrying a fraction of the load. In fact carrying only part of it teaches him to become dependent, to avoid making decisions himself.

There is one caution. Where spots are identified and reserved for rotation, employees in the department are denied the opportunity of promotion to such positions. Unless other, and adequate opportunities for promotion are open to them they will resent the idea and the man who is rotated into the position.

113   Should Employees in a Department Be Prepared for Rotation of Their Superior and Acceptance of a New Leader?

Yes. Preparation is needed because subordinates who have established satisfying or stable relations with their superior may be upset by his loss. When this happens, morale is lowered by fears and frustrations. Disturbed subordinates also are likely to give vent to their emotions and anxieties by attacks upon rotation itself, upon the new man, or even upon their departing superior. Moreover, some members of the department may be resentful because they are not promoted to fill the vacancy. Others also may fear that the spot is to be permanently reserved for rotation, thus denying promotion to them or any other member of the department. Meetings must be held to explain how candidates for rotation are chosen, and to outline employees' chances for rotation or advancement, and to show what steps they must take to merit that opportunity.

Cooperative subordinates can do much to make a rotation successful. In fact, in the right climate they may willingly help teach a new man the ropes. Whether they do this or not, the whole department may have to work a little harder and share results of the new man's trials and errors while he is being oriented. The right preparation puts people in the mood to do this.

114   How Does One Prepare Employees for the Rotation of Their Superior and Acceptance of a New Leader?

Preparing employees involves talking with them long before rotations actually take place, thus giving them a chance to think the matter over and make partial adjustment to events before they happen. It is well, moreover, to go beyond telling about rotation and invite employees to express their opinions about contemplated moves or suggest moves themselves. In doing so they will reveal the extent of their concern over changes and at the same time get rid of some of their tensions.

Assurance that a competent substitute will be sent is useful. Telling why rotation is practiced and showing what all concerned are likely to gain from it, also helps prepare a department for the change. Assurance from the department head that he will always be available to assist the new man or anyone in the department will help further to gain acceptance of the change.

115   When a Man Is Rotated, Is It with the Idea That He Will Eventually Come Back to His Original Job?

Perhaps—and perhaps not. The answer depends on the purpose of the rotation. If a man is rotated to improve his performance in his present job, obviously he will return to his original position when the necessary development has taken place. If, on the other hand, the man is being rotated so that he may gain the breadth and experience required by a more responsible position, he probably will not return to his original position.

Few rotations start out with the definite intention of returning a man to his starting point. A rotated man may remain permanently in one of his new jobs, or he may make a long stay under constant observation and evaluation. When he reaches a position for which he is well fitted, and in which his services are needed, he may remain there for some time maturing, doing good work, and getting ready for another horizontal rotation or for a step upward.

116   How Can Rotations Be Planned or Prepared For to Make Sure They Will Meet Individual Needs?

Three simple steps are helpful in seeing that rotation meets each learner's needs:

1. Review the man's evaluations and audits, or collect comprehensive data on his performance if audits are not available. From this review determine his development needs.
2. Survey positions in the company to determine where the man can get the experience and guidance he requires.
3. Plan the actual rotation move.

117   Isn't There Prohibitive Loss of Efficiency in Department Operations When Established Leaders Are Uprooted and Newcomers Introduced?

Perhaps, but there need not be. To reduce this hazard, rotation should begin while a man is at a fairly low level in the organization. There the problems he faces will not be very complex and other men are available with similar skills and comparable jobs who can take over, or help out if he needs assistance. By the time the trainee has had one or two moves at low levels he learns to adjust himself quickly to new problems and new associates and can handle rotation on higher levels without forbidding losses in department operations. This is specially true if the department he is leaving and the department he is entering have been prepared for the change, as is explained in the answer to Question 114.

If severe losses are feared, a man may be moved to a new department as an assistant to the executive into whose position he will be rotated after six months or a year. This gives the trainee time to learn the ropes, identify major problems, and grow into the full responsibility of the job.

Loss of efficiency also is reduced by careful selection of positions into which men are to be rotated. No spot should be chosen unless it is operating smoothly, with a minimum of problems and with an adequate second line of supervision to back up the newcomer.

118   How Do Men React to Being Rotated?

Under proper conditions they react well. "Proper conditions" means that the general purposes of rotation be explained to trainees; that they know in advance the specific skills they are supposed to develop in each new job; and, as they progress on the job, that they are told how well they are accomplishing what is expected of them. If the learner can help select the position to which he will go, he is unlikely to feel that he is being manipulated impersonally. He is almost sure to welcome the opportunity afforded by a new job.

119   What Happens to a Man Who Does Not Want to Be Rotated?

This depends on why he resists rotation. Does he have evidence that other men have been started on rotation and then forgotten?

Does he fear the personal discomfort of having to learn new things? Is he without ambition? Is health an obstacle to geographic change? Does the man feel that he can learn things faster in some other way? The reason for resistance must be uncovered. If they are unsound, the man should be given counsel to analyze and remove the causes of his anxiety.

Perhaps the question implies that a person who turns down one opportunity for development should not be given another chance. Any such decision, however, should depend upon the man's reason for the earlier refusal, the potential he shows for growth, and the resulting opportunity for service to himself, the company, and society. Another opportunity of a different kind, presented differently and coming at a different period in the man's life may be accepted, though an earlier one was declined. One of the obligations of leadership is to make men willing to realize the best that is in them, and this may mean that some should be given a second chance.

120   Are Rotations Always Lateral?

They usually are lateral. But so long as job changes are temporary and for purposes of development, moves can be made up or down. The determining factor here is the experience which a particular man may need at a particular time. If moves upward were permanent, they would constitute promotion, and if permanent and downward, they would be demotions—and neither of these is part of rotation.

121   How Long Is a Man Left in One Position?

Usually at least six months but not more than two years. The length of stay is determined by the amount a man must learn, his speed in learning it, and the skill of his teachers.

122   How Many Men Should Be on Rotation at Any One Time?

This is hard to say. It depends upon the size of the company, the urgency of the need for development, and the extent to which rotation is the single method relied upon as a means of achieving improvement. Consolidated Edison, a company of 30,000 employees which is known for the excellence of its rotation program, reports that 200 members of management rotated in ten years.

123   **Is the Vacancy Created When a Man Is Rotated Always Used to Give Some Other Man a Berth on His Rotation Program?**

No. The job and its performance may have suffered by having a learner as an incumbent, and it may be necessary to give a permanent, or at least indefinite, appointment to a very able man who will bring the job and its performance back to normal. Moreover, employees or subordinates do not always like the idea of constant change in their boss. Sometimes they need and deserve the stability of a permanent boss, quite as much as a trainee needs and deserves an opportunity to learn.

124   **When a Man Is Being Rotated, Who Is His Boss?**

If a man is rotated within his own department, his boss does not change. There may be some confusion, however, when a man is rotated out of one department and into another where direct supervision changes. His boss is the person designated as his superior in his new department. This person will carry out all the usual responsibilities of a supervisor.

Let us not forget, however, that the man's original supervisor must have played a part in suggesting or arranging the rotation. He therefore will check frequently with the new supervisor to evaluate the man's progress and will work closely with him, the rotation committee, or the personnel or training director to plan future moves, salary adjustments, or any other significant changes. In Consolidated Edison, men are nominated for development by their superiors. Once a man is accepted for rotation by the development committee, his growth is watched over and encouraged by his sponsor. But when a trainee is assigned to a job, his work is supervised by the head of the department to which he goes, and so is his immediate development. But the responsibility for seeing that a man is making progress as he moves from job to job should remain with his original sponsor.

125   **When a Man Makes a Lateral Transfer from One Department to Another Where Salaries Are Higher or Lower for Comparable Jobs, Should His Salary Be Adjusted to the New Level?**

No. Reducing his salary might upset the man's standard of living and prejudice him against the rotation; increasing it might lead him to become unduly enthusiastic over the new position. Since the rotation is temporary, the man is not actually a member of the new department, and his lower salary need not be compared with the salaries of men permanently assigned to the unit.

126   What Is the Cost of Rotation?

In dollars expended, it costs little. In terms of mistakes and failures on the part of the learner, it can be high. The cost is high, too, in terms of time and attention required from both the learner and the supervisor who directs his work. Trainees must be guided if they are to learn quickly and surely from experience, and are to avoid costly errors and mistakes. Guidance takes intelligence, planning, patience, and time. Learners who are thrown unguided into rotations will learn something—but they are likely to learn it slowly and poorly. What is worse, they are almost as likely to learn inefficient ways as they are to learn efficient ones. The values of rotation make it a profitable device, but it demands an initial investment of attention by the learner's superior.

127   Is Job Rotation a Substitute for Promotion?

No. However, all organizations are faced on occasion with the problem of men in middle management who have potential, who are doing outstanding work in their present jobs, and who are expecting new opportunities and challenges. They are qualified to move ahead but there are no openings for them.

Rotations can provide them with opportunities and challenge which may keep them from becoming impatient and in a mood to leave the organization. Seasoned men, ready for advancement at a time when no vacancy exists, find that rotations provide them with the stimulation and challenge of new things, with opportunity for further growth and with assurance that the company is aware of their need and has their interest at heart.

128   Rotation Seems So Simple—Why Don't Companies Make More Use of It?

One reason is that an organization may place too much emphasis upon present-day success and give too little attention to the continuity and future of the organization. If so, executives will avoid even the brief upset or reduction in efficiency that may result when a rotation is made.

Furthermore, not all men respond well to rotation. Stable,

established people often prefer routine and repetition to change, transfer, and new experiences. Such executives both dislike and fear the uncertainties and insecurities of rotation. They are afraid they will not like new work. They wonder whether they will succeed in new environments; and whether they can return to their original jobs if the rotation proves unsatisfactory. They need assurance that they have home jobs to which they can return if need be.

Another reason is that rotations are too often made with little preparation and planning. When this is the case, the candidate may think there is no particular purpose in his job change, and may see no evidence that the new skills he obtains in rotation are needed or will be used. If such inadequate planning leads to failure in one or two initial cases, managers may discard rotation as ineffective.

Also, training men and managers are often not persistent enough in encouraging management to start rotation, even on a small scale. Rotation programs need not be company-wide. A start can be made with even one job-swap within a department. After a few men have had the opportunity for rotation, things move faster for others.

129   In the Operation of the Rotation Plan, What Is the Reaction of the Department Head When Jobs Within His Department Are Being Filled by "Rotation"?

Unless he believes in rotation, has been part of the group that planned and established it, and sees merit in it for himself and his subordinates, he may be resistant or uncooperative.

Don't include a job in the rotation schedule without first making certain of the department head's wholehearted acceptance of the plan and that of the man who is being rotated. If the department head cannot be brought into the planning of the rotation scheme, it will be necessary at least to train him in the values, effectiveness, and methods of the program.

130   Can You Illustrate a Developed Rotation Program?

Yes. The Assistant Treasurer and General Controller and the Controller of Johnson & Johnson have developed and installed an excellent example of such a program in their department. The written plans and policies are given on page 90. They were worked out in weekly staff meetings of the Controller's division.

ROTATION PROGRAM
CONTROLLER'S DEPARTMENT—JOHNSON & JOHNSON

I. *Definition*

    A. Job Rotation is the planned movement of personnel from one position to another in order to develop a variety of skills and a breadth of knowledge and experience. Personnel may be exchanged among divisions or moved into specially created positions for specified periods of time.

II. *Objectives*

    A. The objectives of the program are as follows:

        1. To broaden personnel by presenting them with new and challenging experience and stimulating fresh ideas and approaches.

        2. To help individuals find the field in which their talents are best suited.

        3. To point up areas in which individuals need guidance and counseling.

        4. To provide greater flexibility within the Controller's Department.

        5. To provide trained replacements for promotions or other openings that might occur anywhere in the Controller's Department.

        6. To obtain closer coordination between divisions of the Controller's Department and thereby develop more uniform policies and practices.

III. *Scope*

    A. Initially, the program will start within the Controller's Department of Johnson & Johnson, New Brunswick. If the program succeeds, it is planned to integrate it with Controllers' Departments in Subsidiaries and later with other functions of Johnson & Johnson that have established similar programs.

IV. *Rotation Committee*

    A. The Rotation Committee will consist of two permanent members: the general controller and the controller. These permanent members will choose three additional members who will serve on the committee for two years. The Training Director will serve as an ex-officio member of the Committee.

    B. The Committee is responsible for:

        1. Selecting rotatees.

        2. Planning the sequence of rotational steps.

        3. Reviewing evaluations.

        4. Periodically appraising the progress of the rotation program and recommending change of modifications.

        5. Reviewing the formal training program submitted by the supervisors of the departments into which people have been rotated.

V. *Personnel to be Rotated*

    A. Supervisory and staff personnel in the Controller's Department are eligible to participate in the program. Employees will be selected on the basis of their potential for development as revealed by their past performances, merit rating and personnel tests, their adaptability and their needs and the needs of the organization.

    B. The number of persons in the program at any one time will be limited to the eligibility requirements and the intention to avoid any confusion or dislocation in the operations of the department. Initially, the program will be limited to a few, but other qualified employees will be given an opportunity to participate as experience is gained and as the program develops.

    C. Participation in the program shall be entirely voluntary on the part of the employee selected.

VI. *Period of Rotation*

    A. The period of rotation in any one assignment will vary with each position and with the ability and experience of the person who is rotated. The minimum period is expected to be one year. There is no specified limit as to the number of years during which a person may take part in the rotation program. The period will depend upon his progress, the opportunities for rotation, and the extent to which the program develops.

    B. An employee may move from one rotated position to another, or he may move from a rotated position to his regular position and later be rotated again. In the course of the program an employee may be assigned permanently to the position into which he has been rotated. Employees in the rotation program are eligible for other opportunities for promotion on the same basis as any other qualified candidates.

VII. *Rotation Positions*

    A. All supervisors and staff personnel may be rotated as follows:

        1. Into a regular line job where he is given full line responsibility.

        2. As "assistant to" an executive where he develops a familiarity with the administrative and technical aspects of a highly specialized job.

        3. Into a staff job which gives the man opportunity to deal with new problems less routine than the line job. This position puts him on his own and develops his coordinative skills.

VIII. *Responsibilities of Supervisors*

    A. During the period of rotation, employees will report to the head of the division to which they are rotated. This supervisor is expected to provide them guidance, counseling and supervision. The supervisor may expect some temporary dislocation of his division's activities and some demands on his own time. He is expected to recognize that the program is designed primarily for the good of the organization and the persons who are rotated. To the degree that he corrects and stimulates these men, the supervisor will benefit from fresh insights and useful ideas.

B. The supervisor of a department into which a man is rotated is responsible for developing a formal program for orienting and training the rotatee as to the purposes, policies, procedures and specific functions for which he will be responsible. This program should be submitted in writing to the Rotation Committee before the rotation takes place.

C. In addition to continually guiding the rotatees, supervisors will submit semi-annually to the Rotation Committee a written evaluation of their performance. These evaluations should cover such areas as their ability to grasp operations of the department, their adaptability to subordinates or fellow supervisors, ability to plan and ability to make sound judgments and decisions.

IX. *Compensation and Merit Increases*

A. An employee in the rotation program will receive his regular salary and periodical salary adjustments in accordance with the standard policy.

B. Salary adjustments will be based upon the recommendations of his immediate supervisor. Because employees in the program may be at salary levels other than the rotated job level, salary adjustments should recognize merit rating and performance only.

X. *Cautions to be Observed in Job Rotation*

A. Personnel may feel that rotation is the only way to promotion. This attitude may be avoided by publicizing the policies and purposes of the program and making certain that these are thoroughly understood by all employees in the Controller's Department.

B. Occasionally, the first two or three months of the rotatee's new assignment are vague or completely wasted. This may be overcome by a program planned in advance and carefully supervised.

C. Subordinates may resent frequent changes of supervisors and the loss of stable leadership as a result of the Rotation Program. These feelings may be alleviated by good communications and proper selection of rotatees. In addition, rotation should be spread among departments so that no one department is overburdened.

D. Some individuals may feel that they are being by-passed in the Rotation Program. It is important that all members of the Controller's Department understand the long-range program. It is obvious that all men cannot be rotated at once, and many of the suspicions and fears may be eliminated by an understanding of the over-all program. If some men are not considered for rotation, the reason should be thoroughly discussed so that they are understood and accepted by the individual.

E. There may be some feeling that the Rotation Program is costly and upsetting to the normal operations of the Department. Such problems may be avoided by careful planning and by having all those involved in the program participate in setting up policies and procedures. The cost of rotation must be balanced by the long-term advantages accruing from the development of high-caliber personnel to man the executive and supervisory positions within the Department.

131   How Often Should Personnel Be Rotated on Not Too Technical Jobs?

The purpose of rotation is training. Men should be rotated, therefore, when they have learned that which they set out to accomplish. Specific goals for each step for every man on rotation should be spelled out. It may be that the purpose of an assignment is to do no more than acquaint the trainee with the types of problems faced in a particular position. In another situation, the purpose may be to acquaint the learner with both the problems and their solutions. Or it may be that the rotated man is expected to go beyond an acquaintance with a job's problems and their solutions. He may be expected to develop full ability to handle, without assistance, the problems that arise in the operations he has been studying. The goals and objectives determine the length of stay, which usually varies from a few days to a few years.

Chapter 8

MULTIPLE MANAGEMENT

---

132   What Is Multiple Management?

Multiple management is the direction of a business through formally organized groups instead of through a few executive officers. In its most elaborate development, multiple management supplements the usual Board of Directors with a Junior or Auxiliary Board, a Sales Board, and a Factory Board. The Junior Board is the best known and the most widely adopted aspect of multiple management. Composed of junior executives of a company, the Junior Board has the responsibility and the authority to concern itself with matters of broad company policy and practice, to develop its own projects in any area of the business, and submit recommendations to the Senior Board of Directors for approval and implementation.[1]

133   What Is the Purpose of the Junior Board?

The purpose of a Junior Board is to expose executive specialists within the company to problems which extend beyond or cut across their specialized fields; to give them training in the analysis of problems and the development of practical solutions; to prepare men of junior executive rank for the assumption of top responsibilities; and, finally, to democratize management through broader participation.

134   What Conditions Are Necessary for Junior Boards to Succeed?

Obviously, Junior Boards of Directors can be effective only when they grow out of top management's sincere desire to share

[1] This answer and the answers to the three questions which follow are written by W. S. McCord, Personnel Director of Personal Products, Milltown, N. J. The Personal Products Corp., an affiliate of Johnson & Johnson, has had a Junior Board for several years.

the responsibility for management of the business. There must be complete freedom for the Junior Board in its selection of projects; there can be no sacred areas from which they are barred. Senior executives must be warmly receptive to suggestion and, at times, to searching scrutiny. Junior executives are not long deceived or impressed by a Board which is nothing more than a debating society. Moreover, a Junior Board will soon stop functioning unless its proposals receive serious attention on the part of the Senior Board.

135　How Is a Junior Board Established and What Does It Do?

A typical Junior Board consists of from ten to fifteen members, representing the principal functions of the business. The initial Board members are appointed by the Senior Board. Thereafter, the group perpetuates itself by the election of new members—with or without recommendation by the Senior Board. Members serve for a designated period of time (usually six months to one year), or a certain number of senior members are eliminated each year by lot. The Junior Board establishes its own by-laws, elects its own officers, and sets its own projects. When a project is accepted by the Junior Board, a committee is appointed to investigate and report. Such a committee will consist of Junior Board members and other appropriate persons selected from the company. When a project investigation is completed, the report is submitted to the Senior Board for approval.

136　What Are the Advantages and Limitations of Multiple Management?

ADVANTAGES	LIMITATIONS
1. The Junior Board develops strong feelings of responsibility and belonging among its members.	1. The Junior Board can upset the smooth functional arrangement of the organization unless its authority and responsibility are made clear to and accepted by all executives.
2. Young executives are broadened by contacts with others who represent different specialties and departments.	2. Success of the method depends rather heavily on the board leader's ability. It requires a particularly strong leader.

3. Board activities and their practical nature appeal to many men who resist academic approaches to development.
4. Gives executives who are specialists added opportunity for broad decision making and in taking responsibility for such decisions.
5. Board activities are real, not make-believe exercises. They result not only in training but in reduced costs.

3. Individual growth is likely to be unplanned for, and may go unnoticed by the learner when it occurs.

137 What Kind of Projects Do Auxiliary Boards Undertake?

In the first thirty months of its existence the Auxiliary Board of Permacel Tape Corporation, an affiliate of Johnson & Johnson, investigated twenty-four projects. Of these, sixteen were accepted, three were rejected, and five were taken under consideration. The scope of this work, as well as the results achieved, may be indicated by brief summaries of a few projects approved by the Senior Board of Directors:

PROJECT 1. Revision of order-handling procedures. Complex and sometimes confusing procedures for handling orders had grown up. Through one of its committees, the Auxiliary Board worked out a simpler plan which concentrates authority, improves scheduling, and keeps customers informed of changes in shipping dates. This plan has been in operation about two years, with all anticipated benefits, including a considerable reduction in clerical work.

PROJECT 7. Reduction of shipping costs. The Auxiliary Board developed a plan by which the managers of company-owned warehouses may anticipate inventory needs and thus permit goods to be shipped in carload lots, which is much cheaper than split-car shipment. This plan was tried out, but has been suspended until adjustments can be made in certain warehouses. When adjustments are made and carload shipment is resumed, it will save about $10,000 per year.

PROJECT 10. Installation of slitter rewinders in warehouses. Slitting and rewinding machinery had been maintained only at New Brunswick. If a distant warehouse received an order for tape of a size not in stock, it had to wait for a special shipment from New Jersey. With equipment installed in each warehouse, other sizes of tape can be cut and rewound, thus speeding up service to customers.

PROJECT 16. Merit policy for salary increases. Salary increases had been made by individual decisions which were not consistent in various departments or even within departments. This has been replaced by a plant-wide policy and procedure to be followed in reviewing the progress of office workers, technicians, supervisors and executives and in increasing their salary. This policy has been accepted as fair and reliable.

PROJECT 18. Simplification of price schedules, with reduction in their cost. The Corporation once issued a large and expensive series of price schedules, in a form which demanded extensive and frequent reprinting. The Auxiliary Board has suggested simpler, more compact schedules which can be kept up-to-date at less expense. A detailed plan has been drawn up and approved which will save approximately $10,000 per year.

138   Don't Auxiliary Boards Train Executives Who Quit and Go Elsewhere for Better Positions?

Some of this must be expected. However, the fact that only two members of the Auxiliary Board have left Permacel Tape allays fear that the Board merely trains ambitious men who will promptly seek better jobs elsewhere. One great cause of turnover among junior executives is frustration; another is lack of prospect for advancement. Some junior executives with the highest potential for advancement are able both to serve fully in the narrow specialty where they may be currently assigned and still serve well on projects of broader scope. The Auxiliary Board provides them this opportunity. The Auxiliary Board gives such executives a chance to experiment and achieve in broad new fields. It also provides assurance that good men will not be overlooked and, at the same time, develops a feeling of fellowship, of belonging, of satisfaction as part of the organization. The man who shares that feeling is not in a hurry to quit.

139   What Do Men Learn from Serving on Multiple Management Boards?

They learn the problems of the whole business. Since members are free to investigate any area of the business, they learn about problems in areas that are not so well known to them. In this sense, multiple management broadens men. Board members learn, also, how to work with men whose training and experience are different from their own. Since members serve on management boards voluntarily, whatever learning takes place in this area comes from their own desire to cooperate.

In addition to a horizontal broadening there is a vertical growth. Men learn what the problems of top management are. They better understand top management and also prepare themselves for the day when they may become major executives.

From multiple management boards men learn how to manage —not from books and teachers but from solving the real and practical problems of the business.

Chapter 9

ROLE PLAYING

140   What Is Role Playing?

Role playing, sometimes called "reality practice," is a teaching method originally used and given prominence by Moreno[1] as a therapeutic device under the name of "psychodrama." Role playing is just what its name suggests—playing the parts or roles of other people. In training meetings, either the leader or the group determines the human relations problem to be acted out and members are chosen to take parts. The rest of the group observes the "actors," who carry on a spontaneous conversation.

Role playing may be a simple demonstration or it may be so subtle that in the hands of a skilled user it can be used for group or individual therapy. It is a natural method of learning. Your small son is playing a role—that of a fireman—when he chugs about the floor, ringing bells and squealing brakes in imitation of a fire truck. When he wears your hat, swings your golf club, or puffs at your dead cigar butt, he is playing your role and thereby learning how it feels to be grown up.

For one to whom role playing is completely new, a simple experiment will reveal its potential. As you sit down to dinner tonight, invite your son or daughter to take your part all through the meal. You or your wife should, of course, take the part of the child. You will be surprised at your child's knowledge of your behavior and his ability to imitate it.

Translated into industry, role playing is a method for creating life-like situations and choosing members of a training group to play the parts of the characters. It affords practice in changing roles and in dealing with human relations problems in as near to real situations as is possible without the penalties of failure that might result in the actual situations.

[1]J. L. Moreno, M.D., ed., "Inter-personal Therapy and the Psychopathology of Inter-personal Relationships," *Sociometry*, July and October, 1937.

141   How Does Role Playing Work?

The usual procedure in using role playing is as follows:

A group of supervisors is organized for the purpose of analyzing, discussing, and solving their human relations problems. In the first meeting, the leader sets the stage by explaining the purpose of the meeting and discussing role playing. The leader's objective is to motivate the group to try role playing as a means of solving the most pressing problems of members. He gets the supervisors to state the human relations problems which are causing them trouble, and lists these on the blackboard.

In the second meeting the leader reviews the previous discussion and groups the problems obtained in the first meeting. He may have classified the problems before the meeting and now presents his groupings for their approval. He leads the group to choose the problem they consider most urgent. For example, let's assume this chosen problem is "lining up at time clocks five minutes before quitting time." A specific illustration of this violation is obtained from one of the supervisors. The leader then asks "the" supervisor to describe this employee and the situation. What are the employee's position, length of service, age and home responsibilities, where is the time clock located, what are the rules about lining up at the clocks, and so on? The leader then obtains agreement on when and where the supervisor should talk with the employee: while standing near the time clock, in his office, the first thing in the morning, etc. This is called designing the situation for the group. It is done by getting them to ask questions of the supervisor so that they have the facts they need in order to handle this problem.

The leader usually writes these facts on the blackboard and proceeds to select individuals to play the roles of the supervisor and the worker. This is not done arbitrarily. The leader may ask for volunteers or he may use his knowledge of the abilities of the members of the group and pick men who have sufficient confidence and ability to do a creditable job. He may even have the group select the men to play the roles.

In an area at the front of the room, the leader arranges chairs to represent the physical surroundings in which the proposed action will take place. He reviews the situation and asks the role players to move to the front of the room and act out the handling of this problem. The rest of the group is instructed to act as "observers."

The role playing is halted when the leader feels that the supervisor has demonstrated his method of handling this particular
human relations problem. Usually, the leader first obtains the
group's impression of whether the supervisor who played the part
of the employee played it as an average employee would, and asks
the actors for their comments on the role playing. The leader will
protect the actors' feelings as much as possible yet utilize their
demonstration to give the whole group an insight into principles
and good practices of human relations. Almost invariably, this discussion will give someone else a desire to play the same situation,
using the ideas that grew from the discussion.

Succeeding meetings are devoted to stating a problem, obtaining a specific violation of it, and designing the problem. The
role players are chosen, the problem acted out, and the role playing is thoroughly discussed. Other trainees role-play this same
problem.

This is an outline of the basic way in which role playing works.
However, there are many variations in the method:

1. Roles may be reversed after they have been played and evaluated. (After Supervisor A has played the part of the "supervisor" and Supervisor B has played the part of the "worker,"
   Supervisor B becomes the "supervisor" and Supervisor A, the
   "worker.")

2. Sound recordings of the role playing may be used and replayed
   for discussion.

3. The leader may define the problem for the group by giving
   them a written illustration of a problem with all the necessary
   facts, etc.

In general, these variations will be determined by the leader's
preference and will be used to fit the needs of the group.

142   Why Let a Training Group Design the Role Playing Problem?

The group should be encouraged to build the problem and
establish its setting for two major reasons. First, since the group
has to assume responsibility for defining the problem, its members
will not complain that too few facts are available to them. Second,
the group learns, by experience, to distinguish relevant from
irrelevant facts, thus increasing the ability of members to analyze
their own problems.

143   **How Do You Convince a Skeptical Supervisor That Role Playing Is More Than Play Acting?**

Usually those who scoff at role playing have had no experience with this method or have been subjected to role playing conducted by an inept, incompetent leader. Supervisors who have participated in training classes where the method was effectively used, speak highly of it and do not think of it as "play acting."

Some measures that may be taken to sell a supervisor on the value of role playing are:

1. Encourage him to talk with fellow supervisors who have participated in role playing and have derived profit from it.
2. Invite him to observe role playing.
3. Give him some literature on the role playing method. Encourage him to read it and discuss it with you.
4. Discuss one of his personnel problems with him. Demonstrate how role playing works by role playing this problem with him.

144   **What Are the Advantages of Role Playing?**

Some of its major advantages are:

1. It convinces participants that other people do not always interpret their statements, actions and attitudes as they really mean them.
2. It enables participants to see the effects of their behavior on others.
3. It increases an individual's sensitivity to what others say and to the feelings that lie behind their words.
4. Role playing helps each participant locate his own weaknesses in handling problems of human relations. By practice, it enables him to overcome these defects.
5. It teaches individuals self-reliance in solving problems of human relations.
6. It helps supervisors recognize and understand different points of view.
7. It allows individuals to release pent-up emotions in practice situations, so that they face real life situations in an improved state of mind.
8. It takes training beyond discussion and translates it into action. Participants must act out their changed attitudes, their concepts

of supervision, and their ideas as to what should be done. More than any other method of formal group training, role playing allows people to learn by doing, not talking.

9. It provides practice through which participants develop skill in handling problems of human relations.
10. It permits "dry runs" for anticipated difficult situations.
11. It allows observers to watch and absorb the skills and techniques of other supervisors.
12. Some psychologists define personality as the total of different roles which a person can play. Some of us are inflexible and limited to being just ourselves. We find it difficult to get into the shoes of others, to see and feel life as they do. Consequently we have difficulty in dealing with others. Role playing teaches us flexibility, adaptability, and the power to see life as others see it. It broadens us by forcing us to assume the attitudes and habits (roles) of others.

145   What Are the Disadvantages of Role Playing?

A. A. Liveright[2] enumerates these as follows:

1. Role playing is harder to use effectively than other tools.
2. It's often used inappropriately. In some cases, discussion or presentation of facts would be more effective.
3. Group may place major emphasis on acting rather than problem involved.
4. Group may become so involved in the technique that they forget subject matter and content.
5. Unless effectively introduced, group may resent technique as a childish, kindergarten approach to serious problems.
6. Unless role players are carefully briefed, they may become embarrassed and situation may backfire.
7. A direct question or problem may be more effective and take less time.
8. If parts aren't well cast, people who really don't want to take part may be embarrassed.
9. Group may be antagonistic toward member of group asked to play unsympathetic role.
10. If person really gets into role, it may be difficult to get him out of it later.

[2]A. A. Liveright, *Union Leadership Training* (New York: Harper & Bros., 1951), p. 134.

146   When Should You Use a Sound-Recorder in Role Playing?

Some training men use a sound-recorder to record all skits right from the group's first experience with the role-playing method. In our opinion, this is not entirely satisfactory. Participants need to gain experience in the method, be convinced of its value, and lose some of their fear of the unknown before they have their performance recorded. Once these conditions are met, recordings that are replayed stimulate discussion and concentrate attention on what was said and on the reactions of actors.

147   How Should Role Playing Be Used in Leadership Training?

Role playing may be employed as the sole or principal teaching method in a planned series of meetings in which human relations problems of leaders are presented. These problems may be actual examples drawn from the participants' experience, or they may be prepared by the leader and presented to the group for role playing and analysis. Sound-slide films are available which present typical problems and deal with common situations that are likely to arise. A series of these films may well form the basis of a course for supervisors.

Role playing also may be used to meet specific needs in supervisor training courses that rely primarily upon conference, case study or other teaching methods.

In the latter case, role playing provides examples and experience that may follow discussions of techniques to be used in dealing with specific human relations problems. For example, in the middle of a case study or conference a trainee may say that, "the supervisor should take the employee aside and talk to him about his actions." The leader then asks the man if he would like to show the group just how he would do this, and asks another member to play the part of the employee. Thus, almost spontaneously, role playing becomes a part of the course.

148   What Value Is There in Role Playing for Those Who Do Not Act in a Skit?

Observers are necessary for effective role playing, since they provide a stimulus and supply the candid comments that make the work meaningful and practical for the actors. Observers, on the other hand, profit by the opportunity to witness and analyze demonstrations of human relations in action. They move from the realm of theory into that of practical application. This is the area in which they have greatest competence and are most eager to explore. Their discussion will be more pertinent and more fruitful than it would be were it based solely on oral or written illustration. Sometimes nothing more than a happy phrasing of a difficult thought may benefit the observer. We grant that this learning is less effective than actual doing. But, when properly guided, it can help participants become better supervisors. By watching others attentively and analytically, they learn to recognize some of their own weaknesses and understand their own actions.

149   What Should the Observers of a Role Playing be Watching for?

Observers do not "look for" this or that during role playing. Instead, they observe, analyze, and reach decisions in accordance with suggestions which the leader gives them in advance. In a typical case these suggestions may read:

1. Analyze the way the "employee" role is being played. Is it a representative performance? Does the "employee" act the way an employee would act in this situation?
2. Notice how the "employee" responds or reacts. Does he resent the way the "supervisor" handles him? Does he accept what the "supervisor" says? Do you think he will improve as a result of this discussion? Does he tell his whole story? What emotions are aroused in him by the "supervisor"?
3. Analyze the effectiveness of the "supervisor." What technique, method, approach, etc., does he use to improve the "employee"? Does he talk too much and overpower the "employee"? What does he say or do that significantly affects the outcome of this meeting? Did you feel the "supervisor" kept in mind his purpose or objective in talking with this "employee"?
4. Decide how you would act the "supervisor's" part. In what ways would your performance differ from that of the man who played the role? Be prepared to explain or demonstrate your ideas and give reasons for them.

If more than one supervisor has played the role of the "supervisor," all of these guiding questions can be used. Moreover, observers can be directed to observe and analyze significant differences between the ways in which different men handle the same situation. They do not listen to words alone. They analyze the effect of what the "supervisor" does and says on the "employee" by reading facial expressions or other physical manifestations that indicate pleasure, displeasure, acceptance, irritation, etc. Having done so, they try to decide why the "employee" acts as he does.

150 Where Does One Obtain the Situations or Problems Needed for Role Playing in Supervisor Training?

There is no one source. In general, the leader lets the group decide the situation or problem to be role-played. Sometimes, however, if time is an important consideration and there is a specific problem that the leader is aware that the group is facing or will face in their jobs, he may choose the problem and give all the pertinent facts necessary for role playing. He may even present written problems that are used by other companies.

151 How Can One Sell a Supervisory Group on Role Playing?

This is not as difficult as it may appear. Sometimes situations arise naturally during supervisor training conferences, where all feel the need for acting out a situation. The leader is alert to these situations and gets role playing in use. Although most supervisors will be reluctant to "act" in front of the group, there will always be some who have the necessary confidence in themselves and, with a little encouragement from the leader, readily take part. The leader may ask for volunteers or may choose those who he feels will most readily accept. Before the group knows it, the role playing method is being used. After a few successful experiences with role playing, as subsidiary to the conference method, role playing becomes an accepted method of instruction.

If a series of meetings for supervisors is to be conducted, in which role playing will be used exclusively, one may well begin as follows:

1. Use the entire first meeting to secure a list of the participants' problems, spending whatever time is needed to lead them to be specific. Some will be problems which the trainees can correct themselves, but others will be outside their field of activity. Be sure to get many problems which trainees can handle themselves, as well as those which they cannot.

2. Before the second meeting, list problems which trainees can handle in one group, subdividing the list if necessary. Place those

problems which are beyond the control of trainees in the second subdivision.

3. Present this classification to the trainees at the second meeting. Point out what can be done about problems beyond their control and then direct their attention to the other group. Ask the trainees to select the problem that seems the most troublesome. Suppose, for example, that they may want to know how to deal with the employee who frequently overstays his rest period. Ask someone to give a specific example of a person in his department who creates this problem. Encourage the group to ask questions of this supervisor about the individual and the situation and write these facts on the blackboard. When the group is through questioning, ask for a volunteer to play the part of the employee and another to play the part of the supervisor. If no one is willing to try, the leader should take the "supervisor's" role to demonstrate how the method works.

At this point, the group may not be "sold" on role playing, but the leader has got it into operation and has shown some of its values. From here on, however, the going should be easy. Remember, it is a major principle of selling that getting the product into the hands of the user is nine tenths of a sale.

As in the selling of all training programs, if top management evidences active interest in the training program and the conferees' past experiences in training classes have been satisfying, the role playing method will be easily accepted by the group. However, the group must be motivated by the leader to participate in the method and full acceptance of it will come through its successful use.

152   Can Line Executives Use Role Playing to Train Their Supervisors?

Certainly, if these executives prepare themselves for their work. Preparation will involve:

1. Study of the literature on role playing.
2. Observation of role playing conducted by an experienced leader.
3. Discussion with men experienced in the use of the method.
4. Review of principles of conference leadership. Since a very fruitful part of role playing is the discussion following the demonstration, the leader must know how to effectively draw ideas from the "actors" and the "observers" and lead them to make critical conclusions.

5. Review of individual and group psychology with special emphasis on:
   a. Motivation
   b. Interpreting behavior
   c. Communications
   d. Changing behavior

The line executive who makes this preparation can use role playing to advantage. On the other hand, leaders inexperienced in the use of the method may design a situation improperly, allow the role playing to continue long after the major points have been made, prevent the contributions of members, and do other things which will make both leaders and participants feel role playing is a waste of time. This method is too valuable to be thrown into disfavor by impetuous, ill-prepared leaders.

153   When Would You Use Role Reversal?

Role reversal is the exchange of actors—the one who played the part of the "supervisor" is now the "employee," and vice versa. Use role reversal to assist a "supervisor" who shows little understanding for the "employee's" feelings or reasoning, to help him understand the other person's point of view. Use it, also, to control the "employee" who is overplaying his part and does not enter conscientiously into his role. Finding himself faced with the responsibility of handling the role he has created, he realizes the necessity of entering into a role realistically. Finally, use role reversal to enliven the role playing and to sustain interest.

Chapter 10

THE CASE STUDY METHOD

154 What Is the Case Study Method?

In the case study method participants are given a written report or history, called a case, which they study and then discuss in group meetings. The case summarizes a problem or situation that has existed or now exists in some plant or office. The statement is both comprehensive and realistic; it presents both good and bad practices without identifying them as such, the two commonly being mingled. Though needless detail is avoided, the case presents all the facts required for a fruitful analysis of causes and effects, human motivations, company organization, and the merits and demerits of particular actions or policies. Depending upon the scope of the problem, the presentation means a manuscript whose length may be one or as many as forty pages.

The case is given to participants before the first group meeting so they may study it and prepare for discussion. The leader emphasizes that preparation must be thorough. The more careful, deliberate, and analytical it is, the more benefit will come from discussion. Participants are advised to study the factual information which gives background and basis for decisions, to examine the broad setting of the case, and to determine and analyze the implications of the actions and feelings of the people involved. The problem or problems must be defined and the causes and cures must be determined. The participants should be prepared to give evidence for their conclusions.

In group meetings, trainees are free to direct their discussion into areas that appear significant. Through such free exploration and discussion, they learn to respect the opinions of others, to perceive weaknesses in their own analyses, and to improve their ability to make decisions and to locate problems without having them pointed out by the "professor."

He may curb oratory and digression, but he does not lead the group to recognize and accept predetermined solutions, conclusions, or principles. He takes care not to lecture, but does encourage participants to think by asking them to justify and defend their points of view.

In general, the case method seeks to emphasize the development of judgment, knowledge, and attitudes through analysis and nondirected discussion, with the responsibility for learning resting primarily upon the students. It compels each participant to examine the acts and feelings of people in real situations in order to interpret, analyze, and understand this behavior. The most able participants learn to make generalizations that will guide their own future acts and decisions. They increase their ability to define and solve problems in specific complex situations. This ability then can be applied in handling particular problems that arise in their own departments and companies.

155   What Are the Advantages and Limitations of Case Studies?

ADVANTAGES

1. The case study method trains men to identify and analyze complex problems, and to frame their own solutions.

2. Since each member of a group makes his own proposal, no one man's solution or analysis is accepted without criticism. Learners are exposed to a variety of approaches, interpretations and personalities.

3. Principles, if they are drawn, come from practical cases and are established by the learners themselves.

4. The case study method reduces the overconfidence of dogmatic participants by submitting their ideas to challenging, thoughtful criticism by their equals.

LIMITATIONS

1. Trainees must be successful men of wide experience and sound judgment. Otherwise their analyses are likely to be superficial and their solutions impractical.

2. Some high executives are reluctant to submit their ideas to thorough criticism and resent anything except agreement. Such men must be handled with so much caution that the method may be impractical.

3. Men brought up in the lecture, recitation, or textbook-with-answers tradition may be completely adrift in a discipline that demands analytical thinking but provides no answers and leads to no "best" solutions.

4. Case study also may be criticized as being a piecemeal approach which lacks in focus, since it allows various men to present a variety of ideas and conclusions but avoids using any mechanism that could put the whole problem together as the study comes to an end.

5. "Departmental" men are taught to seek an insight into the over-all problem of the entire business.

5. Like role playing and other off-the-job approaches, this one gives no assurance that classroom success will be duplicated in office, factory or store. Men who understand a problem and frame an acceptable verbal solution still may not know what steps to take or how to take them. Under the pressures of their heavy workloads, conflicting personalities, and loyalty to old methods, brilliant analysts may fail in practical application.

156   Can Cases Be Used in More Than One Way and for More Than One Purpose?

Yes. For years, cases have been used in management training to illustrate and teach principles or practices of supervision. These cases are usually short—a paragraph or two in length. They present an easily discerned problem and describe real or fictitious happenings, with little attention to the circumstances which led to their development or which now surround them. The leader controls the discussion of the case and leads the group toward predetermined principles or practices. This use of cases has sometimes been termed the Case *Problem* Method.

In more recent years, cases have been used in management training for the purpose of developing analytical thinking. These cases, usually more than a page in length, describe actual situations and are written after careful investigation and recording of facts. They contain both important and less significant facts that surround the happenings described. They are written to present broad concepts of administration and human relations problems and to encourage analytical thinking. The leader does not lead the group toward any predetermined principles, practices, or conclusions. This use of cases is referred to as the Case *Study* Method.

These are general categories. There are minor variations in each category, and a combination of both is often employed in industrial training. The instructor will make his choice in view of (a) the purpose of a given course or program, (b) his own ability as an instructor, (c) the type of cases available to him, (d) his attitude towards purposes, methods, techniques, results and other aspects of education that are incorporated in his philosophy of education, and (e) the experience and ability of the learners.

157   What Are the Special Advantages of the Case Study Method?

1. By their very nature, cases appeal to both students and supervisors alike. They have a flavor of reality.

2. Cases are dramatic. They clothe academic ideas and formal principles in a humanistic form and incorporate the strengths and weaknesses of people. The characters in the case live and have real meaning. In fact, characters in cases take on such reality that their names are constantly brought up in social gatherings of the learners and even become synonymous with the error or success in which they have been involved. In contrast to tedious texts on scientific management, cases are the novels and dramas of the work place.

3. The case study method teaches men to think in the complex relationships that envelop all of us.

4. The case study method permits trainees to participate actively in instruction.

5. The case study method gives men a chance to make decisions which may well be beyond the requirements of their present jobs, thus preparing them for increased responsibility.

158   How Should One Prepare to Lead a Case Discussion?

Before actually leading a case, the instructor should study it very carefully. Every phrase and sentence should be scrutinized for every implication. Study of the case should be directed toward four major areas:

1. *The facts as presented in the case.* The leader should have a complete and ready knowledge of all the facts in order to help the group in their analysis. During the discussion he must give his undivided attention to the group, listening to every comment, observing reactions to the comments, being alert to those who want to talk, recognizing misquotation of facts. Therefore, he is not free to refer frequently to the case to refresh his memory.

2. *Implications and meanings of facts.* It is not enough for the instructor to know the facts in the case; he must also examine them. What implications or meanings do they hold, what feelings do they express, what motives underlie them, what is their rela-

tionship to other facts? Advance notes on these aspects of the facts will assist the instructor to perceive the avenue that may be explored by the group. Advance study also prepares him to ask questions that will assist the group to make a comprehensive analysis to weigh the facts with their emotional implications, and to propose solutions for problems that are uncovered.

3. *The identification of problems.* What is the immediate problem in this case? Is there also a long-range problem? Is there more than one problem of either type? By asking himself these questions and justifying his answers, the instructor will prepare himself to help the group locate problems and discover significant facts that support or refute their diagnosis.

4. *Possible solutions.* The instructor must strive to foresee the solutions that may be offered by the group. He should analyze these solutions in advance, to determine how they may be developed and justified during discussion. What weakness do these solutions have? What effect will they have on the organization? Are they easily put into effect? How?

After studying the case, with particular attention to these four areas, the instructor is ready to develop questions that will assist members of the group in their analysis. He also feels confident in his knowledge of the case and is ready to concentrate his attention on what the group thinks and says, and to use their comments to develop their thinking, understanding, and values.

159   How Does One Select Cases Appropriate for a Case Study Program?

Judgment and common sense will play an important part in the selection of cases. Determine the objectives of the training program, consider the needs of the trainees, and examine all available cases. No one knows why a given case is effective in one course or class but not in another. However, we do know that cases must fit the experience, intelligence, and maturity of the group that studies them. Cases must not be too complex or difficult for the group to analyze. Long cases that cover details of operating procedures of a number of departments are not appropriate for persons inexperienced in case study or for groups with limited administrative experience. The first few cases in a case study program should be relatively short (3 to 5 pages), should describe situations of interest to trainees, and should present problems that can be easily grasped. These factors must be judged by past experience with the trainees and from the way other groups have reacted to the material. Cases that deal with a variety of functions in an organization should be gradually worked into the program as the participants grow in ability.

160   Are Case Studies Most Realistic and Effective When They Are Developed by Company Trainers or Line Executives, and Are Built upon Real Experience Within the Plant?

Not necessarily. Internal cases are sometimes undesirable for the following six reasons:

1. The trainer who builds the case may be involved in the actual situation. If so, he is not likely to be objective in his selection of facts or the manner in which he reports them.
2. The trainer may distort the case and the facts in order to get some preconceived conclusion from them, and thus deny some other equally valuable result.
3. Even though the trainer who builds his own cases may not be personally involved or have an emotional bias, his trainees may think otherwise. If so, they will not discuss the case openly and freely.
4. Home-built cases can seldom be discussed fully and freely without seeming to reflect on someone present or at least in the company. Such cases therefore may not be adequately examined. If they are, people still on the payroll may feel hurt. Defenses and loyalties also may be aroused, preventing impartial discussion.
5. When cases are written locally, each conferee may try to identify the persons involved instead of dealing with facts and problems of general significance.
6. Complete reliance upon home-built cases limits the opportunity for gaining knowledge of other industries with other operating problems and procedures.

Since the problems of administration tend to repeat themselves in a variety of circumstances, many cases written about one company will apply almost equally well to others. We therefore have found that using cases based on other companies is realistic and effective. Indeed, so much so that trainees often believe that cases taken from outside were drawn from their own company and must be assured that this is not true.

161　　How Do You Start Discussion of a Case?

There are two well-tried methods. In the first, the leader begins by asking trainees if they have any questions on the case. Someone is almost certain to ask for more facts. It frequently happens that the individual who asks for this additional information has not studied or analyzed the case thoroughly, or perhaps puts more emphasis upon and desires more of the type of facts with which he is most familiar (financial reports, sales goals or achievements, etc.). In any event, the leader will ask the questioner why he desires the information, what difference the information will make in his analysis, or whether the information is not already contained in the case. Such questions will force the man to think and will stimulate others to discuss the need for such information. Soon the general discussion is rolling well. At the same time the leader may have suggested better reading of the case or better thinking about why certain missing information is needed.

Starting a discussion in this manner is most effective with groups which have participated in only a few case studies and so have not yet learned to read the case carefully, to solve problems with available facts, or to realize just what they would do with additional information. New trainees soon learn, too, that the leader does not have additional facts for them.

Another way to start is to tell the group you are ready to begin or to ask for a comment: "Who would like to get us started on today's case?" Once someone in the group has broken the ice, even with a question, the discussion is under way. The important thing to remember in starting a discussion is that the leader should not tell the group when to start. Nor should he provide a leading opening. Let the trainees decide or find out for themselves how the case should be tackled.

162　　How Important Is the Leader in the Case Study Method?

He is very important. The success of case studies as a teaching method depends upon:

1. His self-control. Can he keep from expressing his own opinions?
2. His use of thought-provoking and penetrating questions to help trainees think, analyze, weigh, and reach conclusions.
3. His ability to maintain an orderly discussion without dominating it.
4. His ability to clarify or to help members of the group in clarifying their ideas.

5. His ability to distinguish between facts and feelings about those facts, and to get others to see that difference.

6. His unwillingness to guide or lead the discussion toward a particular solution.

7. His sincerity in being permissive—his patience with discussion that appears to be "off the beam."

8. His understanding of the fact that he knows no more than others in the group.

9. His genuine desire to help students analyze situations and express their own ideas and opinions about them.

Unless the leader understands his role and plays it properly, the case study method will not be effective.

163   Can You Give Examples of the Kind of Questions Used When Leading a Case Study?

It is hard to suggest illustrations of meaningful questions without being able to refer to a specific case. There are certain typical questions, however, that can be used with almost any case. Here are a few examples:

Can you point out to the rest of us where you found this fact in the case? This question is used when a trainee states as facts items that are not in the case. This question directs the man and the group back to the source to help them find and utilize data. Sometimes a trainee states as fact something arrived at by inference. It is then important to the group to understand the man's reasoning so that they may either profit by it or point out weaknesses for his benefit. Sometimes, too, the man has misquoted facts or twisted them unconsciously to justify his position. He may become aware of this through this type of question and the discussion it provokes.

Would that really solve the problem? The man has proposed a superficial solution, or his solution applies only to one detailed or relatively unimportant part of a complex problem. This question helps him to realize the inadequacy of his solution and directs his attention toward fundamental issues. It may lead him to tell why he thinks he has solved the problem, thus opening up areas of his own reasoning to class examination.

Can you explain what you mean in more detail? The man may be fuzzy in his thinking or may fail to express his ideas clearly. It usually happens that when he tries to explain or illustrate what he means, he becomes aware of his own loose thinking, or others may pick up his idea and develop it. Eventually the man may either express his idea effectively or realize that he has no significant contribution to make. This question makes him and the group aware of the need for clear thinking and effective expression.

Would what you propose be easy to do? This question is directed to persons who offer glib solutions, clichés, or easy generalizations. When the participant analyzes the means by which he must accomplish something, and the effect his action is going to have upon the persons involved, he is compelled to think in concrete, specific terms. Prompted by this question, he may for the first time take into account the things that may interfere with his proposed action, weigh their importance, and find a practical way to put his proposal into effect.

How would you go about doing this? This question accomplishes the same purpose as the preceding one. It is sometimes used as a follow-up question to lead the trainee directly into specific analysis and step-by-step planning.

If you did have the additional fact, how would it influence your decision or future action in this situation? This question may be asked of trainees who habitually call for more facts than are needed to solve problems. Such persons try, sometimes subconsciously, to evade analysis of the cases as they are presented by demanding additional information. For these trainees, and for others who are merely inexperienced in making decisions, this question serves four purposes:

1. It redirects attention to the facts presented. Has their scope or significance been overlooked?
2. It compels trainees to evaluate the facts which they think are needed. Are these data essential, desirable, or really unnecessary?
3. It leads trainees to realize that business problems must often be solved on the basis of limited information. There simply isn't time to make exhaustive inquiries.
4. Since *all* the facts cannot be accumulated, the question prompts trainees to use the information they do have to the best advantage. That, of course, is the basis for practical, effective decisions.

How do you reconcile your statement with the arguments advanced by John and Joe? Reference to what others have said emphasizes the need for listening. Moreover, this question indicates that there is more to listening than merely hearing what another person has said. To be worth while, listening involves hearing what is said, understanding it, interpreting it, and relating it to one's own ideas. By these means each participant learns from the others, even though he may question the evidence they advance and disagree with their conclusions.

164   Should the Leader Tell the Group His Solution to the Case?

Groups inexperienced in the case study method often want the leader to give his solution. This is natural since, during most of our educational lives, we have been taught that the teacher has the answer. We look to the instructor—who often has the answer printed for him in a teacher's manual—to determine whether we are right or wrong.

Answers in case studies are not so important as the methods used to arrive at workable solutions. The case study method seeks primarily to develop effective thinking through analytical discussion and weighing of all available facts. In concluding a case study, the leader may point out facts that were skimmed over or neglected during the discussion, indicating their significance to him. When pressed, he may occasionally go further and give his opinion about a solution. When he does this, he makes it clear that he is only offering an opinion, not stating *the* solution of the problem. This is as far as he should go.

165   Suppose the Leader Regularly Provides Solutions to Problems Arising in Case Study. What Effect Does This Have?

Obviously, members of the group learn to depend on him, not on themselves. He stifles creative thinking and discussion, since learners know he is eventually going to give them *the* solution. And, of course, he may be wrong. If so, he probably will find himself arguing with the group to defend his position.

Trainees attempt to preguess the teacher. They size him up and offer solutions they think he will accept in terms of the solution he has offered in earlier cases. When they get back into their industrial situation, there is no leader to provide approved solutions and no book of answers to which they can refer. Giving answers does not prepare men to think and act on their own responsibility.

166   Can the Case Study Method Be Used More Effectively with Some Subjects Than with Others?

The case study method was originally used in the law schools for two purposes, to give students a knowledge of law and to teach them analytical thinking. It has been used for more than twenty years by the Harvard Business School in the teaching of graduate students in Business Administration, and is now also employed at Chicago, Stanford, Columbia, and other universities. In these institutions, many subjects relating to business are dealt with, and some form of case study is used in the presentation of the subject matter. Universities also use this method, along with lectures and other techniques, to help bridge the gap between business theory and practice.

Cases are most effectively used when the purpose of training is to teach understanding of human relationships and leadership skills rather than technical knowledge and know-how. If the engineer were to acquire formulae and his fund of general scientific knowledge through the case study method, he would be forever-and-a-day learning the fundamentals. On the other hand, the problems he encounters in gaining acceptance and cooperation from his fellow workers and from other staff and line men would be profitable subjects for the case study method.

167   Are There Any Groups with Which the Case Study Method Is Most Successful?

Not for certain. In our experience we have found it a very successful method with members of middle management and top executives. Success is determined by the number of cases in a program, the selection of cases appropriate to learners' needs, and the quality of the instruction, rather than the level of the group. If cases are selected to fit the intelligence, experience, and maturity level of the group, the method can probably be used at any level.

Top level executives seem to like the case study method because no one preaches to them or gives academic answers to their problems. They are allowed to develop their own answers with the help of other experienced executives. Because of this, the case study method may be more appropriate for top management than the conference or lecture method. It may be less successful at lower levels, when trainees are less experienced, less accustomed to responsibility, and sometimes less able. Still, the facts at hand do not allow us to make an unqualified answer to this question.

168   Do Participants in a Case Study Program Always Feel Frustrated or Resentful During the Early Part of the Program?

Since all of us have been educated in a system in which the teacher knows the answers, or the answer is in the back of the textbook, most participants in a case study program feel some degree of resentment toward the method or the instructor when the latter refuses to tell them whether they are right or wrong. However, after trainees have had enough experience with the method to recognize and accept their role and responsibility, this resentment disappears.

An article describing how one leader assisted his group to overcome their feeling of frustration appeared in a recent issue of the Harvard Business School Bulletin:[1]

Professor Joe Bailey had the unique privilege of serving as "defender of the faith" when he'd only been teaching at Harvard Business School for a month. His first class, having reached the stage between frustration and despair at ever coping with "these ungodly cases," challenged him as a body with a vehemence never before encountered—nor since, for that matter—to defend his existence. Just what in the name of Heaven was the teacher's function?

True to the case method, he let them talk. The gist of their gripes ran like this:

"The class may leave a case with many points of importance undetected and undiscussed."

"Class discussion often ends with our conclusions confused, scattered, unassorted."

"We often may be reasoning wrongly and arriving at erroneous estimates."

As the leader of a case discussion should, Professor Bailey pointed out the unexpressed inferences—what they wanted to say, but didn't:

The *teacher* (Bailey) should put the conclusions together in a neat package for the class.

The *teacher* should straighten out the students.

This went on for almost three hours. The complete case for the defendant, Bailey, was made in question form. . . .

"If I tell you what points you've missed, will you come to rely on me to do this? Do you want to so rely? Whom will you rely on after graduation? If you seem to be reasoning wrongly, should I merely say so? Or, should I then go on and reason correctly for you? If I don't convince certain students, do I merely say they're wrong and assure the others that I'm right?"

It is a remarkable commentary on the case method of instruction that this

---

[1] "The Business of Teaching," *Harvard Business School Bulletin,* Summer, 1952, p. 95.

"rebellion" of the students really constituted an attempt to put the teacher on a pedestal whence he could hand down professional dicta to be accepted as is, or else. And the defense (triumphant, by the way; a chastened class went on to set a brilliant record) consisted of knocking down the pedestal; of making the teacher a humble searcher for facts too, rather than an infallible encyclopedia of not-to-be-questioned knowledge.

169   How Can a Teacher Become Competent in the Case Study Method?

Anyone who wants to become a leader of case studies must first realize that the job is a very dynamic one. The leader must be adaptable, versatile, alert, and responsive to what is happening before him. He is not leading or forcing the group to accept any predetermined principles or follow any preconceived courses of action. He is trying to help them to probe deeply, analyze carefully, weigh and evaluate feelings and emotions involved, and to recognize weaknesses in their own conclusions. This is no easy task, and it demands skills and abilities that are not easily defined. However, it seems that anyone who wishes to become competent in the case study method should:

1. Gain experience in conference leading, in supervising role playing, and in leading group decision conferences.
2. Study readings such as those listed in the case study section of the bibliography.
3. Observe case studies being conducted by competent instructors.
4. Gain experience and knowledge in the work area of his students.
5. Take university courses in social psychology, group dynamics, and industrial sociology.

170   How Large Should a Case Study Group Be?

It should be large enough to obtain diverse ideas and viewpoints and small enough to allow participation from all who desire to express themselves or can be led to do so. Some case study groups are as large as 100 people; others have as few as 10 or 12. Both extremes have their limitations. Groups that are approximately 40 in number appear to be best. Forty people can exchange ideas freely and often, and all members who desire can participate. Differences in educational and business background are great enough to insure contrasting opinions, and the group is not too large for orderly discussion.

171   Since a Number of Advanced Management Training Schools Use the Case Study Method to Educate Top Executives, Do You Feel That It Is the One Best Method to Use?

If we were permitted to use *only* one method in the group training of top executives, we would choose the case study. In training anyone, however, be he top executive or production employee, the method to be used will depend on the objectives of the training, the ability of the instructor, the ability of the group, and the educational philosophy of the person responsible for training. The real need is to appraise all these factors and then select the training method that promises to be most successful. Lectures, conferences, panel discussions, etc., can be used effectively with top executives, and for some purposes (imparting knowledge, solving immediate problems) they serve better than the case method.

172   What Do You Do When a Whole Case Study Group Will Not Talk?

The answer to this is *keep still.* Groups inexperienced in the case study method expect the leader to prod them, guide them, or carry them along. Silence means that they are waiting for his cue to tell them how they should start their discussion or whether they are on the right track. The effective case study leader will do neither. He will remain silent . . . even after silence becomes painful. Someone will open or reopen the discussion when it finally becomes clear that the leader is not going to do it for them. Silence is an effective device for making trainees take the initiative.

173   Should the Case Which Is Distributed for Discussion Be Followed by a Few Written Questions to Stimulate Discussion?

Sometimes an instructor using the case study method may prepare written questions to help participants make a thorough analysis. Trainees review them when they are preparing their analysis of the case. The questions are not "loaded"; they do not lead to preconceived statements of problems or solutions; they have no right or wrong answers. Their primary purpose is to encourage the student to explore areas of the case that may normally escape his attention. Obviously, such questions are most helpful to students who have had little experience with case analysis. Others probably will not need them.

174   Should Case Studies Be Led by Line Executives?

Yes. Especially case problems. As indicated in Question 156, these are cases prepared for the purpose of obtaining discussion in which the group will discover and accept certain predetermined principles or practices of supervision. Line executives are especially qualified to handle case problems that will add to or improve the skills of their supervisors. The abilities needed to conduct these case problems effectively is essentially the same as that required to lead successful conferences with subordinates.

Cases which are primarily prepared for the purpose of developing analytical thinking—such as those used in the Advanced Management course at Harvard—are more difficult to lead. A competent line executive can handle them successfully, but only after adequate preparation. However, because of the amount of time needed for preparation and their unfamiliarity with the method, line executives may well hesitate to lead such case studies.

175   How Does a Leader Know When the Discussion of a Case Has Been Good?

The only real, final proof that discussion has been good is improved job performance by members of the group. This, however, may be slow in coming—not because of weakness in trainees, but because opportunities to reveal progress cannot be made to order. While waiting for them, the leader may get some idea of his own and the group's success by asking himself these questions:

1. Did everyone participate? If not, why not? How can those who were silent be encouraged to take part in the future? Participation usually is an indication of interest and learning.
2. Was the group interested in the discussion? Was talk lively or did a considerable number of trainees appear bored? When interest is high, learning takes place readily.
3. Did the group stick to discussion of symptoms rather than trying to ferret out basic causes? The deeper the group probes, the more fruitful is the discussion in terms of improved understanding.
4. Was there evidence that members of the group listened care-

fully to what others were saying? As a result, did any of them change their analyses or conclusions? Although some persons are easily swayed, such changes are the best available evidence that members of the group have listened thoughtfully to their fellows.

5. Were many of the significant facts in the case brought out and evaluated? This is direct evidence of active thinking on the part of the participants.

6. Did the group continue to discuss the case after the formal meeting was over? If interest is high and the case keeps on living for the participants, then discussion has indeed been effective.

7. Was the group offering clichés or generalizations as solutions to the problems in the case? Shallow or sluggish thinking is evidence that the discussion has been superficial—easy but unrewarding.

8. Did the group appear to solve the case immediately and then act as if there were nothing more to discuss? This is a natural reaction from inexperienced groups and indicates limited success. Real progress is made when trainees continue to revert to the problem, trying to amplify their analysis or to improve their solutions.

9. Did participants relate the case to similar experiences in their own actual work? Did they reveal increased insight into their own problems as a result of the discussion? If trainees relate discussions to their own work situations, and profit by them, the case study is beginning to bear fruit.

Chapter 11

STAFF MEETINGS FOR DEVELOPMENT

176 **What Are the Purposes of Regular Staff Meetings?**

Regular staff or departmental meetings serve four major purposes:

1. *They are a device for training and development.* Staff meetings impart information, develop attitudes and skills, and lead to planned changes in participants. Changes are brought about in participants not only by telling and showing, but also—and more importantly—by exchanging points of view, assimilating ideas, observing, experiencing, listening, and interacting with other individuals who earn their livelihood doing similar work. In staff meetings, training and development take place as information about the company or its men is presented, top policy decisions are explained, present procedures are analyzed, new projects or problems are discussed, and decisions are reached. Furthermore, additional training is achieved as assignments to prepare special reports are made, as the chairmanship of the meetings is rotated, and as outside specialists are brought in to contribute to the discussion.

2. *They are a device for obtaining participation.* In staff meetings men are encouraged to express their ideas and, through discussion, assist in the formulation of policies and procedures that directly affect them. Thus they develop a feeling of kinship, learn to understand each other, gain practice in working harmoniously and develop group identity. Participants and their ideas are given the recognition and attention that is essential if supervisors and subordinates are to be cooperative, happy and productive.

3. *They are a formalized, regular vehicle of communication.* Meetings facilitate communication both upward and downward. They provide a vehicle through which top management may regularly communicate timely, well-planned announcements of business conditions, departmental operations, and personnel changes.

This strengthens lines of authority since supervisors receive information and pass it on to the next appropriate level in their own staff meetings or through other media. Also, staff meetings offer top management an opportunity to know through upward communication about operating problems or conditions that lead to problems before they become serious.

4. *They are a method of obtaining sound decisions.* Group analysis and discussion of operating problems leads to sound and acceptable decisions. When a group composed of members experienced in current operating problems examines a proposed solution, many of the contingencies which might occur are foreseen and provided for. Also, the final plan becomes acceptable to members of a group, since they help formulate it. Moreover, men who discuss actual, urgent problems are impelled to make prompt, workable solutions.

177   Aren't Staff Meetings Primarily Designed for Communication, Not Development?

Yes, the stated purpose of staff meetings usually is communication. The department head meets with his key men primarily to discuss operating problems, to pass on information which they need to accomplish their jobs, and to learn what help his subordinates need. Other values, however, can be achieved, and development is one of them.

178   Who Should Attend Staff Meetings?

Literally, a staff meeting is one held by a department head with members of his staff—the men who report directly to him. However, this traditional concept of the staff meeting does not meet the needs of today's dynamic, complex industrial society, and progressive department heads are seeking to expand and modernize these meetings. One common method of doing this is to invite others to attend regularly or occasionally. These men may be representatives of other departments or persons who are subordinate to members of the department head's staff.

When representatives from other departments attend staff meetings, communications between departments is made timely, cooperation is obtained, team work is encouraged, and decisions are reached quickly. They also improve in quality, since they are based upon consideration of a variety of viewpoints.

When department heads encourage their staff members to bring subordinates with them from time to time, the latter receive recognition and opportunities to observe and participate in the problems and planning of "higher management." This builds understanding of management and promotes company loyalty.

In some companies a representative from the training and development department is invited to staff meetings. He participates actively in the meetings and observes the men in action, gets first-hand knowledge of their problems, helps them apply principles taught in supervisor training classes, determines further training needs, and evaluates his training programs. As a result he contributes to the effectiveness of the meeting and improves the coordination and effectiveness of his training programs.

179   Isn't It Hard for Department Heads to Hold Weekly Staff Meetings Because of the Limited Number of Subjects Appropriate for Discussion?

Frequently, when supervisors are encouraged to hold weekly staff meetings, they reply that they wouldn't have anything to talk about. Actually, they have an abundance of subjects for profitable discussion—subjects that fall under the general heading of management information and departmental problems and practices. Here is a partial list of specific subjects other than operating problems discussed in the weekly staff meetings held by one department head in a medium-sized New England plant during a six-month period:

1. What part shift foremen should play in the orientation program.
2. Policies and procedures on pay day and the method of payment.
3. The policy on temporary employees.
4. The importance of removal notices in relationship to Unemployment Compensation cases.
5. Records of labor turnover.
6. Current labor market and conditions.
7. Policy concerning paid holidays.
8. Additional benefits available through group insurance.
9. Orientation instruction given by the Industrial Relations departments.
10. Policy on payments to employees on day of injury.
11. Plans for tours by plant employees and their guests.
12. Present and future operational requirements.
13. The possibility of cutting the two trips of the coffee wagon down to one trip.

14. The problem of seated employees blocking stairways during changes of shift.
15. The possibility of a Christmas party for all employees.
16. The desirability of having members of the local fire department attend plant fire brigade meetings to demonstrate artificial respiration, accepted methods of combatting fires and care of equipment.
17. Ways to improve incoming phone calls concerning absenteeism and tardiness especially on night shifts.
18. Changes to be made in regard to use of bulletin boards.
19. Solicitation practices.
20. Duties and responsibilities of foremen.

The training and development director can encourage reluctant department heads to hold regular meetings by helping them find appropriate subjects for discussion and make plans for weekly or bi-weekly meetings for a six- or twelve-month period.

180   What Climate Should the Leader Strive for in His Staff Meetings?

The climate which gets the most growth and development from subordinates is one wherein they—

1. May discuss failures and errors freely without incriminating or belittling themselves.
2. Feel that staff meetings are to be used for analyzing weaknesses as well as for creative thinking and taking credit for things well done. They must feel that failures and successes are shared as a group.
3. Understand fully that there is a complete freedom of expression and no resistance to minority opinions.
4. Learn respect for their superior's ideas and for the consideration he gives to theirs.
5. Respect one another and become more and more willing to compromise their ideas with different points of view.
6. Feel informal, relaxed and interested, yet handle problems in a businesslike manner.
7. Feel that their ideas are invited, needed, and used by their superior.
8. Take pride and confidence in their own accomplishments as well as that of the group.
9. Participate democratically in planning and take decisive action

upon important subjects. Meetings that become known as mere talking sessions lead to frustration, disinterest, and disrespect for the meetings and the leader.

181   What Preparation Should a Supervisor Make to Lead an Effective Staff Meeting?

Effective staff meetings require careful planning. The rule that an instructor spends twice as much time preparing as in actual teaching also applies to the department head who leads staff meetings. To prepare for a staff meeting, a supervisor should consider and have the answer to five questions:

1. *What should his men be told?* The department head may decide that his supervisors need to know about such things as personnel changes in the department or company, production and sales volume for the week, policy statements from top management, recent operating decisions, this week's waste, cost, or turnover reports, union activity, production quotas or goals for the next week, new projects to be undertaken, and other related facts.

In order to assemble, select, and present this information, the department head or his secretary should maintain a file containing all memos or reports which may be of value to his staff. As he thinks of subjects that are appropriate for discussion in his staff meetings, he jots down a note and inserts it in this file. These subjects may have come from observations of the men's performance, from readings, from discussions with his own superior, from discussion with other operating men, his subordinates, or staff specialists, or even from his future plans for the department.

2. *What unfinished business from the last meeting needs to be reviewed?* From notes or minutes of the previous meeting, the department head finds that some subjects either were not discussed or were left for further consideration. Are they to be discussed in the next meeting? Have some men been given special assignments upon which they should report?

3. *How can the department head assist his men in this staff meeting?* The department head can best answer this question by reviewing his men's weaknesses and planning specific steps to overcome them; most of these steps should be those which can be taken during the course of meetings. For example, suppose some men do not participate freely; the department head decides just how he will draw them out and encourage them. Also, the whole

group may profit from an example showing how to communicate an unpleasant decision to subordinates.

4. *What upward communication shall he encourage?* Since upward communication is not necessarily spontaneous, the superior must plan to obtain it. He should plan to ask questions that will draw his men out and remind them of things concerning which they should report, such as: How are things going in your departments? Have you noticed any change in your stewards' attitudes? Are many employees taking advantage of the new sick leave policy? How are employees reacting to the new incentive plan that we adopted a month ago? Such questions serve to check on former decisions and to discover conditions that need attention before they become serious.

5. *What specific problems should be discussed?* This is the heart of the meeting, from which the most fruitful results must come. The leader must present and introduce for discussion the most pressing problems in his department. These usually arise from product and system changes, reorganization plans, sales forecast changes, need for new equipment, back orders, waste, costs, personnel needs, and policy changes.

182   What Should the Leader of Staff Meetings Avoid if He Wants to Encourage Participation and Growth?

The leader should take care not to—

1. Dominate the discussions.
2. Show, too early in discussion, which one of two or more opposed opinions has his approval.
3. Use tones, gestures, and grimaces that reveal irritation, displeasure, or disagreement.
4. Present an unrelieved series of dull and uninspiring subjects. He should introduce a few "hot" subjects which are sure to provoke participation.
5. Present subjects which interest only part of the group.
6. Establish rigid time limits for the meeting.
7. Belittle opinions that are not clear, well expressed, or, in his opinion, sound.
8. Limit discussion to the subjects on his agenda.
9. Ignore timid participants who might well be drawn out by a question or two.

183   I Am a Division Superintendent. What Will My Supervisors Get from Staff Meetings?

They will get:

1. Information on items that affect their daily work and the progress of their company.
2. Opportunity to express ideas on subjects related to their work.
3. Exposure to other points of view.
4. Experience in reaching cooperative decisions.
5. Respect for the ideas of others.
6. A feeling of departmental solidarity.
7. General stimulation and incentive.
8. Self-confidence and self-assurance.
9. Assurance that you and they will continue to meet at a regular time and in a definite place.

184   How Long Should Staff Meetings Last?

The length of staff meetings will depend on their frequency, the amount of participation desired, the subject matter to be dealt with, the pressure of work in the department, and the leader's awareness of values in his staff meetings and his ability to achieve those values.

When a staff meeting is looked upon as a training device and discussion is encouraged, the length of meetings may vary. However, it is best to establish a reasonable length of time, such as one hour, which the leader will observe without being arbitrary.

185   Shouldn't We Call Staff Meetings Only When Urgent Problems Are to Be Discussed?

No. Staff meetings serve a number of purposes, only one of which is the solution of problems. They also are means of communication, and provide broad training whose ultimate objective is to keep problems from developing. Meetings make subordinates feel and work as a team and draw from them the creative, constructive, new ideas that are the lifeblood of any organization. If time is scarce, meetings may be short, but they *should be held regularly*. Otherwise, they become unplanned and unwelcome interruptions to a supervisor's busy schedule. Training also is most effective when it is continuous, pleasant, and planned, and regular staff meetings meet these requirements.

186   What Training Will Help Executives See the Value of Regular Staff Meetings and Use Them?

Principally, two courses: conference leadership and communications. The former is designed to inform executives of the need and value of conferences and meetings and to develop skills of leadership. Such training gives executives the confidence to meet with their key men and shows them the need for regular gatherings.

Communications training demonstrates the need to keep supervisors informed and the value of helping supervisors feel that they are participating in management. Executives also learn about the devices that are available to them for communications. One of these devices, staff meetings, is the core of any communications program.

187   How Valuable Are Staff Meetings When Compared with Regular Supervisor Training Classes?

These training devices, of course, serve different purposes. In staff meetings, participants discuss specific operating problems that arise in their day-to-day activities, doing this under the guidance of their immediate superiors. Both of these factors stimulate supervisors to do their best and offer them direct help in their daily operations. On the other hand, supervisor training classes are usually led by specialists in administration, supervision, or in technical areas of a supervisor's job. The training offered is broad, and much of it is meant to teach general concepts rather than to meet specific needs.

Since both types of training are necessary, we cannot say that one is more valuable than the other. The unique value of training in staff meetings lies in the fact that it offers training in policy and decision making, and training in cooperative group discussion which is difficult to offer elsewhere. In addition, staff meetings lead supervisors to improve their performance as leaders and form the base upon which other training can be added.

188   How Do Staff Meetings Fit into a Training Program for Supervisors Conducted by the Personnel Department?

Staff meetings and training classes supplement each other. Through discussions of practical operating problems in staff meetings, supervisors become aware of their training needs and request formal training. The department head also is able to determine formal training needs of his staff from their performance in regularly conducted staff meetings.

The department head can often utilize opportunities presented in staff meetings to give his supervisors practice in applying the skills they have learned in supervisory training. Thus staff meetings can be proving grounds of what has been taught in supervisor training classes. Staff meetings enable the boss to tell whether or not his supervisors have grown as a result of training.

189   Should the Chairmanship of Staff Meetings Be Rotated?

Staff meetings are usually led by the department head—the man in authority. However, when downward communications is not the major objective of the staff meetings, the chairmanship is rotated among those who attend regularly. This is an excellent device if a department head is striving to develop leadership among his subordinates and improve their ability to conduct meetings. Specific advantages of rotation are:

1. Subordinates learn how to lead meetings, gaining knowledge that will help them deal with their own subordinates.
2. Subordinates have a chance to play the role of their superior and obtain insight into his responsibility.
3. Subordinates develop skill in planning and organizing.
4. Subordinates obtain increased understanding of each other.
5. The superior is able to observe each man in action and secure a basis for evaluating and counseling his men.

Disadvantages of rotation are:

1. Meetings may not run smoothly, since subordinates commonly lack the experience and skill of their superior.
2. Many superiors find it hard to yield their position to a subordinate even temporarily, and some cannot resist the temptation to take over the meeting.
3. Some men are so inept at conducting meetings that they lose the respect of their associates and embarrass themselves.
4. The superior may have to spend more time to prepare the leader for the meeting than if he led it himself.

190   What Training Can Be Done Best Through Staff Meetings?

Staff meetings are admirably suited to train executives and supervisors in:

1. *Making decisions.* Current problems are presented and analyzed, possible solutions are discussed, and final decisions are reached. Through this process of verbal exploration under the guidance of an experienced supervisor, the group learns how to collect facts and weigh them before making a decision.

2. *Understanding operating procedures and policies.* New procedures and policies are established and old ones are discussed, interpreted, and revised. In this process, supervisors learn not only what the procedures and policies are but the intentions and purposes behind them.

3. *The philosophy of management and techniques of supervision or administration.*

4. *Methods of obtaining agreement.* Opinions are sure to vary when operating problems are discussed and solutions are proposed. These opinions must be weighted and reconciled, and solutions must incorporate the best ideas and judgment available. However, when each man has an opportunity to present his own ideas and is led to understand the reasoning behind the final decision, agreement and acceptance can be easily obtained.

5. *The responsibilities of an executive or a supervisor.* Through discussion of operating problems, procedures, and techniques of supervision, subordinates will gain a full realization of their responsibility and authority.

191   Should Minutes of Staff Meetings Be Kept? If So, for What Purpose?

This generally is a good practice. Minutes, which form a written record of what took place in the meeting, serve these purposes:

1. They remind individuals of assignments.
2. They inform absent participants what took place while they were away.
3. They inform others in the department and in related departments of the activities of the department.
4. They form an official record of decisions reached.
5. They assist in planning future meetings.

Usually one of the regular participants is given the responsibility for preparing and distributing the minutes, which should be approved by the leader of the meeting before they are duplicated for distribution.

192   How Far Down the Line Should Staff Meetings Be Held?

All supervisors and staff men in a department—those who are considered to be on the management team—should be regular attendants at staff meetings conducted by their superior. Indeed, in some organizations the meetings are held for production employees. First-line supervisors meet once a month with their employees to tell them of changes, operating problems, production schedules for the coming month, waste reports, and to discuss matters of interest to them and the company. Staff meetings can help to produce sound employee attitudes, to solve operating problems, and to develop personnel, and should be used at all levels for these purposes. In the lower echelons, the meetings may be brief and less frequent, but they should be held regularly.

193   Are There Some Cautions You Can Offer the Executive Who Asks His Group to Solve Problems in Staff Meetings?

Staff meetings are an excellent means for solving common operating problems of a department. However, they do sometimes fail in this purpose. To guard against such failure, these cautions should be observed by the leader:

1. The leader should take care not to express his own ideas too freely, lest his men withhold their own ideas. If they do, a truly cooperative solution cannot be reached.
2. The leader should define problems carefully, and should limit them to facilitate comprehension. A problem properly limited and defined often takes on new meaning, and the solution is then easily found.
3. Men should be informed of the subjects to be discussed before the meeting so that they can be prepared to enter into fruitful, penetrating discussion and thus reach sound solutions.
4. Written procedures should not be developed during a staff meeting. It is best to ask members of the group to prepare a rough draft and present it for discussion.
5. The leader should make sure that problems are appropriate to the group. Is it one they can solve and should be expected to solve?
6. The problem may require research and study in which the group cannot profitably engage.
7. Since people need experience in solving problems, the leader

should not be discouraged by his group's inability to reach sound, clear solutions the first few times they try to do so. They probably have learned to rely on the boss, and must overcome this.

Chapter 12

MISCELLANEOUS DEVELOPMENT METHODS AND PROGRAMS

---

194 How Is Counseling by Staff Specialists or Outside Consultants Used in Development?

This is a service rendered by skilled counselors working outside the line organization. It is an individualized method wherein men with problems are free to talk over their affairs with skilled listeners who help get executives to see their problems clearly and the manner of their solution. It is a method which helps provide insight into one's own behavior. Some companies use the service of consulting psychologists for this purpose, others have internal counselors.

195 What Values Are There to Counseling?

ADVANTAGES	LIMITATIONS
1. Counseling enables executives to secure help with personal problems involving home, children, themselves, their work, or their superiors.	1. Counseling requires considerable skill on the part of a counselor.
2. Counseling also can deal with internal business problems too delicate for executives to discuss with their superiors. This method also gets at problems involving jealousies, fears, personal ambitions, and with the relationships of one executive to another. Such problems might otherwise be suppressed, with serious results.	2. The method may be time consuming.
3. Counseling provides individualized help to meet highly individual needs.	3. Counseling frequently deals in confidences which are difficult to keep and dangerous to reveal.

4. Counseling is useful for complex, difficult problems that individuals must be skillfully led to see and solve for themselves.

4. Some critics feel that counseling should be unnecessary if line executives are fully available and acceptable to subordinates who wish to confide in them.

196   What Is Refresher Training?

It is both a review and a bringing up to date. Refresher training for personnel interviewers, for example, would review, in some interesting way, the generally known and established concepts about recruitment, selection, and placement. It would, however, go beyond and bring the learners up to date by discussion of such things as the patterned interview, the group interview, use of stress situations, role playing in interviews, etc.

197   What Are the Cooperative Courses Given by the General Motors Institute?

This is a program through which an industry offers college degrees in engineering and business administration.

The program covers five years. The first four include alternating periods of work and instruction, the fifth year involves full-time employment plus completion of a study or research report on some plant project related to one's field of specialization. During the full five years the learner is an employee of the plant which chose him to attend the Institute.

The course follows the typical college pattern with emphasis upon cultural breadth. Sixteen course hours in English, speech, economics, modern plays, psychology, etc., are required. There are student activities, loan funds, counseling, social fraternities, and the usual activities of college life.

The curriculum covers industrial and mechanical engineering and business administration. The mechanical engineering course allows majors in: Automotive Engineering, Body and Sheet Metal Engineering, General Mechanical Engineering, Tool Engineering and Die Engineering. The degree in Industrial Engineering may be taken with majors in General Manufacturing, Body Manufacturing, Methods and Processing, Foundry Technology, Welding Technology.

The Business Administration Course allows majors in Accounting, Sales and Service, Personnel, Materials Control.

These courses and a two-year program for dealers are described in a General Motors booklet entitled, "Cooperative Programs," issued annually at Flint, Michigan.

198   What Is Home Office Training?

Companies whose employees are scattered geographically frequently bring them to the home office for training. These conferences or institutes last from a few days to several weeks and are used both for new and experienced employees. Strengthened social and psychological ties with the front office usually develop from this type of training. Distance is bridged; fear and suspicion of the unknown reduced. The home office and the policies that emanate from it get better understanding and acceptance.

Home office training is common with sales forces and in the insurance business.

199   What Is "J.R.T."?

This term refers to Job Relations Training. The program, consisting of ten sessions of two hours each, was very popular in World War II. It was in effect a training program in human relations. There was also J.M.T. (Job Method Training) and J.I.T. (Job Instructor Training).

200   What Is the "Buddy" System of Orientation?

It is a plan under which a new employee is assigned, after formal orientation, to an experienced worker who takes the new employee to lunch on the first day—both as guests of the company. The sponsor or buddy shows the newcomer where to get uniforms, tools, first aid, information, and assistance of all kinds. He provides the personal, friendly, ever-present reassurance the new worker so much needs, reassurance which the supervisor, because of his many responsibilities, cannot offer continuously during the first day or two.

201   How Are Committee Assignments Used in Development?

Many companies have management boards, policy and coordinating committees, and other high-level groups which deal with problems to be solved at executive levels. Primarily designed to do work, these groups may also be used to develop the abilities and personal qualities of executives. Some organizations try men out on temporary committees before assigning them to permanent committees with greater responsibilities.

202   **What Are the Advantages and Limitations of Committee Assignments?**

ADVANTAGES

1. Group activities enable men to become acquainted with the problems and operations of divisions with which they may have been unfamiliar.
2. Committees and similar groups enable men to practice the art of working together effectively and without friction. Under able, tactful chairmen, they often develop cooperation, understanding, and even friendship between men who have been at odds.
3. Participants gain experience in solving problems that exceed the responsibility of any one executive.

4. Group membership cultivates a feeling of "belonging." It also gives status and develops a sense of responsibility.

LIMITATIONS

1. Committee meetings can be time-wasters.

2. Committees can be set up to help executives escape their responsibility for making decisions.

3. Committees are frequently not given enough authority and their recommendations are sometimes ignored. Both faults lead to frustration and sometimes to irresponsibility.

203   **What Is Meant by Loop Training?**

This is rapid rotation from department to department for newly hired college graduates. It is a sort of intensive, on-the-job orientation and may take from two weeks to two years. Sometimes the trainee's first permanent assignment is determined at the time of hiring, as it is with engineers or salesmen. "Looping" in that case serves only to orient the newcomer to the company, its departments, services, personnel and policies. In other cases where a man is not hired for a specific assignment, looping gives the trainee a chance to try out various jobs and determine for himself which one he is best fitted for. It also gives supervision an opportunity to observe the new men and determine which ones they would like to request for permanent assignment in their departments. When the trainee and supervisor for whom he has worked agree on the first permanent assignment, looping has served its purpose.

204   What Is the Syndicate System of Development?

The Syndicate System was devised in England. A syndicate, or committee, of nine is established to make a thorough investigation into some broad and fundamental aspect of business, such as the use and effect of incentive systems or the compatibility of Christian ethics and the profit motive. The syndicate devotes several weeks to a full-time intensive study of the problem, reviewing the literature, calling in experts to testify, and visiting commercial houses or industries to observe their practices. Members then prepare a report and present it to the other executives attending the college, meeting in an all-day session. Analysis of the report and defense or criticism of its findings then proceed in open forum.

205   What Advantages and What Limitations Are There to the Syndicate System?

ADVANTAGES

1. The syndicate method is exceptionally thorough. It trains participants to use observation and research methods, to employ consultants and other authorities, to select and utilize data, and to collaborate in investigation as well as in preparing reports.
2. Presentation of report provides experience in give-and-take communication.
3. Reports are well accepted and given serious consideration, since they are knowingly proposed by practical-minded men.
4. Participation in a syndicate gives men status within their own organization.
5. It is a device for training both the audience that listens and the syndicate that prepares and presents the report.

LIMITATIONS

1. The method is time consuming.

2. Requires stimulation and guidance from someone well informed about sources of information and methods of investigation and presentation.

3. The recommendations made are academic, in the sense that the men on the syndicate do not have responsibility for the consequences of their findings, as does an executive back in his office.

**206   What Are the Steps in Selling Top Management
on an Executive Development Program?**

1. As a first step, be sure you yourself know the values to be secured from development. Some of the major ones are:

   a. Orthodox methods of management succession cannot furnish industry with either the quantity or the quality of executives it needs. Formal development programs are taking the place of unplanned experience as a means of securing competent executives.
   b. Executive development prepares a reserve group of men ready to fill openings caused by resignation, discharge, sickness, death, and retirement.
   c. It improves all executives on their present jobs.
   d. Development broadens the specialist and prepares him for administrative responsibility.
   e. Through the executive audit that usually precedes development, management gets a picture of the strong and weak points of its management team.

2. When you are sure you know the values you seek from development, be certain you can prepare and administer a successful program. In other words, review your own preparation for the work.

3. Talk frankly with your management. Be sure they know what you propose to do and what support you will need from them.

4. Make plans to inform people at all levels about development work and for securing their support of it. In this you should rely upon friendly members of top management to explain training, to use its services, and to promote their use by other executives. Ask these same friendly executives to help plan courses, to open and close them, and to occasionally teach their specialties. Fortify them with the information and first-hand experiences they will need to represent you before other executives who do not understand what development is and how it can help.

5. Let members of the opposition know what you are doing, ask their opinions, and give them a chance to tell why they oppose your ideas. Find out whether they are resistant to all training or whether they may be willing to support certain programs. Get them to talk about their own problems and suggest how development can help. Many an opponent of training has been won over by one or more programs tailored to his needs.

By all means invite the opponents of development to visit your classes, where they can see what they oppose, and persuade them to follow up on your results. Thus they can see for themselves, and unless they are deeply prejudiced, they will find development more valuable than they thought. Being determined critics, they also may be able to make valuable suggestions for improvement.

6. Persuade major executives to visit outside schools and colleges doing good development work, where they can see what development is, what other companies are using it, and what results can be expected. If executives cannot visit schools and colleges it will help to circulate flyers and catalogs describing the courses.

207   What Is a Task Force? Is It a Training Device for Supervisors?

A task force is a term used to describe a working committee of supervisors or staff employees. It is a training and development device for supervisors. The characteristics of a task force are:

1. It is small in size and unified in makeup, since it usually contains three to six members of approximately equal status and experience.
2. The members are drawn from several departments of the organization.
3. The task force is organized for the purpose of studying and solving one particular problem.
4. When this problem has been studied and a report has been made to management or an action completed, the task force is disbanded.

A task force serves two major purposes: (a) it analyzes a current problem of the organization and makes recommendations to solve this problem; (b) it provides supervisors with an opportunity to broaden their experience and participate in solving problems of management that are not a part of their day-to-day activities.

208   What Is the Supervisory Method Known in England as Joint Consultation?

Joint consultation means the same thing as participation. It is a device of management in which employees have the opportunity to be informed of what is going on and to share in the decisions that affect them. It is implemented through staff and employee meetings in which subordinates have an opportunity to express their points of view and assist in the formulation of policy and practices.

209   What Is the "Phillips 66" Method of Training?

It is something like the buzz sessions of group dynamics. The method is frequently used after a speaker has made a presentation to a fairly large group. Thereupon the group, sometimes consisting of several hundred people, breaks up into units of six or more to propound one question to the speaker.

Now and then the six-man teams are given a question by the speaker or the chairman and the teams meet separately to arrive at a team answer. When the small units reassemble, their answers are reported to the whole group.

210   What Is the Carrier Cabinet?[1]

The Carrier Cabinet is a group of approximately 165 Carrier executives who meet once a month to review and discuss progress, problems, and plans of the business. Its stated objectives are as follows:

1. To disseminate information on corporation matters and the general business situation and to establish a chain of supplementary communication with the rest of the organization.
2. To give management personnel the first information on all important developments, whenever possible.
3. To develop management abilities and attitudes in order to provide a reserve of qualified candidates for promotion to more responsible positions.
4. To obtain, to the extent possible, the benefits of broad participation in the discussion of management plans and problems and thereby encourage the free flow of suggestions and comments.
5. To promote profit-consciousness and a determination to get maximum value for all money spent.
6. To stimulate thinking and to furnish inspiration for both performance and production.
7. To promote better acquaintance among management people.

[1] This question was answered by the Vice President in Charge of Personnel Division, Carrier Corporation, Syracuse, New York.

8. To promote a high degree of cooperation among organizational units and individuals.

9. To answer questions in the minds of management personnel.

Membership in the Cabinet is by invitation of the President, upon recommendation of a division head. Those who belong have important management, technical, or communications responsibilities.

The President presides at all meetings, and the agenda includes an explanation of the financial report, a review of general business conditions, and a summary of actions taken by the Board of Directors at its latest meeting. Also, various members are called upon to present subjects of current interest, including descriptions of the operations of their own divisions and departments. A question-and-answer period is included in each session, with provision made for submitting written questions in advance. Programs are planned by a committee which is made up of representatives of all divisions of the corporation.

Twice a year, the attendance at Cabinet meetings is expanded to include all "exempt" employees of the corporation who are located in Syracuse. The total number of people involved is slightly in excess of 1,000.

The Cabinet usually meets on the last Monday of each month, immediately following the Board of Directors meeting on the previous Thursday. The group convenes at 5 p.m., takes time out for dinner at the company cafeteria at 6:30 p.m., and remains in session until about 9:30 p.m. Attendance is obligatory except when a member is ill or must be out of town on important business.

211   What Is the Meaning of Observational Assignment?

It is a little like rotation in that a man is assigned to a new position or a different department primarily for the purpose of learning. The observation may last for a day or a month, or longer.

Observational assignment is different from rotation in that the trainee is not expected to achieve any degree of skill or proficiency in the operations. He seeks only general knowledge and understanding of what goes on and why. Usually, observational assignment is used to acquaint a man with the work and problems of a department with which he must closely coordinate his own activities. Men in finishing divisions of manufacturing concerns are frequently assigned observational spots in the processing departments that handle the product before it reaches final assembly or finishing stages. Production supervisors in Johnson & Johnson have, for example, been assigned brief tours with field salesmen so that they may see the destination of the product they make and the problems faced by salesmen.

212　What Are "Memory Joggers?"

They are monthly calendars in booklet or diary form, useful for reminders and day-to-day entries. Inside one or both covers of the booklet there are reviews of simple management principles. Memory joggers are available from the National Foreman's Institute.

213　How Does One Determine Whether Executive Counseling Methods Produce Improvements?

Counseling for improvement should be undertaken only when the subordinate's history and record have been carefully studied and an informal plan laid out by the counselor. After the study it may be determined that the purpose of the interview is to arouse initiative in the subject, or to teach him the responsibilities which one going into supervision must assume, or to improve his attention to detail. Whatever the purpose, it will be carefully and specifically defined in the counselor's mind and will result from a thorough observation and study of the employee's work habits. When counseling is carefully thought out, and specific objectives are set, it is easy enough through follow-up observations, merit rating, and further counseling to determine what the results have been.[2]

214　Does the Flat Organizational Structure of Sears Roebuck Have Any Bearing on Development?

Certainly. It reduces the layers of authority through which communications must pass on the way up or down. Each layer, as Burleigh Gardiner points out, is a small filter station sifting and distorting the information as it passes along. In the flat structure, communications flow more freely up and down and travel more directly through fewer filters. This means that information is more available throughout the organization making less need for training classes to provide it.

So it is with leadership. In the flat organizational structure,

[2]For a fuller discussion of this subject see Earl G. Planty and Carlos A. Efferson, "Counseling Executives After Merit Rating or Evaluation," *Personnel,* March, 1951.

workers and leaders attain a closer harmony. The first line boss, being at the bottom of a chain of only three or four superiors, has more authority than he would have at the bottom of a chain of six or seven superiors. His morale is higher and he gets an opportunity to learn by actual practice. Less training is needed.

Size and complexity have brought many problems. Confusion, lack of interest in the job, impersonal attitudes toward workers, frustration with red tape and distant controls, failure to assume responsibility lest higher levels of management overrule the decision, frictions between the line and innumerable staff and service departments, and over formal organization—all can shackle or destroy individual spirit and initiative. Where there is a long chain of command, the training staff is busy teaching men how to live within the artificial framework they have constructed. In the flat structure which more nearly approximates the natural work groups, problems are fewer and training is less needed.

215   What Are the Sloan Fellowships at Massachusetts Institute of Technology?

They are part of the Executive Development Program of M.I.T.'s School of Industrial Management. This program is designed to meet the needs of young executives who, through several years of industrial experience, have demonstrated unusual general ability and leadership and the capacity for rapid growth towards high levels of management responsibility. A limited number of fellowships are granted annually, following a nationwide competition. The program is supported by special grants from the Alfred P. Sloan Foundation and is usually referred to, therefore, as the Sloan Fellowships.

The twelve-month program of study is at the graduate level. It attempts to provide understanding of the complex human, economic, and business relationships that must be considered in setting policies and programs for the long-range success of industrial enterprises. It offers a broad background in related fields including Business Administration, Personal Relations, Economics, Finance, Marketing, Production Management, and Accounting Control. In addition to classroom instruction by regular faculty members, a variety of special educational means are used, including (a) a series of more than fifty conferences with leading industrial executives, government representatives, and labor leaders, (b) several weeks of group field trips, (c) orientation seminars in a broad range of technical fields, and (d) individual investigations.

Fellowships are available only to men who have been nominated by their employers. Primary factors considered in the selection of men are:

1. A substantial record of achievement in the candidate's own field or specialty.
2. Evidence of his effective performance in the management components of past and present assignments.
3. Personal qualities appropriate to high level management responsibilities.
4. Evidence of his recognition of responsibility to his associates, to the enterprise, and to the broader community of which he is a part.
5. Evidence of his intellectual capacity and vigor.
6. Assurance that he will have opportunity to progress into constructive leadership in his company.

The fellowships carry cash stipends and tuition grants which are intended to supplement the financial support provided by employers.

216   Where Can We Send Sales Executives for Training?

Most of the schools offering short courses in general management are suitable places, since the principles they teach are applicable to all areas of business. The National Association of Sales Executives has recently offered a sales administration course in cooperation with Rutgers University at New Brunswick, New Jersey. Their program runs for two years, meeting two weeks each summer. The Industrial Management Institute of the University of Wisconsin offers a series of six one-day conferences for sales managers. The meetings are held one day a month and are devoted to the following subjects:

1. Organization and Administration of the Sales Department.
2. Selection and Training of Sales Personnel.
3. Sales Forecasting.
4. Sales Promotion and Advertising.
5. Compensation of Salesmen.
6. Analysis and Control of Sales Costs.

The Personnel Group, National Dry Goods Association, New York, publishes an up-to-date list of schools and colleges offering courses in retailing and related fields. The list also includes correspondence schools giving courses in merchandising, salesmanship, etc.

217   Is the Conference Method as Desirable as the Lecture Method When Training New Salespeople in the Retail Field?

The value of any method of training depends partly upon subject matter and partly upon the experience and needs of trainees. The chances are that both the lecture and the conference method will need to be used if a sound job of training is to be done.

It is not too difficult to teach a new employee to fill out a sales slip, take inventory, care for merchandise, and other mechanics of the job. Such training demands that factual information be presented clearly and effectively. When a salesperson comes to work, he seldom knows how to do these things, but he does realize that they are necessary and important. For this reason, and because he wants to keep his job, he usually is willing to accept and follow instructions. The lecture, fundamentally a one-way means of communication, is, with variations and additions, the simplest and most effective means of giving the new employee the know-how required for making a start in the motor and manual phases of his job.

We all know too many workers, however, who are rich in know-how but poor in performance because their personalities and attitudes prevent efficient use of their knowledge. An effective training program must remove these barriers. In other words, it must teach the skills essential to every job and at the same time develop the understandings and attitudes which will make sure that the trainee puts those skills to work.

For this second purpose, the conference method is superior to lectures because it is a two-way means of communication which arouses the trainee's interest and capitalizes on the knowledge and experience the trainee already possesses.

Typically, of course, the new employee has no knowledge of the company's policies and practices in such fields as customer relations. Still, anyone who is old enough to be hired at all has an accumulation of good and bad ideas, habits, convictions, and prejudices about greeting people, answering questions, replying to criticisms, and other acts which properly come under the heading of courtesy to customers.

Since this knowledge has accumulated without plan and often without regard for its effects upon other people, it generally is an obstacle to success. Modification, correction, and re-orientation are needed before the employee can accept or even understand the way management wants things done. Accomplishing this calls for a meeting of minds on matters which often are subject to emotion and prejudice. The most effective means of accomplishing this is the conference method. This form of two-way communication lets the trainee ask questions and raise objections as they occur to him. It gives the trainer the chance to discover and dispose of these obstacles to agreement. The very fact that you listen to an employees' opinions makes him responsive to yours.

Teaching methods can be combined to advantage, even in presenting factual information such as sales-slip procedure. The lecture, supplemented by a demonstration, effectively teaches the new employee what to do and how to do it. Except in rare cases, however, it neither induces him to accept these mandatory instructions nor arouses a desire to follow them precisely and intelligently.

One of the most effective means of gaining acceptance, of course, is to establish why each step is logical and important. When this is done by lecture—telling the trainee—the instructor is often put in the position of insulting the intelligence of the more capable trainees by emphasizing the obvious. But when the trainer employs the conference method technique, and *asks* the why of points which the group can answer, he develops acceptance and interest by acknowledging that the trainees have worth-while opinions and by giving them a chance to express these opinions.

It is difficult to visualize an effective training program which does not utilize both methods: the lecture to impart essential information, the discussion to show its importance and to develop the attitudes and acceptance essential to good performance.

218   **What Kind of Training for Sales Leadership Can Be Offered Inside the Company?**

The best way to answer this question is to cite the program of a six-day leadership institute for divisional sales managers which was offered by the Ortho Pharmaceutical Corporation of Raritan, New Jersey. The program was conducted by inside professional training men and by sales executives.

ORTHO PHARMACEUTICAL CORPORATION'S
DIVISION SALES MANAGERS' PROGRAM
St. Simons Island, Georgia

Monday—March 17th
9:00—10:30 a.m.—How to Organize Sales Groups, Divisions, and Larger Units. Introduction to organization.
10:45—12:30 p.m.—Advanced Principles of Organization in Sales.

1:30— 3:00 p.m.—Defining the Divisional Sales Manager's Job. Purpose, use and method of preparing a job description. Practice in writing divisional sales manager's job description.

8:00—10:00 p.m.—Case Study in Sales Organization.

Tuesday—March 18th

9:00—10:30 a.m.—How to Evaluate Men. Fundamental principles discussed, illustrated and applied.

10:45—12:45 p.m.—The Work Analysis Method in Evaluation; its use and improvement. How to observe the salesmen at work. What to look for in a salesman's work and how to find it. Application of fundamental principles of evaluation to typical work analyses.

2:00— 5:00 p.m.—Workshop in Evaluation of Salesmen.

8:00—10:00 p.m.—Case Study in Counseling.

Wednesday—March 19th

9:00—11:00 a.m.—Case Study in Orientation and Training.

11:15—12:45 p.m.—Orienting New Salesmen.

2:00— 5:00 p.m.—Workshop in Evaluation of Salesmen

Thursday—March 20th

9:00—10:30 a.m.—Panel discussion of Counseling for Improvement From the Work Analysis. How to develop and use individual strengths of salesmen. How to inform men of weakness; how to get them to accept the criticism; how to help them correct specific weakness.

10:45—12:45 p.m.—Role playing in Counseling: Application of Principles and Methods.

2:00— 4:00 p.m.—Role playing in Counseling: Application of Principles and Methods.

8:00—10:00 p.m.—Case Study in Counseling.

Friday—March 21st

9:00—11:00 a.m.—The Work Analysis method of reporting performance. Use of the work analysis sheet, and other methods for improvement and follow up.

11:15—12:30 p.m.—Self-Development for Divisional Sales Managers.

2:00— 5:00 p.m.—Ortho Sales Managers' Problems. Group discussion and upward communications.

Saturday—March 22d

9:30—12:30 a.m.—Ortho Sales Managers' Problems.

As will be seen, the meetings used role playing, cases, the conference method, and panels. The trainees also had two free afternoons in which they joined, workshop style, to plan their own merit-rating forms for salesmen.

219   How Does One Start a Sales Training Program from Scratch?

The Air Reduction Sales Company has developed a sound and unusual program of this sort. The following statement concerning it has been provided by the Special Assistant to the President, who developed the program:

When our Sales Vice President gave me the job of organizing a sales training program, my first question was "What is a sales training program?" Definitely, the job had been assigned to a greenhorn in this field.

It took seven steps and three months to produce a program.

Step 1—The Company librarian was consulted and she made available a few books and a dozen or so articles on sales training which had appeared in business magazines.

These enabled me to gain general familiarity with the subject of sales training.

Step 2—Short discussions were held with the Vice President and other department heads in sales to find out what, in general, they expected sales training to accomplish in our Company.

These discussions suggested the broad objectives of our program.

Step 3—Through the cooperation of the Sales Vice President and others in our Company, a list was prepared of six industrial companies which were known to have sales training programs and whose sales efforts —as with us—were in the industrial field. One-day visits were then arranged with each of these companies.

These visits produced considerable practical information regarding the various media used in sales training programs.

Step 4—Eight of the Company's District Sales Offices were visited and individual conversations held with thirty to forty managers, supervisors, salesmen and technical sales representatives.

These pinpointed the specific needs of our sales representatives in the field, as outlined by the men themselves.

Step 5—The problem now was one of study, analysis, and selection. The objective was to select those methods and tools already successfully used by other companies which seemed best suited to our organizational setup and most likely to deliver what was needed.

The conclusions of this study were included in a forty-page report which outlined the sales training program recommended for our Company.

Step 6—The Sales Vice President circulated this report to all his department heads and district managers, with an invitation to comment and make suggestions.

This turned out later on to have been a very desirable step. It gave most of these individuals a second opportunity to participate in the development of the plan. It helped to give them a proprietory feeling towards this activity, which is the essence of our Company's program.

Step 7—The suggestion of department heads and district managers were then incorporated into the plan.

The program was now ready to be launched. Inasmuch as all the key people in the sales department were already familiar with the plan, it was simple to get the program started. All it required was a letter by the Company's president to every member of the sales force announcing it and explaining what it was intended to accomplish.

What are the features of Air Reduction Sales Company's sales training program?

The Company's program is known as the "Sales Development Program." This name was selected to serve as a constant reminder that the objective of the program was to increase sales through greater efficiency in the personal promotion of the Company's products.

The Sales Development Program is carried out through two main vehicles.

1. A bulletin known as the *Sales Development Program Review,* is published every month except July and August. Each issue includes three articles. One article always deals with one of the Company's products and the second with a process. The third article may deal in some phases of salesmanship, with one of the markets for the Company's products, how salesmen can assist in making the Company's *direct mail advertising* more effective, or with some other similar topic. All articles are written by Company people and are edited by the Program Director. A strenuous effort is made to make these articles as accurate, informative, and as clear as possible, and to keep them free of extravagant claims.

Each issue of the *Review* includes a quiz sheet which all participants are required to fill out and return to their district managers. The questions are of the "true" or "false" type. Most of them relate to the subjects covered in that particular issue, although some review questions are always included. Occasionally the men are given problems to work out.

2. At the end of every month a sales development program meeting takes place in each of the District Sales offices. The district manager presides at these meetings. The corrected quiz sheets are returned to the men and questions which gave trouble are clarified. Each of the subjects included in the *Review* is then discussed under the leadership of a man who had been notified of his assignment two weeks prior to the meeting. These discussions further amplify the *Review* articles. Their main purpose, however, is to translate technical information into sales situations which actually exist in a particular district. In other words, the keynote of these discussions is "now that we have this knowledge, where and how are we going to use it?"

Subjects which lend themselves to physical demonstrations are demonstrated by other individuals, who likewise receive advanced notice of their assignments. Occasionally, practice sales ("role playing") are held. A sales situation is assigned to a few men ahead of the meeting so as to enable them to prepare themselves carefully. Films which demonstrate applications of the Company's products or which deal with the Company's markets are occasionally shown.

The monthly district meeting is the drive gear of the Sales Development Program, and this is graphically illustrated in a picture which appears every month on the inside cover of the *Review*. The program is under the direction of a Director who reports to the Sales Vice President. A Sales Development Program Committee which includes the Sales Vice President and all product sales managers, as well as two district managers (on a one-year rotating basis), controls general direction to the program.

220   What Is the Incident Process of Case Analysis?

There are many variations in the use of the case study method. The incident process of case analysis, developed at the Massachusetts Institute of Technology by Professor Paul Pigors, is one of the most practical and useful adaptations of the case study method for lower and middle management personnel. Professor Pigors describes the method and its values below:[3]

The Incident Process, as developed at M.I.T., varies from accepted case method practice primarily in that (a) group work starts at a point much nearer to actuality, and far less advanced, than a finished case report, (b) role playing is built into it, (3) as soon as group members get the hang of the method, they take turns in preparing and presenting cases (the teacher, or "expert," is then "kept on tap, not on top," and joins with other class members in asking questions and making decisions on cases about which he has no advance information), (d) a process of thinking is practiced which follows the same sequence as that needed by a leading participant or by an arbitrator whose decision is binding on the parties to a dispute.

221   How Does the Incident Process Method Work?

In brief, this way of thinking about actual role playing situations proceeds as follows:

At the first meeting (preferably of a small group) the discussion leader describes the aims and procedures of the method. He also explains about assignment of roles. Cases are presented by two-man teams. These consist of a *Leader* (who is responsible for selecting and preparing a case, presenting the Incident, and providing information) and an *Observer* (who helps with the preparatory work, takes notes during discussion, and writes a report that

[3] This answer and those for the two following questions were prepared by Professor Pigors for use in this book.

includes preliminary evaluation of group work on the case).[4] For each case, discussion members are assigned to the collective role of a management representative, union leader, or arbitrator. This sets the tone for responsible thinking because it shows how determinant their decision would be for future developments in that situation.

1. *The Incident.* The Leader reads aloud (or distributes in writing) a brief statement of some precipitating incident; perhaps incipient trouble, a potential turning point, a complaint, or an unsettled grievance. Such a start on case analysis has always proved challenging to group members. They see its similarity to what happens when actual difficulties crop up and demand decision. An example of an actual incident is as follows:

"One day the treasurer (and vice president) was walking through the shop. He noticed that a worker whom he passed was tying a knot in an oil rag. A few seconds later a knotted oil rag hit him hard in the back of the neck." If you were in his place, what would you do now?

Most of our Incidents are taken at the stage when a misunderstanding has grown into an unsettled grievance and gone to arbitration. (There are special advantages in having management representatives "learn by doing" the kind of thinking that is appropriate for an arbitrator.) A sample Incident at this stage is as follows:

"The Union claims that on January 27, 1951, Assistant Foreman Hermann violated the contract by performing production work." What is your award?

2. *Fact-Finding.* When confronted with such a scanty statement, the need for fact-finding is obvious. By conducting what amounts to a group interview with the Leader, members get information about *what* happened, *where, how,* and to *whom.* This makes it possible to visualize the immediate context of the Incident. Other questions bring out the larger context, so that this climactic point can be seen in relation to the existing labor agreement, corporate policies, established procedures, accepted practices, precedents and previous understandings or decisions (if any) in similar situations.

This challenge to recreate a case situation, starting from the merest sketch of a climax, has never failed to bring immediate and

---

[4] At M.I.T., both these roles are taken, in rotation, by all members. In industry, the Leader should always be a representative of line management. But there are obvious advantages in having the Observer's job done by a member of the personnel department.

sustained response from group members.[5] At the end of this stage in analysis, a considerable variety of facts has usually been brought out. What then?

3. *What Has to Be Decided, and How?* Group members have an opportunity to notice that a mass of facts, as such, is relatively useless. How can it be handled most efficiently? Unless the conferees have unusual ability or considerable experience in case analysis, they need help from a skilled discussion leader at this stage. The most effective kind of help is provided *not* by having an "expert" analyze the case for the group but by helping members to help each other do the job, after they recognize why the job requirement has been formulated in this way.

Genuine discussion usually begins only in this phase of analysis. The nature and value of this group activity are highlighted because they come immediately after the questions and answers exchanged between individuals and the Leader. Such dialogues often lead to individual insight, based on information that was sought by that person. Other members who were thinking along similar lines also benefit. But only full discussion can ensure a composite view, in which individual points of view are explored, tested, and integrated to form group insight. When this stage is slighted (because the time allowed for a meeting is too short), its importance is illustrated in reverse. Key facts that were brought out as information get entirely left out, by some members, when making their decision. And the "reasons" given (under an arbitrator's discussion) have included judgments such as: "The Foreman was overambitious."[6]

Unless the point to be decided is worked out in discussion, it is rare that all members of a group can see it clearly, even though the Incident indicates it, in general. For example, in the abbreviated Incidents cited here, we should redefine the issues as follows:

a. When provoked to take direct action, what can a *staff man* properly do that might strengthen his organization as a whole?

[5]For example, under the unfavorable conditions of experimenting with much too large a group (120 members) at a single session, when this method came as a complete surprise to them, the Observer noted that there was no pause even before the first question, that relevant questions were answered at the rate of about two a minute for more than half an hour, and that some members still had questions to ask when this phase had to be shut off for lack of time.

[6] Evaluation of this stage, by discussion members themselves, in relation to decisions made in the next phase, shows clearly how wide the gap often is between factual information that has not been sought by a given individual, and insight into the meaning of facts. Management representatives can never afford to overlook this distinction when planning for communication with employees.

b. Did this supervisor overstep his recognized functions, within the meaning of the existing labor agreement?

4. *Making and Testing Decisions.* In deciding a live issue, group opinion is seldom unanimous, even after discussion. Entrenched attitudes, misconceptions, preconceptions, and differences in value scale exert a strong pull on the minds of members. In making and testing decisions, case students get a vivid demonstration of the fact that no one thinks with absolute objectivity, or solely in the context of a single situation. In a series of meetings, they get practice in controlling prejudice and in using their cumulative experience constructively.

When members are ready to commit themselves, we encourage independence by asking them to write their decision, or "award" (often just "yes" or "no" on the issue), to jot down their reasons, and sign the paper which they then turn into the Observer. To get a total picture of group opinion, the Observer tabulates these decisions, on the spot if possible, so that the result can immediately be announced. To develop the possibilities of integrating differences, each sub-group goes into a huddle, consolidates their view, and elects a spokesman who then summarizes it for the benefit of those in other sub-groups who differ. After using these group resources we offer a further test by having the Leader announce the decision that actually was made in the case situation. In an arbitration case, he also summarizes the "discussion" (reasons) written by the official arbitrator. When he has the facts, he tells the group about the immediate sequel of events, after the actual decision.

5. *Evaluating and Generalizing.* To round out our analysis, we then think back over the situation as a whole, asking questions whose general tenor is: "What can we learn from this case?" For instance: in that situation, might anything have been done better, by any of those participants, to prevent misunderstandings or to settle disagreements at any earlier stage? How might that kind of difficulty be prevented in similar situations? How effective were corporate policies? Were they clearly understood and interpreted with sound judgment by all management representatives who needed that kind of guide for decision?

During a series of meetings, we ask periodically: "In working on this case together, have we exhibited any of the forms of behavior that obviously impeded progress in the work situations which we have analyzed? If so, what are we going to do about it?"

222   What Are the Values of the Incident Process Case Method?

When such a process of case analysis can be carried out repeatedly, by the same small group, the possibilities for learning are limitless. Members practice the skills of leadership (including planning for group activity). They also gain experience in getting and sifting facts, in speaking clearly and in listening intently, in formulating issues, summarizing, weighing evidence, and in thinking independently and decisively, yet flexibly and cooperatively. When serving as Observer, each member gets concentrated practice in watching others apply in action what they know in theory, in making mental notes to amplify written notes, and in preparing reports that need to be clear, concise, and illuminating. In short, case analysts constantly work at the skills needed to raise efficiency in human relations. In this way, responsible individuals at any stage of experience can learn to be increasingly effective as *members*. Each can see that, far from being belittled or submerged by taking part in group activity, he becomes more of a person when he merges his insight and experience as a member, enlisted with others in working toward mutually desired goals.

223   Our Sales Department Conducts Regular Conferences of Its Division Sales Managers. Could Our Training Director, Located in the Personnel Department of the Company, Be of Help with These Meetings?

Decidedly. In one recent case a development specialist from the personnel department was invited by a sales manager to attend a meeting of Division Sales Managers and offer suggestions for improvement of the meetings.

The development specialist turned in a seven-page report, part of which (the "Specific Observations") is given below. Following this report the development specialist was asked to help organize and carry out a two-week training course for these same sales executives.

1. The program established a time schedule, but no subject matter. Would it help the conference participants in preparing themselves for the meetings if they knew in advance what subjects were to be covered? A certain degree of flexibility could still be maintained.
2. Assignment of certain subjects or whole meetings to division managers for them to prepare and conduct would give the opportunity for

participation that both you and they are after. It would also provide valuable practice in the leading of meetings.

3. In any instance where there are many subjects to be covered and many facts to be presented and digested, it would be helpful to have the high points prepared in advance for distribution during or after the meeting. This insures that everyone gets the same story, that attention is focused on the major issues, and that the men have material for later review.

4. In connection with such give-away material, it is unwise to distribute a mass of material at the beginning of the meeting because it necessarily dilutes attention. Conference participants leaf through the pages, not following the discussion. Limit distribution to the minimum necessary to accomplish the purpose. This will sometimes mean handing out one chart at a time.

5. The general objective of the program should be defined in the initial meeting. Then everyone will know precisely where he is going and he can better concentrate on the steps along the way.

6. The use of the conference method, which is extremely democratic, calls for considerable tact and finesse on the part of the leader. He must guide discussion to helpful conclusions without appearing to dictate; otherwise, he might just as well lecture and be done with it. There were a few times in the early meetings when he invited the group to express an opinion and then rather abruptly rejected that opinion. One of the most striking of these, because it was a critical point in the whole conference, occurred when we asked the division managers whether or not they thought we were training salesmen properly. Their answer was, yes,—even after they had seen the chart material which we had presented. Obviously, this was not the answer we wanted, so we rejected it. It might have been more effective if we had taken the time to lead the division managers to tell us themselves that there was a great need for better training.

7. It is hard for a conferee to listen to a lot of discussion and still sort out the principal points. It is for this reason that conference leaders make considerable use of blackboards, easels, and charts to highlight the major problems or conclusions, and to facilitate learning. There were many instances in the conference when a blackboard would have been helpful to everyone concerned.

8. When charts are used, they should generally present one idea clearly. A profusion of information on one chart can be confusing.

9. In the first two days of the conference, there was limited opportunity for participation. On Monday; for example, we listened for the full morning. Monday afternoon was largely listening. On the third and fourth days, this situation improved considerably. Obviously, we can not eliminate lecturing and presentation from these meetings. It might help, however, if we spaced lecturing with general discussion, limiting the straight lecturing to a half hour in any one instance.

10. When the conference leader is soliciting ideas he will have better success if he reserves his own conclusions to the end. When the boss states his own stand categorically and then invites discussion, he is deceiving himself.

11. In a long conference, with full morning and afternoon sessions, there is a great need for change of pace. This, again, points to the need for charts, blackboards, easel presentation, a mixture of conference and lecture, role playing, and cases. Above all, there must be opportunity for the conferee to do more than sit and soak up words.

12. This observation was in my notes for Monday of the conference: "So far, the approach taken by the leaders of the meeting has been primarily critical and somewhat pessimistic. For that reason, probably, what little response the group has made has been largely defensive. Is it possible that the presenting of problems without criticism might lead to a fuller and more constructive discussion?"

13. When we are hearing reports of committee investigations, the meeting room should be so arranged as to put the committee chairman conspicuously at the head of the meeting. In this connection, it might be well if the members of top management present split up instead of concentrating in one impressive group at the head of the table. They offer more competition than most chairmen can face.

14. The division managers' reports became repetitive after about the third man had reported. Would it be possible, if these reports have a real value, to combine them in advance of the meeting and issue them as a single joint report, thereby, eliminating repetition and also avoiding comparison of division managers.

224   What Training Should Supervisors in a Retail Store Receive?

This depends on the needs of the supervisors. Their requirements can best be ascertained by someone who observes them in action, interviews them and others in the organization, and uses additional tested techniques to determine training needs. In general, the needs of retail supervisors are no different from the needs of supervisors in industry and training courses designed to meet specific needs of supervisors in industry can be adapted to similar needs of retail supervisors.

The School of Industrial and Labor Relations of Cornell University undertook a joint study with Loblaw, Inc. to develop a training program for supervisors in the various Loblaw stores.[7]

[7] New York State School of Industrial and Labor Relations, Cornell University, "Improving the Supervision in Retail Stores," Extension Bulletin No. 7, October, 1950.

The basic course was taught by line supervisors, using the conference method. The subject titles and objectives of each conference are set forth below.

Conference No. 1—Responsibilities of the Loblaw supervisor.
1. To help supervisors fix in mind their exact duties and responsibilities —what they must know and be able to do in order to live up to the requirements of their jobs.
2. To give the supervisors confidence in what they know and what they can do, and the assurance that performing most of their duties can be done right so often that good habits are established, thus freeing their minds to plan improvements.
3. To develop within the conference group the view that most of the supervisor's duties lead to the need to understand and deal with human beings.

Conference No. 2—Overcoming difficulties in carrying out supervisory responsibilities.
1. To determine the duties and responsibilities that create difficulties for Loblaw supervisors.
2. To set up a method for analyzing these difficulties in order to determine their causes and possible remedies.
3. To encourage Loblaw supervisors to take an active part in removing the difficulties, thus making their own work easier.

Conference No. 3—What Loblaw employees expect of their supervisors.
1. To enable each supervisor to see that, in fulfilling his responsibilities as a supervisor, he is helping employees to develop their own capabilities and to get what they want out of life.
2. To assist the supervisors in analyzing what some of the real wants of employees are so that they may fully appreciate these wants.
3. To translate realization of employee wants into a definite method of showing employees how they can satisfy their wants by willingly contributing their efforts to the organization.
4. To set the foundation for the next conference, in which a definite approach to constructive criticism will be developed, based particularly on the material in this conference.

Conference No. 4—Helping employees to satisfy their wants.
1. To develop an approach to constructive criticism that is constructive first, and, if necessary, critical afterward; that stresses the right way to do things, that touches on the wrong way only if necessary for comparison.
2. To agree on reasons that are acceptable to employees as well as to supervisors; that explain why certain courses of action are right and others wrong—reasons that, whenever possible, are based on gain or loss to the employees rather than on impersonal policies or the dictates of a supervisor.

   3. To develop more firmly the recognition that, through helping em-
      ployees to satisfy their wants, supervisors can more easily assure that
      the needs of the organization will be met.

Conference No. 5—Helping an employee adjust to a new job.
   1. To discuss the supervisor's responsibilities in inducting a newly em-
      ployed worker into the Loblaw organization, or any employee into a
      new job and a new social group.
   2. To consider the new employee's and the supervisor's feelings in mak-
      ing the new adjustment involved and the kinds of information that a
      new employee needs to feel at home on the job and to do a good job.
   3. To agree on what the supervisor must do to help the employee get
      started right, and how the supervisor can follow up; and on some of
      the special problems arising with a new employee and how these
      problems can be met.
   4. To stress the significance of correct orientation as related to turnover
      and grievances.

Conference No. 6—Eliminating causes of complaints and grievances.
   1. To arouse in the supervisors an alertness to remove potential causes
      for complaints before grievances develop.
   2. To develop a recognition that most grievances do not pop up sud-
      denly, but have an underlying cause that can be diagnosed and ad-
      justed with relative ease if sighted and acted on promptly.
   3. To outline, with the aid of the group, ways in which the supervisor
      can prepare himself to prevent the causes of grievances from arising.
   4. To call to attention the fact that an ignored or unrecognized griev-
      ance may result in substitution of other or additional grievances, thus
      increasing the difficulty of final solution.
   5. To emphasize prompt attention to complaints and symptoms of
      grievances.

Conference No. 7—Handling grievances when they do arise.
   1. To examine situations in which individual and group differences of
      aims, interests, and purposes are revealed, and the care required of
      the supervisor in order to reconcile individual purpose and co-
      operation to the group effort.
   2. To focus attention on the problem of uncovering the real cause
      underlying stated grievances, inasmuch as the grievance advanced by
      the employee and the actual cause of his unhappiness may not be
      the same.
   3. To illustrate, using the grievance as a concrete situation, a method of
      getting to the root of and attempting to remedy problems that arise
      through misunderstanding or bad practice in relations between
      people.

Conference No. 8—Developing good work habits among employees.
   1. To develop a concept of "discipline" that will embody the ideas of
      preventive as well as corrective discipline, and to define discipline as

instruction and training designed to "correct, mold, strengthen, and perfect" employee performance on the job.

2. To discuss means and incentives that the supervisor can use to encourage employees to maintain and improve good habits, and to correct bad working habits.

3. To agree on the importance, before taking any disciplinary action, of first having all necessary information and of deciding what purpose the action is intended to accomplish.

4. To emphasize the importance of selecting and judging any form of disciplinary action on the basis of whether or not it represents the best way to achieve the desired purpose.

5. To consider the application of disciplinary measures to individual employees in a constructive manner that will improve human relations.

Conference No. 9—Why employees work for Loblaw's.

1. To cause the supervisors to think concretely of the specific things done by Loblaw's to make it a desirable place to work.

2. To bring to light facts about the Loblaw organization so that the supervisors will be able to talk about it and think about it definitely and with justifiable enthusiasm.

3. To enable the supervisors to "sell" themselves on the good qualities of the organization for which they work, and to make contributions toward further improvements.

4. To show the supervisors how the good qualities of the Loblaw organization justify them in thinking and saying that the employee can satisfy his wants by working for Loblaw's.

In short, the conferees aimed first at a clear understanding of the supervisor's responsibilities, most of which center upon getting things done through other people. They proceeded to the identification of responsibilities presenting the greatest problems. Next they developed a framework for analysis of supervisory problems. Finally they went ahead to discuss problems of motivation, orientation, grievances, discipline, and morale as they apply in the retail store.

PART III

TYPES OF DEVELOPMENT

Chapter 13

EXECUTIVE DEVELOPMENT

225   Who Are Executives?

For the purpose of this chapter we define executives as the top-level men in any organization who are specifically responsible for the making of policy as well as its administration. They are the presidents, vice presidents, works managers, plant superintendents, controllers, treasurers, office managers, and directors of functions such as purchasing, research, personnel, legal, manufacturing engineering, customer service and warehousing, etc. Usually, they are so high up in the organization that they are supervisors of supervisors. In most cases, they supervise bosses who in turn direct the work of other supervisors. Also included in the term "executives" are top-level staff men who may be advisors to other executives—specialists, for example, engaged in organizational planning, electronics research, or population studies. These staff men may work alone or have assistants. They are usually professionally trained and are considered as executives because their research studies or recommendations play a major part in setting policy and controlling operations.

226   What Is Executive Development?

Executive Development is the planned improvement of high-level managers in those understandings, attitudes, and activities that enter into or influence their work and their work relations.

227   Why Do Executives Need Development?

Executives need development to fit them for even better performance in the jobs they now hold, to prepare them for the changes and challenges that are sure to come in the future, and to add to their years of service to the company. Participation in continuous development activities slows up the aging processes, physical as well as mental. Executives who follow a continuous program of development therefore protect their own well-being and welfare, reduce the loss of efficiency which comes with the years, and find new ways to utilize the abilities that result from long years of experience.

228 Is Executive Development Timely in Rapidly Expanding Companies?

Development is always timely, but it is most timely when it seems to be least needed; that is, before expansion takes place. Any company which delays development programs until it finds itself building new plants, adding new products, and entering new sales territory is asking for trouble and sacrificing results. At such a time all hands are working under pressure; few hours and little thought can be spared for jobs other than those of the moment. Development is therefore either "crammed" or neglected, compelling men to take on jobs for which they are not ready, or forcing the organization to hire outsiders who also may be unprepared.

Development is just what its name implies. It is not and cannot be sudden transformation. Growth in understanding, technical skill, ability, and creative imagination takes place step by step, often with long pauses for practice and assimilation of things that have been learned. This requires at least relative calm, during which the company operates on an even keel. If such periods are used to advantage, the frantic need for development during expansion can be reduced, leaving men free to apply the abilities they have developed for just such emergencies.

229 What Is the Place of Executive Development in Relation to an Established Personnel and Training Program?

It is too soon to say where the function known as executive development will eventually come to rest in the ideal organization. At this time, it seems certain that development must report fairly high up in the organization. It seems equally certain that development is a personnel function. In companies whose personnel director is a vice president or board member, the person in charge of executive development should report to him. To have him report elsewhere can only lead to competition and conflict with other human relations and human resources functions assigned to the personnel department. If, however, personnel is a routine activity having little prestige or authority it may be necessary to have executive development report elsewhere until the personnel functions of the company come to maturity.

When executive development is placed in the personnel department, it can function side by side with training, now well established with other human resources activities as the responsibility of personnel. In fact, in cases where training is well established, highly regarded, and professionally led, it may well be that executive development and training will and should merge.

At any rate, training and executive development must work in close relationship and willing harmony.

230   Who Is Responsible for Executive Development?

Since executive development involves matters of basic policy, it is the responsibility of top executives. They must decide that programs are to be conducted, and must give them support. Each executive or administrator must then outline systematic development plans for his assistants. These individual plans may be *worked out* with the assistance of staff training men or development specialists. The plans may be *carried out* by the department head or he may share this responsibility with staff units such as a training or personnel department, with outside educational institutions, or with individual experts acting as consultants. The degree to which any executive "farms out" the work of training will depend upon the time he can spare and the nature of the attitude, understanding, or skill that is being improved. Some skills and understandings which the executive does not himself possess will of course have to be developed by others. While the actual teaching in executive development may be delegated—some of it, certainly, must be delegated—the primary responsibility for seeing that development opportunities are provided and taken advantage of lies with the chief executive.

231   Are There Any Assumptions or Preliminary Propositions Which Must Be Adopted in Order to Establish an Executive Development Program?

There are. No program or executive development can get under way unless an adequate number of leaders in top management either accept its ability to meet their needs, or determine to give it a thorough trial. As a working basis, at least, these men must accept four propositions:

1. Progress or growth can be furthered and made effective by planned attention to it on the part of the individual himself, his superiors, and the training staff.
2. Development is basically an individual matter. The development program, therefore, must be highly individualized.
3. Age is no insurmountable barrier to learning new things. One can teach an old dog new tricks. The best "trick" of them all is the discovery that he can develop these new tricks himself—and can enjoy doing so.
4. Each manager must accept the responsibility for developing one or more possible successors to himself, as well as men who will advance to other high positions in the organization.

Men who are successful executives today must be led to see that the skills and abilities that got them to the top may not be the ones they will need most in the decades ahead. Success in the modern business world is a temporary prize that can be held only so long as each leader sees newly evolving forces and adapts his thought and actions to them. Executive development helps mature, successful business leaders to perceive these new forces as they arise, and long before they become apparent to less alert competitors. Such leaders may, in effect, be more alert and skilled in adaptation in their late 50's and 60's than they were as young men.

232   What Thinking Should Be Planted in the Minds of All Top Management Before Starting an Executive Development Program?

Everyone involved must realize that worth-while development comes slowly. Small results may appear in a few months, but important ones probably will not be evident for three to five years. Even then it will be difficult to measure results or relate them positively to any one development activity. Top executives must have a strong faith in education and a full, enduring confidence in the person who directs the program. Moreover, top management must be willing to improve itself. It must become willing, if it is not already willing, to have younger, well-trained executives question its policies and challenge its decisions. Most important of all is top management's acceptance of the fact that development can improve the performance of even highly successful and able executives, and can add many years to their periods of competent service. In both ways it more than repays the time, thought, and money devoted to it.

233   **How Does One Select Executives Who Are to Be Developed?**

No selection should be made because *all* executives who are worthy of being kept on should be developed according to the needs of their present jobs. Some will need help in public speaking, others will need help in developing conference leadership, decisiveness, consultative management, planning, report writing, public relations, money management, budgeting, organization, and many other general or specific areas. Development is not only for a few who are failing and must improve to hold on, nor for those at the other end of the scale who already have gone far in the company. It is for all whose present job performance can be bettered. After an individual participates in programs that bring him a very high level of success in his present job, and after he shows that he has potential for promotion, some of his training may be geared to the needs he will face as he moves upward in the company. Major emphasis, however, should be placed upon helping each man to do his present job better. Under this plan, development becomes a need for all executives.

234   **Who Selects the Executives to Be Developed for Promotion?**

As stated in the answer to the previous question, there is no selection. All executives should be developed. However, some will have more potential than others and it may be desirable for them to participate in some broader program of development in addition to routine development programs offered to all executives. The highest operating official in the department determines who will participate in such programs and recommends the training.

235   **How Can You Lead the "Busy Executive" to Realize That an Advanced Management Course at One of the Universities Will Help Him and His Company?**

Let's begin by analyzing this man's reluctance. It may rest partly upon self-satisfaction, partly upon the self-flattering feeling that he cannot be spared, partly upon fear of revealing his weaknesses, and partly upon the fact that he has allowed himself to become submerged in details. He also may be unfamiliar with courses, and may think them "theoretical," with little practical value.

Assume that the last two factors are most important. The training director may begin by discussing the steps a "busy man" may take to free himself from pressure. Later, after the executive has spelled out the steps that should speed up his work, begin to suggest that certain university programs are reputed to do just that for other businessmen. Repeat that suggestion, though not too often, and show the executive catalogs from Harvard, Columbia, The Wharton School, and other outstanding institutions and discuss selected offerings with him. It may be well to discover, with the executive, that certain courses really are as useful as they are reputed to be.

If possible, he also should be induced to read articles discussing university courses, to talk with other executives who have taken them, and to visit one or more schools where he can watch programs in action.

236   What Are a Few Ways to Convince Members of Top Management That They Themselves Need Today's Training?

Many specific suggestions are available. From the following list select the ones that seem to fit the individuals that are being approached.

1. Overcome their lack of interest by getting them to help plan and conduct training for their subordinates.
2. Keep them aware of courses, programs, visits, tours, rotations, etc., that are available to men of their level. See that they know of other men who are taking advantage of these developmental opportunities.
3. Enlist the aid of the men's superiors, who may not be so resistant to growth plans.
4. Offer a two-hour conference on the subject of "Self-improvement—Need for It and Ways of Achieving It." Or approach the subject indirectly under a different title if that seems necessary.
5. Results of employee surveys or middle management opinion polls help to reveal needs for development. Men who are overconfident may be urged into improvement when they learn what the surveys show concerning the opinions of their subordinates or associates.
6. Establish evaluation and merit rating plans, and counsel with the man evaluated. After a superior has pointed out a man's weakness, lead the subordinate to ask what he can do to im-

prove himself, and then get him to help plan his own developmental program.

7. Include a heading such as "Will to Improve," in the executive audit or merit rating scale. See that the top managers are rated and counseled on this factor.

8. In determining merit increases and promotions, presidents and vice presidents may be led to consider their subordinates' open-mindedness and willingness to grow.

9. Approach the problem directly by asking top-level managers, at the appropriate time, what development they think is needed for men like themselves.

10. Get high executives to visit training conferences in which useful subjects of which they know little are being discussed and mastered by their associates or subordinates.

237 How Can High-Level Management Be Induced to Cooperate in Development Programs Instead of Approving Them "in Principle" or for Others?

The problem is closely related to the one considered in Question 236, because men must be convinced that they need development before they will cooperate in it. There also are various types of cooperation, ranging from casual and intermittent to constant and enthusiastic. It is obviously desirable to secure the latter type.

To accomplish this, the man in charge of development will work to get the executives to understand his program, and then get them to participate in planning and organizing it, and finally in accepting his offerings for themselves. He should meet occasionally with top management, explaining the problems of development, his plans to solve them, and results already achieved. He should invite executives to take part in planning development programs and even in teaching them. He should repeatedly but tactfully offer assistance to busy executives in all areas of development —their own as well as that of their subordinates.

238 Is There One Best Approach That Will Sell Executive Development to a Division of a Company When None of Its Management Has Had Training?

People who have had little training themselves usually respond best to practical, realistic approaches. They want to see and benefit directly from the results rather than be told about them. Probably the best approach in this case is to find some place in this division where errors, failures or weaknesses are bothersome. Poor management may permit excessive breakage of dishes in the cafeteria, may let new employees "ride" and wear out the clutches on machines they operate, or may lead to loss of shipments because cartons are sealed poorly or stencils are illegible. There may be failure to delegate authority, unwillingness to accept responsibility, or poor understanding of the executive's own motives or those of others. If the training man can make himself available and his services known, so that he is invited to help executives solve any of these practical problems, he has broken the ice. If his help makes a real contribution, his services will be valued and will be sought more and more frequently. In time—and the length of time will vary—he can suggest specific and later general projects in executive development.

239   In General Who Determines What Training Major Executives Need and Receive in Industry?

At the moment, training given within industry is usually determined by committees made up of company executives. Committee members are influenced by the opinions of chief executives, training directors, and any specialists whose subjects are being taught. Custom, or courses that have been successful in other industries also influence offerings. Sometimes a single executive sees need for a certain improvement among his own executives. He establishes training to bring about this improvement. Other executives observe his success, discover that they too have similar needs, and transplant the original course, with whatever adaptations are necessary, to their own situations.

240   Can a Person Direct or Conduct Work in Executive Development Although He Himself Does Not Hold High Rank in the Organization?

He can, and in most cases he must. His position is much like that of the personnel expert who recruits and hires professional men and administrators who will operate several levels above him. Any development man who is fit for his job can teach or administer teaching for executives whose positions are higher and more responsible than his own. Such a man earns respect by his ability to guide and stimulate the growth of others, not by the level at which his name appears on the company's organization chart.

Especially in schools of business, many a professor successfully teaches graduate students whose age, salary, and over-all accomplishments exceed his own.

241　In an Executive Development Program Is It Possible to Start at the Top with the Big Boss, or Must Development Be Inaugurated with the Little Fellow?

It is quite possible to start at the top. Some programs do so in one of two ways:

1. A committee, drawn from the top echelon of management, decides what training is needed for its own members and others at their level. The committee organizes content, and in some cases may even teach. Training in this case is aimed at the top level and starts there.

2. A training director, outside consultant, or major executive especially assigned to the job may prepare a program, usually for middle or lowel levels, and invite top management to preview, edit, and improve it before it is carried out. This subterfuge brings development to the attention of men at high levels who might shrug it off if the purpose were not disguised.

Other programs start at lower levels. These programs usually provide skill training for employees or supervisor training for beginning supervisors. The reception given training at the bottom levels is frequently very good. Younger men are inevitably found there; they have their futures ahead of them and their ambitions are stronger than they will be later on. In addition, young men are closer to their formal school years; they learn faster and respond better to training.

Because of these factors, some training men prefer to start training at the bottom and encourage development to grow horizontally and upward. It does so in two ways: older men, observing that promotions and opportunities come to young fellows who take training, and that training makes their work easier, request it for themselves. Training also grows upward as young, trained men advance to higher and higher positions and take their understanding of, and support for, training upwards with them as they go.

242　At What Level Should an Executive Development Program Begin?

We used to think that development had to start at the top. Although that still is a most desirable level, we must admit that top executives are more likely to approve development for others than they are to accept it for themselves. It also would be unwise —yes, harmful—to do nothing for any of the executives in a company until the needs of highest executives are met. The place to start, therefore, is where we can. Some successful executive development programs began at the "assistant to" level and have spread both upward and downward. Others—and they include some of the finest development programs in American industry— gained a foothold far down in the organization. Then, as they proved their value, the programs were requested by higher and higher levels of management.

Fortunately, development is not a highly formalized activity, like classroom education. Any executive who wants to coach, counsel, train, or rotate his subordinates should be free, and almost always is free, to do as he wishes. Moreover, a departmental climate that encourages improvement may be just as important as organized activities. This climate is something the boss himself creates as a result of his basic wishes and attitudes. If they are right he almost inevitably produces a situation, or atmosphere, in which men are encouraged to improve their work and themselves. If the bosses' attitudes are neutral or negative, this favorable situation does not arise. In this sense, development may start—or be introduced—at any level in the organization.

243   What Are the Initial Steps in Organizing an Executive Development Program? What Is to Be Done First?

These questions assume that the preliminary spadework has been done. That is, top executives have decided that a program of executive development shall be put into effect. They have selected a man to plan, establish, and manage the program, and have given him wholehearted support. He is ready to go—but how does he start?

His first task is to make an executive appraisal. Unless already fully prepared for his work, he will begin by studying several good appraisal programs, such as those of Detroit Edison, Esso Standard Oil, and U. S. Rubber. Since the leader will want to be sure of understanding and support from the top, he may circulate these plans among executives who will help develop the appraisal plan for his own company. He almost certainly will offer and lead one or two conferences on the executive audit—what it is and how it is conducted. He may wish to isolate one step in the audit, such as the actual evaluation of men, and hold a series of conferences on how to rate and evaluate executives. To make these conferences effective, he will probably use films such as those developed by Ford and Esso Standard. He almost certainly will use some role playing to strengthen men in their ability to judge others.

Out of these meetings may grow a form for evaluation, or at least some common agreement on what skills or habits are to be rated. At this point the director of the program will organize a committee and establish with them the actual process, forms, and methods to be used in conducting the appraisal, so that it can be essentially uniform throughout the company. Having done so, he will announce his next steps, the method agreed upon, participate as much as necessary in making the appraisal, and follow up on its accomplishment.

244　In What General Areas, or Fields, Do Executives Need Development?

Many authors have summarized the development needs of executives, in statements that range from general to ultra-specific. One of the best general statements lists four areas of general, or even universal, need:

1. Increased ability in self-understanding and continued growth in the understanding of others.
2. Understanding of the dynamic social and economic forces at work in America today, accompanied by a realization of the ways in which industry influences these forces, and how social and economic forces, in turn, react upon industry.
3. Knowledge of and skill in applying scientific management.
4. Technical know-how in various functional specialties—sales, research, manufacturing, etc.

This list does not imply that every executive is weak in all these areas, or even in any one of them. But each field is so important, so complex, so endlessly changing, that even the strongest executive needs further development.

245　Specifically, What Do Executives Need to Do Better?[1]

Specific deficiencies which executive development programs attempt to correct are frequently indicated by actions of the executive such as these:

[1] The answer to this question comes from "Developing Leadership for Tomorrow's Tasks," by E. G. Planty and Carlos A. Efferson, *Dun's Review*, January, 1952. Used by permission of the publishers, Dun & Bradstreet.

1. The executive indulges in snap judgments, does not study problems thoroughly before reaching decisions.
2. He may not delegate responsibility as often as he should for his own good and that of people below him.
3. He also may delegate vaguely so that subordinates are uncertain as to what they are responsible for.
4. The man may need to appreciate that his lack of technical knowledge is limiting him.
5. He may handle confidential information carelessly.
6. He is tactless in his dealings with associates, subordinates, or superiors, limiting acceptance and support for him and his projects.
7. The executive may not realize that his own personal preferences and experiences influence his evaluation of facts. His decisions therefore are subjective, though he may pride himself on objectivity.
8. He may be unable to organize effectively.
9. He is not fully aware of what competition is doing, too confident and secure in his present efforts.
10. He may be unable or unwilling to take the over-all view of problems, considering them merely as they affect himself or his own department. He may think department-wide instead of company-wide.
11. He may not participate in social, professional, civic, or fraternal activities, and may not encourage others to do so, lessening community understanding and respect for business.
12. He may dampen free exchange of ideas and criticisms; he may not respect opposing views or opinions.
13. He may take too much time to reach decisions. Such a man may try to get too many facts, in the mistaken belief that abundance gives them significance. He may go from problem to problem, seldom taking time to settle one before becoming immersed in the next. Through being overcautious, he may subconsciously seek to avoid decisions by putting them off by one means or another.
14. The executive may not make full use of his associates or subordinates in framing policies.
15. He may have stopped growing. Instead of welcoming new methods, products, and ideas, he tries to do his job as he did it years ago.
16. A man may constantly seek simple or "correct" answers, not realizing the complexity of forces that affect executive decisions and the likelihood that answers, even when carefully thought out will be compromises.
17. He may be unable to establish the climate of respect and cooperation in which subordinates do their best work.
18. He may need increased personal security and healthful enjoyment from life in order to be at his best in business.
19. He may not keep his associates adequately informed of his activities.
20. An executive may think too much about details; too little in terms of broad problems and policies.

21. He may not be at his best in the presence of superiors. Many a man of native ability stammers, hesitates or becomes dogmatic in the presence of high executives.

22. He wants too much conformity of thinking among subordinates; rewards those that follow him more than he does those that sometimes question his opinions.

23. He may appear to seek his own advancement more than that of the company or his subordinates.

24. He is confused about his own motives.

25. He is too aware of limits of his authority, thus failing to pick up loose but important ends.

26. People say he does not practice what he preaches.

27. He may fear to tread on the toes of men in other departments. Because of this exaggerated desire not to hurt the feelings of others, he sometimes makes faulty decisions or shows indecision.

28. An executive, like lesser men, may be swayed by prejudice. Thus he may regard all professors as impractical theorists and all college graduates as overconfident upstarts. At the other extreme, he may doubt the ability of any man without a college degree.

Executive development attempts to eliminate these and many other deficiencies.

246   How Is Executive Development Carried On?

It is carried on individually and in groups, and is handled both in the company and outside.

	INDIVIDUAL METHODS	GROUP METHODS
Methods best suited for on-the-job and in the company	Job progression Job rotation Understudies Vacation or leave-of-absence fill-ins Coaching and counseling Guided experience Consultative management	Committees and task forces Bottom-up management Consultative management Syndicates Conferences
Methods equally appropriate for on-the-job and in the company, or for out-of-plant	Psychological evaluation Counseling	Lectures Forums Panels Syndicates

schools, courses, con- ferences, refreshers, seminars, etc.		Conference programs Case studies Role playing Debates Workshops Psychiatric group study
Best done outside the plant	Psychiatric counseling	Courses for credit to- ward college degrees Highly specialized tech- nical courses required by only one or two men in any given company

247   What Is the Best Type of Executive Training?

There is no one best type, under any and all conditions. Executive training meets a wide variety of needs, as it must for people who differ in habits, attitudes, and reactions and who work under a variety of circumstances and pressures. The most we can hope to do is to find a type of training that will be acceptable to a given person, and will bring him early and permanent improvement, with the least possible disturbance of his daily work. If these requirements are met it makes little difference whether the method employed is job rotation, nondirective case studies, counseling, lectures, syndicates, conferences, role playing, or guided experience.

Content will vary as much as method. Some executives need one thing and some another; to prescribe in advance for all is to meet the needs of virtually none. Each man must get what he requires by a curriculum as well as a method selected to meet his demands.

Although there never will be one best type of training for executives, experience undoubtedly will develop a limited range of desirable patterns. Those who are discouraged by this prospect of continuing variety may take comfort from engineering and medicine. Here are two long-established subjects, much older and therefore more firmly fixed than executive development can be for many years to come. Yet no two schools of engineering or medicine offer identical programs, nor are they ever likely to do so.

One of the greatest dangers executive development faces is the insistence of some directors of development upon uniformity in content and method. Mostly, those who try to oversimplify and oversystematize executive development are newcomers to the field of learning who try to apply the disciplines of accounting, engineering, or other exact sciences to human growth and development.

248 What Special Experience or Training Best Equips a Man to Teach Executives or to Direct the Program?

Obviously, the man should know as much as possible about learning, particularly adult learning. Training or experience in other fields such as chemistry, accounting, economics, production management, and a host of other fields do not particularly fit a man to determine what teaching method will return the most results for busy executives in a given period of time and in a particular subject. If a person with some specialty other than education is chosen to direct the program, he will do well to become as familiar with learning and teaching as a well-planned reading program and attendance at evening schools will permit.

249 Will You Outline the Advantages of University Development Courses in Contrast to Similar Work Within Commercial or Industrial Organizations?

University courses provide no general substitute for development within the business organization, but they do offer seven outstanding advantages:

1. Where development activities are undertaken within the plant, operational pressures and tensions often intervene to upset the training schedule. Even when this does not happen, the individual who leaves his office for an hour or two in the classroom may be tense, worried, or impatient to return to his desk. Work at a university removes men from these troublesome everyday pressures.

2. The university brings together in one class men from a variety of occupational fields and industries. Their attitudes and business practices range from old-fashioned and even reactionary to modern, or even ultraprogressive. These contrasts provide a stimulating and varied environment that cannot be obtained within a single plant.

3. High-level executives are normally reserved and conservative in expression. When removed from the constant and critical scrutiny of their associates, they are likely to put aside some of

this caution and participate more freely. As a result, they profit more fully in the university environment.

4. Academic men, secure in their own authority and positions, can deal with successful and sometimes overconfident executives as training men or line executives in their own plants seldom feel free to do. The professor enjoys much the same prestige and power possessed by outside consultants in contrast to internal advisers.

5. Few business organizations can afford to hire a staff of outstanding educators and experienced training men large enough to conduct all essential executive development activities within the factory or office walls. Small organizations may have to rely entirely upon universities and consultants.

6. Even where funds are available, men skilled in promoting human growth and development, and able at the same time to deal with major business executives in their own language, are not always available.

7. Outstanding universities have assembled staffs of teaching specialists which even the largest industry cannot hope to reproduce. Such staffs combine a breadth of knowledge and skills needed to cope with almost any problem. Moreover, these resources can be drawn upon on short notice, if problems that have not been anticipated demand solution. This would require weeks or months and a great waste of effort if it were attempted within one business organization.

250   Can You Compare—or Contrast—the Values of Individual and Group Methods of Executive Development?

Again we encounter the rule that no one method is best. For some tasks, individual approaches are best; for others, such as the development of skill in public speaking or in conference leadership, group meetings are essential. Beyond this there is great variety in the limitations, preferences, and aptitudes of people. The man who travels much can seldom take part in group activities; the executive who stays in the home office can do so and may welcome the chance. Certain executives broaden and grow through case studies; other men of comparable age, formal training, and job responsibilities will learn little from cases but will respond well to role playing or syndicates.

We conclude, therefore, that the method of training must fit the subject being taught, the man, and the conditions under which he works. It is fortunate that a wide range of individual and group methods is available, and that the men responsible for executive development can use those methods according to need.

251   In Developing an Executive, Is It Better to Give Him a Small Area in Which to Operate as a Full-Fledged Executive or to Make Him an Assistant to a Man of Wide-Ranging Authority?

Ideally, an executive should have the advantage of both experiences. The first assignment teaches him specializations and how to handle full responsibility. Work as an assistant broadens him and teaches him how to coordinate the actions of various special units into complete unified actions involving the work of several divisions of the company. Traditionally, specialization has come first. Management has not been willing to trust the decisions of young men in upper-level, over-all areas until they have proved themselves or their potential in some specialty.

252   How Can a Corporation Treasurer, Age 56, Train Younger Executives in His Department and Himself at the Same Time?

The top man's best chance to achieve mutual development is to invite younger executives in his department to participate in problem solution and department management. In both activities he will be able to counsel his men about practical problems with which he has had much experience. At the same time the superior will expose himself to, and broaden himself by, the thinking of younger men. He will learn how to secure and use their best ideas while they come to know and use the skills his experience has developed.

Regular weekly staff meetings are an essential part of this approach. In them, problems can be discovered, solutions explored, and knowledge exchanged through the group, without regard to superior-subordinate roles.

253   Isn't There a Danger That Executive Development Will Prepare Men for Advancement More Rapidly Than Opportunities Can Arise?

A careful study of organizational needs will enable management to balance the number of men developed for advancement with promotion opportunities. Besides, not all people should be developed for advancement. This type of development should be restricted to those who show unquestionable ability to handle more responsible work, in the fields where needs are likely to arise in the reasonably near future. Turnover of executives, ages, retirement, policies, growth of the company, and other factors help to determine how many men should be groomed for promotion.

Admittedly, it is bad to prepare men for promotions and then let them wait with no clear prospect for advancement. Under such conditions some persons become discouraged and others become impatient and hunt new jobs elsewhere. For this reason, and because there always is need for improvement at executive levels, development should first aim at improved performance in existing jobs and leave training for advancement to a later time. This provides immediate satisfaction, confidence and respect, yet leaves the way open to further progress for those who unquestionably deserve it. They usually are so few that no embarrassment of riches results. There is hardly one of us who cannot improve his daily performance in some manner. In making himself as nearly perfect as possible on his present job, a man gains immediate satisfaction, confidence, and respect among his equals.

254   Don't Men Sometimes Become Frustrated by Having to Wait for Advancement?

Yes. Good men who are ready for promotion are likely to feel lost if they wait long for promotion. During this period, the wise senior executive will keep in close touch with these men, encouraging them, inspiring them, and making them see the delay as a profitable opportunity to learn new skills and acquire broad vision. The better the men the more they need the challenge of varied and increasingly difficult assignments, backed by the reassurance of personal counsel while they wait for the promotion that is sure to seem long overdue. The company should also attempt to remove needless uncertainties and avoidable delays. Properly planned promotion plans based on studies of turnover, separations and retirements make advancement predictable rather than something that happens somehow and sometime, though no one knows just why or when. Planning may also reduce the gap between readiness for advancement and the availability of an appropriate job.

255   When Does One Give Up on an Executive and Drop Him from Classes and Activities?

Never, so long as he stays on the payroll. One may give up on trying to prepare a man for advancement, but if he is worth keeping at all, one should never stop helping him to do a better job in his present assignment. Since changes in methods, technology, and even company and departmental policies take place endlessly, executive training must go on without end, just as it goes on for all others in the company.

Some authorities doubt that it is ever wise to write a man off irrevocably and finally as nonpromotable. As we have explained, early learning and development take place at an irregular rate which is characterized by periods of enthusiastic growth followed by intervals without apparent progress. During these "plateau" intervals the trainee assimilates what he has learned, tries it out, gains confidence in using it. Some very fine executives have seemingly marked time like this for five or ten years before entering upon another cycle of growth, development, and achievement. To write them off during those intervals of seeming stagnation would have been a costly and unfair mistake.

256   How Do You Handle Executives Who Have No Potential for Promotion?

This question is anticipated and partly answered in Question 255. For a long time—perhaps five to ten years—we assume that the executive does have potential but has not revealed it. Meanwhile, we seek to improve his performance in the job he now holds.

But suppose he never does snap out of his doldrums; he still is not hopeless and a candidate for separation. Every company needs a reasonable number of average men in its executive ranks—men who do the routine, daily work adequately; men who have reached their peak and are either unable to go higher or cannot be interested in doing so. These people should be accepted at their appropriate levels. They should be trained *to do their present jobs better* and to keep up with the growing body of new knowledge that becomes yearly available in any area. They should neither be forced to work for promotion nor belittled for their failure to seek it.

**257   Why Do Some Able and Successful Executives Fail
After They Have Been Promoted?**

Men sometimes achieve outstanding success in one situation
and under one superior but fail elsewhere. A good candidate for
an executive position is one who has been trained in adaptability
and versatility to the extent of doing well under different men and
in different departments—with different problems. The man who
stays in one place too long becomes attached to his job, his associates, and frequently to his boss. In contrast, the one who learns
to do well under different men, in different departments, and at
different tasks, lacks these emotional limitations. Rotation, therefore, becomes an essential part of every well-planned development
program.

In the Consolidated Edison Company (of New York), for example, a man who is being developed for executive responsibility
serves, through rotation, with several different executives, and
learns to work well with all of them. Success in a single situation,
in a single kind of work, or under a single regime is not a full
guarantee of success under different conditions. Rotation is the
best single device to avoid such danger.

**258   How Does the Director of Training (or a Line Executive)
Develop a Demoted Executive?**

The time has passed when a man who does not make the grade
after promotion could be summarily fired. Much time, thought,
and money go into the development of an executive before he is
advanced; these and the man himself must be salvaged. Several
measures will make this possible:

1. Realize that the transition from up to down will be difficult.
The man's pride, his prestige, feeling of importance and even of
belonging may be injured or destroyed. Persuade his superior to
make a special effort to reassure the man and convince him the
company intends to keep him and to use his abilities. This will
produce a situation or a climate in which the man can see a secure
and ultimately satisfying future for himself.

2. Make sure why the man is being demoted; if the company
was at fault in advancing him too rapidly or getting him into a
position requiring greater talents than he possessed, admit the
fault frankly. If the fault is his, find out what skills, understand-

ings, or attitudes he lacks. Help him to develop these skills if he needs them in the position to which he is being assigned.

3. Consult often with the demoted executive to assure him of your own and the company's good intentions. Let this man's associates know that the company values his service and intends to continue to do so. Saving the man's pride, helping him face his failure, discovering his strengths, and building satisfactory performance upon them—these are steps that must be taken to assure his service to himself and his company and make possible whatever future development may be in order.

4. Finally, the fact that a promotion has failed will prompt the director of development to take steps to prevent similar errors in the future, (a) find out what was wrong in the man's selection, (b) try out men via rotation before they are given full responsibility, (c) train the man fully on the responsibilities of the new job both before and as he assumes it, and (d) counsel the newly promoted man regularly on his performance.

259   What Kind of Man Should Teach Executives and Direct the Development Program?

The question obviously assumes that the teacher-director will be a member of the organization in which he works. His status therefore will be lower than that of men whom he teaches and advises. At best, one of them probably will be his direct superior.

This relationship imposes some stringent requirements. The development director, whatever his title, cannot be management's hired man. He must be the kind of person whom management respects as its equal *in his particular field*. He must deserve and receive the confidence of top-flight executives, for he is in effect molding their successors and remolding them. Unless they trust him to do a good job, they cannot accept his work.

These points deserve emphasis. The good development counselor tries not to exert undue influence, but he must exert some. With minor exceptions, his advice influences which film shall be shown, which professor or consultant is brought in, what books read, what magazines circulated, and what courses or other helps presented. The director is the company's specialist in his field, and executives must rely upon his advice.

The qualifications of the director will vary with his functions. If he is to do a large part of the actual training, he should have specialized in human growth and development, and the arts and sciences that contribute to them. He should be fully familiar with the psychology of learning—especially adult learning—which includes group dynamics, sociometry, role playing, the case and syndicate methods of instruction, general teaching methods, and curriculum construction. He also should have had ample practice. A man who is to teach experienced, successful business executives, or teach others to teach them, must himself be an experienced and successful teacher. He also should have considerable skill as an administrator and should have a working knowledge of commerce or industry.

If the director of executive development is able to rely upon university professors, consultants, and executives of the company for the actual work of instruction and advising, he need not be so skilled in teaching. He must, however, be well grounded in the psychology of learning and in the problems and objectives of human development. He also must know good and bad teaching when he sees them, and must have great ability to plan, coordinate, and promote learning—the last including the power to arouse and maintain enthusiasm. With these qualities, the director can do a good, or even a creative job of buying educational services for executives who seldom will know just what they need but will be properly critical if they do not get it.

260   To What Extent Should Outsiders Be Brought in to Help Develop Executives?

As with many other problems that arise, the answer depends on circumstances. If a company has no full-time, professional educator or training director, much of the work of development must be done by outsiders. If a company does have such a man, he will conduct some of the development work himself and will prepare others in the organization to do so. This will reduce the number of calls that must be made upon outside experts.

Even when there is a well-developed training department, however, there will be occasions when no one within the organization will be able to present certain information, or develop certain skills or attitudes. Speech correction, for example, is a highly technical field in which no insider is likely to possess experience and competence. There also will be occasions when people who have the necessary knowledge are not good teachers, or are unable to devote the time and energy required by a particular project. When this happens, it will be necessary to go outside the organization.

Furthermore, some executives respond more readily and willingly to outsiders than to men within the organization. Work with such executives obviously should be done by outsiders.

261　Why Not Let Line Executives Do All the Developing?

This is a good idea—to the degree that they have the time, the interest and the ability to do all the training and development. Sometimes, however, line men lack interest and skill in teaching. Training is first necessary to develop their enthusiasm for teaching and their ability to do it.

Sometimes, too, there are skills desired in subordinates which superiors themselves do not possess, and a line man is not likely to teach his subordinate to do something which he does not understand or cannot do. If, for example, a line man does not like staff services, does not see their need in the business nor understand how to use their contributions, he cannot teach his subordinates a healthy respect and proper use of staff and service departments. In like manner one who resents unionization, dislikes union leaders, and considers unions a threat to his own authority, is not able to build or teach employee-management cooperation, mutual respect, and true industrial democracy. To overcome this limitation, skills and understandings not possessed by line executives must be taught by others.

We do not do our best toward improving over-all management efficiency if we limit our task to each man's passing on what he himself knows and does well at present. For this reason line executives cannot do all of the teaching.

262　Where Can I Find Out Details About Executive Development Courses Offered by Universities and Professional Management Societies?

Write to one or more of the following institutions and ask that you be informed regularly of their programs of executive development.

1. Director, Advanced Management Program, Graduate School of Business Administration, Harvard University, Cambridge.
2. President, American Management Association, New York.
3. President, National Industrial Conference Board, New York.

4. President, American Society of Training Directors, Eli Lilly and Company, Indianapolis.
5. Director, The Executive Program, The School of Business, The University of Chicago, Chicago.
6. Director, Executive Program in Business Administration, Graduate School of Business, Columbia University, New York.
7. Director, Graduate Division, Northwestern University, Chicago.
8. Director, Conference on Executive Policy and Coordination, Wharton School of Finance and Commerce, University of Pennsylvania, Philadelphia.
9. Coordinator, Management Problems for Executives, The University of Pittsburgh, School of Business Administration, Pittsburgh.
10. Industrial Management Institute, University of Wisconsin, Madison.
11. Director, Executive Development Program, University of Georgia, Athens, Georgia.
12. Director, the Houston Executive Development Program, University of Houston, Houston, Texas.

Courses given by university and professional management groups provide some measure of substitute where plant executive development programs do not exist, and offer a very fine supplement to them even where they are at their best. More and more business executives are asking what formal schooling is available to provide executive development for them. The list above attempts to answer this question.

In general, the list has been confined to recognized schools and colleges, including primarily those programs that are truly of an executive nature, that endeavor to develop broad administrative techniques or points of view rather than specialized occupational skills. There are abundant facilities to teach men accounting, sales, engineering, etc. But facilities to train top leaders in coordination, logical processes of thinking, and in human, social, political, and industrial values and vision are scarce. Only such programs have been listed.

Another factor in determining our selection has been the length of the program. Long courses or degree-conferring programs, however excellent they may be, have been omitted in favor of short programs, evening courses, or conferences which the busy executive may be able to fit into his all-too-vigorous schedule.

263 **What Would You Think of a Training Program for Top Management in a Smaller Manufacturing Firm Which Covers the Principles of Scientific Management?**

Such a training program would be good, especially if a discussion of propositions regarding the scientific management of men were included. The generalizations about work relations, below, illustrate what is meant by scientific principles in the leadership of men.[2]

1. Work is a group activity.
2. The social world of the adult is primarily patterned about work activity.
3. The need for recognition, security, and sense of belonging is more important in determining workers' morale and productivity than the physical conditions under which they work.
4. A complaint is not necessarily an objective recital of facts; it is commonly a symptom manifesting disturbance of an individual's status position.
5. The worker is a person whose attitudes and effectiveness are conditioned by social demands from both outside and inside the work plant.
6. Informal groups within the work plant exercise strong social control over the work habits and attitudes of the individual worker.
7. The change from an established to an adaptive society tends continually to disrupt the social organization of a work plant and of industry generally.
8. Group collaboration does not occur by accident; it must be planned for and developed. If group collaboration is achieved, the work relations within a work plant may reach a cohesion which resists the disrupting effects of adaptive society.

264 **How Can We Teach Top Management to Assign Authority and Responsibility?**

In staff meetings or face-to-face conferences, discuss the principle of exceptions and the role of the executive. Circulate books, readings, and literature which point out that the executive confines his actions to the unusual, the novel and the difficult—that the bigger a man is, the more he is willing to and the more he must delegate to his subordinates. Show the difference between the

[2] D. C. Miller and W. H Form, *Industrial Sociology* (New York: Harper & Row, 1951), p. 72.

production worker who does things himself, the supervisor who gets others to do them, and the executive who decides what is to be done and supervises those who get things done.

Sometimes a formal approach to the study of organization is helpful. A few training meetings on the principles of organization usually lead into the creation of organizational handbooks with charts and clear definitions of duties and responsibilities. Good jobs of this kind have been done recently by SKF and Koppers Coke.

Devoting a session or two in the training program to delegation of authority and responsibility would be helpful. In their staff meetings, some executives regularly review the duties and responsibilities of all in the department. Industrial and commercial jobs are usually in a dynamic state of change. New duties are constantly added and old ones subtracted until a particular job sometimes grows out of all proportion. Annual reviews help keep this growth under control and help keep superiors aware of job loads and work responsibilities. The subject of delegation is easily worked into such a discussion with helpful results.

It helps to have policies clearly stated in writing. Decisions become more automatic, and timid superiors will trust subordinates with responsibility for making more of them where policies have been established in advance. The training man may well inaugurate a program of reviewing written policies, or of writing them if none exist.

Another approach is to find out why the executive is reluctant to release authority and responsibility. It may well be that his subordinates are not competent, have failed and embarrassed him when he did give them freedom. If so, here is a need for training these men to better handle the responsibilities that have been given them.

265   What Can Be Done by the Training Director to Train the General Manager?

Although classroom training, rotation, university programs, and other formal devices are of great help, much can be done individually. In some cases the training director is so close to the president that he can suggest special assignments to strengthen the general manager. Where he is not close enough to volunteer suggestions, the president sometimes asks the training director what special development or coaching would be most useful for his subordinates. In two cases known to the authors, a president and a board chairman sit down with the training director about twice a year and ask, "How am I doing?" In such a case the training man is at liberty to suggest development activities for the president's immediate staff. He may work at the problem in three ways:

1. From above, by getting the president interested and skilled in auditing and in developing his subordinates, one of whom will be the general manager.
2. On the general manager's level. Here the training man offers formal programs and individual coaching and counseling to the general manager and all others at his level.
3. From below. Here the training man tries to improve the general manager's subordinates because some of this new skill flows upward and because, as the subordinates take more and more responsibility, the general manager has more time for self-improvement.

266   We Have a Major Executive Who Has No Interest or Skill in Developing His Subordinates. What Can We Do with Him?

First, try to get him to see and accept development as his responsibility. His superior's counseling with him on this should help. His job description should be reviewed and the responsibility for developing subordinates should be played up. He might be sent to attend one of the seminars of the American Management Association on the job of the chief executive. Such seminars usually make the responsibility for developing leaders one of the chief responsibilities of the executive. When the man understands and accepts his responsibility he should be helped to see how the actual developmental work is done. For this, he might be asked to attend one of the many good seminars on executive development. These usually last from four to twenty hours, are offered by the various management societies and universities, and provide good motivation and some knowledge of technique. Such conference programs can be had by writing to the following:

1. American Society of Training Directors, Eli Lilly and Company, Indianapolis.
2. Society for Advancement of Management, New York.
3. American Management Association, New York.
4. National Industrial Conference Board, New York.
5. Industrial Relations Research Association, University of Wisconsin, Madison.

6. School of Industrial and Labor Relations, Cornell University, Ithaca, N. Y.
7. Department of Industrial Engineering, Columbia University, New York.

Certainly a few basic publications should be made available to him. See, also, the bibliography for a listing of pertinent material.

267   How Should Men Who Have Failed Be Handled to Get the Most Development from the Experience?

Failure is caused by many things, and the specific cure for each case is different. Failures may be due to inadequate technical knowledge, personality weaknesses, inability to handle a large quantity of work, the boss's method of supervision, or poorly defined responsibilities. However, we can generalize and say that we should:

1. Analyze the situation (job requirements, quality of supervision given the man who has failed, pressure of work, etc.).
2. Determine the cause or causes of failure (inadequate training, personality conflicts, temperament unsuited for the job, poor judgment).
3. Discuss the man's failure with him and get him to realize that he has failed and in what manner.
4. Encourage him to improve where he is weak. Offer your support to assist him to improve.
5. Get him to outline a program of improvement.
6. End constructively. Review his strengths and outline how you plan to use the good qualities which he possesses.

Failure on a single development assignment should not condemn a man irretrievably. Many good men fail now and then. Those who do should, however, have the experience looked into carefully to determine causes, and development thereafter should be planned to overcome whatever specific deficiencies are discovered.

268   What Responsibility Does an Executive Have for Improving Himself?

He has great responsibility, perhaps even full responsibility. However, it is not enough to say this and let it go at that. The problem is to get men to see this responsibility and act upon it.

Executive audits and the counseling which follows aim to kindle the spark, interest, and self-responsibility for improvement. Having thus roused the interest in the man, development activities assist him in satisfying his needs. Before growth takes place from any of these activities, however, the man must wish it. Most executive development activities aim to fortify this desire where it exists and create it where it is absent.

269   What Would You Consider a Rather Full and Complete Executive Development Program?

Perhaps the experience of Johnson & Johnson and its affiliated companies can be used in reply. Although it is broad, the executives of Johnson & Johnson do not consider their program complete. It does reflect a belief that executive development is a continuous process which is accomplished most fully through each executive's day-to-day work with his subordinates, supplemented by other developmental activities. Among the latter are:

Review of Economic Conditions. This is a bi-monthly review of economic conditions, provided by the Econometrics Institute. One of their executives reviews business conditions with emphasis on textiles, rubber, and other areas of primary interest to the company, although he also covers general economic trends. Board members and those who report to them attend these reviews.

Multiple Management. In three of our companies we have an Auxiliary Board somewhat like that of McCormick and Company, Inc. In one company, four members of the present board of directors were promoted to their positions from the Auxiliary Board.

Role Playing. A role playing program has been given for plant superintendents in Johnson & Johnson, for the board of directors of one subsidiary, and for executives of another. We are encouraging further use of this device.

Case Studies. Four series of case studies were offered to major executives. Two sessions were led by professors from Harvard and Northwestern Universities. One affiliated company has offered a similar program to middle management, our training director has started another program in our engineering division, and one group of divisional sales managers has used case studies.

Evening Dinner Meetings. This is an arrangement of regular dinner meetings for board members, directors, vice presidents, and the echelon directly beneath them. We have held five or six dinner meetings each year, for purposes both social and educational.

Specialized Conferences. Each year Johnson & Johnson holds specialized conferences, lasting two or three days, for personnel directors, controllers, material handling specialists, production and sales specialists, and other professional or technical men from subsidiary companies.

Harvard and Columbia Advanced Management Course. We have had thirteen men in eight sessions of these courses; they include five board members and eight others who are works' managers or other major executives. In addition, we have used a similar course at the University of Western Ontario and at Northwestern University.

Wharton School of Finance. We have enrolled thirteen executives, including a president, six vice presidents, and other seasoned executives, in the course in executive management given each summer at the Wharton School of Finance, University of Pennsylvania. Our Vice Chairman of the Board took an active part in establishing this course.

Reading. A seventeen-hour course in improvement of reading has been prepared and offered. It provides group and individual instruction for executives burdened with heavy reading loads. The course, designed to improve speed and comprehension, relies upon the Science Research Associates Reading Accelerator, and the Harvard Reading Films and Teaching Aids. It has almost doubled reading speed with no loss of comprehension.[3]

Conference Leadership. We have a ten-hour course in conference leadership which is considered fundamental for our executives. It has been asked for and given to boards of directors, to office executives, to plant superintendents, and to others.

Public Speaking. Over one hundred executives have taken a sixty-hour course in public speaking. Professors of speech from several metropolitan universities join operating businessmen in teaching it within the company.

In-Plant Conferences. Recently we decided that communications was one of our major problems. We started with the executive committee of the board and came down through the board of the parent company to the boards of all subsidiaries with a series of conferences designed to review and improve communications. In another series of conferences, most of our major executives devoted twenty hours to the study of interviewing techniques. Still another series of conferences has been offered on finance and investment. These dealt with the way money was raised, stock was issued, and profit was made. The series also gave individual financial guidance to executives who might wish to invest in real estate, insurance, stocks, or bonds.

Psychiatric Group Study. A vice president in charge of production asked for a course in human motivation for his superintendents and works managers. A psychiatrist from the Cornell School of Industrial and Labor Relations prepared and conducted the course, in which executives tried to get better understanding of themselves and each other.

Out-of-Town Conferences. One of our executive committee members arranged a four-day conference for merchandising executives of all com-

[3] W. V. Machaver and W. A. Borrie, "A Reading Improvement Program for Industry," *Personnel,* September, 1951.

panies. Held at a mountain hotel, the conference enabled professors from the Wharton School and a vice president from a major distributing firm to lead discussions on operating cost and marketing. At another conference, our presidents met for a day under the guidance of two outside specialists to discuss executive traits and qualifications and how to measure them. Other conferences have been held on sales training, manufacturing problems, insurance, etc.

Short Courses, Seminars, School and College Programs. Some of our personnel directors have attended a six-week summer session in personnel administration at the School of Industrial and Labor Relations at Cornell. We have sent men to the University of Wisconsin's Industrial Management Institute, to the Rensselaer Polytechnic Institute Seminars, and to Princeton Conferences. We have had a Sloan Fellow studying at Massachusetts Institute of Technology, and have used the Executive Round Table at New York University. Several of our Chicago executives are earning advanced degrees in Administration in the University of Chicago's evening program. During the past few years, under a tuition refund plan, there have been 280 course completions at Rutgers University. We actively participate in American Management Association conferences and those of the Industrial Conference Board.

Job Rotation. We are encouraging job rotation where it is feasible. It has been tried in office and production. The moves are made with the idea of broadening and strengthening experience.

Counseling. A great deal of executive development is done through individual counseling on personal problems which leads easily into general development of the individuals involved.

Staff Meetings. Regular staff meetings are encouraged everywhere, and the leaders are trained to handle the weekly or fortnightly meetings so that the greatest training and development result. This may be our most useful single training device.

Johnson & Johnson encourages professional, public, and community service. Its executives serve on local school boards, Borough Councils, United Fund Committees, university teaching staffs and committees, hospital and Chamber of Commerce Boards, committees of professional societies, and a host of other service groups. This we consider a legitimate public service and good community relations. In addition, it is a fine development opportunity for men learn to serve with, or lead, voluntary groups of citizens. Here authority, power, and the prestige of position are of little avail, and men must learn to sell themselves and their ideas on their merits—a lesson not easily taught in the authoritarian hierarchy of most businesses.

Finally, carefully planned executive audits, including a personal developmental program spelled out for each executive, form the base for participation in the developmental activities listed above.

No executive, of course, participates in all these activities. With the assistance of his superior, each man chooses those of most value to him. These activities only supplement the day-to-day contacts, coaching, and guided experience, all of which go on constantly. In line with Johnson & Johnson's practice of decentralization, there is no required company-wide "program." Each subsidiary company is encouraged both to participate in activities established in the parent company or in any of the subsidiaries and to undertake whatever additional development work it chooses.

270   How Much Time Should an Executive Be Expected to Spend in a Training Course?

Some training programs take seasoned executives off the job and even out of the plant where they spend full time for as much as a year. Where the executive handles a full time job and is not sent out of the plant for study, fifty to a hundred hours yearly is a good average in formal training activities. Many conditions determine how much time will be given to development:

1. How demanding is the executive's job? How much time can he spare from it?
2. Is he failing and making trouble? Is his need for improvement urgent?
3. Or is the development to improve a few weaknesses on his present job or to get him ready for the next one?
4. Is the learning to be spaced over a period of time or concentrated and accomplished quickly? A vice president who is to become president next year and whose development has not been planned and progressing in orderly fashion for some years will spend more time in training than one who is expected to reach the top ten years hence.
5. What is the best rate for learning what the executive needs? Some learning because of its nature must proceed slowly.
6. What is the age and experience of the executive? Younger and less experienced men might be expected to devote more time to development.
7. How willing is the executive to spend time in training?

After answering these questions, one is in a position to determine how much time an individual should devote to development work.

271   **Isn't It Better to Do Executive Development on an Individual Basis?**

Both individual and group approaches should be used.

Much of the top level development must be individualized (see the chapter on Guided Experience) but surely not all of it. Executives brought together in groups for case studies or conference discussions learn things from one another that cannot be learned so well in other ways. Just being part of a group that is meeting for the purpose of learning provides a kind of stimulation and a satisfaction lacking in individual work with executives. The need for an audience also requires some courses like communications, public speaking, and conference leadership to be taught in groups.

272   **Is It Best to Build an Executive from Within an Organization or Acquire Him from Outside?**

It is best to build from within. In so doing, you are likely to have a man ready when you need him. He will be trained to meet your own needs and will understand your philosophy of management, your technical problems, your personnel, and your product. He will have proved himself in your own climate and the risk of failure will be less. If you build your own executives and reward them with advancement, you encourage all levels of management to do better in the hope of obtaining similar rewards.

Sometimes, in order to challenge present executives, to raise standards of performance, to bring in new ideas, or to obtain special skills that are not easily developed inside, it is necessary to bring in a few men from the outside.

Chapter 14

SUPERVISORY DEVELOPMENT

273   Who Should Receive Supervisory Development?

Supervisory development should not be limited to a selected few. In-plant training, rotation, school and university courses, and all forms of development should be available to all who are eligible. When all supervisors enjoy equal opportunities for growth and improvement, a few will emerge whose ability and ambition will be recognized as superior by their fellow-employees. These superior persons deserve promotion and advanced opportunities for learning.

274   How Do You Avoid Making Supervisors Feel That They Are Going to School When They Attend Supervisor Training Classes?

Most training directors believe that training is a valuable service and deserves no apology or camouflage. Instead of spending time in an all-too-obvious attempt to disguise what they are about, they face the reality that most adults in industry do not like the experiences they have had with schools and with "school learning." Training directors, therefore, work with energy and insight to develop teaching methods (nondirective conference, role playing, group dynamics, case study, syndicate system, etc.), appropriate to the maturity level and judgment of adults. Supervisors show little resistance to learning when teaching is planned professionally for adults. The instructor who does this soon creates a sense of pride in his trainees because they are taking advanced courses and are preparing themselves for better things. This method removes or decreases the insecurity, fear, and resistance to growth and change.

The other approach—that of beguiling the trainee into believing that he is solving problems or reviewing a training program for his subordinates—rarely results in the trainee's recognition of his own need for development. In fact, casting reflection, even indirectly, upon the value of schools for successful adults merely strengthens the learner's resistance. More and more, men who are engaged in training recognize their responsibility to create respect for and acceptance of the development of adults in industry. These men lead supervisors to take pride in their wholesome willingness to learn new things—to "go back to school."

275　　**Recognizing That the Specific Objectives of Any Supervisory Training Program Vary in Individual Organizations, What Are Some of the Basic Goals Which You Believe Such a Program Should Strive to Attain?**

Goals depend upon the needs of company and of individuals. What one shop or office needs may be unnecessary in others, or may even conflict with their practices and policies. However, generally accepted objectives of supervisory training are, first, develop supervisors who can carry out the functions assigned to them with maximum satisfaction to management, to their subordinates, and to themselves. Second, insure the vitality and continuity of the organization by assisting each supervisor in the discovery and utilization of his potential abilities.

276　　**What Kind of Formal Training (General Rather Than Specific) Is Desirable for All Supervisors?**

This is a good question because it indicates that there are training needs common to all leaders of men and women at work. In this country we probably place too much emphasis on programs developed locally to fit specific needs, and too little on skills, understanding, and attitudes that are necessary for all supervisors. An unusual training program to meet these general needs has been worked out by Wittenberg College and the industries of Springfield, Ohio, through their Chamber of Commerce. All believe that, "To be successful the supervisor must have a solid foundation in five basic areas of knowledge: Personal Development, Human Relations, Economics, Company Operations, and Technical Operations." Their program takes supervisors from their jobs for one week and registers them at Wittenberg College in specially arranged courses designed to help the supervisor gain this foundation in the first four areas. The five basic areas are outlined[1] as follows:

[1] Curriculum Outline of Management Development Program, Dr. Gerald Saddlemire, Wittenberg College, Springfield, Ohio.

Personal Development. The supervisor must first look at himself—a management man—and recognize his position as a leader. He must work constantly toward self-development—in his thinking, in his ability to convey ideas to others, and in the way he plans and organizes the work in his department.

Human Relations. The supervisor is constantly in contact with other people; the employees who work under him, representatives of the union, his superiors and other members of the community. He must, therefore, have an understanding of human relationships—recognize individual differences, know how people learn, and have the ability to maintain good morale.

Economics. The supervisor should be aware of the relationship between his job and conditions in the community and the nation as a whole. This implies an understanding of the American competitive system and the economic truths that lie behind the operation of a business under that system.

Company Operations. Sound supervision also implies a knowledge of company structure: how it is organized, how it distributes products, and how policy is developed and carried out. Since class members will represent many different companies in Springfield, this area of knowledge will be considered in general terms.

Technical Operations. Finally, there is the supervisor's technical knowhow—his knowledge of machine tools, materials and the routine procedures affecting the operation of his department. These subjects should be presented at the works level where specific, local application is possible. . . .

This is a remarkably good statement of the general needs of supervisors, and training men might well establish similar programs cooperatively with other industries and local educational institutions. If this procedure is not feasible there are suggestions in the Wittenberg outline for the development of a good program within one's own industry.

277   What Specific Subjects Do You Include in a Course in Basic Supervisor Training for New Supervisors?

The following program shows the subjects, frequency, length, and instructor for each meeting of a basic supervisor training course for newly appointed production supervisors in the Johnson & Johnson organization.

JOHNSON & JOHNSON

BASIC SUPERVISOR TRAINING PROGRAM

DATE	SUBJECT	TIME	LEADER
Feb. 22	Introductory Session	11:00–12:00	Vice President—Manufacturing
Feb. 27	Duties and Responsibilities of Supervisors	9:00–11:00	Executive Counselor

Feb. 28	Morale and Motivation	1:00– 3:00	Training Director
Mar. 5	1. Principles of Organization	9:00–11:00	Assistant Training Director
	2. Functions of Staff Departments	11:00–12:00	Assistant to Vice President—Manufacturing
Mar. 6	1. Communications	1:00– 3:00	Assistant Training Director
	2. Research Activities	3:00– 4:00	Director of Research
Mar. 12	Quality Control	9:00–11:00	Assistant Director Quality Control
Mar. 13	1. Inducting the New Employee	1:00– 2:30	Training Director
	2. A Case Illustration	2:30– 3:00	Production Superintendent
	3. Orientation	3:00– 4:00	Training Instructor
Mar. 19	Laws of Learning and Training Responsibilities of Supervisors	9:00–11:00	Assistant Training Director
Mar. 20	1. Production Control	1:00– 3:00	Plant Manager
	2. Market Research	3:00– 4:00	Market Research Director
Mar. 26	1. Analyzing and Controlling Costs	9:00–11:00	Plant Manager
Mar. 27	1. Giving Orders and Directions	1:00– 3:00	Assistant Training Director
	2. Daily Personnel Problems	3:00– 4:00	General Foreman
Apr. 2	Correcting and Improving Employees and Supervising the Woman Worker	9:00–11:00	Assistant Training Director
Apr. 3	1. Handling Employee Problems	1:00– 3:00	Assistant Training Director
	2. New Developments in Handling Materials	3:00– 4:00	Superintendent
Apr. 9	Waste Control	9:00–11:00	Plant Manager
Apr. 10	1. Labor Legislation and Union Contract	1:00– 3:00	Assistant Personnel Director
	2. Personnel Practices	3:00– 4:00	Assistant Training Director
Apr. 16	Selection and Placement	9:00–11:00	Director of Placement
Apr. 17	1. Personnel Evaluation	1:00– 3:00	Assistant Training Director
	2. Plant Administration	3:00– 4:00	General Manager—Manufacturing
Apr. 24	1. Work Simplification	1:00– 3:00	Industrial Engineer
	2. Time Study	3:00– 4:00	Industrial Engineer
Apr. 30	1. Safety	9:00–10:00	Safety Director
	2. Housekeeping	10:00–12:00	Superintendent
May 1	Self-Improvement	1:00– 3:00	Assistant Training Director
May 7	Plant Tours	9:00–12:00	Training Instructor

278   What Particular Cautions Must Be Observed in Training Supervisors?

1. Supervisors are experienced men. They feel they know their job and their training needs. Allow them to participate in planning their training programs.

2. Supervisor training classes that allow for group discussion seem to be most acceptable and productive. Limit the amount of lecturing.

3. Supervisors respond best to training that appears practical and not academic. Use illustrations and examples to teach concepts or practices of supervision drawn from their world of work. Avoid the theoretical and academic approach.

4. Supervisors have job responsibilities which they carry with them into training classes. It is with reluctance that they spend two, three or four hours in training classes away from their job. Keep training periods relatively short—60 to 90 minutes at the maximum.

5. Supervisors prefer to plan ahead for training classes. Establish a schedule at the beginning of the course. Give them a copy of it. Don't deviate from the schedule. Avoid haphazard planning of training meetings.

6. Supervisors don't like a schoolroom atmosphere so develop an informal atmosphere in the class. Treat them as adults. Avoid the traditional teacher-pupil role of strict discipline, formality, home work, rote learning and tests.

7. Supervisors like to feel that the instructor knows and understands their problems. Visit them on the job. Show an interest in their work.

279   What Skills, Attitudes, and Understandings Are Essential When New Supervisors Are Responsible for Employees with High Seniority?

These new supervisors need all the general techniques necessary for any supervisor. In addition, they need to know how older, experienced workers react to newcomers; how any combination of men or women, constituted as a group, reacts when new leaders are imposed upon them; what strengths and assets the experienced employees have and how to capitalize upon them; what their weaknesses are, how great a handicap they represent, and what can be done about them; how rapidly old timers can be expected to change; the best method for accomplishing a change, and how to determine when changes are being made too fast; what training or other activities will facilitate integration of the old and new workers.

280 Should Top Management Review and Adopt Training Programs Which Are to Be Presented to Supervisors?

It is not necessary for top management to review and adopt all supervisor training programs. Top management should determine the fundamental attitudes, skills, and philosophies of management to be taught to their supervisors. After these are agreed upon, the training director develops programs to meet the needs of supervisors within this general framework. The training director works with the superiors of the men who will receive the training in the development and execution of the program. Periodic review by top management of supervisor training programs is valuable. It serves as a check on whether the programs are meeting the needs of management and also reiterates the interest and support of top management in supervisor training.

281 How Can the Foreman Be Helped on the Job to Solve His Own Current Problems? In Other Words, What Organizational and Communication Facilities Can Help Him Learn Through His Own Experiences?

Careful counseling by his superior, particularly if he has a highly successful one, is of greatest help. The plant superintendent who helps his foremen solve their own problems is actually engaged in training. A good executive counsels regularly with his men about their strengths and weaknesses, their successes and failures. He does this in such a manner as to encourage growth and improvement.

Foremen get a great deal of help in solving their problems by sitting in on weekly staff meetings where they hear other supervisors report and help solve group problems. An open flow of communication, both up and down, provides the foreman with the information he needs to recognize his problems and to assist him in their solution. Formal training classes and circulation of pertinent reading matter are also helpful.

282   Can Supervisors Who Belong to Union Organizations Work Effectively on Behalf of Management?

The first line supervisor is always in a difficult position. He must be loyal to his superiors and his company. He also feels responsibility to other supervisors at his own level and on many occasions must favor his subordinates. In some situations, usually untenable, supervisors are expected to exhibit such a degree of loyalty to their management that they always support and defend management's position, even to the extent of refraining from constructive criticism in management meetings where unworkable policy is being determined. Common as it is, this extreme and blind loyalty is fruitless. It sometimes happens that supervisors, faced by the dilemma of divided loyalty, claim to represent and defend their subordinates when they are in management councils, and represent management when in the presence of subordinates.

Some supervisors are "oriented upward"—that is, they are much more conscious of, and seek more ardently, the respect, recognition and approval of their superiors than of their subordinates. Others are "oriented downward" and consistently seek to be a part of the groups they lead. Overbalance in either direction is undesirable. When a supervisor is a member of a union and must maintain loyalty to it, as well as to his subordinates as individuals and to his superiors, his problem is complex indeed. The best solution provides that management train supervisors in loyalty to the business—a sane, open-minded loyalty coupled with encouragement to speak out concerning abuses, inconsistencies, and failures in respect to their needs and wishes.

283   How Are In-Plant Foremen or Supervisory Clubs Useful in Developing Supervisors?

The officers and program committees of these clubs are usually drawn from the ranks of supervision. These men get experience in organizing and planning programs to meet the needs of their co-workers. Likewise, the programs usually meet specific needs of supervisors. The most urgent problems of industry are problems in human engineering. It is important for supervisors to know each other on a personal basis. Supervisory clubs offer them opportunities to know each other socially and to encourage friendly relationships.

Supervisory clubs serve as a medium for exchange of ideas and philosophies among all supervisors. Many programs planned in the

supervisory clubs require presentations by members. These presentations encourage supervisors to improve and continually raise
their standards of performance.

284   What Kind of In-Plant Program Do Supervisors' Clubs Offer?

The following schedule illustrates the program offered by a
supervisors' club in the Johnson & Johnson organization during a
recent year. This club meets bi-weekly for one and a half hours
after working hours. The programs are planned by a program committee of club members, who serve for one year.

DATE	SUBJECT	LEADER
Sept. 4	A Fair and Just Taxation	Vice President—Manufacturing
Sept. 18	A Sound Dollar	Tax Consultant
Oct. 4	Integrity in Government	Sound Government Committee Chairman
Oct. 16	A Vigorous Two-Party System	Sound Government Committee Representative
Nov. 6	A Resourceful and Respectful Foreign Policy	Assistant to President
Nov. 20	Ancient and Modern Taxation	University Professor
Dec. 4	Case Study (Government)	Director of Manufacturing
Jan. 8	Ideas for Straight Thinking Reducing Straight Thinking to Four Simple Principles	Division Leader, Member of the Club
Jan. 27	Ideas for Straight Thinking Making Precise Observations Defining Real Problem and Consider-ing Possible Solution	Division Leader, Member of the Club
Feb. 5	Ideas for Straight Thinking Securing Evidence on Possible Solution Drawing Conclusions	Division Leader, Member of the Club
Feb. 19	Aspects of Surgery	Director of Clinical Research, Johnson & Johnson
Feb. 26	Case Study (Orienting a New Employee)	Training Director
Mar. 5	Case Study (Problems of Expansion)	Training Director
Mar. 18	Case Study (Counseling)	Training Director
Apr. 2	Aspects of Surgery	Director of Research
Apr. 22	Aspects of Surgery	Director of Industrial Medicine
May 6	Case Study (Selecting a Man for Promotion)	Training Director
May 26	Case Study (Managing One's Superior)	Training Director
June 3	Review of Meetings Introduction of New Program	Chairman of Training Committee

285   What Are the Major Problems Met by In-Plant Supervisors' Clubs?

Supervisors' clubs may become informal pressure groups. When not properly guided or directed, the group may want to resolve company problems and issues that are more rightly handled in on-the-job conferences with their superiors. Some participants attempt to interest these organizations in solving their own personal problems. An approach of this kind can only lead to increased friction, dissatisfaction, and departmental conflicts.

Another major problem is to maintain a continuing interest in the club. There must be a nucleus of supervisors who spark the club, develop sound, interesting programs, and keep all members participating actively. Conscientious program planning and opportunity for member participation help to maintain interest.

Through active participation in the club, the training director can do much to forestall and overcome such problems.

286   Where Can One Obtain Short Cases That Can Be Used to Teach Good Supervisory Practices?

Short cases, usually no more than a paragraph or two in length, are effective teaching devices. They describe an occurrence in sufficient detail to illustrate a supervisory practice or principle. They are used primarily to stimulate discussion. There are three main sources of such cases:

1. Prepare them yourself. They are not difficult to write and may be drawn from actual experiences in the company. Supervisors can relate any number of incidents which may serve as case material. Not long ago, the authors prepared a number of short cases for use in a supervisor training class for department heads in a hospital. The following is a sample case:

> A new supervisor of nurses is hired, the third in four years. She is an excellent woman, strong in all areas. She sees weaknesses in previous systems and previous supervision of the department. She institutes revised systems and improved supervision. But her subordinates resist her, block her reforms, dislike her and her program.
>
>   a. What may be some reasons for this?
>   b. What should she and her subordinates do about this condition?

2. Write or visit the training departments of large companies. Most of them use written problems for discussion purposes in su-

pervisor training and usually are willing to share their materials. Universities that offer management training programs commonly develop "case books" which can be purchased or borrowed.

3. Purchase books, periodicals, or films that contain case materials. Examples of these are:

a. The film strip, "Human Relations in Supervison," produced by Armstrong Cork Company and distributed through the Text-film Department of the McGraw-Hill Book Company, Inc., New York.

b. George R. Terry, "Case Problems in Business and Industrial Management," Wm. C. Brown Company, Dubuque, Iowa, 1949.

c. *Supervision*, Supervision Publishing Co., Inc., New York.

287　What Methods, Other Than Formal Classes, Have Been Effective in Supervisor Training?

In addition to formal in-company classes, the following training methods may be utilized:

Guided Experience
Correspondence courses
Technical and management conferences sponsored by reputable
　organizations outside the company
Evening courses conducted by nearby schools and universities
Plant visits for observation and discussion with other supervisors
Periodicals that relate to supervisors' jobs
Membership in professional societies
Outside psychological consultants who counsel supervisors
Staff meetings led by one's superior
Specific work assignments under the direction of one's own su-
　perior or other experienced executives
Job rotation
Acting as substitute for the boss when he is over-busy or absent
Going "upstairs" *with* one's superior
Committee assignments
Membership in the company supervisors' club
Individual counseling and coaching by superior or others in the
　organization
Merit rating and the performance review that follows it
Service on boards and committees of governmental, school, and
　civic bodies

288   Are Correspondence Courses Recommended?

Yes, when there are not enough candidates to merit establishing a course within the plant or local schools. The advantage of the correspondence method is that it can provide training for almost any need, thus relieving the training director from setting up training for one or two individuals only. The weakness of such courses is the lack of personal contacts and stimulation by the teacher and other trainees. Lacking this incentive, many registrants lose interest and fail to complete their courses, through no fault of the schools. Training directors who use correspondence courses should counsel with their men frequently and provide the interest and attention that will stimulate the learner to finish his course. Some correspondence courses now provide monthly meetings of trainees under trained instructors. In these sessions course problems are invited and discussed.

289   Where Can I Obtain Information About Correspondence Courses for Supervisors?

There are two national associations which publish literature describing accredited courses for home study.

1. The National University Extension Association publishes a "Guide to Correspondence Study," which lists all colleges offering correspondence courses and the courses offered. The guide may be obtained by writing to the National University Extension Association, Bloomington, Indiana.
2. The National Home Study Council, Washington, D. C., publishes a directory of accredited private home study schools and courses.

290   What Media or Medium Prove Most Effective in Leadership Training When the Trainees Are at Diverse Corners of the Country and Cannot Be Brought Together in Worth-While Groups for Longer Periods Than a Day or Two a Year?

1. A lending library. To promote its use the training director should get out a monthly flyer describing one or two new books each month. Personal letters recommending planned reading programs will create interest and stimulate use of the library.

2. Subscriptions to *Factory Management and Maintenance, Fortune, Modern Management, Supervision,* or to sales, personnel, or other specialized publications also stimulate reading.

3. Use supervisory information services such as those offered by the Research Institute of America and the National Foremen's Institute.

4. Use correspondence courses. See Question 288.

5. Make effective use of the day or two when the men are together to stimulate their will to learn. During the few days available yearly for training, conferences on the following should be held:

a. Self-evaluation. What am I like? What can I do to improve?
b. Self-help through reading. What is available to me? How can I make use of it?
c. Self-help through courses at local schools and colleges.
d. Self-help through communication with the home office.
e. Self-help through professional, civic, political, or other community service or memberships.
f. Help through my supervisor. What help can I expect from him? How can I make better use of his service?

291   Is It Advisable to Repeat or Review Supervisory Training Programs for Groups That Have Completed Them?

Yes, because everyone forgets. Even those skills in which we are proficient deteriorate unless checked upon and strengthened by guided practice. It is estimated, for example, that reading speed may decline as much as 40 per cent over a period of years and that refresher training usually restores it to its original point or even improves it.

Mere repetition of what has been taught should be avoided. When supervisors have had introductory conferences or lectures, a change in method to role playing or case studies may cover the same subject matter without the appearance of repetition.

Training should take place continuously, both because of forgetting and because of the vast variety of knowledge, attitudes, and skills now necessary for supervisors. It takes years to cover what a supervisor needs to know concerning methods, economics, machine operation and maintenance, human relations, labor relations, incentives, costs, and the social order. In fact, training is a continuous process—for life.

292   How Much Does a Man Learn from the Example of His Superior?

Since man is a natural mimic and since those in authority have an aura of right and acceptance surrounding them, a person does learn from the example of his superior. The amount, however, cannot be measured. However, we know that most effective learning involves more than observation; it requires participation, experience, and understanding. Therefore, while the value of example should be recognized, it should not be relied upon as the sole method or even as the principal method for developing subordinates.

293   Do Some Companies Make Long-Range Training Plans for Their Supervisors? Can You Describe Such a Plan?

It seems logical that companies should formulate long-range objectives for supervisor training and then carry out plans that will meet them. Actually, few companies do this. Most of them appear to work from yearly plans governed more by immediate needs than by long-range requirements and goals. Some companies, however, assign the responsibility for developing long-range plans for supervisor training to the training director or to a training committee.

The following plan for training supervisors in the fundamentals of supervision is designed to meet both immediate and long-range needs. It was developed by a committee of line men, with the assistance of the training director of a textile company which has a number of separate operating units in different locations.

I. HUMAN LEADERSHIP

Leader: This course will be conducted by the Training Director or the Industrial Relations Manager of each individual plant.

Content: It will consist of basic human engineering principles. Such subjects as human drives, security, recognition, belonging, giving orders, relationship between supervision and employees, handling grievances, etc., will be covered in this course.

Number of Meetings: Five to ten conference meetings will be required, depending on the progress of the group. The course should be handled by the informal conference method and must be followed up by constant exposure of supervision to staff meetings, personal conferences, and all other reasonable means of interpreting and applying the principles set forth.

Refresher: At least once a year.

II. Job Relations Training

Leader: Industrial Relations Manager, Superintendent, or Plant Manager.

Content: This course covers various elements needed to help supervisors in the development of skills and getting results through the people they supervise, not only as individuals, but as a team. This course is desirable and should be included, but should be used only to the extent that it covers subjects other than those in the Human Leadership conference sessions.

Number of Meetings: Ten meetings, one hour each.

Review: Every two years.

III. Job Instructor Training

Leader: Industrial Engineer, Industrial Relations Manager, or Training Director.

Content: This course has as its objective how to get an employee to do a job correctly, quickly and conscientiously. It will use the content contained in the JIT course of the Training Within Industry program.

Number of Meetings: Ten one-hour meetings as a minimum, twenty as a maximum.

Review: Every two years.

IV. Job Methods Training

Leader: Industrial Engineer or Methods Engineer.

Content: This course is intended to develop skills in the improvement of methods of doing various jobs. It will use the content contained in the JMT course of the TWI program.

Number of Meetings: Ten to twenty meetings of one hour each.

Review: Every two years.

V. Costs

Leader: Plant Manager, Superintendent or Cost Accountant.

Content: Economics of textile industry and our company. Discussion of factors affecting material, labor and overhead costs. Preparation and interpretation of cost reports.

Number of Meetings: Ten to fifteen one-hour meetings.

Review: Regular review of cost developments and reports as well as principles.

VI. State and Federal Labor Laws

Leader: Industrial Relations Manager.

Content: Review of Labor Management Act with some background of old National Labor Relations Act, Fair Labor Standards Act, State minimum wage laws, regulations of Industrial Commission covering working conditions and hours of work.

Number of Meetings: Eight one-hour meetings.

Review: Review yearly and as particular needs require.

The following subjects are also included as a part of this plan and are analyzed in the same manner as the subjects already listed.

ANALYSIS OF TEXTILE DATA
ADVANCED HUMAN RELATIONS
POLICY DEVELOPMENT
BASIC MACHINE DESIGN
PROPERTIES OF COTTON FIBRE AS RELATED TO MANUFACTURING
QUALITY CONTROL
REVIEW OF GENERAL PROBLEMS
SAFETY
LABOR TURNOVER AND ABSENTEEISM
GENERAL EDUCATION

The sixteen courses described above do not constitute the total, all-time educational needs of supervisors in this organization. The courses are, however, the initial, presently important subjects in which they feel instruction is needed. As progress is made with these courses, and as new problems arise in the plant, the need for new and advanced study will no doubt arise. In addition, the committee emphasizes that courses and staff meetings alone do not constitute their only means of supervisor development. Some of their units have already taken advantage of many supplementary devices, such as outside courses at summer schools, encouraging supervisor attendance at special lectures and professional meetings, recommendations of readings to individual supervisors, personal coaching, etc., and these activities will be continued.

In addition to the foregoing plans the textile company described had listed all of its supervisors and indicated which of the seventeen courses each had completed. At a glance management could see where any supervisor stood in relation to completing the full program.

294   What Type of Supervisor Training Should Be Done in the Department Where the Man Works and by His Superior?

The immediate superior of a man is responsible for his development and training. In the development and training of his subordinate, he should utilize the Training Department, when one exists, and all useful outside training programs and activities to their fullest degree. He probably can give most effective training in his own department by:

1. Holding regular staff meetings for his subordinates.
2. Observing his work and counseling him frequently on it, especially during his first few months as a supervisor.

3. Being thoroughly familiar with what is taught in supervisor training classes, and by giving his supervisor specific work assignments which will allow him to practice what he is being taught.

4. Letting the supervisor observe him in the handling of grievances or other personnel problems of a departmental nature.

5. Explaining departmental policies, practices and work methods.

6. Appointing his subordinate now and then to represent him, to take his place in his absence, to "go upstairs" for him.

7. His needs should be analyzed and met, as explained under Guided Experience, Chapter 5.

295   What Do You Do with a Supervisor Who Accepts the Gospel but Does Not Practice It—Who Attends All Meetings, Agrees with Results of Conferences on Human Relations and on Getting Along with People, But After the Meetings Is Still in the Same Old Rut and Follows Practices of Thirty Years Ago?

In formal classes use role playing, case study, or other non-directive approaches in which the trainee is not given ready-made principles and platitudes. In the nondirective methods learning is internalized—it gets into the bone and sinew and becomes a guide to thought and action. Nothing is poured out for the learner to repeat without understanding or full acceptance. Encourage the man's own supervisor to discuss with him the subject matter taught, to set up specific situations so that the trainee may apply what was taught and to coach and counsel him on his performance to help him understand and apply the concepts learned in training.

In this way, a good climate for growth and development is established and the man soon learns that in order to win the approbation of *his* supervisor his actions must conform with accepted concepts of supervisory practice.

296   How Can I Stimulate Our Supervisors—Men with 10 to 15 Years of Service—to Prepare for Their Own Advancement and to Develop Replacements?

Train them. Set up a conference or series of conferences in which this very question is asked. Suggest that the men pool their opinions and make practical suggestions. A discussion in which supervisors are asked to tell how they train understudies will be stimulating and helpful. For those who are not doing any training it is a revelation to find that some are attempting it. If responses threaten to be barren, the training director may invite in a few men who are outstandingly good at developing understudies to salt the discussion. After a good meeting or two on how to train understudies a conference may be devoted to self-development. A brief summary of material covered in such a conference, given as part of the Johnson & Johnson Training Program, follows:

SELF-IMPROVEMENT

Basic Principle: The more an industry practices scientific management, the more a man's success depends upon his own efforts toward self-improvement and the less it depends upon luck, favoritism, and personal friendship. Some things to be done in your own program for self-improvement follow:

1. Analyze yourself. Make a list of what you consider to be your strong and weak points. Ask friends or relatives to help out. Recall the criticism and praise you have received about your limitations and your abilities.

2. Set a vocational goal. Decide what success means to you. Set an immediate objective and one to be reached a few years hence.

3. Strengthen yourself:
   a. Lay out a program to use your strengths; volunteer for assignments which call for their use.
   b. Take improvement courses.
   c. Plan a reading program for *self*-improvement.
   d. Get a variety of experience; seek job rotations, transfers, or promotions to which you believe yourself entitled and for which you are qualified.
   e. After gaining experience, find an area in which you can develop a specialty that will utilize your abilities, bring satisfaction, and still provide challenges.
   f. Know your field and get known in the field. Join professional associations, attend conferences, read journals.
   g. Find a sponsor who is interested in you, seek his help and advice, and follow it.

4. Perform every job just as successfully as your ability allows. Review it after completion to make sure what you have learned.

When men who are not interested in self-improvement are being evaluated and counseled, their superiors should discuss directly and frankly the importance of self-training and the development of understudies. If each supervisor's performance on these two factors is rated and discussed it will help him to realize the importance of keeping himself alert, and of preparing at least one understudy to take his place.

297 Should Supervisor Training Classes Be Held on Company Time?

Most companies recognize their responsibility for the training and development of their management group. As a result, more and more companies are holding training activities on company time. This practice seems to have the following advantages:

1. All men who need the training are able to attend.
2. Participants are encouraged to improve. It is plain that any management which pays men to spend time in class wants and will reward their progress.
3. Training is accepted as an integral part of supervisor's daily responsibilities. It is not something extra that must be done after working hours. It is just as important to the organization as other work activities.

298 Is It Better to Give All Supervisors in One Department Supervisor Training in a Single Group, or to Have Them Participate with Supervisors from Other Departments?

If the purpose of training is to teach men to understand and handle problems that are peculiar to one department, then it is best to include only the supervisors from that department in a given class or program. If the objectives of supervisor training are broader than this, however, and include teaching of general principles of administration, participants will profit when men from various departments come together in one group. Some values of this latter method are:

1. Supervisors learn that their problems are not limited to individual departments.
2. Men are exposed to various points of view and opinions.
3. Participants develop friendship with and understanding of supervisors in other departments. Both become valuable in their daily operations when they need to get cooperation, information, or assistance from other departments.
4. Such training classes focus attention on company objectives. Thus they afford a counterbalance to departmental loyalty, which can be detrimental when it is carried too far.

299   **Some Supervisory Groups Meet Monthly on Company Time to Discuss Current Topics of Interest to Management. What Are the Values of Such Meetings?**

The supervisors of the Ortho Pharmaceutical Corporation at Raritan, New Jersey, where such monthly meetings are held, have listed the values as follows:

1. Meetings encourage thinking about problems broader than those of the immediate job.
2. Participants gain broader perspective and knowledge, dig deeper into the meaning of supervisory responsibility, and come to a realization of what a "good" supervisory job is.
3. Discussions develop a recognition of the value of teamwork— that all are working toward the same goal.
4. Conferees gain more respect for opinions and decisions of men in other fields.
5. Supervisors are able to compare their ways of handling problems with associates.
6. Individuals learn that group consideration of problems often leads to better decisions than those reached by men thinking alone.
7. Meetings give top management a chance to present its problems and ideas, as well as to discuss changes in plans or policies. Through discussion, supervisors obtain a better understanding and knowledge of their company and become identified with the business.
8. Supervisors discover that other supervisors have problems like their own, which may be reduced or solved by group discussion.
9. The discussions clarify policies and this results in greater uniformity of application.
10. Individual supervisors find out when and how they are deviating from company practice. Grievances are brought into the open where they can be discussed constructively by the group.
11. Supervisors become acquainted, both socially and as men of varying capabilities who must—and can—work together.
12. Discussions help individuals to present their ideas clearly and coherently, and give the men practice in talking before a group.

300   **What Is the Best Method for Training Supervisors?**

There is no one best method. Undoubtedly the daily on-the-job training given to a supervisor by his superior is the most practical, fruitful and acceptable. However, on-the-job training is limited by the ability of a superior to teach subordinates adequately, the superior's knowledge of sound supervisory practices, and the available time that can be devoted to the training of his men.

Assigned readings, training classes, committee assignments, observations of other supervisors, staff meetings, and plant visits and tours also add to the growth and development of supervisors. Analyze the training needs of your supervisors and utilize the methods that will meet these needs most effectively.

301   How Do You Determine What Training to Give Supervisors?

Training needs of supervisors may be determined by a variety of means. Not all of these must be used in any one situation, but all give insight into training needs.

1. Ask top management.
2. Hold personal interviews with supervisors.
3. Use the results of merit ratings, made by the superiors of the supervisors to be trained.
4. Organize training committees to study the needs of supervisors. These committees should be composed of members who will receive the training, as well as representatives from top management and the training department.
5. Observe supervisors while they are carrying on their supervisory jobs. This observation should be made both by the man's immediate superior and by training or personnel specialists.
6. Study personnel reports and records, such as minutes of grievance meeting, labor turnover, absenteeism, safety records, etc.
7. Study cost reports, on-the-job training results, maintenance records, labor turnover and similar technical reports.
8. Consult with individuals in staff departments who have work relationships with the supervisors for whom you are planning a training program.

These will furnish a general indication of the training needs of supervisors, but they will not tell the full story. It is important to analyze the findings of each of the foregoing devices in order to determine the causes of the conditions which it reveals. These causes will indicate the specific training needed by the supervisors.

302   When Does Supervisory Development Begin?

There are two possibilities. When a new supervisor is hired or when an employee is promoted to his first job in supervision, he usually receives orientation from the training or personnel department, from his superior, or from both. This is the beginning of the plan for the man's development as a supervisor. From this point he receives on-the-job coaching and guidance from his superior, attends formal supervisor training classes, and engages in other planned training and development activities. Some organizations, however, believe that development should begin before promotion. They establish pre-supervisory training programs to prepare the prospective supervisor for his responsibilities. In this system supervisory development begins before the man is required to put his abilities to practical use, and before he can establish habits or procedure that will require correction.

303   When Do You Suggest That Training Be Started for a New Production Supervisor?

It is wise to train the prospective supervisor before he assumes supervisory responsibility. To do so gives him courage and confidence when he needs them most. Pre-supervisory training also enables the man to get help before he makes errors which would be costly to the company and would linger in the memory of both subordinates and superiors. Besides, men have more time for training before they take over their supervisory responsibilities than they have afterward; they are also much more open-minded and eager to learn. Finally, pre-supervisory training usually eases the transition from worker to supervisor.

304   Should All Employees in a Department or Organization Be Selected on the Assumption That They May Become Supervisors?

No. Such a procedure would be impractical and inefficient. However, a number of positions serve as appropriate training spots for prospective supervisors. It is important that these positions be filled by employees who have qualities that will enable them to grow into management positions.

305   What Methods Can Be Used to Select Supervisors from Within the Organization?

Selection should result from the assembly and study of all available information regarding the candidate. This information may include:

1. Results of a patterned interview or a regular interview with an experienced interviewer not otherwise involved in the selection.
2. Careful study of the candidate's work history in the company, including interviews with supervisors and others with whom he has served in a staff relationship.
3. Review of previous evaluation or merit ratings that may be on file, training class or school results, etc.
4. Results of psychological tests.

When assembled these data may be submitted to a committee of three: the supervisor under whom the candidate will work, a representative of the personnel department, and a representative of management in whose selective powers both the others have confidence. This committee studies both the findings and the candidate. If they are satisfied and wish to proceed, the candidate should make the final decision regarding promotion.

306   In the Selection of a New First-Line Supervisor, Should Past Productive Performance Be a Determining Factor?

Past productive performance may reveal energy, drive, and the will to work. It may also reveal technical know-how and motor skill. These are useful qualities in a supervisor, but they represent only part of the over-all requirements for the job. The supervisor himself does not do the work; he gets others to do it. This means that he must combine ability to do the work with ability to lead people—and in that, command of job routine may not be very important. Sometimes, in fact, men who have too much job or technical skill make poor supervisors or executives. They rely too heavily on their technical ability and do not develop the broader skills of understanding, cooperation, teamwork, and motivation. Such men are constantly drawn back by their technical knowledge to the operations and routines of the process. They neither comprehend fully nor assume their responsibilities to plan, coordinate and control a wide variety of operations. They are frequently "detailists" and therefore lack a broad, long-range point of view.

307   When Supervisors Fail, Is the Primary Cause Poor Selection or Poor Training After Selection?

Who can say? Failures may be due to poor selection, poor training, or to poor working environment. Obviously, not all persons are leaders. Careful selection will help to choose those whose native abilities, previous education, and experience make them most likely to succeed. Training can improve natural ability and the skills that have already been learned at school and at work. It cannot *create* natural ability. As for environment, a good man, well prepared, may fail if the mechanics, resources, and personalities involved in a new job are hostile to success. Such factors are almost certainly at fault if a series of well-selected, well-prepared men fail in a given job. In such a case, development is indicated—development of those men responsible for the climate of indifference or hostility toward the growth and improvement of men.

308 How Do You Handle the So-Called Unpromotables After Having Selected and Promoted the Persons Most Likely to Succeed as Supervisors?

Keep on training them to improve their performance on the jobs they hold. Stress improvement for jobs they now occupy. If you are sufficiently sure that the men will not be promoted, put your whole emphasis upon improvement of present duties. The proper kind of counseling after merit rating will make supervisors aware of their strengths and weaknesses and the likelihood of their being promoted. When they are passed by, the fact will not come as a surprise to them.

309 How Does a Fast-Growing Organization Get Its Supervisors When Time Is Lacking to Develop Them from the Ranks?

To meet an immediate need for supervisors, you may have to hire them from outside the company. Use the recruitment techniques you would use to find other management specialists. Contact employment agencies and colleges, and run advertisements in newspapers and technical and professional magazines. However, by establishing a pre-supervisory training program or a supervisor trainee program now, you will make men available as future openings within the organization occur.

310 What Steps Are Involved in Establishing an Effective Pre-Supervisor Training Program?

The success of a pre-supervisor training program depends to a great degree on the amount of planning before the program is put into operation. The following steps, taken in the order presented, help to insure the success of a pre-supervisor training program.

1. Determine the first-level supervisory needs of the organization by obtaining supervisory turnover records for the past five years. Also estimate the number of supervisory positions that will be created and will have to be filled because of the expected growth of the business. Analyze these data. From this analysis project the supervisory needs for the current year and the next few years.
2. Establish a testing program to assist in selecting candidates for supervision. Sometimes a committee of senior supervisors interviews candidates and helps select them.
3. Establish a training program which involves both classroom instruction and on-the-job training. This should be done in cooperation with a committee of senior supervisors.
4. Recruit candidates from the present employee group. Use the company house organ to explain the program and ask present supervisors to encourage good men to apply.
5. Supplement those who meet your standards with competent young men recruited from outside the company.
6. Place the desired number of candidates in training.
7. Fill all first-level supervisory positions with men chosen from this group.
8. Review your supervisory needs periodically to determine whether the number of trainees is adequate to meet your future needs. If it is not—recruit more candidates.

311   What Should We Teach a Supervisor So That Employees Will Accept Him When He Goes into a Department as a New Supervisor?

Besides teaching him sound principles and practices of supervision, train the new supervisor to become acquainted with all his workers. This means that he should learn their names, interests, and backgrounds, and should show a personal interest in them. He should invite their ideas and suggestions on department operation, change work assignments gradually, and should refrain from instituting major changes in operating procedures until the group has had an opportunity to know and respect him. He must sell himself by his present actions, not by his past achievements.

312   **How Can the New Supervisor Be Encouraged to Think as a Member of Management Rather Than as an Operator?**

When a supervisor has been appointed from the ranks, there is usually a period of three to six months during which he is "in transition." He feels that he is neither fish nor fowl. His allegiances are with his previous associates; he enjoyed satisfying relationships with them and was proficient in his work. It is natural for him to continue to think and feel as he did when he was a worker. He cannot change these attitudes quickly. During the course of normal day-to-day contacts, conferences, and staff meetings, however, the new man's immediate superior can lead him to understand the philosophy of management and become an accepted member of it.

Formal training also can hasten this process during pre-supervisory training, or as soon as possible after the worker becomes a supervisor, the training director should enroll him in a conference course on duties and responsibilities of a supervisor. This course is an essential part of any basic training program for supervisors, even when they are experienced. In its sessions the teacher brings out or gets the group to specify the responsibilities and duties that make the supervisor's job different from that of the operator. Good discussion questions for this purpose are:

> "Why is it more difficult to supervise now than formerly? What factors make supervision less difficult?"
>
> "Why is supervisor training necessary? What does it contribute?"
>
> "What are the duties and responsibilities of supervisors?"
>
> "What tools or services has management provided to help supervisors do their job?"

313   **Should Promising Candidates from the Ranks of Workers Be Included in a Training Program for Experienced Supervisors?**

Generally, it is not good practice to include prospective supervisors in a training course designed and executed for experienced supervisors. However, if workers are selected after careful evaluation and their appointment to a position in management is imminent, they may be included in a regular training program for supervisors if their number is small and if the reason for their inclusion is accepted by the others. If supervisors-to-be form the majority of the group, or join it without explanation, the operating supervisors will be upset by the implication that they need the same training given to men without supervisory experience.

As a general rule, special classes should be set up for new supervisors. When this is done, the subject matter can be designed to meet their specific needs, which are different from those of experienced supervisors. A more unfettered discussion and exploration of the subject matter will result when all members of a group are on the same basis.

314　Why Do Supervisors Tend to Resist Training Classes? What Can Be Done About It?

Veteran supervisors tend to resist training for the same reason that we like to continue in our life pattern. Once we develop a method of performance it is natural to use it. Some supervisors also resist training because they think they will be "shown up" in the training meetings. Some of them may have limited formal schooling, which increases their feeling of inadequacy in a classroom.

What can we do about supervisors who resist training? Allay some of their fears by a detailed explanation of the purpose of training; show how it differs from the training offered in the public schools. Emphasize the fact that veteran supervisors who will attend the classes have had little formal education. Get their superiors to talk with them, encouraging them to participate in the training. During the actual training classes, utilize these veteran supervisors as much as possible; give them the recognition that their length of service with the organization deserves. If a few of these who have resisted training become enthusiastic, they will help win over the others.

315　How Do You Get Old-Line Foremen to Attend Supervisor Training Classes?

Have the supervisors of these foremen encourage them to attend the class. Develop a personal relationship with these old-line foremen. Visit them on the job and get them to help plan and establish the training program. Invite their participation in the program as instructors. Once you have recognized their experience and knowledge you have gone far to break down the barrier that is keeping them out of the training classes.

Another device that has proved satisfactory is to train the subordinates of old-line foremen before offering training to the foremen themselves. When the subordinates go back to their departments from training classes, they are encouraged to carry on discussions of the training class material with their foremen. Soon the foremen ask for the training given their subordinates, and are indignant that you are not directing your attention to them rather than to lower levels. This indirect approach is effective, but it requires more time.

316   How Can Training Men Get Supervisors to Attend Classes, Accept, and Then Practice What Is Taught?

There is no single method except continuous hard work. The approach must be different for every trainee and for every program. Some valuable suggestions are the following:

1. If possible, make the training voluntary.
2. Let the trainees or their immediate superiors have a part in planning the program.
3. Start with programs that are most likely to be received with enthusiasm and progress to those that are necessary but less attractive.
4. See that the trainees know what is being taught and feel a need for it.
5. Make sure that the teacher is competent to teach and has prepared himself well. Make sure that his teaching is interesting, spirited, vital, meaningful, and individualized.
6. Use some "top brass" to open the program and comment upon its value.
7. Use a teaching method that encourages the trainees to participate actively in the learning.
8. Get out good publicity about the course before it begins, while it is underway if it continues for some time, and at graduation.
9. Send to trainees a written or printed notice or invitation, announcing content, dates, place, etc.
10. Give a certificate, signed by a representative of top management, to those who complete the course successfully.
11. Even if you, as director of the program, would rather be a production vice president than a teacher, don't let your feelings be known. *You love teaching.* It is your life work. Be proud of it. Enthusiasm is contagious, so is despair or regret.
12. Base promotions and pay increases, in part, on participation in training classes.

317　Can You Outline Some of the Basic Arguments Used to Sell Supervisor Training to Top Management?

Without attempting a formidable and all-inclusive answer, we would rely upon the following methods, to be employed casually, informally, and over an extended period. Great care should be given to timing and the manner of presentation.

1. Point out the great speed with which science is bringing about changes in our lives—changes in methods, production, and human relations. Suggest that change is always with us and that those who live most happily adapt themselves most easily to it. Also explain that adaptation to change requires knowledge of the change—a knowledge best provided through training.
2. Remind your superiors of the excellent training programs that competitors are using to improve the performance of their leaders. Get copies of their training programs. Route them over superiors' desks.
3. Emphasize the feeling of neglect and exclusion which many supervisors have. Point out that supervisors who are to do their best job must identify themselves with the company and its policies and progress. Show how training helps attain this identification.
4. Find specific areas of error or failure within the company, such as too many returned goods because of errors in packaging and shipping, too much breakage, too many accidents. Indicate how training programs would bring improvement or show how, in other instances, they have improved similar situations.
5. Start discussions with top management about the strengths and weaknesses of supervision. Lead them to recognize common weaknesses of supervision. Ask what plans and policies they have to improve their managers.
6. Arrange visits to plants in which top management can see good programs in operation.

318　What Kind of Training Programs Are Usually Offered to Supervisors in Industry?

The Illinois Training Directors' Association recently completed a survey of supervisor training programs in twenty-six companies in the state. The courses and the number of companies conducting each course are shown below.

	Number of
Course	*Companies*
Human Relations	20
Job Instruction	18
Safety	16
Supervisory Responsibilities	13
Job Improvement	10
Organization Relationships	10
Work Simplification	10
Union Contract	9
Cost Control	9
Self-Expression	8
Testing and Counseling of Supervisors..........	8
Mental Hygiene	3
Labor Legislation	3

319   What Are the Characteristics of a Good Supervisor Training Program?

A good supervisor training program has the following characteristics:

1. It is geared to meet the needs of supervisors.
2. It is taught by competent, well trained instructors.
3. It is a continuous program.
4. It consists of formal classroom meetings and guided experience activities on the job. (See Chapter 5.)
5. It covers all levels of supervision.
6. It is integrated into the normal activities of the office and the plant.
7. It utilizes to full advantage outside training facilities and activities.
8. It makes the line organization responsible for seeing that supervisors have training.
9. It has the active support of the top man in each department.
10. It allows for maximum participation by supervisors both in the formulation of the program and in the learning.
11. It is flexible and adaptable and so meets ever-changing needs.
12. It covers not only the technical parts of the job but the social, psychological and economic relationships as well.
13. It improves the performance of management.

Chapter 15

MANAGEMENT TRAINEE PROGRAMS

---

320 **What Are the Merits of College Graduate Recruitment of Executive Talent?**

In general it is much better for a company to develop its own executives from within than to hire seasoned men or high potential juniors from the outside. This is especially true when newly hired juniors start well up in the organization or are placed on "escalators" that lead them rapidly upward.

Although the practice of recruiting high potential men from outside is sometimes necessary, it should be undertaken only when it is clear that qualified people cannot be found in the organization. Even then, there must be a full understanding that newcomers will have to prove themselves and earn their advancement step by step. Such outsiders should not be provided learning opportunities which are in excess of those given to men within the organization who have similar potential or who are ready for advancement. We cannot go into details here, but many of the difficulties that arise in factories and offices can be traced to the natural antagonism toward outside imports or "crown princes." Indiscriminate outside recruitment of talent frustrates home-grown men, who think they merit advancement but are passed over. A national personnel conference recently concluded that many ills in the textile mills of the South can be cured most effectively by developing middle management from men in the ranks of the cotton mills rather than by college recruitment.

All this does not imply that business should not scout the colleges for able graduates. It does suggest that scouting should not take the place of an equally careful talent hunt within the organization. Both methods can yield results if men from the colleges and insiders are placed on an equal footing and are given an equal chance to earn advancement.

321 **Have Most Large and Medium Sized Companies Established a Training Program for College Recruits? What Is Included in Such a Program?**

It has long been true that companies, large and small, actively recruit college graduates and offer them a planned, although sometimes informal, training program. In recent years, because of a scarcity of technical and scientific personnel, there has been increased emphasis on this college recruitment. Although this may be the primary reason for the present intense interest in the subject, many companies hire college recruits for general management training and not to fill specific positions. Following a specified training period, they are placed in positions which are mutually agreeable to the men and the company.

In general, the future leaders of a company will come from its college recruits. Consequently, they are selected carefully and in many cases receive planned on-the-job and classroom training. The training program usually includes:

1. Orientation to company philosophy, personnel and general policies, company organization, and products. There are meetings with major executives, plant tours, etc.
2. Try-out experiences. The trainee is assigned to a series of jobs in the various departments of the company so that he may understand the operation of the business, learn the interrelationship of the major functions, and be in a better position to decide on his choice of work.
3. Specialized training. After the two steps above, the trainee is assigned to the department where he eventually will work and is then given intensive, specialized training in most areas of this department.

322 **Why Should We Offer Special Training for College Recruits?**

College recruits are new members of the organization with considerable theoretical knowledge, but little or no experience in how to apply it. Therefore, they need specialized training in order to help them become familiar with the operations of the company and adjust to its organization. Training assists them, through try-out and similar experiences, to choose the type of work for which they are best fitted in the company. They learn to apply the principles and theories taught in college. Specialized training starts them constructively toward a leadership role. It prepares them for their first step in business at a time when their aspirations are directed toward the higher management positions they may eventually occupy.

323   What Is the Greatest Problem in Developing College Graduate Trainees?

The greatest problem for the young man is adapting his thinking to a new environment. He was trained, if the school was a good one, in problem solving, in creative thinking, in profiting from varied, new experience. He has, however, had little experience with the routine of day-to-day administration and follow up. During his first years in industry he may feel his skills are unused, that a routine clerk could handle his responsibilities, that he will never get to solve complex, challenging problems or to participate in setting company or department policy. But this is the reality which he will face and must succeed at during his orientation years in industry.

It is not wise to start college youngsters half way up the ladder, nor to advance them with inordinate speed through lower but very important rungs of the ladder. It is, however, equally unwise to place college trained young men in low level jobs and ignore them. These years are the crucial ones for the trainee and for the company that has invested in him. Trainees require more expert guidance during this apprenticeship than at any other time. They need counsel to prevent frustration, to hold open the visions of the future, to help them in the inevitable adjustment from the idealism of classrooms and textbooks to the reality of the workplace. They need occasional committee assignments or participation in task forces, or multiple management boards to keep alive and make stronger their creative powers and their broader visions. Above all they need help in discovering *what can be learned* at their first job and in accomplishing it. The supervisor who has been properly trained to receive one of these college-trained men knows what a learner should get from his first years. He may use a list such as the one below, to see that his protégé is really learning.

1. Attitudes and habits of thought and action at the worker level.
2. How to deal with operators and production workers.

3. A broad view of the company—its organization and its leaders.

4. A "feeling" for its climate and preferences—what will work in this particular company and what will be resisted.

5. A knowledge of early experiments and projects that have failed and an opportunity to analyze why they failed and whether they should be tried again under different circumstances.

6. An opportunity to stand aside and watch and think and even plan for the future—an opportunity that the trainee may find little time for after his advancement gets underway.

7. An opportunity to build community contacts and participation in civic, welfare, fraternal and service groups, not only to obtain from them personal satisfaction and security but also to learn about his company from the outside.

324   What Should Be Done to Get Management Trainees Started Right?

Trainees should be informed of the objectives, duration, and mechanics of their training program. Orienting them to their job, its importance, and its relationship to other jobs in the organization is equally important. Their duties, responsibilities, authority, and status should be discussed with them, and they should be made familiar with the organization chart, personnel policies, and similar information. They should be informed of some of the doubts that they will probably have and the usual problems they will face. They should be told to whom they should go for counseling and guidance. Every effort should be made to prepare them to begin their new job with anticipation and confidence.

The trainees should be introduced to all those with whom they must work. These men should be oriented to the trainees: what they are to do, why they are in the department, and should be given a few personal facts about the new men. The trainees should be given an opportunity to tour those areas of plant and office which influence their work or in which they express an interest.

An illustration of a formal program which is designed to help trainees get started right follows:

ORIENTATION PROGRAM FOR MANAGEMENT TRAINEES

MANUFACTURING DIVISION
JOHNSON & JOHNSON

The following schedule has been planned as an interesting and comprehensive introduction to our Organization. Please feel free to ask any questions that come to your mind during the course of the week's activities.

FIRST DAY

TIME	ACTIVITY	LEADER	PLACE
9:00–10:30	Take complete physical examination	Company Doctor	Medical Department
10:30–11:00	Complete personnel records	Records' Supervisor	Records Department
11:00–12:00	Explain orientation schedule	Training Director	Personnel Conference Room
12:00– 1:30	Luncheon		
1:30– 1:45	Discuss general policies of Manufacturing Department	Vice President— Manufacturing	Vice President's Office
2:00– 4:30	Discuss company organization, including personnel, plants, and products; personnel policies and practices.	Assistant Training Director	Personnel Conference Room

SECOND DAY

9:00– 9:30	Discuss objectives of Manufacturing Department.	Production Manager	Production Manager's Office
9:30–12:00	Tour	Members of Training Department	Museum, Cotton and Gauze Mill, Plaster Mill
12:00– 1:00	Luncheon		
1:45– 3:00	Receive welcome and tour Baby Products plant	Plant Manager	Plant Manager's Office
3:45– 5:00	Receive welcome and tour Shipping Center	Director, Customer Service	Director's Office

THIRD DAY

8:45–10:00	Discuss organization of Personnel Department	Assistant Personnel Director	Personnel Conference Room
10:15–11:15	Discuss selection, placement, and counseling policies	Director, Selection and Placement	Personnel Conference Room
11:30–12:00	Discuss Transfer Policy	Employment Manager	Employment Manager's Office

12:00– 1:00	Luncheon		
1:00– 2:00	Discuss Company train- ing activities	Training Director	Personnel Confer- ence Room
2:15– 3:15	Discuss labor relations policies	Labor Relations As- sistant and Plant Steward	Personnel Confer- ence Room
3:30– 4:30	Discuss Wage and Sal- ary Administration policies and practices	Director of Wage and Salary Ad- ministration	Personnel Confer- ence Room

FOURTH DAY

9:00–10:00	Receive welcome and tour Orthopedic Products plant	Plant Superintendent	Orthopedic Products Plant
10:30–11:30	Receive welcome and tour Elastic Goods plant	Plant Superintendent	Elastic Goods Plant
12:00– 1:00	Luncheon–Research Center		
1:00– 2:30	Tour–Research Center	Research Chemist	Research Center
3:00– 5:00	Discuss General Offices organization and functions	Assistant Controller	Controller's Conference Room

FIFTH DAY

9:00– 3:30	Tour Engineering De- partments and dis- cuss functions of each department	Director, Central Engineering and his staff	Director's Office
3:30– 5:00	Discuss sales and mer- chandising policies	Director, Sales Training Manager, Field Forces, Hospital Division Director, Surgical Dressings Division	Sales Conference Room

325   What Are Your Suggestions for Establishing and Operating an Effective College Recruit Training Program?

Suggestions are:

1. Establish a committee made up of senior executives, including the personnel or training executive, to plan, coordinate, and control the program.
2. Define the specific experiences the trainees will have in each of their assignments.
3. Help trainees to carry their weight and to produce during their training period. Assign them to productive work.

4. Assign trainees real projects for study and analysis.
5. Make the on-the-job training experiences long enough to be meaningful to trainees.
6. Supplement the on-the-job experiences of trainees with class-room instruction, counseling, planned reading programs, and outside training experiences.
7. Let trainees participate in activities such as grievance meetings, foremen's meetings, departmental staff meetings, special assign-ments, training classes, etc., so that they are a part of manage-ment.
8. Offer trainees opportunities to receive counsel and guidance from qualified employees in staff and service positions.
9. Encourage trainees to express their opinions about the training program to members of the trainee committee.
10. Review the progress of trainees frequently. Members of the trainee committee should do this at least quarterly. Trainees should be informed by their immediate superior of their prog-ress on each task.
11. Encourage trainees to complete their training program before accepting opportunities within the company for permanent posi-tions.
12. Give trainees pay increases during the training period.

326   Can a Small Company Successfully Set Up a Development Program for College Recruits?

Yes. Although more publicity has been given to the training programs for college recruits in large organizations, many small companies successfully execute such programs. These programs are usually informal, personal, realistic, and involve small numbers of trainees.

An excellent illustration is given below of a program[1] for train-ing college recruits in an accounting division of a small company (450 employees).

ACCOUNTING TRAINEE PROGRAM

ETHICON, INC.

Objectives of the Program.

1. To provide an opportunity for junior accountants to become familiar with several related areas of accounting work in our organization, in

[1] This program was prepared by the Treasurer-Controller of Ethicon, Inc., New Brunswick, N. J.

order to broaden their understanding of the accounting effort as a whole and furnish the company men with diversified experience.

2. By exposure to the different phases of accounting work to give the trainee an opportunity to select the field of work in which he is particularly interested. Every effort would then be made to place him in that area for permanent assignment.

3. To obtain an evaluation by three supervisors of the trainee's ability to adjust himself to different areas of accounting effort, and thereby result in a more objective valuation as to the trainee's potential for future development.

Qualifications of Trainees. Trainees will consist of (a) clerical employees who have evidenced an interest in accounting and are taking advanced courses in order to improve their knowledge of accounting, (b) college graduates now employed as junior accountants, and (c) junior accountants hired from the outside specifically for the purpose of entering into the trainee program.

Trainee Assignments. An accounting trainee may be assigned in one of three areas:

General Accounting Department
Cost Accounting Department
Tabulating Department

Trainees will be assigned regular work in the section in which they are employed, and the work will be subject to the same review as that of any other employee in the department.

Time Schedule. A trainee will be assigned to each section enumerated above for the following periods of time:

General Accounting Department—approximately six months
Cost Accounting Department—approximately six months
Tabulating Department—approximately six months

At the end of the training period, the trainee will be assigned to a specific department. Every effort will be made to assign the trainee to the field in which he is particularly interested.

Methods of Paying. The trainee will be paid at a rate established for the trainee position. Merit increases, while he is in the trainee program, will be granted by the immediate supervisor of the trainee with the approval of the treasurer-controller. Salary will be reviewed at least twice a year.

Responsibilities of Supervisors. While it is recognized that each supervisor has a responsibility to train and develop his subordinates, this responsibility takes on great significance in the case of trainees. In order to attain the outlined objectives it is necessary that the training of participants in the program be based upon a planned schedule.

Supervisors must recognize that the trainee program is built, first, for the benefit of the trainee and the organization as a whole, and, second, for that of the individual department and supervisor. While the trainees are to be treated in the same manner as any other new employee, the purpose of the training program requires special attention of the departmental supervisor.

Reports of Progress by Supervisors. It is expected that each supervisor of the trainee will submit a progress report to the treasurer-controller every month, covering the trainee in his department. During the first month of the trainee's employment the supervisor will meet with him weekly to discuss his progress and every second Friday thereafter. The treasurer-controller will discuss with the trainee his progress quarterly. All progess reports and counseling results will be put in writing and maintained in the trainee's personnel folder in the treasurer-controller's office. The supervisor may delegate the responsibility of guiding the trainee to a qualified person in his department, but he will not relinquish his over-all responsibility for the trainee's performance.

Trainee Reports. Prior to transferring the trainee from one department to another, the trainee will write up his understanding of the work performed in the department from which he is being transferred. The purpose of this write-up is to evaluate the understanding that the trainee has acquired in the period of his assignment and in some degree provide the supervisor with a measure of the effectiveness of his training program.

In addition to the above general outline, a specific listing of the work assignments in each section was prepared. The following illustrates the assignments made in one department of the division.

TRAINEE WORK ASSIGNMENTS

GENERAL ACCOUNTING DEPARTMENT

I. ORIENTATION   2 days
   A. General discussion of the accounting operation
   B. Formal orientation tour.

II. SALES REGISTER   1 week
   A. Distribute daily invoices
   B. File invoices for posting
   C. Discuss procedure accounts receivable
   D. Prepare journal entry, net sales, and class of trade report

III. CASH RECEIPTS ALLOCATION   4 days
   A. Distribute daily cash
   B. Prepare monthly journal entry
   C. Explain cashier's function

IV. ACCOUNTS PAYABLE AND CASH DISBURSEMENTS   2 weeks
   A. Study procedure manual
   B. Assist and perform all steps in processing invoices
      for vouchering

    C. File vouchers
    D. Prepare journal entries
    E. Check customers' statements
    F. Process vouchers for payment

  V. WAGE PAYROLL   2 weeks
    A. Process employees' time cards
    B. Summarize and extend weekly time sheets
    C. Post withholdings and deductions
    D. Prepare daily variance reports
    E. Prepare weekly distribution
    F. Prepare monthly summary and journal entry
    G. Review payroll records and prepare special reports

  VI. ACCOUNT ANALYSIS   3 weeks
    A. Prepare regular monthly analysis of accounts
    B. Make out special reports

 VII. JOURNAL ENTRIES   3 weeks
    A. Make standard monthly entries
    B. Make miscellaneous adjusting entries

VIII. FINANCIAL STATEMENTS   6 weeks
    A. Prepare commercial expense reports
    B. Prepare balance sheet
    C. Prepare company profit and loss statements
    D. Prepare profit and loss by product group
    E. Make miscellaneous reports

  IX. QUARTERLY CLOSING   1 week
    A. Prepare quarterly reports to parent company

  X. SPECIAL ASSIGNMENTS   3 weeks
    A. Handle correspondence
    B. Prepare charts and graphs
    C. Approve vouchers for payment
    D. Do other special projects as assigned

  XI. MISCELLANEOUS   2 weeks
    A. Reconcile bank statements
    B. Process intercompany transactions
    C. Post and balance subsidiary ledgers
    D. Prepare miscellaneous billings
    E. Process and code miscellaneous debits and credits to
       customers' accounts

                                  TOTAL 24 weeks

327   **What Are the Chief Problems Faced by Management Trainees When Put into a Development Program Which Places Them on Production Jobs for Learning Purposes?**

Experience with counseling management trainees shows that they are principally concerned with such things as:

1. Their responsibilities.
2. Their status within the organization.
3. Their need for occasional counseling and talking it over.
4. Their future.
5. Their lack of knowledge about how their work fits into the general scheme of things.

Frequently, trainees run across firmly established but awkward situations within the department where they are in training. Discussions with the department head do not bring about what they feel are the desirable changes. As a result, the trainees are confused and feel a divided allegiance to the man who hired them and to the man for whom they are working. They want it made perfectly clear to whom they must report. They want to know whether they have a voice in problem solving where they are temporarily assigned, or whether they should accept established but not necessarily effective work methods?

It often happens that the trainees meet with resistance from supervisors who cannot, because of their own limitations, advance further in the organization. Such supervisors do not understand how trainees fit into the scheme of things. They regard them as "fair-haired" boys of top management and resent their intrusion. As a result, it is difficult for the trainee to obtain the cooperation of these supervisors or to be accepted by them.

Many trainees feel the need of an opportunity to discuss these and other daily problems with a skilled counselor. To have an occasional talk about their progress, shortcomings, strengths, and goals becomes increasingly important as the trainees advance in the program and questions and doubts rise in their minds.

Trainees are also often concerned with the over-all picture of the operations of the plant. They want to know how their jobs or special projects tie in with the final picture or finished product. And they want to feel they will wind up, whenever possible, in areas of work which interest them most and for which they are best qualified.[2]

[2] This question was answered by J. F. Buckley, Assistant Training Director, Johnson & Johnson, New Brunswick, N. J.

328   What Should We Look for When Selecting Junior Executives Who Can Go Way to the Top?

In the absence of certain scientific tools to help us, the very practical approach of William B. Given, Jr., is helpful.[3] Mr. Given has developed a job specification to help select young men who would advance in management. To him, leadership is quite likely to come from a man "who gets a real 'kick' out of sticking his neck out—but not from a desire to show off; who is keen to try a new way; who enjoys proving that the boss is all wet; who has the common sense to ask for outside help when he needs it, and the instinct to seek out the right person for that help; who has unlimited confidence in the future, but is realistic about the terrible things that can happen; who gets pleasure out of doing things for others; who is challenged by tough problems; who will be a useful citizen; who realizes that all men want and need friendships; who is not afraid of being afraid."

329   How Can You Keep the Man Happy as a Trainee Until the Opening for Advancement Occurs?

As long as men are faced with challenging, worth-while activities which lead toward acceptable objectives, and salary adjustments are made, they are willing to mark time for advancement up the organizational chain. Therefore, the training and development program must be planned to involve more and more complex tasks that will hold the interest of the trainees, and salaries must be reviewed regularly.

One of the best developmental devices to maintain the interest of trainees and at the same time profit the organization is job rotation. Assignment to another position at a comparable level, with clear-cut reasons for the change, is the "shot in the arm" that can hold capable juniors until openings for advancement occur.

330   How Do You Keep the Competition Among College Recruits from Becoming Rough and Disastrous?

The questioner has experienced a different kind of training program for college recruits from those with which we are familiar. There is competition among college graduates the same as

[3] William B. Given, Jr., "Experience in the Development of Management People," in *Development of Executive Leadership*, ed. by Marvin Bauer (Cambridge: Harvard University Press, 1949), p. 82.

among all levels of management. It may be more pronounced with college recruits since each is striving to earn a permanent position. However, this does not mean that competition will have disastrous effects on the men. The emphasis in training is on accomplishing each assignment to the best of the trainees' abilities. It is upon learning and not upon permanent jobs or promotions dangled constantly like a carrot from a stick in front of their noses. Also the training program is not used as a selection device from which only the hardy survive. Careful selection through testing and interviewing will provide qualified candidates. These are then trained through realistic, meaningful, well-planned work experiences which will help almost all to succeed to the best of their abilities, and without jealousy and harmful competition.

331 Don't Most College Recruits Leave a Company After They Receive Their Training?

The experience of most companies which have conducted management trainee programs for college recruits does not confirm this. Frequently, the only men we see who have participated in a management trainee program are those who have left their company for one reason or another. It is easy to conclude from this limited evidence that college recruitment and training is costly and of little value, since the trainees do not stay with the company.

The best college recruits are eager, aggressive, ambitious, and capable young men. They are anxious to learn and eager to prove their mettle. Some company training programs fail to offer a series of challenging, guided experiences and, as a result, these companies do lose more trainees than they should. If the college recruit's training program is properly planned, if counsel and guidance is given to the participants, and if placement is made after a stated training period, a company will be able to hold its trained men.

332 What Type of Training Program Would Be Most Effective for Teaching College Trainees Basic Business Economics?

Assuming that these individuals have an understanding of basic economic and accounting principles as a result of their college training, a guided analysis of specific company economic problems would prove most effective. For example, the trainees might participate in a conference-type review of the deliberations necessary in choosing the location of a new plant, the purchase of a major piece of equipment, or the planning of a large advertising campaign. Such a review would indicate to the trainees the effect of taxation and government fiscal policies on their company, how profits are used and why they are necessary, an explanation of company pricing policies, and the cost and methods of raising capital, to mention a few of the many facets of business economics. Such a program would have a two-pronged effect: a review of the application of the principles of economics to business problems, problems with which many of the conferees are familiar, and a more thorough understanding of the company's operations and problems.

333   Who Teaches College Recruits?

Since the primary method of training college recruits is through work assignments in operating departments, the line supervisors for whom the trainees work carry the heaviest instruction load. Also, the training department usually conducts orientation and supplementary training programs that are coordinated with the on-the-job training.

334   What Is the Usual Length of a Training Program for College Recruits?

There is no set length for college-recruit training. Many companies expend considerable time and effort to train college recruits and their training programs frequently last at least a year and some companies extend the training for five years. The length of the period depends on the nature of the job for which the recruit is being prepared. Technical training programs usually take the longest. After the recruits have passed the trainee stage, they are given the same training opportunity as other executives. No other group in industry receives such extensive training.

335   How Does a Management Trainee Program Fit into a Development Program for All Members of Management?

A management trainee program is preliminary to a general management development program. The latter serves experienced executives in an organization while the former is directed at employees who are in training for management positions.

In its later stages, the trainee program merges with, or leads into, participation in the company's regular management development program for experienced executives.

The following is an excellent description of how a management training program fits into a management development program:

MANAGEMENT DEVELOPMENT PROGRAM[4]
FOR THE
MANUFACTURING DIVISION
(Johnson & Johnson, New Brunswick)

In order to insure its growth and effectiveness, the Manufacturing Division of Johnson & Johnson at New Brunswick has instituted a management development program for all its management personnel. The program aims to improve supervision and leadership in management positions and to develop a reserve of trained executives for future needs. It places stress on the activities that will contribute to the growth and development of the individual and the strengthening of the Company. The Management Development Program provides for a systematic appraisal and a continuous improvement of the total management force of the Manufacturing Division.

I. OBJECTIVES:

    A. To provide development activities that will help management personnel to meet the growing challenges of their jobs and to progress within the Manufacturing Division in accordance with the policy of promotion from within.

    B. To develop the abilities of each executive to handle higher-level responsibilities.

    C. To develop greater breadth and flexibility in management personnel.

II. ADMINISTRATION:

The program will be administered by the Management Development Committee consisting of the Production Manager, the Plant Managers, the Assistant Personnel Director and the Training Director.

III. OPERATION OF THE PROGRAM:

The program includes the following steps:

    A. Recruitment of men of high potential for management into the Manufacturing Division.

    B. Determination of short- and long-term organizational needs of the individual mills and of the Manufacturing Division.

    C. An annual audit and evaluation of the present management force.

    D. Individual and group development activities.

IV. PHASES OF THE PROGRAM:

The program is divided into four phases. The preliminary step deals with recruitment and selection. The orientation and intermediate phases of the program involve only personnel brought into the division as trainees. The advanced phase of the program involves every member of management throughout his career with the division.

[4] Prepared by the Management Development Committee, Manufacturing Division, Johnson & Johnson, New Brunswick, N. J.

A. *Preliminaries*:

1. Recruitment
   a. When trainee positions open up, they will be posted within Johnson & Johnson and subsidiaries. Qualified trainees will be recruited from within the Company, if available.
   b. If it is necessary to go outside the Company, trainees will be recruited from the colleges. Preference will be given to recent graduates who possess the training, character, and potential that will enable them to move into the ranks of management.

2. Selection
   a. Initial screening is the responsibility of the Selection and Placement Director who will use psychological tests and careful interviews in his work.
   b. Final selection is the responsibility of the Management Development Committee. Each applicant will be interviewed by at least three members of the Committee. The Selection and Placement Director will be present in an advisory capacity. The final decision to hire will be made by the Committee as a whole.
   c. The Selection and Placement Director will inform each applicant that he is accepted or rejected for the program.

3. Qualifications
   a. Age. 20-28
   b. Sex: Male
   c. Education and Experience: College degree or equivalent. Major in Business Administration or Engineering preferred. Academic class standing and participation in college activities will be seriously considered. Summer or part-time employment in industry is a favorable factor. Experience may substitute for a degree where the candidate is already a company employee.
   d. Appearance and Health: A general impression of neatness, poise, alertness, and good health is expected of the candidate.
   e. Self-Expression: The candidate is expected to express himself clearly and forthrightly.
   f. Personal Qualities: The Committee will look for evidence of ambition and initiative, of creative and analytical thinking, insight, maturity, and leadership.

B. *Orientation Phase of the Training*: A six months' program for selected trainees chosen both from inside and outside the company.

1. The successful candidate will be trained for at least six months in a designated mill.
2. The objectives of this training are
   a. To familiarize the trainee with as many of the production departments as possible.
   b. To enable him to learn the policies and techniques of various line supervisors and to get practice in the supervision of a manufacturing department.
   c. To enable him to learn the functions of staff departments in the Manufacturing Division.

3. The Training Director is responsible for the initial orientation of the trainee. In addition, he will interview the trainee at three-month intervals to evaluate his progress, offer counsel and receive the trainee's suggestions and criticisms. A record of these interviews will be submitted to the Production Manager and the manager of the plant in which the trainee works. Whenever the trainee is transferred from one department to another, the Training Director will sit with him and his new supervisor to review his progress in the program.

4. Every three months the Plant Manager will formally evaluate the trainee's progress and performance. The rating will be guided by his own observations and those of the supervisors to whom the trainee has reported. A copy of this evaluation will be transmitted to the Training Director who will be guided by it in his periodic interviews with the trainee.

5. The Plant Manager is responsible for the on-the-job training of the trainee, but the trainee will report directly to the supervisor to whom he is assigned at any given time. He will be assigned various projects in line and staff departments that will give him a broad but intensive and realistic experience in the activities of the mill.

6. The Training Director, in consultation with the plant managers, will draw up a check list of the information and skills the trainee is expected to acquire during the Orientation Phase. It is expected that his job assignments will cover all the items that appear on the check-list. Prior to transferring to another department, the trainee and his supervisor will initial those items on the check-list that both believe have been adequately covered.

7. Completion of the Orientation Phase

   a. The trainee is eligible for a merit increase six months after he begins the Orientation phase of the program. He is eligible for another review six months after he enters the Intermediate Phase of the program. Thereafter he is subject to the general policy with respect to merit increases.

   b. After six months, the Plant Manager may recommend for the Committee's approval that the trainee is ready to move into the Intermediate Phase of the Management Development Program. If the Committee approves, he ceases to be a trainee and is given the title of Assistant Foreman. The Committee, if at all possible, will at this time assign him to a mill other than the one from which he came.

C. *Intermediate Phase*: A program for trainees who have passed the orientation stage and who now carry the title Assistant Foreman. The aid is to provide a variety of specialized training experiences.

1. In the Intermediate Phase the Assistant Foreman may be assigned a production unit to operate or be delegated special projects under the supervision of a foreman. In general, he will be rotated into those activities that will provide for his further managerial development and use his abilities for the advantage of the company.

2. He will participate in the basic supervisor training program, followed by other group training activities that will develop his technical, administrative and human relations skills. In addition, he will be given the opportunity to visit outside plants, attend professional meetings

and conferences, and engage in other activities that will contribute to his over-all development.

3. During the Intermediate Phase, the Assistant Foreman will be periodically interviewed and evaluated as described in the Orientation Phase, Par. 3.

4. At any time during the year, the Assistant Foreman will be eligible to apply for posted jobs in line or staff supervision within the manufacturing division. When appointed to such a job, he becomes a member of the regular management force and is eligible to participate in the Advanced Phase of the Management Development Program. Henceforth his status and opportunities are precisely those of any other management member of the Manufacturing Division.

D. *Advanced Phase*: A broad and continuing Management Development Program available to all members of the management force including the rank of Assistant Foreman. The program consists of four elements:

1. Organizational Analysis: To determine the short- and long-range needs of the entire Manufacturing Division. The analysis will be made periodically by the production manager in consultation with the plant managers.

2. Preparation of precise, up-to-date job descriptions: To determine the responsibilities for each management position and the qualifications of the man who is to fill the position. The descriptions will cover: (a) General Duties, (b) Specific Responsibilities and Authority, (c) Relationships, (d) Man Specifications.

3. Annual Performance Review: Each supervisor is to be evaluated by his immediate superior (plant manager, general foreman or foreman) aided by the Training Director and members of the Personnel Department.

a. The purpose of the review is to appraise the supervisor's strengths and weaknesses, assess his potential and determine the development activities that will improve his present performance, help him keep pace with the increased demands of his job, and prepare him for future assignments.

b. At scheduled periods annually, a member of the Training Department will sit with each reviewing supervisor to assist him in appraising the performance of his subordinates. The interview will attempt to cover every facet of his job according to the duties outlined in his job description. The evident strengths and weaknesses of the subordinate will be analyzed. He will be appraised in terms of his mastery of his recent job and his readiness for promotion. On the basis of this analysis a tentative program of development activities will be drawn up for the ensuing year.

c. A draft of this interview will be written by the Training Director and submitted to the reviewing supervisor for his approval and use as the basis for counseling with his subordinate. As the result of this discussion, the reviewing may amend the original appraisal of his subordinate. He will return the performance review to the Training Director with the statement that he has discussed it with his subordinate.

d. A final version of the performance review (with names omitted) will be coded and prepared by the Training Department in duplicate. One copy will be retained in their files, the other delivered to the Plant Manager.

4. Development Activities: On- or off-the-job programs designed to help each supervisor to perform at the top of his potential on his present job and to prepare him for advancement within the Manufacturing Division. These activities will vary with the needs and abilities of the individual supervisor.

   a. Informal Development Activities: The opportunities within the organization for broadening the experience and stimulating the growth of executives are limitless. Imagination and careful planning will create many devices in addition to such activities as:
      (1) Participating in Task Forces or Profit Committees composed of members of definite departments, to study and solve specific problems.
      (2) Participating in Job Rotation Program.
      (3) Handling delegated assignments to be completed under the guidance of the superior.
      (4) Attending Plant Manager's Staff Meetings or meetings of other levels or departments.
      (5) Helping in the preparation of a plant or department budget.
      (6) Sitting in on various steps of grievance meetings.
      (7) Studying regular or special reports circulated to him from other departments (Personnel, Sales, Research).
      (8) Leading discussion of the Annual Report with his subordinates.
      (9) Leading conference of groups in which he normally participates as a member.
      (10) Receiving circulated copies of periodicals he normally does not see. (For example: *Harvard Business Review, Management Digest, Advanced Management, Fortune.*)
      (11) Visiting other departments in Johnson & Johnson or departments similar to his in other Johnson & Johnson mills or affiliates.
      (12) Attending meets of Econometrics Institute.
      (13) Attending Executive Dinner meetings.

   b. Outside Development Activities
      (1) Attending conferences of other Johnson & Johnson divisions. (Personnel, Controllers, Sales, etc.)
      (2) Attending Seminars or Workshops sponsored by the American Management Association and similar organizations.
      (3) Taking evening courses at Rutgers and elsewhere.
      (4) Visiting outside plants.
      (5) Taking Dale Carnegie Public Speaking Course.

   c. Johnson & Johnson Group Development Activities: Participating in management programs conducted by the Johnson & Johnson Training Department. For example: those being offered at the time of this writing:
      Reading Improvement

Effective Job Organization
Case Studies in Administration
Business Manners
Effective Supervision
Employment Interviewing
Memo and Report Writing
Handling Personnel Problems (Role Playing)
Conference Leadership

V. CONCLUSION:

The Management Development Program is founded upon the belief that when a company stops getting better it stops being good. The program offers insurance against the effects of expansion, competition, and complacency. It repudiates the idea that time and experience alone will solve the problems of the future. Management Development is a planned effort to help each supervisor and executive find the place in the organization that will provide best use for his talents. It aims to stimulate the growth and improvement of our entire management force.

Chapter 16

GENERAL EDUCATION

336   What Is General Education?

General education is designed primarily to meet the social, recreational, cultural and avocational needs of employees. It is complementary to, but different in emphasis and approach from, special training for a job. General education encompasses the common knowledges, skills, and attitudes needed by each individual to be effective as a person, a member of a family, a worker, and a citizen. A decision as to whether a particular course or program is general education depends on the purpose and intent of the learner rather than on course content or methods of instruction. A course in typing, given after office hours, may be designed primarily to train employees in this occupational skill although it may be pursued by some employees as an avocational activity. In the latter case, it is essentially general education.

In some companies, general education runs largely to such subjects as home decorating, personal problems of everyday living, creative writing, literature, design, ceramics, photography, home care of the sick, first aid, and handicrafts. In other companies there is more emphasis on vocational courses. The program usually does not include courses designed to improve the employee's performance on his job, but may include those that will prepare him for advancement. There is less company direction than in traditional employee training.

General education contributes to the continuous educational needs of employees by means of courses or activities that lead to new hobbies or new vocations. It provides socializing experiences that meet basic needs by enabling people to express their personalities and develop their creative capacities through dramatics, painting, design, or similar activities, and by providing fundamental knowledge which prepares employees to assume increasing responsibility.

337   Who Participates in a General Education Program?

General education programs are usually designed to meet the needs of all employees, and all are invited to participate. In some companies, however, members of the employee's family who are at least eighteen years of age also are eligible to take part. This practice seems to be growing, probably because business organizations recognize the value of good community relations and the importance of the attitude that an employee's family has toward the company.

338   How Do You Determine What Subjects to Include in a General Education Program?

Include only those subjects which the employees desire. Determine these desires by questionnaires or personal interviews. However, those in charge of the program have a responsibility to suggest subjects and offer samples or previews from which employees may choose. Worth-while results will be achieved only if the subjects are made inviting and the choice of what to include is left to the employees.

339   What Are the Steps in Beginning a General Education Program?

Assuming that such a program is desired in a company, the first step is to obtain management's approval and permission to use company facilities for it. Then learn what can be established at little or no cost to the company. In every plant there are employees who have hobbies or specialties and who are willing to share their knowledge without charge. Many films also can be obtained at no cost, or merely by paying transportation. If necessary, begin with courses that require no appropriation, letting success with them become evidence that can be used to secure a reasonable appropriation to continue, and expand, the program. The second step is to choose members of the employee group who will represent various departments and levels of employees to serve on the General Education Committee. Someone from the training or personnel department usually serves as secretary on the committee. The third step is to hold meetings of the committee to determine how the committee will function and to make the decisions involved in running any training program. The fourth step is to determine the specific courses that are to be offered immediately. The usual method for determining the immediate needs is by questionnaire or personal interviews. The fifth step is to publicize the courses, enroll interested employees, and run the courses. The program is now under way.

340   What Are Some of the Subjects Taught in a General Education Program?

The subjects that may be taught in a general education program are limitless. The Hawthorne Club Evening School, which offers courses to employees of the Hawthorne Works of the Western Electric Company in Chicago, lists seventy-five courses under the following headings in its *Bulletin* for 1952-53:

Applied Mathematics, Business English, Art and Literature, Electricity and Magnetism, Effective Speaking, Psychology, Accounting and Manufacturing Costs, Calculating Machines, Blueprint Reading, Drafting and Machine Courses, Manufacturing Practice, General Telephony, Crossbar Telephony, Step-by-Step Telephony, Radio and Television, Typewriting and Shorthand, Athletics, Camera Club, Car Repair, Decorative Handicrafts, Home Owners' Forum, Fundamental Economics, Sewing, First Aid.

An example of the courses offered under one of these general headings is:

Home Owners' Forum: Interior Decoration of the Home, Carpentry, Furniture Finishing and Refinishing, Upholstery, Advanced Upholstery, Home Plumbing and Repairs.

The Hawthorne program shows the great variety of courses which are possible in a general education program and indicates the emphasis which one company gives to its content. Here one sees handicrafts, technical and related subjects and some avocations, with a minimum attention to the arts and sciences. Other companies put the emphasis upon broad cultural fields. An example is the "Great Books" Program—planned particularly for the reading and study of the classics—which constitutes part of the general education program in some companies.

341   Is It Advisable for an Employee Committee to Run a General Education Program?

Yes, because of these advantages: (1) Employees are in a position to determine the general education needs of fellow employees, who feel free to talk with them and express their desires. Courses will be offered which meet these desires of employees as expressed by them and not those that management feels they should be interested in taking. (2) An employee committee removes all fear that courses are intended to indoctrinate employees with management's thinking. The program is accepted as one developed by employees to serve their own interests. (3) The committee provides developmental experience for its members, enabling them to take on broader responsibilities than they can assume in their jobs.

342   What Are the Functions of a General Education Committee?

A general education committee comprised of representative employees drew up the following list of its functions:

1. Determine the interests of employees in specific courses, and, where interest is great enough, make such courses available.
2. Successfully administer the general education program.
3. Establish the minimum and maximum number of persons to enroll in each course.
4. Determine the fee for each course, if a fee is required.
5. Decide the number of courses to be offered and the time and date of each one. The committee will be guided in its selection by the convenience of such dates and times for the greatest number of interested persons.
6. Allocate all funds of the program.
7. Select and evaluate instructors.
8. One member of the committee will maintain all records of the program and a record of all funds. This person shall be a member of the training department.

Although the duties of a general education committee may vary from company to company, this list covers its usual tasks.

343   How Large Is a General Education Committee and How Does It Operate?

There is no single answer to this question. No committee should be so large as to be unmanageable, yet it should have the broadest possible representation of departments and levels. In one company of 2,000 employees, the General Education Committee consists of seven members: two each from wage and salary, one supervisor from office and one from manufacturing, and one member of the training department. The training department representative acts as secretary and maintains all records, and sends committee members communications dealing with meetings, policies, and activities of the committee. When a committee member resigns, his replacement is selected by the remaining members of the committee. The permanent chairman and secretary are elected annually by committee members. No officer may succeed himself in the same office. All decisions are determined by majority vote.

344 Where Do You Obtain Instructors for a General Education Program?

Instructors for a general education program are usually drawn from within the plant or from the community. When subjects like blueprint reading, mechanical drawing, fundamentals of electricity, practical law, and secretarial practice are presented, the instructors can usually be found within the plant. When subjects are broad and cultural such as modern civilization, creative writing, design and illustration, personal problems in everyday living, flower arrangement, leather craft, corsage craft, ballroom dancing, gardening, harmonica instruction, etc., the instructor is usually drawn from the public schools or services within the community.

General education programs are no better than the quality of the instruction offered in them. Therefore, select your instructors carefully and help them plan their courses to meet the needs of your employees. The most highly qualified instructors frequently come from the high schools, vocational schools, business schools, colleges and university extension divisions in your community.

345 I Have Very Limited Education in the Humanities— Literature, Science, History and the Arts. What Can I Do to Improve Myself in These Areas?

There are a number of specific activities which will give you an appreciation and some understanding of the humanities. Here are some:

1. Join a book club and read their selections.
2. Attend plays and good movies.
3. Travel to historic spots, national parks, shrines, and monuments.
4. Join an evening discussion group.
5. Engage in community activities—welfare, political, social.
6. Listen to selected radio and television programs.
7. Take courses in the humanities in nearby colleges.

8. Participate in church affairs.
9. Endeavor to paint, play a musical instrument, or join a dramatic or choral society.
10. Visit museums, art centers, and libraries.
11. Read thoroughly two periodicals like *Readers Digest, Time, Life, or Harpers.*
12. Read the classics or join a "Great Books" course.
13. Join a community concert association.
14. Purchase a phonograph and some good music.
15. Regularly read a good newspaper like *The New York Times, The New York Herald Tribune,* or *The Christian Science Monitor.*

It is not suggested that you engage in all of these activities. Rather, pick a few and concentrate your attention on them.

Your motivation in this matter is important, too. If you can become so interested in some area of general education that it becomes a vital satisfying part of your life, then your education lives and breathes and stimulates itself. For example, concern over one's community may lead to studies of modern cities, architecture, sanitation, and even of civilization itself. From this it is a short step to philosophy and ethics—to the purposes of life itself.

346   How Do you Publicize General Education Courses?

Use bulletin board postings, articles in the company paper, announcements over the public address system, departmental meetings, individual contacts, direct mailings, and course catalogs to make known the opportunities. We have found that bulletin-board postings are the most convenient and one of the most effective devices to keep employees informed on general education courses. A sample bulletin-board posting follows:

NEW GENERAL EDUCATION COURSES

Listed below is the schedule of the four new courses offered under the General Education Program, which will begin the week of March 16. If you are interested in taking any of these courses, you can obtain a Registration Blank from your Committee Representative, or send your name and department name to the Training Department.

Beginner's Contract   Monday nights, beginning March 16 for 6 weeks, from
    Bridge   7:00 to 9:00 p.m. The instructor will be Mr. George Graham of Personal Products Corporation.

Umpire's Class　　Tuesday nights, beginning March 17. Tom Curran, Recreation Manager, will conduct the six sessions.

Interior Decorating　Wednesday nights, beginning March 18. There will be no class offered on April 8. The instructors for the six sessions will be Miss Mildred Burdett and Mr. Theodore Weiss.

Ballroom Dancing　　Thursday nights, beginning March 19. The six sessions will again be conducted by Miss Dee and Mr. Reamer of the Arthur Murray Dance Studios. This class is open only to those employees who registered for the previous class and could not be accommodated.

Additional descriptive material about the classes will be posted in a few days.

All registrations must be in to your Committee Representative, or to the Training Department by Tuesday, March 10.

General Education Committee

After the course is in progress, obtain pictures of participants and prepare human-interest stories in connection with the course for insertion in company publication or for bulletin-board postings.

347　Are General Education Programs Conducted on Company Time?

Courses in general education are usually offered on the employee's own time, and for a nominal fee.

348　What Are Information Racks?

Information racks are usually wooden holders or bins which contain selected readings, usually in pamphlet form, which are purchased by the company and then made available to employees at no cost. Information racks are located in easily accessible spots where employees will have frequent opportunities to choose from the available readings.

349　What Are Information Racks Used For?

Information racks are used to offer employees their choice of reading materials covering a broad range of subjects. The racks are an excellent device for making reading material available which broadens employee interests, stimulates their development and improves employer-employee relations without the employees feeling that the readings are being forced on them.

350   How Are Information Racks Administered?

In most companies the operation of the information rack program is given to the personnel or industrial relations department. The person in charge of the program will usually choose a committee of three or more members of the company to select the material to be used in the information racks. This material can be obtained through commercial firms which prepare and sell materials for use in employee information racks or from a wide variety of other sources.

Chapter 17

ORIENTATION TRAINING

351   **What Is the Difference Between Induction and Orientation?**

For many years these terms were used synonymously, but they are clearly distinguished today. Orientation is the planned and guided adjustment of employees to their company, their departments and their jobs. It includes a series of informal and formal activities which help employees gain a fuller understanding of their company as it relates to them. These may be summarized as follows:

1. The actions of the employment department during the initial screening and selection process
2. The formal orientation class
3. The induction of a new or transferred worker into his department by his supervisor or fellow workers
4. General education classes which acquaint employees of long service with company operations and policies
5. Company handbooks
6. Letters from top executives welcoming new employees
7. The employee magazine
8. Plant tours
9. Bulletin board statements

Although orientation encompasses all the activities that assist employees to adjust to the company, induction comprises the specific activities by which line supervisors help new or transferred employees adjust themselves to conditions as they exist in their departments. It is accomplished by the appropriate line supervisor of the department in which the employees work. It usually begins on the first day an employee reports to work, and may continue for a number of days. It involves a discussion with the supervisor concerning working conditions, rules of the department, computation of pay, location of the locker room, etc., as well as introducing him to fellow workers, taking him on a tour of the department, and assigning him to a job instructor.

352   Who Should Be Oriented?

Every newcomer to an organization—be he one who will assume the lowest-level position or a new top executive—should participate in a planned program of orientation which will assist him to adjust to the organization. No one should be omitted.

353   Why Should a Company Institute a Planned Program of Orientation for New Employees?

There are two major reasons for instituting such a program. First, to reduce costs, which is done in at least two ways:

1. The highest turnover rate in most companies is among those employees with less than three months' service. Conservative estimates indicate that a company spends at least $300 to recruit, hire, and train a new employee. Planned orientation programs reduce turnover and cut down losses from it.
2. Planned orientation helps new employees to overcome feelings of fear, ignorance, or awkwardness which often cause costly damage to equipment and materials, as well as accidents. Learning time—and costs—are also reduced when employees feel secure, confident, and at ease in their new situations.

Second, to improve employee morale, loyalty, and job satisfaction. These contributions of a good induction program are well outlined in a memorandum sent to all supervisors in the ATF Corporation:[1]

Here's What Proper Induction Does for You and for the New Worker.

1. It gives you a chance to explain your position before the worker is misinformed by others, and since first impressions are lasting ones, this is an advantage which should be realized.
2. It reduces waste time on employee's part—he will know what to do and where to go with his problems. He will be more secure, satisfied, less frustrated with unrecognized anxieties. He won't bother other workers with questions so often.
3. It builds up a reserve of morale to a point where the worker has some resistance power to rebuffs or disappointments which he must inevitably meet on his job. It helps keep workers from quitting before they can give the job an honest tryout.

[1] "ATF's Induction Program, A Man Meets His New Job," *Management Record*, March, 1952, p. 92.

4. It reduces ill will, disciplinary action, and dismissals caused where the employee did not know the rules or consequences of violating them. It reduces the "take a chance" attitude. Proper induction will help build job satisfaction which helps counteract the activities of those present, even in the best of industries, who complain, criticize, and destroy good will.

5. People fear the unknown. New workers are timid, sometimes afraid. Oftentimes this fear, which may be subconscious, acts as a block or barrier so that the new worker never realizes his top production level until his fears are removed by slowly accumulated knowledge and understanding of the [unknown] new job. [Proper induction helps remove this barrier at the outset.] Unless assistance is given, this accumulation of knowledge and elimination of fear of the unknown may take many months.

354　　What Are You Trying to Accomplish in Orientation Training for New Employees?

In general, the purpose of orientation training is to reduce a new employee's fears, awkwardness, uneasiness, and ignorance so that he can apply himself wholeheartedly to his job and at the same time develop good attitudes toward it and the company. Workers are most impressionable at the beginning of their employment. The company has an opportunity to develop a firm basis for cooperative understanding with them. Why leave this to fellow employees of the new worker, who may or may not share management's feelings and goals?

Specifically, orientation seeks to give the employee:

1. A knowledge of company and departmental rules and regulations.
2. A knowledge and appreciation of, and a desire to use, company services.
3. A knowledge of what the company is, what it does, and the importance of its product.
4. A knowledge and realization of the place and importance of the individual worker in the company.
5. A sense of being at home, and a friendly attitude toward the boss and fellow workers.
6. A feeling that the worker can expect fair and impartial treatment.
7. Confidence and pride in the company.
8. A feeling of freedom to ask questions and to criticize. Freedom from suppressed antagonisms and hostility toward the company, secured through inviting free expression.

9. An attitude of personal responsibility for job, product, and company.
10. A realization that employee and employer are interdependent.
11. A feeling of responsibility for waste and cost.
12. An appreciation of the necessity for regular attendance at work.
13. Knowledge and practice of safety and health rules.
14. Knowledge and appreciation of pay deductions, insurance, etc.
15. Knowledge of company lines of authority.
16. Knowledge of where to get personal, social, and job needs satisfied, and the feeling of freedom to do this.
17. An understanding of major problems of the company and a realization that everyone is expected to help solve them.
18. A feeling that the head office and the immediate supervisor are O.K.
19. Realization that management respects the personal liberties of each employee.
20. A positive, constructive attitude in all job relations.
21. An early mastery of the job skill involved.
22. Satisfaction with the job and confidence that there is little possibility of unjustified discharge.

355   How Does the Orientation Training for Workers Differ from That for Supervisors?

Orientation instruction is similar in that the need exists in both groups, the over-all purposes are the same, and discussion can be effectively used. The major differences appear in content and in the amount of time devoted to class instruction. The supervisor's job responsibilities require him to be better informed about company policies, practices, regulations, products, organization, history, benefits and philosophy than is the production worker. The supervisor also needs to know company practices as they apply to both the hourly and salaried workers, since he must be able to interpret and apply them to both groups. All this, of course, demands increased instruction time.

356   Is Early Training in Developing an Open Mind a Key to Making a Good Executive?

Open-mindedness is certainly a strong factor in executive success. It enables a leader to analyze alternative solutions in the problems he handles daily. Management involves the power to construct or to elicit from others a variety of solutions, and the skill to select the one that is best in a given set of circumstances. Men with closed minds seldom see beyond their own first impressions or solutions.

Training in open-mindedness is good at all ages and at all levels in society. It is difficult to teach however and is best approached indirectly through case studies, syndicates, and role playing. Lecturing, telling, or scolding will certainly not suffice!

357   How Should Executives Be Oriented?

The orientation of executives should be a well-planned program that will be carried out over a period of time. Because of the level of their responsibilities and the nature of their work, they need to meet more people, know more about the history of the company, be better informed on past and present work procedures of their department, know rules and regulations more fully, be better informed on physical layout and products, and know more about the community than other new employees. Consequently, their orientation program will be both more intense and more comprehensive. As part of their orientation program new executives should:

1. Attend the orientation class.
2. Have a guided tour of the whole plant.
3. Receive a packet of written materials that contains information on the company's history, philosophy, products, practices, and policies, the union contract, company organization charts, the house organ, and the employee handbook. The packet should also contain a map of the city and the plant, a list of civic organizations and other pertinent facts about the city, and an explanation of privileges and benefits that apply to the company's executives.
4. Visit staff meetings held in related departments. Such visits should be scheduled and organized by the superiors of the new executives.
5. Meet other executives.

358   Where Does Orientation Begin?

In some companies it begins with students in high school. A large telephone company, a surgical supply house, and hundreds of other companies hold annual open houses for high-school students and their teachers, at which orientation to business and the world of work begins. Some companies bring students in for after-school, week-end, or vacation work that is primarily designed to interest them in the companies. Other corporations distribute their publications to teachers, school and public libraries, doctors and dentists (for use in their offices), taxi drivers, barber shops, and other spots where the casual reader or visitor may pick them up and read them.

Public relations activities such as these are early steps in orientation. Newspaper and radio advertising, proper reception of job applicants, filling out application forms and holding employment interviews are also preliminary parts of the orientation process. In fact, all the major steps of recruitment involve elements of orientation. Formal orientation proceeds from these beginnings into classroom orientation and then to on-the-job induction.

359   What Knowledge of the Company and the Job Precedes the Orientation Class? Where Does the Employee Get This?

Even before the worker applies for a job, he has some information about the company. Through his friends and neighbors or from a newspaper advertisement, he has obtained some facts and has developed some attitudes—it is a good place to work, working conditions are pleasant, the pay is high, there are many employee benefits, the supervisors are fair, etc. As he applies for a job, the friendliness of the receptionist, the convenience and comfort of the waiting room, the length of the wait before he is interviewed, the attitude of his interviewer, test administrator, and medical examiner, the initial contact with the supervisor, and the helpful guidance of the record clerk all create lasting impressions on a new employee. These impressions constitute first-hand knowledge gained about the company. They are far more real than anything the employee may have been "told" about the company. To him they *are* the company.

The specific knowledge about the company which a new worker receives before the orientation class is determined when the orientation program is planned. Each company should carefully determine the responsibilities to be assumed by the employment department, the orientation instructor, and by supervision. The amount and kind of knowledge to be given before the orientation class will depend on when the orientation class is held, the amount of time involved in the hiring procedure, the level of the job that the applicant is being interviewed for, and upon other variables.

360   How Does a New Employee Get Informed of What the Orientation Procedure of the Company Is? Who Does This?

It is common practice for the employment manager to tell the prospective employee about the orientation program after the decision has been reached to hire him. In some companies, an outline of the procedure is given to him by the employment manager at this time. In at least one company an induction training schedule is mailed to all new people after they have accepted a position. This company feels that all new employees have a natural curiosity about what is going to happen to them in their first few days of employment and that mailing home an induction outline gives them the feeling of "being taken care of." The following is a sample induction training schedule.

ORIENTATION TRAINING SCHEDULE

TRAINING PROGRAM FOR: Miss Jane Jones
POSITION: Filing Clerk, Claims Clerical Department
SUPERVISOR: Miss Mary Brown

This is your Induction Training Schedule. Please bring this with you when reporting for work. Feel free to ask questions at any time about anything you do not fully understand.

FIRST DAY—MORNING

1. *Report to Our Office*
   Keller Building
   4105 Broadway

Take elevator No. 11 to 14th floor. Our Receptionist will be waiting to greet you at 8:00 a.m.

2. *Registration*
   You will complete various employment forms.

3. *Induction Training Schedule and "Our Customs"*
   The Personnel employee will go over this training schedule with you. It tells you what your activities will be during your training period.

   You will also receive your copy of *Our Customs*. This booklet is given to all of our new employees. We hope it will help you become acquainted with your company.

4. *Tour of Office Facilities*
   During this tour the office facilities will be explained.

   REST PERIOD

5. *Read and Discuss "Our Customs"*
   During this period you will start reading your copy of *Our Customs*. The information in this booklet will be thoroughly explained to you. Do not hesitate to ask any questions you might have.

6. *Tour of the Office Department*
   This is a "get acquainted" tour. You will see where the various departments are located in our office.

7. *Meeting the People in Your Office*
   During this time you will talk with your supervisor and meet the people you will be working with.

Lunch Period

FIRST DAY—AFTERNOON

Job Training
During the afternoon you will be in your department. Your supervisor and training will start training you in how—

    a. Your department works with the other departments
    b. Your job relates to other jobs in your department
    c. To do your job

SECOND DAY

Job Training

THIRD DAY

Job Training

After the third day your on-the-job training will continue until you have completely learned your work.

Training never really ends, however. After you have mastered your job you will have opportunities to learn others and improve your possibility for advancement.

Although your training will be as thorough and complete as we can make it, you will still have questions—all new workers do. We want you to ask questions about things you do not understand. Our business requires highly efficient operations. We cannot afford mistakes because workers do not understand their jobs.

During your first few weeks with us you will participate in four sessions where you will learn about our history, organization, and way of doing things. The information given in these sessions will be found in *Our Customs*.

361   If an Orientation Class Is Held, Who Should Teach It?

It should be taught by someone from the personnel or training department who is a good instructor and who is friendly and understanding, has a pleasant personality, and is adaptable. He must make the employee feel at home, encourage his questions and ideas, and show a personal interest in him. Probably in no other industrial training program is the personality of the instructor so important.

Formal orientation is individualized teaching. The instructor must fit his material to the employees' needs and adjust his presentation skillfully to meet them. Routine presentation accomplishes no more than a good employee handbook and fails to utilize personal relationships to build worth-while attitudes.

It has been our experience that women make successful orientation teachers. A secretary, an ex-school teacher, an employment interviewer, or a receptionist may have the necessary personal traits, and with some coaching and guidance can become a successful orientation teacher.

362　Is It Best to Have a New Worker Attend the Orientation Class the First Day of His Employment?

Some formal orientation training should be accomplished during the employee's first day and before he reports to his department. Unless this is done, the training program has no real control over the first impression which the new employee gets of the company. Busy supervisors who have more than one new man reporting for work on a single day can hardly give the individual attention that each new employee needs. After a brief talk, they usually turn him over to an experienced employee for further induction or for on-the-job training. The new employee is then put in the position of learning about the company, department, etc., from a fellow worker who may or may not be sympathetic toward him or the company. It is much better to hold an orientation class on the first day of work and have it taught by someone whose loyalty to management is unquestioned and who is skilled at reducing normal tension involved in undertaking any new job.

363　How Do You Get All New Employees to Attend Orientation Classes?

Whether new employees attend orientation classes will depend on:

1. *The attitude of top management toward the value of such classes.* High executives must approve such classes, or it would not be a part of the orientation program. A written statement explaining why they value the classes highly will help convince the rest of the organization. If possible, this statement should specifically require all new employees to attend such classes.

2. *The attitude of the supervisors.* If supervisors have not been sold on the value of the orientation classes, they will find reasons for not sending employees to them. In supervisor training classes, teach them the value of formal orientation and the need for requiring all new employees to attend. Encourage them to visit classes and ask for their ideas on the content.

3. *The attitude of the new employee.* During the hiring process, tell the new employee about the orientation classes, convince him of their value, and tell him when he will participate in them.

4. *The method of scheduling attendance.* Attendance is hardly a problem when the classes are held before the new employee reports to work. After he has filled out his records and has been placed on the payroll, he can be sent to the orientation class. If this is not practical, the individual who prepares his records (usually a record clerk) may tell him when he is scheduled to attend and give him a written reminder. The orientation instructor and the records clerk should cooperate to see that all new employees are scheduled to attend orientation classes.

364 How Many Orientation Meetings Should There Be for New Employees?

Some companies hold one meeting; others hold several. The most common practice is to hold one meeting. The number of meetings is closely linked to the size of the organization, which in turn determines the amount of information to be presented.

365 How Many Persons Should Make Up the Orientation Class or Group?

For best results, ten or fewer. A small group enables the orientation teacher or leader to give individualized instruction. In some companies, however, so many new employees are hired daily that orientation groups must be larger. Still, every effort should be made to keep the group small enough to permit discussion and participation by all. We have learned in supervisor training that a group of ten to twenty is the most desirable size when you expect the members to participate actively. The same limitations would also be true for orientation training.

366 Why Is Participation Important in the Orientation Training Class?

Participation is especially important in orientation because:

1. New employees need to express any fears and anxieties they may possess; only after doing so can they respond wholeheartedly to their new situation.
2. Teaching must be geared to the needs of trainees. As newcomers, what questions do they want answered? No teacher can

anticipate these questions and unless new employees participate, the information they most desire may not be forthcoming.
3. New employees learn what the company expects of them by
analyzing their own responsibilities. The rules, regulations, and
policies of the company will seem fair and the employees will
be willing to abide by them after they have made this analysis.
4. Feelings of friendliness and personal interest are developed
when new employees express themselves freely in the training
class.

367　Why Are Flyers or Give-Aways Provided in the Orientation Class? What Do They Include?

The use of "give-aways" in orientation classes has two major
purposes. First, they serve as a reference for what was taught and
provide additional information about the company which the employee may acquire on his own time. When they are given out in
the orientation class, the instructor can interest the employee in
reading them by pointing out pertinent passages or reading ex-
cerpts. Second, when taken home by the employee, they help
orient his family to the company. The attitude of an employee's
family toward the company can directly affect the man's action
on the job. The company should capitalize on the natural curiosity
of the new employee and that of his family concerning the company and supply them at this most impressionable time with materials that will encourage good attitudes.

It is common practice to give a new employee some of the following written material about the company:

A company handbook
A map of the company and the department where his job is located
Organization charts
Summary sheet of pertinent facts about the history and products
of the company
Statement of the philosophy of the company
Insurance booklet
Safety manual
Copy of the house organ
The union contract
Suggestion system booklet
Health booklet
A sample of the product
Training policy statement
Bus routes or timetables

If the company handbook is properly prepared and up to date, the need for a number of separate "give-aways" is reduced.

368 Are Plant and Office Tours a Part of Orientation?

Guided by an orientation teacher or a supervisor, new employees often tour areas of the plant or office other than those in which they will work. Such tours, which generally last one to two hours, acquaint new employees with the layout of the plant, the offices, and the flow of work. They come to realize the part their department plays in the operation of the business. A tour of each worker's own department is an integral part of the orientation, and is conducted by the line supervisor.

369 What Should Be Pointed Out on a Plant Tour for a New Employee?

Requirements will vary with the size and type of the company, the employee's job demands, the amount of time devoted to a tour, and the personal needs of each employee. Things commonly touched upon include:

1. The names and locations of the operating departments.
2. Location of the offices of people of whom the employee will hear, or with whom he will deal.
3. Location of parking lots, restricted areas, conference rooms, cafeteria, pay telephones, bus stations, medical department or first aid station, fire alarms, bulletin boards, time clocks, elevators, fire-fighting equipment.
4. Standards of housekeeping, quality and workmanship.
5. Work flow and the processing of products, from the raw material to the finished article.

370 Should an Exhibition and Story of Company Products Be Part of the Orientation Class?

Yes. The products which a company produces or distributes are its real reason for being. Employees should know these products, respect them, and be able to talk intelligently about them. However, if a company has a great many products, individual employees can become familiar only with those on which they work and the most important members of the list as a whole.

An exhibit is an excellent teaching device. It enables employees to see and handle products, read labels, and discuss them. Products too large to be displayed can be illustrated by mounted posters and diagrams or by slides.

Through discussion growing out of actual examination, employees can be led to see the value of advertising, the need for quality, the importance of the customer, their part in the final product, the growth of the business, etc. All this develops pride in the company and understanding of each worker's responsibility.

371   Is a Company or Department Map Usually Given to New Employees Who Are Being Oriented?

No. In small companies a map or plan of the plant is not needed. In larger ones, it may be needed but is seldom given to new employees, either as a separate sheet or in the employee handbook. Many employers provide only drawings which show the location of services (cafeteria, laundry storage, medical department, parking areas, recreation facilities, etc.) used by most employees. There is general agreement that plant tours are more effective than maps, yet it seems that the latter would be useful to new employees in large, complex plants and to supervisory and technical employees whose work requires them to move freely from one part of the plant to another.

372   Are Films Used in Orientation Classes?

Yes. Some companies have developed excellent sound films to acquaint new employees with the community, the company, its services, and its products. These films are usually fifteen to thirty minutes long and are most valuable in companies that hire large numbers of new employees.

The orientation film can be a very helpful supplementary teaching device, but it should not be thought of as *the* orientation device. Although a picture can have considerable appeal and do an excellent teaching job, the discussion developed by even an inexperienced instructor is worth more than any film.

373   How Is the Employee Handbook Related to Orientation?

It is a part of the orientation program. On his first day, the handbook is usually given to the new employee by the employment manager, the line supervisor, or the orientation instructor. The employee is encouraged to read the book, to let his family read it, and to keep it for reference. The handbook generally contains detailed information about the company, employee benefits, safety regulations, rules, products, employment conditions, and so on, all of which must be dealt with in orientation.

374 What Part Does the Union Play in Orientation?

In most companies, the union takes no active part in orientation. Union officials may be consulted at the time the program is organized to learn their ideas about the needs of new employees, but they usually contribute little more. Any company which desires harmonious relations with its union teaches new employees nothing that can be considered anti-union and will utilize the union wherever possible to assist new employees to get off to the right start. If employers seek constructive union participation, however, they may find that orientation provides suitable opportunities.

375 Should Office and Wage Personnel Attend Orientation Class Together?

No. It usually happens that employee benefits, hours of work, and other items are discussed in such a class, and these differ for each group in spite of management's intention to be impartial and fair. The instructor facing a mixed class will have to state the practice for each group and explain why differences exist, and the explanation may not be acceptable. Suppose, for example, that wage employees receive one week's vacation after one year of service and two week's after five years, while salaried employees receive two week's vacation after one year. How can the instructor explain this difference so that wage earners will consider it fair? Almost inevitably, emphasis is switched from the actual benefits to which new employees are entitled to the difference between the benefits received by various groups. Instead of building good attitudes toward the company, therefore, this sort of orientation would develop a feeling of inequality and unfairness. When groups are homogeneous, however, discussion is directed at the benefits, rules, policies, etc., affecting a particular group, and little or no attention is given to differences.

376   **Should the Orientation Class Instructor Follow Up His Classroom Instruction?**

If the orientation instructor has done his job properly, he will have developed a good relationship with the new employee, who is favorably disposed towards him. When this relationship exists, the employee will express feelings about the company, his job, and the treatment he receives—feelings which he is unwilling to express to others. Therefore, it is good practice for the instructor to have a planned follow-up, at least during the new employee's first few weeks on the job.

An informal visit with the employee at his place of work is very effective. There the instructor can discuss the worker's attitude toward his job, answer his questions, and show a general interest in his well-being. Through such contact the instructor may learn of ways to improve company practices and his own teaching and can do much to develop or maintain a favorable impression of the company.

377   **What Is the Sponsor System of Orientation?**

A recent issue of "Personnel Executives' Newsletter"[2] answers this question as follows:

Sponsor System

Unique procedure for easing new employees into job routine with minimum stress was disclosed during recent P.E.N. interview with Benno Bordiga, Director of Manufacturing at Olympic Radio and Television Inc. [New York City]. Sponsor system, initiated at Olympic by Mr. Bordiga, is so successful that new-employee turnover [during first three months] was reduced from virtually 100% to 10% according to estimates. Here's how it works:

Each department has one or two sponsors, chosen from ranks on basis of ability to get along with people. Sponsor meets new arrival in personnel department, accompanies him throughout plant in informal orientation tour on way to assigned department; once there, sponsor introduces him to foreman, shop steward, and fellow employees.

Sponsor becomes new worker's "bosom companion" for remainder of day, possibly longer, during which time he is given help in adjusting to new job and surroundings, familiarized with employee facilities and programs, and made to feel "at home" generally. Fifteen days later new employee is granted friendly, informal interview with top official, encouraged to come to front office for advice whenever he wishes.

[2] Published by Deutsch & Shea, Inc., New York.

Besides nearly eliminating turnover of personnel and surviving critical three-month starting-period, sponsor system also serves as excellent communications medium between various levels at Olympic. For example, an employee survey found that most sponsors feel link with management as result of distinction of wearing badge, other privileges.

378   Should Each New Employee Meet His Department Head and the Plant Manager During His First Days in the Organization? (Neither of These Men Is the New Worker's Immediate Superior.)

Yes, this is good practice, even though the employee may have been interviewed by the department head during the selection process. The department head should meet with the new employee and discuss his job and the company within the first few days the employee is on the job.

Depending on the size of the organization, the new employee should meet the plant manager within the first week or two. In one organization of a thousand employees, the plant manager holds a group meeting for fifteen minutes with all newly hired employees two weeks after they are on the job, and not only talks to them but gives them an opportunity to ask him questions. This approach is not as effective as an individual interview, but it may be more practical for a busy executive. It shows that top management is interested in all employees, brings the new employee and the "head man" together, assists in developing a good relationship between workers and management, personalizes management and the company, and gives the employee a chance to be heard.

Department heads and plant managers, through the simple device of meeting and talking with new employees, can do much to develop the "we" concept in employees and dispel the "they" concept of top management as impersonal, inhuman figures who are more concerned with profits than with the feelings, needs, and aspirations of the workers.

379   When Labor Is Scarce, the Only Available Employees Are Often of Poor Quality, and They Do Not Respond to Progressive Instruction. How Can This Obstacle Be Overcome?

Manufacturers are sometimes forced to work with substandard material and must change their processes and reduce speed and efficiency. The same is true of people. Even poor students can learn, but they require special techniques and long-continued effort. Experience has shown that employees recruited when labor is scarce may require stronger motivation, more individualized instruction, and longer learning periods than do those hired in periods of plenty. Orientation training is a must for such inferior employees, since individualized, well-executed orientation helps motivate them and prepare them to become acceptable workers. If possible, jobs should be simplified or deskilled so that each inexperienced worker learns only a portion of the task. This reduces demands upon his learning ability in keeping with his limitations. Orientation leaders and job instructors must be selected carefully and trained to meet the needs of substandard workers.

380   How Would You Propose to Improve the Quality of Employees Coming into Industry from High Schools? We Find the Present Quality Low. Moreover, Everybody Seems to Want a Good Living Without Doing Good Work.

Many people disagree with this low estimate of today's youth. In one plastics factory where youth were held in low esteem by many of the supervisors, one of the authors interviewed factory and office supervisors to learn just what was lacking in the preparation or in the attitudes of high school graduates hired into the business. Uniformly, the performance of recent graduates was criticized for a variety of reasons until the interviewer met the office manager and treasurer of the company. He had established in his department a six month's orientation-to-industry program which was given to all young employees. This man and his associates reported that the program was highly valuable, that his turnover of high school graduates was nil, and that records for production and cooperation were highly commendable. It may well be that young people coming fresh from the schools into business and industry need more formal orientation than they are getting, both to the responsibilities of work and to the requirements of the job. Children once learned at home what it meant to work, but that is no longer true. Industry may have to do the teaching once done by circumstances and by parents.

Industry also can help students in schools to learn about business. Many firms now invite teachers as individuals or groups to spend a day or two, or even a summer vacation, observing or working in business. Many businessmen take part in vocational guidance courses and in other classroom activities.

381   Do Employees of Long Service Need to Attend a Class in Orientation?

Yes. Like new employees, they are more than likely to need information about policies, procedures, employee benefits, and services that directly affect them. They have forgotten some of these during the years and, since the organization is dynamic, it is sure to have made many changes which old-timers do not know of or perhaps do not understand. One company presented an orientation program for employees with three or more years of service. The participants were asked to answer about twenty true and false and completion questions during the first meeting. These questions dealt with employee benefits, company products, rules and regulations, and employee services. The majority of the employees attending the training answered less than half the questions correctly. Try this device in your company to find out whether experienced employees know what they should, or are in need of training.

Other facts which show that long-service employees need orientation classes include the following:

1. Some of them began work before orientation training was instituted, and so have never had a chance to learn about the company in a systematic course in which all the facts relating to their conditions of employment are presented for discussion and analysis.

2. If long-service employees have not participated in orientation classes, they resent the amount of information possessed by new employees. Feeling that they should have the same chance to learn that newcomers enjoy, veterans may become envious, resistant, and discontented.

3. Misconceptions and misinterpretations of rules, procedures and policies, as well as negative feelings toward management or the company are often revealed when employees take part in discussion during orientation classes. A frank discussion relieves the employee's feelings and gives the leader a chance either to change the employee's interpretation or to bring about a correction of policies or action when management is in error.

4. Observations and interviews during and after orientation classes show that veteran employees are interested in learning about their company, and are enthusiastic and pleased with the training.

382 How Do You Inform Line Supervisors of What Is Taught in the Orientation Class?

1. Appoint supervisors to serve on the training committee that establishes the orientation program.

2. Prepare and distribute a digest of the content of the orientation course to all supervisors.

3. In basic supervisor training classes, discuss the orientation responsibilities of the company, the conduct of orientation, and the relationships between each step of orientation.

4. Invite supervisors to visit orientation classes in order to observe and help teach new employees.

Any orientation program loses its effectiveness if it appears disjointed and unplanned to the new employee. When those responsible for orientation do not coordinate their activities, important parts can be overlooked or are assumed to have been handled by someone who is not responsible for them. As a result, the course is incomplete.

383 How Is a Check List Used in an Orientation Program? Please Give an Example of a Check List.

Check lists outline the steps to be taken by the employment manager, the orientation instructor and the line supervisor. The lists serve as reminders of what should be done in each part or stage of orientation. They are also used as controls to make sure that all pertinent facts of orientation are covered.

The following is an example of a check list prepared for line supervisors:

ORIENTATION—SUPERVISORY
(Check List)

EMPLOYEE:......................... DATE:.............................
DEPARTMENT:..................... SUPERVISOR:.......................

First Day (or week)

____ 1. Personal welcome
____ 2. Supervisor's name and position
____ 3. Departmental organization
____ 4. Employee's name (actual)
____ 5. Name (wishes to be called by)
____ 6. Your interest in his work and welfare
____ 7. Housekeeping
____ 8. Personal cleanliness and dress habits

____ 9. Uniform (women)
____10. Dressing and rest rooms
____11. Safety rules (specific hazards)
____12. Fire regulations
____13. First aid facilities
____14. Plant rules
____15. Absenteeism
____16. Tardiness
____17. Smoking privileges
____18. Parking facilities and rules

___19. Snack wagon and schedule
___20. Bulletin boards
___21. Shifts (starting time and ending time)
___22. Weekly work schedule
___23. Pay week
___24. Job product and relationship
___25. Pay day

Second Week
___1. Any questions (general)
___2. Careful handling of material (cost)
___3. Any questions on:
   a. Company policy
   b. Seniority
   c. Moving from shift to shift
___4. Importance of his job in regard to:
   a. Production
   b. Quality
   c. Effect on other employees
   d. Total process

Third Week
___1. Suggestion system

___26. Identification button
___27. Method of pay
___28. Production expectation
___29. Importance of job
___30. Training program
___31. Introduction to instructor or operator

___2. Location of Suggestion Box
___3. Any questions on:
   a. Group insurance
   b. Workmen's compensation law
   c. Vacation policy
   d. Holiday policy
___4. Avoid excessive waste
___5. Reduction of seconds
___6. Any questions on training
___7. Any further questions (general)

When placed on incentive
___1. Essentials of point system
___2. Pay calculation in detail
___3. Posting sheet
___4. Any questions on pay

384   Are Employees Paid While They Attend Orientation Classes?

The accepted practice is to pay employees while they attend such classes. This is understandable and reasonable. The company is going to profit from orientation through reduced turnover, shorter learning time, improved morale, increased understanding, and by reduction of errors and waste during the early days of employment. To obtain these dividends, the company is willing to invest a small amount of the employees' time in orientation classes.

385   I Have No Training Department to Rely On. How Can I Get Supervisors to Orient Their Workers?

Try to relieve your supervisors of some of this responsibility. Isn't there someone in the employment office—a secretary or clerk —who can be trained to lead an orientation class? Your supervisors are responsible for inducting new men into their departments and training them to do their work. If you can relieve the supervisors of some parts of orientation they may be willing to do an effective job of induction and on-the-job training.

Convince supervisors that orientation is important. In your staff meetings discuss why they should induct their new workers. Review your turnover. Is there high turnover of employees who have been on the payroll only a month or two? These findings may help you to sell supervisors on the importance of giving proper orientation.

Help supervisors outline a program of orientation. Define their responsibility. Spell out exactly what facts are to be covered and suggest ways of putting them across. Help them develop mock-ups or displays that can be used in orientation.

In general show an active interest in orientation training and make sure that all parts which have been agreed upon are included. Use the same techniques to get supervisors to do proper orientation that you use to get them to carry out other job responsibilities.

386   Should a Company Prepare Its Own Orientation Sound Film?

Yes. Commercial production of orientation films is expensive, since each must be made to order. When a company prepares its own, the cost is relatively small. There is usually someone who has photography as his hobby and he can do an adequate job of picture taking. Someone from the advertising or sales department or the editor of the company magazine writes the narration. Shooting the pictures and dubbing-in the voice is accomplished quickly, but planning the sequence and preparing the narration take longer. A professional film maker would dub the voice in for a reasonable fee. The over-all cost, exclusive of time, should be less than $500.

387   What Is the Recommended Procedure for Induction by the Immediate Supervisor?

The immediate supervisor of a new worker should:

1. Give him a personal welcome— Let the new employee know your name and position—be sure you know his name, and the name by which he likes to be called.

2. Explain department organization—let him know that you are the one most interested in his welfare—that you will do everything possible to make his employment pleasant and profitable.

3. Show him around the department. Explain the operation of the department. Discuss his responsibility for cleanliness and the safety and welfare of fellow employees. Give him information on departmental rules—fire safety—job hazards. Take him out on the job—point out hazards of machinery and layout. Point out fire exits. Show bulletin boards—tell him to watch posting for information and guidance.

4. Tell him about lunch periods. Use of cafeteria—schedule—kinds of food sold. Parking facilities. Dressing rooms—when open and closed, and similar provisions for employees.

5. Tell him how absenteeism and tardiness affect production and even another employee's pay. Whom to notify if unable to report for work. Explain shift starting and ending time—weekly work schedule.

6. Explain the smoking privileges.

7. Give job information—what you will consider satisfactory on-the-job performance. Check starting pay. Explain pay calculation.

8. Explain policy on uniforms.

9. Explain training program as it applies to new employee—explain normal learning time.

10. Introduce new employee to employees with whom he will work and to job instructor. Explain position of job instructor.

Chapter 18

TRAINING FOR BREADTH AND CHANGE

388   Do Development Programs Really Change the "Old Hands?"

Yes, but changing the thinking habits and skills of older people is more difficult than with younger employees. Some of the difference between the learning speed of young and old people is due to motivation. The younger person has a greater motive to improve. His future is ahead of him; his ambition generally is stronger than it will be later on in life.

389   How Should We Motivate Development for Older People?

To motivate older employees, appeal, tactfully and not too directly, to their pride in long years of service with the company and their desire to see the business of their choice keep up with competition in knowing and using new methods. Relate the teaching to their previous experience. Associations should come easier for them, having a richer and more varied background to draw upon. Then go on to point out how they can use the new skills and ideas. Young people learn many things in preparation for their futures. Their hopes are high; they will learn things that they *may* be able to use later on. Older people are practical minded. If they don't see a reasonably immediate use for what is being taught, they are reluctant to learn. Be sure to give the older employee more opportunity to suggest what he wishes to learn and how he desires to accomplish it. The youth, fresh from school expects to be told what his courses and assignments are to be.

It is well to consider the fear and anxiety with which older people, many with little formal education, return to school. Plan to arrange social conditions and the physical set-up so as to put the old hands at ease as quickly as possible. Arrange the experiences which you have chosen to produce the learning in a gradual progression from easy to difficult. This helps the trainee to experience the success in his early attempts which carries him on to greater efforts and more difficult achievements.

Lastly, do not overlook the fact that it helps older people to adjust to new ideas if they are asked to serve as teachers for things they know well. It builds their confidence by reassuring them that part of their know-how is useful. Thus fortified, they find it easier to consider some of the new things that training classes will introduce.

390   How Can We Get Presidents and Vice Presidents to Be Willing to Learn and Try New Things?

There is a reluctance to change in all of us, and as we grow older, this reluctance becomes stronger. However, we live in a dynamic society and change is inevitable. Top executives must be encouraged to try new and better things and to prepare themselves to meet the challenges of a competitive society in which business conditions and practices change from day to day. Here are some of the ways they can be encouraged to keep up:

1. De-emphasize the novelty of new prospects or new policies—disguise them in old clothes, so to speak.
2. Give executives assignments on committees and task forces that will put them in contact with new ideas.
3. Teach them the inevitability of change by sending them selective readings on the subject, by bringing in outside lecturers to discuss it, or by introducing discussion of change in general leadership conferences or other meetings they attend.
4. Where the workshop or syndicate methods are used in formal training, try to see that conservative executives elect projects that will draw them into new situations.
5. Get the executive's superior to make job assignments that will result in contacts with new ideas.
6. See that those who do new things, and are adaptable, growing, and open-minded, are rewarded. This encourages others to follow their example.
7. Encourage executives to visit other plants, or attend conferences and conventions where they can see and discuss new ideas.
8. Prepare future executives, through counseling, to expect change and to welcome it.
9. Encourage the use of executive audits which will be useful in revealing to the executive his fear of new things or his lack of knowledge about modern-day business conditions.

10. Make sure that the director of development has a program for introducing presidents and vice presidents to new things. Perhaps their reluctance to change comes from not knowing what it is they might change to and its advantage over their own ways.

We must be certain to recognize fully the services and contributions of older employees. Not all their old ideas are obsolete, and those that are may have served well in their day. We must also recognize the need for stability. This grows from holding a stable job long enough to understand and be at home in it. Stability comes from understanding of one's tasks, one's superiors and one's own place in a firm, steady net of job relationships.

391   Many Technical Men (Engineers, Etc.) Are in Executive Jobs. Their Interests Are Often Purely Technical. How Can They Best Be Stimulated to Take an Interest in Administration and Leadership?

Periodic, formal appraisal followed by a discussion[1] of the man's strengths and weaknesses and his promotional possibilities is an excellent device to make him conscious of his limitations and to get him thinking about how to remove them. During the discussion that follows evaluation, specific courses of action for the man to follow are outlined.

Another way to broaden specialists into administrators is to send them to a course in Advanced Management. Still another device is to bring the specialists' attention to articles written by top executives on the need to prepare themselves in other fields. A quotation used frequently in Johnson & Johnson to encourage specialists to see the need for leadership skill comes from Robert Wood Johnson, Chairman of the Board, Johnson & Johnson.[2]

It is important to note that for many years we have chosen our management from men who have been educated as technicians and specialists. Unfortunately the graduates of our great engineering schools and the products of our American universities were not equally well educated in the great science of human leadership. Recently it has become apparent that the greatest technical skill is worth little unless men and women can be persuaded to carry out the decisions essential to making that skill effective. We are now discovering that a scientific and technological understanding of a

---

[1] Earl G. Planty and Carlos A. Efferson, "Counseling Executives After Merit Rating or Evaluation," *Personnel*, March, 1951.

[2] Robert Wood Johnson, *But, General Johnson*, Princeton: Princeton University Press, 1944.

subject does not of itself develop or produce ability to lead large groups of people into enthusiastic day-in and day-out response. This means that we must have new management—management not only skilled in the techniques but equally well grounded in the field of human leadership.

Frequent reading of this quotation in J & J meetings and conferences, and printing it on small cards and distributing it, seems to get understanding among technicians and a willingness to learn about leadership and administration.

392   How Can We Help People Sell Ideas to Their Superiors?

This is a matter of upward communications. Some executives complain that their subordinates propose new ventures involving expenditures of hundreds of thousands of dollars and support their recommendations with bare, orally presented evidence or brief written reports. In such cases, development conferences devoted to selling ideas to the boss will help. Start with a review or clear statement of the problem, plus a presentation of a few clear-cut examples. Continue with an analysis of the difference between selling one's boss and selling one's subordinates. Then there will be some "Do's," "Don't's," and cautions. The meetings will include some role playing in which a subordinate tries to get his boss to accept a new idea. A good case-study reference[3] for such a course points out that:

1. The technological changes the authors studied involved the making of new personal relationships among the people involved.
2. Objection and resistance grew up around these changes in personal relationships more than they did around the mechanical or physical changes.
3. Until relationships were understood, accepted, and functioning well, technical progress was seriously retarded.
4. Whether or not the change was accepted depended in large measure upon the supervisor's skill in understanding different viewpoints and in building satisfying new relationships.

The authors do not generalize about methods for introducing change. The reader, however, might conclude that his boss may resist some changes more from fear that personal relations will be disturbed than from disinterest or lack of confidence in technical or mechanical changes that are advised.

[3] Harriet O. Ronken and Paul R. Lawrence, *Administering Changes*: Case Study of Human Relations in a Factory. (Boston: Harvard Graduate School of Business Administration, Division of Research, 1952).

Chapter 19

SKILL TRAINING

---

393   To Whom Does On-the-Job Training Apply?

The majority of the working force in this country is made up of workers who perform jobs which are limited to a few operations and which do not require extensive technical knowledge or a variety of skills. Examples of such jobs are salesclerk, cashier, and records clerk. Workers can be trained best in these and similar positions by a program of on-the-job training.

394   Is On-the-Job Training Really Needed?

Although considerable attention is given to the training of employees in the skilled trades, the great majority of workers in commercial and industrial enterprises who perform semiskilled operations receive little or no planned, organized training. These "unskilled" workers usually are left to their own resources or to the gracious or reluctant attention of fellow employees to learn their jobs. However, each worker in an organization has an influence on the cost of doing business. Without proper training, his full value is not realized or, worse still, if he does the job incorrectly he causes waste and costly errors. Replacing him with another employee is no solution since the new worker is no better fitted to learn the job under these same conditions than was the other worker.

Properly trained workers reach peak efficiency quickly. As a result, they obtain greater satisfaction from their jobs; accidents, turnover and costs are reduced; and damage to equipment and products is decreased. On-the-job training offers management a program for utilizing its human resources to the fullest, thereby increasing the profit potential of the organization.

395   How Does One Know When an Organized On-the-Job Training Program Is Needed for New Workers?

On-the-job training is a continuous program that applies to all new workers. It is not a program that is turned on and off as emergencies arise. When the labor market is tight or when an organization has to expand rapidly the value of an organized on-the-job training program is readily recognized. However, there are many evidences of wasted time and increased costs that could easily be eliminated through proper job training. The following are illustrative:

1. A high rate of turnover among short-service employees.
2. Excessive waste or spoilage after a new worker has completed his learning period. Sometimes the same condition is observed with experienced workers when the job has been slightly changed, or when they have been transferred to a different job.
3. Excessive accidents and a poor safety record, especially among newly hired or transferred workers.
4. Close supervision required of workers.
5. Supervisors doing the work of workers.
6. Lack of experienced workers to assume positions of more responsibility.
7. High labor costs.

When these are analyzed and causes ascertained, inadequate on-the-job training is most frequently found to be the major cause.

396   Can You Give Me a Specific Illustration of How to Determine the Need for, and How to Establish, a Skill Training Program?

This is well illustrated in Johnson & Johnson's Chicago factory, where a program for fork lift truck drivers was recently established. Their Training Director reports as follows:

Our Fork Lift Truck Driver Program was established to meet a need which the drivers themselves actually felt. Often, their competence had been a target for criticism from pedestrians who felt that, in many cases, the trucks were not being operated safely. To combat this, the drivers, after consulting with their foremen, appointed a committee, which drew up a set of rules to govern the operation of the lifts. The Safety, Shipping, and Training Departments, working with this committee, drew up the training program for new drivers as we now have it. This program is the result of a particular group of employees recognizing the need for training and, working with management, establishing the program.

Always working with the regular drivers, we gradually set our physical and skill requirements for drivers, determined the teaching material to be covered, designed our obstacle course to simulate actual driving conditions, and determined how we would evaluate the progress of trainees. When the entire course was prepared, the regular drivers agreed to act as a pilot group to help us evaluate the program. It was emphasized to the drivers that this help was needed. In order to promote their interest, we had a contest on the obstacle course for the regular drivers, with prizes awarded for the best scores. This served to eliminate any feelings of insecurity that may have been present and stimulated wholehearted cooperation and participation.

The program is now functioning actively and we feel that it has accomplished a great deal in improving the performance of our drivers, both old and new.

397   What Are the Steps in Establishing a Job Training Program?

The following is a detailed account of the steps by which one company established an on-the-job training program.[1]

1. *Estimate of Personnel Needs.* First, it was necessary to estimate the needs for new personnel and, therefore, for job training, for the next year or two. Those who have seriously tried to make a fairly scientific estimate of such needs know that this is a difficult, yet an essential task. No company can afford the idle machines or excessive labor costs that result from inadequate estimates of personnel changes and additions.

The estimate of personnel needs for any given department was made cooperatively by the personnel director, the department foreman, the head production man in the plant. Even the big boss himself—the general manager —had a voice in the final decision.

2. *Setting Up the Organization for Training.* After personnel needs were estimated, we had the problem of setting up a new organization or revising an old one to assure the efficient training of new people in ample time for service. A large proportion of our supervisors had had JIT (Job Instruction Training) during the war; certain people had been used as instructors more often than others; a few even had job breakdowns to follow in their teaching. In spite of all this, we decided to start from scratch and completely reorganize the entire training procedure. We then had to answer these questions: (a) Who would be instructors, operators, or foremen? (b) To whom should operator-instructors be responsible—the foreman, or the one man in the plant who will be appointed JIT instructor and head of the on-the-job training program? (c) If this staff man who coordinates the training activity within the mill has anything to do with trainees on the floor, where will his respon-

[1] Adapted from a speech by Carlos A. Efferson, Staff Consultant, Kaiser Aluminum and Chemical Corp., Oakland, Calif., before the Midwinter Personnel Conference of the American Management Association, Chicago, February 26-28, 1951.

sibility start and stop, as compared with the instructor's authority and responsibility for the learner? (d) Who shall instruct the foremen and the instructors in the art of on-the-job teaching? (e) How would we prepare this coordinator of training to carry out his new duties?

We decided to use experienced operators, not foremen, as on-the-job instructors, since the typical foreman is so busy acting as supervisor that he does not have time to teach. This meant that we had to select with great care a few outstanding operators who would be trained as instructors or trainers.

We also decided that each operator-trainer would be completely responsible to the line foreman of his department. Experience has repeatedly shown that this is the only way to operate an on-the-job training program successfully over a long period. In other words, the foreman is boss of both learner and operator-trainer, with no dilution or division of authority.

We also had to define the duties and authority of the staff man in charge of the job-training program. We decided he would:

a. Train foremen in how to instruct.
b. Train operator-instructors in how to instruct.
c. Assist them in job breakdowns and methods of instruction.
d. Keep progress charts on each learner, using information secured from the foreman or the operator-instructor, if this job was delegated to the latter by his foreman.
e. Call periodic meetings of responsible officials in various departments in order to get understanding and agreement as to the progress of present learners, and especially to see if more learners should be hired. In other words, the staff man should stimulate his associates to continue their educated guesses as to the number of people who should be in training.
f. The head of job training should be responsible to the plant personnel director.
g. The plant head of job training would have no authority over the learner at the machine, the operator-instructor teaching the learner at the machine, or the foreman. He would merely carry out to the best of his ability his work of educating, advising, keeping control and progress sheets, and preparing the over-all picture of training in the entire plant for responsible officials. If he encountered severe opposition or action contrary to the general plan, it was not his responsibility to tell the operator-instructor or the learner what to do. Instead, he should first try to straighten matters out on a friendly and nonauthoritative basis; that is, on the basis of service. If this effort proved unsuccessful, he should take the problem to the plant personnel director. The latter would take it to the boss of the foreman, who would work directly with the foreman in getting agreement as to what should be done.

It has been our experience, time and again, that authority cannot be united with the staff function--and the man in charge of on-the-job training must be a staff man serving several departments. This means, of course, that on-the-job training must be thoroughly understood, endorsed, and supported by the top men of the plant. They provide the authority needed to deal with problems.

3. *Deciding How Each Job Ought to Be Done.* The next step was to decide how the jobs ought to be done, so that instructors can properly teach them. I do not imagine that we are alone in finding out through experience that, even in long-established plants and processes, and certainly in newer and expanding plants, there can be great disagreement about very important phases of almost any job, and how it ought to be done. Situations frequently arise in which foreman, operators, and technical experts hold conflicting opinions, which often become charged with emotion. The learner who is dropped into such a conflict is bound to be confused, embarrassed, and even alarmed, and the trainer is in an even more difficult position. He can please only one party in the argument, and in doing so will offend all the others.

This problem can be serious, yet the remedy is relatively simple. Someone —preferably the superior of the foreman—must bring the conflicting parties together, let each one state his case, and lead them to agree upon one way in which the job can be done well without trying to establish that method as *final* or *best*. The job then may be taught in accordance with this decision, though with freedom for established workers to continue with other methods so long as they prove successful.

These concessions save individual pride, and they allow realistically for operators who will go quite contrary to the generally accepted method and still do superior work. Avoidance of finality also permits the group to work out details that are not clear even when the general method is agreed upon. Details also may be allowed to vary, especially if that is the price of securing general agreement.

4. *Teaching Instructors How to Instruct.* First we gave a course for all foremen in the plant, teaching them how to instruct operators. The course was—and still is—substantially the JIT course. All foremen take it even though they will not actually instruct, since they must know its content in order to supervise operator-instructors and learners. Next, we gave the same course to selected operator-instructors. They and the foremen then agreed upon a teaching outline for use in training learners on each job.

In a couple of our plants where operators on a few jobs were needed quickly, we departed from this practice and trained only foremen and operator-instructors concerned with these critical jobs.

5. *Putting the Trained Organization into Action.* Especially during the last war, many American industries failed in their job-training programs because they did not give primary attention to the simple and very obvious step of supplying administration for the job-training program. They thought all they had to do was to teach people how to instruct then let them go ahead on their own.

Putting a serious job-training program into complete and effective action on the floor is an administrative task that must be initiated and followed through by no less a person than the head of the production function in the plant. He must make sure that the persons selected as instructors are actually doing the teaching, and must see to it that the proper breakdowns have been made and are being followed. Under him, the training supervisor must carefully observe the newly appointed instructors to detect those who are unfitted for the work or reveal inadequate training. The production superintendent also must go down the line with his foremen to see how they are coming along with their part of the program.

Just giving a course in how to teach is of practically no value, if we don't apply scientific administration to the job of putting over the training program. We cannot leave training to chance any more than we can leave quality or cost to chance.

6. *Controls and Follow-Up.* Control measures which can be used in the follow-up stage of job-instruction training include:

a. A learner progress sheet. This takes the form of graphs of both quality and production, showing the degree to which the trainee has mastered his job at the end of each week. This sheet also should bear a line representing the standard or average learning time, permitting a quick comparison to determine whether the learner's progress is good, average, or poor.

b. Separate weekly or biweekly departmental meetings for the purpose of evaluating the progress of the learners and also to revise estimates as to the number of new operators that should be hired and trained. This meeting should be attended by the operator-instructors, the co-ordinator of job training, and the foreman.

c. We have found one device to be very helpful in reviewing the training situation in a given department. It is simply a board on which every regular operator and trainee is represented by an individual card, which is either pasted or tacked on to the board. For your regular operators you can place such information as parts of the total job which the operator is qualified to handle, draft status, age, and other such information. At the bottom of the board, on the cards representing the individual learners, appears such information as date of hiring and the date when learning should be completed.

Our experience has been that some kind of visual presentation is most advisable. It hastens decisions and conclusions that would otherwise be talked about for hours before all persons concerned got a picture of the situation.

d. Even when good operator-instructors are experienced and excellent, and where the foremen do their part fully, the staff coordinator of training should help the operator-instructors to keep their job breakdowns up to date, and should continue to emphasize in one way or another the importance of the human element in supervision of the learner.

398   What Is Meant by a Learning Period in On-the-Job Training? How Do You Determine the Length of a Learning Period?

A learning period is the average length of time it will take a worker to come up to minimum standards of performance for a specific job. No scientific measuring tools can be used to establish this period; it generally is set by the supervisor departmental after consultation with experienced employees and staff specialists in training. If the plant is unionized, the union representative in the department and the supervisor will establish the learning period jointly.

Although learning periods are established subjectively, organized on-the-job training provides records of employee progress which are an adequate basis for decision.

399   What Preparation Should an On-the-Job Instructor Make Before Teaching?

An on-the-job instructor should make the same preparation that any teacher makes before teaching. He must plan what is to be taught and how to teach it, must assemble instructional materials, and must then organize them logically or psychologically to make sure that the teaching area is properly arranged.

In planning what to teach, he uses the job breakdown, which tells how the job is to be done. He also decides how he is going to put the worker at ease and arouse his interest.

The on-the-job instructor has been taught to use the four-step method to teach the job. He plans what he will say and do to carry out each step in teaching. He also may have to practice the job himself in order to demonstrate it properly. He also decides what part of the job he will teach first. What is the best order of presentation?

He obtains all the necessary teaching materials (instruments, tools, raw materials, charts, diagrams, etc.) and checks to see that they are of proper quality or in good working order and readily accessible for use in teaching.

He arranges his teaching workplace so his materials are placed conveniently and the learner is in the proper position to observe him when he demonstrates the job.

These are the usual things he does when he prepares to teach. However, one of the most important activities of preparation is to try a "dry run" of teaching an employee. He can do this in the privacy of his own home, using his wife as the learner, or at the shop or office, using the actual job and following his teaching plan with a fellow employee. Learning by doing will give him confidence and an opportunity to check on his teaching plan before using it with a new employee.

400   What Teaching Procedure Should Be Used by an On-the-Job Training Instructor When He Teaches a Worker?

During World War II, millions of job instructors were trained to use the four-step procedure of teaching known as JIT (Job Instructor Training). This procedure is now universally accepted as the best way to teach a worker how to do a job. A description of this procedure follows:

1. *Prepare the Worker.* Since learning takes place best and most quickly when the worker is not tense and frightened because of his new job and the new surroundings, the instructor should make every effort to put the learner at ease.

The instructor should endeavor to interest the learner in the job by showing its importance in relation to the finished product, the advantages of the job to the employee, the possibilities for self-improvement, etc.

The instructor should discover, by observation and questioning, how much the new employee already knows about his job. Without this information, the instructor will not be able to adapt his teaching to the needs of the individual learner.

2. *Present the Operation.* It is essential that the instructor adhere closely to the recommended procedure in this step.

Working from an operations sheet and clearly developing one step at a time, the instructor should both tell and show the new employee how to do the job, stressing key points, knacks, quality standards, and safety precautions. This step should be repeated as often as the complexity of the operation requires. Next, the instructor should perform the job while the learner tells him what to do in each step. By this means the instructor discovers any points on which the learner is weak or confused, and can take care of them at once.

3. *Have the Worker Perform.* When the instructor is sure that the learner has mastered the steps and key points, he should have the learner perform the job, stopping him only when a mistake is made. Finally, the instructor should have the learner perform

the job, explaining what he is doing and why. This step should be repeated until the instructor is sure that the new employee has mastered the details of the job.

4. *Follow Up the Instruction.* After this initial training, the instructor should make himself available to the learner at any time that questions arise, and should insist that the learner come to him and no one else for help. In addition, the instructor should check with the learner at regular intervals (every hour or two during the first week, but with decreasing frequency thereafter) until the learner is able to do the job effectively alone.

A major purpose of the follow-up is to maintain standard procedures. It is assumed that one satisfactory method has been adopted for each job. It is this method that has been described in the operations sheet and has been taught to the new employee. Instructors should insist that the new employee follow this method without deviation until such time as a change may be approved by the supervisor and has been put into writing to replace the original operations sheet. This rigid adherence to standard procedure is absolutely essential to the success of the training program.

401   What Is a Job Breakdown and How Do You Make One?

A job breakdown is a detailed step-by-step statement of the right way to do a job. It is a tool for the instructor's use, helping him to prepare for his teaching, to teach the proper method of doing the job uniformly, and to teach in a well organized manner.

It is relatively easy to prepare a job breakdown for teaching purposes. The following procedure is effective:

1. Observe or perform the job carefully and completely. Write down the major steps as they take place. Each of these steps must be a logical segment of the job or operation and one that advances the work.
2. Observe or perform the individual steps again, looking for and writing down each motion, knack, technique, and safety precaution necessary in each step. These items should also be kept in logical sequence.
3. When this statement is completed, test it by either doing the job or observing someone who is following the procedure given in the breakdown.

The following is a sample job breakdown.

JOB BREAKDOWN

JOB   Labeling Machine Operator   OPERATION   Operating Labeling Machine

STEPS	*KEY POINTS*
(Operations necessary to complete job)	(Knacks, hazards, inspections, special information)

Operation

1. Start operation of Labeling Machine by pressing "On" button of Labeler Control Switch #1 (see diagram).*

  1. a. Place first bottles in machine star wheel after backlog is sufficient.
    b. Inspect first dozen bottles for faults in labeling, such as:
      (1) Incorrect type of labels
      (2) Off-center labels
      (3) Excessive glue around labels
    c. If any of these faults appears, stop machine by pushing red mushroom-shaped button to OFF position. Call Line Specialist.
    d. If bottles come through without labels, remove from conveyor and place in backlog on inner side of conveyor.

2. Turn job selector switch of Operator's Blower Control to "Hand" position.

  2. Hand position is used for supplying backlog to Filler. When operating on Hand Position, Blower operates independently of filler.

3. Press "On" button of Operator's Blower Control to put Blower into operation.

4. Turn job selector switch of Operator's Blower Control to "Automatic" position.

  4. Do this as soon as sufficient backlog (about half the capacity of the conveyor) is accumulated for Filling Machine. Automatic position places Blower in series operation with Filler. Switch remains at Automatic during continuous operation and when operator leaves front of machine.

5. During Operations
   a. Inspect application of labels to bottles

  5. a. (1) Observe front of Labeling Machine (which applies back labels to bottles) to see:
      (a) That guide bar is in position on top of labels.
      (b) That fingers holding the labels are functioning properly.
      (c) That there is a sufficient supply of labels.

* Not shown.

STEPS	KEY POINTS
(Operations necessary to complete job)	(Knacks, hazards, inspections, special information)

(d) That labels are applied properly.

(2) Look into mirror to observe back of Labeling Machine (which applies front labels to bottles) to check same items as in "a" above.

b. Inspect front and back labels as bottles leave Labeler.

b. Front labels are inspected in mirror to right of Labeling Machine. If faults listed in (1) through (6) below occur on only one or a few bottles, remove these bottles from line and place in machine backlog. If faults continue, stop machine by pushing OFF button on Control Switch #1, #3, or #4. Then call Line Specialist.

Faults:

(1) One or both labels missing.
(2) Labels improperly placed.
(3) Off-color labels or misprints. See samples provided.
(4) Blank labels.
(5) Double front or back labels.
(6) Soiled labels.
(7) Excessive glue around edges of label. Stop Labeler by pushing OFF button on Labeler Control Switch #1, #3, or #4. Then call Line Specialist.
(8) Incorrect labels for specific items (e.g., lotion labels on bottles of oil). Stop Labeler as in (7) above. Call Line Specialist.

402   How Should the On-the-Job Instructor's Work Be Evaluated?

The supervisor or coordinator of training has several means of evaluating the effectiveness of the on-the-job instructor. The most important of these is frequent observation of him while he is teaching. The following questions suggest what the supervisor should note:

Was the instructor patient and tolerant with the learner?
Did the instructor follow the four-step method of teaching?
Did the learner appear to respond favorably?
Did the instructor use terms understandable to the learner?
Was the learner encouraged to ask questions?
Did the instructor explain "Why"?
Did he emphasize what not to do?
Did the learner appear enthusiastic and confident?
Did the instructor do too much telling?
Did the instructor correct the learner tactfully?
Did the instructor observe the learner carefully and correct errors immediately?
Did the instructor ask meaningful questions to determine whether the learner understood?
Did the instructor criticize the learner unduly?

The on-the-job instructor should maintain records of performance. Each day's production should be recorded and a continuous record of production for the learner maintained and reviewed by the supervisor. From this record the supervisor can determine the learner's progress and compare it with that of previous new employees. Furthermore, the instructor should prepare written reports at certain specified times during the learning period. These reports should indicate the strengths and weaknesses of the learner, his progress, and any other pertinent facts about him or the learning period itself. These progress reports and the learner's production record will also help the supervisor to evaluate the instructor.

403   Should Job Instructors Receive a Bonus?

When a regular employee is used as a job instructor he should receive a bonus for his extra work. This recognizes his added responsibilities, gives his job prestige, and stimulates him to do a good job. The usual method of compensating the instructor for teaching is to add an amount to his hourly rate.

**404　　Our Company Is Small and Has No Training Depart-
ment. Who Should Coordinate Our On-the-Job Training
Program?**

This responsibility usually is assigned to a staff man in order to
relieve the line executives of time-consuming work of training instructors, maintaining records, and coordinating training. The man
you choose as training coordinator may be your office manager,
an industrial engineer, or some other staff specialist who has an
interest in training and is willing to learn more about it. He should
know the supervisor and the processes, and should have proved
that he can get along with people. All this means that selection
should be based on the man himself, not on his job or—even worse
—on the amount of time he has available.

**405　　What Is the Function of the Training Department in On-
the-Job Training?**

In general, the major function of a training department is to
offer guidance and counsel in developing and executing training
programs for all members of the organization. In on-the-job training the training department usually has the following specific responsibilities:

1. It helps formulate the individual on-the-job training programs.
2. It helps select and prepare training instructors.
3. It assists in preparing job breakdowns and teaching plans.
4. It observes instructors to see that proper techniques and methods are used, and gives help and guidance when necessary.
5. It maintains learners' progress records.
6. It evaluates the individual programs as well as on-the-job training as a whole.

**406　　What Are Some of the Difficulties Faced by an Employee
When He Is Learning a Job—Difficulties Which the Instructor Can Help Him Overcome?**

An employee faces difficulties which vary in complexity according to the task to be learned, his own experience and ability,
and the skill and attitude demonstrated by the instructor who
teaches him. A sympathetic understanding of these difficulties will
help the learner overcome them and so make the learning process
more effective. Some of these difficulties are:

1. Fear of the unknown. Every new job contains elements of the unknown. Usually a new employee is unsure of himself in this situation and feels awkward and self-conscious. He needs assurance, praise, and helpful guidance to help him overcome this natural block to learning.

2. Sensitivity. A learner usually tries hard to make good and so is keyed up emotionally. Although this is a positive factor in learning, it can make the new learner easily disturbed and frustrated by failure. Also, an employee responds to even slight evidences of dissatisfaction or satisfaction when he is learning.

3. Unfamiliar terms. Since we learn through association, the language we use in explaining a job can defeat our objective of teaching the learner how to do it. Use terms that are easily understood or make their meaning clear.

4. Fear of machines or equipment. Fear of physical injury is prevalent among women and men who are to learn to operate production machines. Noise, size, and speed of the machine create an emotional reaction that makes them hesitant and reluctant to learn. Sympathetic understanding of this fear, not ridicule, and carefully planned acclimatization of the learner will do much to help them overcome this fear.

5. Feeling that he is an outsider. When new employees are placed in an on-the-job training situation, they are usually in new surroundings and working with employees they do not know. They don't feel accepted. The instructor can help them to overcome this feeling, which retards learning, by introducing them to fellow employees and acting as their sponsor.

6. Fatigue. When an employee learns a new job it may require the use of muscles and abilities not employed in his previous work. He therefore expends extra effort and becomes tired in a relatively short time. The instructor should recognize this difficulty and adjust the learning program to provide rest and relief from fatigue.

7. Appearing ignorant. The new learner usually hesitates to ask questions for fear of seeming ignorant. The instructor should encourage questions and show by his attitude that he is glad to answer even the most elementary or "foolish" questions.

8. Interruptions or diversions. When the learner is able to concentrate on the instruction and he is not distracted, his ability to learn the operation is improved.

9. Lessons that are too long or too complex. Teach the employee one operation at a time and do not take up the next operation until he has fully mastered this one.

407   **How Do You Compare the Treatment of an Employee During and After Job Training?**

DURING TRAINING

AFTER TRAINING

1. The worker is being paid to learn the job, not to produce. The emphasis must be on learning, not on production.

1. A worker is expected to turn out work in acceptable quantity and quality. He is being paid to produce.

2. The worker is under close supervision and guidance and receives specific instruction in how to perform his job.

2. An experienced worker requires very little assistance or guidance from his supervisor on how to do his job.

3. The worker may work with inferior equipment or material in order to get suitable opportunity to practice the skill he is learning.

3. A worker uses standard equipment and materials.

4. At first the worker may perform only the simplest elements of the job, regardless of sequence, while the instructor handles the difficult ones. This assistance is gradually reduced as the worker acquires skill in each operation.

4. A worker performs every operation and must follow a certain sequence of operations in order to do his job properly.

5. The worker is paid a lower rate than a trained worker—a trainee's rate.

5. A worker is paid on the same scale as other experienced workers.

6. A worker's efficiency is measured by the progress he shows in understanding the job and acquiring the necessary skill to accomplish it.

6. A worker's efficiency is measured by his output.

408   **What Are Some Objections Which Supervisors Make to Organized On-the-Job Training?**

Supervisors usually react favorably towards on-the-job training, especially if they have had a part in planning and organizing the program. A few supervisors, however, see no need for organized job training and usually give one or more of the following reasons for this attitude. The questions in parentheses may be used to reveal weaknesses in their arguments.

1. The people we get nowadays can't profit from such instruction. They don't know how to take responsibility and are not anxious to learn. It's best to let them shift for themselves; the good ones will stay and the others will leave. (Can we expect all our workers to be anxious to please us, do just

what they're told, and to accept responsibility? Don't we have a responsibility to do all we can to help employees become effective members of our organization? How much does worker turnover cost, and can the company afford it? Are you sure potentially good workers aren't leaving? How can you tell?)

2. I don't need a program for on-the-job training. I give all my new workers to Jim Doaks. He's been here twenty years, knows everything about the job, and can take care of them. (But does Jim know how to pass his knowledge on to others? Does the most experienced worker make the best instructor? How is Jim's effectiveness measured objectively? What do the workers trained by Jim say about him?)

3. I don't have to do on-the-job training the way you suggest. I've got enough to do already, seeing that the job is done right, hiring new workers and just getting the product out. (Wouldn't a little planning in job training lessen some of these burdens? Will the supervisor be expected to plan a job training program alone, or will he get help from a staff specialist? Will training not help give him command of his job, instead of letting it run him?)

4. These operations are so simple I don't need to train anyone to do them. (Are they being done in the best possible way? Does the supervisor have to correct workers for mistakes? Does he ever have to do the work that workers should have been able to do without assistance?)

409   How Do You Teach a Long and Difficult Operation to an Employee?

Break the job down into its constituent operations. Define them and determine which are most easily learned. Teach these to the learner first, regardless of whether they are in the sequence of actual job performance. The instructor does the hardest parts of the job and the learner the easiest ones. As he gains skill he is taught one additional operation—the next most difficult one—and so on until he masters the entire job.

410   How Can We Overcome Specific Obstacles or Faults That Are Commonly Revealed by Learners?

The best way to answer this question is to list some common faults and possible remedies:

How Learners Act	Here's How to Help Them
They are slow	Recognize that no two employees will learn at the same rate. Don't rush them—take it easy and teach at the rate that fits each learner. Thorough learning is more important than rapid learning.

They are nervous	Get them to telling about their experiences and interests. Make it plain that you have confidence in their ability. Get their minds off themselves.
They are confused	Remember that starting on a new job is apt to be confusing. Give instructions clearly, simply, slowly. Have a definite plan in instructing, and follow it.
They make mistakes	Don't show annoyance—you must expect mistakes. Let learners know that mistakes are expected. Encourage learners to ask questions freely. Demonstrate each operation, then let each learner perform it. Stop him as soon as he makes a mistake and demonstrate again.
They lack enthusiasm	You must "sell" them on the job and its importance. Show them how their part fits into the over-all scheme of production.
They are scared	Remember how you felt on your own first job and act accordingly. Be sympathetic; take an interest in your learners and convince them that they are among friends.
They seem "dumb"	Don't show impatience—any beginner may appear "dumb." Don't try to teach too much at one time. Be patient—repeat and repeat and repeat.
Some act "cocky"	This is probably a cover-up for nervousness or uncertainty. Refuse to become angry. Be calm and don't attempt to "knock it out of them." Overlook their attitude.

411 How Costly Is an On-the-Job Training Program?

An on-the-job training program is one of the least expensive training programs that can be established, since the instructor's pay is the only major cost. He is paid at least his regular rate of pay while he learns how to teach, prepares job breakdowns, and teaches. Since he is not producing on his regular job, his pay must be charged to training. On the other hand, in order to make an objective analysis of the cost of job training, comparisons of the following should be made in a department before and after the installation of a job training program for new or transferred workers:

Amount of waste and spoilage or returned goods
Number of accidents

Records of production
Records of turnover, absenteeism and grievances

From this analysis it is usually found that the savings exceed the instructor's wages. In addition to these tangible cost savings there will also be intangible values such as greater employee job satisfaction and more constructive and helpful worker attitudes that can't be measured objectively.

412   What Is Trade Training?

Trade training is that training given to a young man (usually 16 to 24) to prepare him to be an accomplished craftsman in a skilled occupation. Trade training is now generally referred to as apprenticeship training.

Trade or apprenticeship training differs from other types of on-the-job training in the degree of skill to be developed, the knowledge to be acquired, and the length of the training. Most apprenticeship training programs last four years and combine shop practice with classroom instruction in related subjects.

Apprenticeship training programs are jointly established by the employer and the employees (or their elected representatives) and the term and conditions of the employment and training of each apprentice is stated in a written agreement and registered with the State Apprenticeship Council.

413   Where Can I Get Assistance in Setting Up a Trade Training Program?

There are three main sources of help:

1. Most large companies have established apprentice training programs and are usually willing to share training materials and experiences.

2. Vocational schools can be of considerable help in the organization and planning of an apprentice program. They are primarily concerned with the training of young men for the trades and are thoroughly familiar with apprenticeship. The vocational schools may also be able to supply you with apprentices and conduct classes as part of your program.

3. The Federal Bureau of Apprenticeship in Washington, D. C., is the national administrative agency in the Labor Department

which is responsible for carrying out the objectives of the national apprenticeship law. This bureau offers consultive service and supplies literature dealing with the establishment and operation of apprentice programs. Each state also has a State Apprenticeship Council as a part of its Department of Labor. This council will give direct assistance on a consultive basis.

414　We Have a Mechanical Department of 80 Men, Rather Equally Divided Among the Trades. Should We Start an Apprentice Training Program?

Although an apprentice program is usually thought of as one conducted by large organizations that hire hundreds of craftsmen, it is also true that small organizations can effectively utilize such programs. The small organization needs craftsmen and cannot rely on the large organizations to train their men for them. In times of high economic activity and widespread employment, qualified craftsmen are not available in the labor market and the small organization, unless it has an apprentice programs, finds itself utilizing second- and third-rate men for positions demanding the skill of highly trained craftsmen.

Yes, establish an apprentice program even though it includes only a few men for the most critical craft in your company. Such a program will have the following advantages: (a) You will have skilled craftsmen when you need them, (b) apprentices start producing from the very beginning of their training; therefore, the cost of the training is relatively low, (c) training can be geared to the company's specialized needs, and (d) the cost of the training program will be lower in the long run than that of recruiting skilled craftsmen who still need to be trained to meet the company's specialized needs.

415　What Is Vestibule Training and When Is It Used?

Vestibule training refers to job training which is given within the organization yet away from the operations area. Here the employee is taught how to do the job with actual equipment, without being on the production line. This type of training is usually used when there are many similar production machines, or operations for which a number of employees are to be trained.

416   What Are the Advantages and Disadvantages of Vestibule Training?

The specific advantages and disadvantages of vestibule training are given by George D. Halsey[2] as follows:

The advantages are:

1. Specially trained instructors, whose whole attention is given to instructing.
2. The possibility of better progression from simple parts of the task to those more complex.
3. More nearly ideal conditions for learning, especially if the actual department is too noisy or involves safety hazards.
4. Better control can be maintained to make sure that the trainee is taught the approved method of doing the job.
5. There is less temptation for the learner to sacrifice quality in order to make the same speed as other workers.
6. Trainees who are definitely unsuited by aptitude to the type of work for which they were selected are quickly discovered and their transfer or separation effected.

The possible disadvantage of this type of training are:

1. With the passage of time, there is a tendency for the instruction and equipment of the vestibule school to lag behind the actual situation in the shop.
2. The emphasis in the vestibule school tends to be upon successful completion of a task, and too little attention is given to the time element involved, a condition that is definitely unrealistic.
3. A retraining period is required on transferring the employee to the shop in order to orient him to production speeds and operating conditions; this period frequently is a discouraging one in the absence of the sympathetic instructor, and it results in a heavy turnover on the part of employees on whom the company has already spent considerable money.

[2] George D. Halsey, *Training Employees* (New York: Harper & Bros., 1949), p. 141.

Chapter 20

DEVELOPMENT FOR RESEARCH, SCIENTIFIC, AND TECHNICAL PERSONNEL

417 **What Type of Development Activities Do You Believe Should Be Provided Research Scientists and Engineers Who Do Not Wish to Move into Management Positions?**

Orientation to the company and to the specific functions in the business would be useful. Refresher and advanced technical training should also be given. If the scientists supervise any assistants, they should have supervisory training. If they do not supervise, some training in coordination and cooperation and human motivation would suffice.

418 **How Can You Train Research People to See Over-All Problems of Management?**

Training courses devoted to orienting supervisors and technicians to the different functions of the business are frequently used. In such cases each division prepares and presents a two- or three-hour story, telling of its responsibilities, methods of work, problems, and results.

Another way to expose research men to over-all problems is by putting them on committees where they will have an opportunity to work and cooperate with other divisions. Multiple management is also helpful. Through it, junior executives see the full scope of the business as well as the services rendered and problems faced by functions other than their own. Rotation of researchers into and out of other divisions permits them to serve in manufacturing, purchasing, personnel, etc. Also, rotate the men within research to help keep their minds broad and alert and prevent narrow specialization within their own field. Methods of training like the case study, the syndicate system, workshops, and role playing are particularly useful in broadening individuals.

As an incentive, the superior will put high values on cooperation, teamwork, and breadth of vision when he evaluates his men's
performance.

419   How Can I Train Graduate Engineers to Fill Executive Positions in Export Territories?

Find out what it is they must do in executive positions which
the typical engineering school training has not prepared them for.
Generally speaking, their new possibilities will require the skills
of coordination, cooperation, teamwork and social relations. They
will be active in public relations, governmental and civic relations,
and in labor relations.

In general, engineers need training in dealing with intangibles
—sentiments and emotions. Their so-called "practical" approach
is quite unsatisfactory for dealing with social and individual problems. Dr. Alfred H. Williams, President of the Federal Reserve
Bank of Philadelphia, says that the essentials of business leadership are:

1. Technical competence (in a specialty)
2. Broad intellectual interest (in history, literature, government,
   sociology, etc.)
3. Social intelligence, which includes skill in
   a. Defining problems
   b. The fruitful conduct of discussion
   c. The art of compromise
   d. Implementing the principles of group administration
   e. The art of exposition

The engineer probably has enough technical competence, but
he may need help with points 2 and 3 of Dr. Williams' outline.
Some of these things will be taught through rotation, case studies,
role playing, and a general education program.

420   Do the Experiences and Training of Research Men Make Them Different from Other Businessmen? In What Way?[1]

The background factors which cause an individual to choose a
scientific career, as opposed to a business career, in themselves
indicate a somewhat different interest and approach to problems.

[1] This question and the three which follow have been answered by the Director
of Research for Ethicon, Inc., New Brunswick, N. J.

When rigorous and specialized scientific training is added to these background factors, the knowledge, attitude, and experience of scientific workers may be markedly different from that of businessmen.

Today, the training of most scientists does not permit them to obtain any formal teaching in the fields of economics, social science, or the various subjects of business administration. Furthermore, unless they have served as teachers during their later scientific training, they have had no experience in problems of supervision. The very terminology and concepts of business operations are frequently wholly unfamiliar to them. As in science, business has its own jargon which to the uninitiated scientist may be as incomprehensible as the terminology of science is to the businessman.

Furthermore, the way of thinking, the critical approach to problems, the effort to classify and to establish general principles from detailed observations appears to be an attitude of the scientist which is not always found in the businessman, although one might speculate that such an attitude could well prove beneficial in solving administrative problems. Nevertheless, observation has shown that some businessmen are annoyed at or do not understand this attitude of their scientific colleagues. Lastly, the scientist is ever ready to try a new approach, to "experiment" and is impatient with "routine" thinking. To him, some of the methods and procedures of business appear unscientific and fruitful objects for experimental alteration. He is frequently amazed and disgruntled that his business colleagues do not share his views.

421   How Do These Differences Influence What Should Be Taught Research Personnel or How It Should Be Taught?

To begin with, the language employed and the terms used in teaching should be based on the assumption that the scientist is unfamiliar with business terminology. Preliminary to discussion of any problems in administration, it should be ascertained whether a brief elementary discussion of general business concepts and principles should be given in order to provide a suitable foundation upon which to base executive training.

The methods of teaching are not necessarily affected by the individual's background. Methods that have proven effective for persons of high ability in the business world should prove equally effective with the research worker. It might be noted that the teaching methods and program selected should provide active rather than passive participation, since most scientists, after their college years, are accustomed to acquiring new knowledge by discussion, preferably argumentative discussion, as well as through reading and the more formal lecture method.

Perhaps more time needs to be devoted to the reasoning behind the concepts presented in the executive training program for scientists. They are, as a rule, logical thinkers (this does not necessarily distinguish them from good businessmen) and their training is such that they do not like to accept concepts, statements, or theories without having an opportunity to examine the data on which such concepts, statements, or theories are based. Their acceptance of ideas will depend upon the ability of the instructor either to present logical and well-documented background material or have the scientists develop such material themselves, as part of the training program. Such a procedure is familiar to trained scientists. This makes difficult the teaching of social relations where conventional, objective data are not often available. They do not readily accept the idea that emotions and feelings are facts.

422 **Are There Any General Cautions a Training Man Should Observe in Setting Up Training and Development Work for Research Personnel?**

Although it has been pointed out that, in general, the training and experience of many research workers is deficient in areas related to business management, the instructor should avoid making the mistake of being too elementary. Often only a definition of terms is needed to enable the scientist to grasp readily the more complex concepts. Because of his habit of continuous study, he may well be prepared to move more rapidly in the course than many other executives. The scientist's mind is adapted and trained for continuous learning because his progress in his chosen field depends upon his ability to study, learn, and use a rapidly increasing body of facts, theories, and ideas. Thus it may irk him if the training and development program moves too slowly or too much time is spent on things which are obvious once the terminology is clear. The scientist, too, may learn the words and facts in administration and conclude too quickly that he is able to apply and use his knowledge. He will not realize that administration is a matter of skill and social insight that goes beyond knowledge.

The instructor must welcome searching questions and discussion. He must accept the fact that his ideas will be challenged and be prepared to defend them in an impersonal manner. Scientists do this among themselves and expect to do it even when the subject is not a scientific one.

423   When Research Personnel with Technical Training Become Supervisors or Administrators, What Are Their Major Problems?

Obviously, the problems will vary with the background, experience and personality of the individual. In general, however, the major problem is one of supervision. As more administrative responsibility is placed on the scientist, the more his problems become those of human relations and the less they relate to technical matters. He often finds himself at a loss when dealing with supervisory problems. He may find it difficult to explain and "sell" his ideas to nontechnical men in other departments. Although he will not sense it himself, nor agree to it if it is pointed out to him, he may not "hear" his subordinates. He may become impatient with business routines and procedures and seek more direct methods to achieve his goals. These inevitably create problems which, in general, fall into the human relations field.

As an administrator, the scientist may be called upon to perform functions for which he has had little or no training such as: budgeting, job and salary evaluation, training of sales and other nonscientific personnel, and participation in committees or other conferences where he must exercise judgment based only partly on technical knowledge. These problems stem from a lack of broad training in economics, business management, and social relations.

Frequently, the scientist will deal with all these problems satisfactorily but may need the assurance of a proper training program that his methods and judgments are correct. He dislikes the feeling that he is "flying blind" without at least a little training in an earthbound cockpit.

424   Do You Believe That Research People Need Less Training, Counseling, Psychological Testing, and Personnel Services Than Production, Sales, Etc?

Certainly not. Basically, the research man's need for human relations and supervisory training, attention, counseling and participation in management is the same as that of other specialists.

A good many of them think of themselves as different and not in need of personnel services, however, and research directors are still contributing to the fallacy. This attitude on the part of leaders in research denies their men legitimate promotion and transfer opportunities into other divisions of the company and into general management of research departments. Research men are the last holdouts in industry against training, development, and the use of personnel services which might improve cooperation within their departments and increase their teamwork with others. Management can in future look to increased tension, friction, and problems in the direction of research personnel and in their working relationships with other departments unless training and personnel services are accepted and used in scientific and technical areas of the business.

Chapter 21

PROMOTING SELF-DEVELOPMENT

425 Isn't It Wise to Leave All Development to Self-Initiation?

It would be, if the men would really undertake it and if they knew how to proceed. Most people, however, must be encouraged to learn, even though the encouragement may be no more than the establishment of a warm and friendly climate in which self-development can take place spontaneously. When development activities are sponsored by the company, one of the main objectives is always to make men increasingly interested in self-improvement.

Development work certainly would be harmful if it led men to rely wholly upon the company or its program for learning and progress. Company programs encourage men to assume more and more responsibility for their own improvement, and so are a device for getting men to do what the question indicates—namely to become self-reliant and endowed with initiative.

426 What Kind of Evidence Do You Seek in Order to Decide Whether a Man Is Interested in Self-Development?

Whether he buys and reads good books and periodicals.

Whether he uses the plant or public library to keep himself up to date in the fields with which he is familiar or to introduce himself to new ones.

Whether he voluntarily registers in correspondence, night school, or university courses.

Whether he takes advantage of training courses offered by the company.

Whether he attends professional and managerial conferences and belongs to the associations.

Whether he visits other companies and other men working in his field.

Whether he appears to have realistic educational and vocational goals and plans for working toward them.

Whether he was guided toward his present position by earlier goals and vocational plans.

Whether he tries to evaluate himself and improve where he is weak.

Whether he seeks and uses the evaluations of others (psychologists, tests, his boss) to formulate a program for self-improvement.

Whether he is alert to get all the learning possible out of his own job, eagerly accepting new and challenging assignments.

Whether he encourages and accepts suggestions for improvement.

Whether his self-improvement is broad, extending into health, leisure, and general education, or is limited to job improvement.

Whether he attempts to and does learn from past experiences and mistakes.

Whether he spends some of his spare time with people who are intellectually stimulating.

427   How Does a Training Man Get Men Interested in Their Own Development?

The fact that his company shows interest in an employee and wants to develop him stimulates the man's own interest in development. People are more interested in development and in assuming responsibility for it when the company supports training and development work. Well-administered company programs also consciously aim to make men increasingly self-reliant with regard to their own improvement. Training programs that teach executives how to counsel with subordinates who have been merit-rated help the latter to see the need for development. In these counseling sessions self-help activities are discussed—correspondence courses, reading, night schools, self-evaluation, travel, community service, and other techniques that can be used by individuals without company help. In fact, the superior who is well trained in counseling, will lead the employee to suggest these activities himself.

The company should recognize and reward those who have improved themselves, at the same time informing people throughout the organization that independent development is encouraged and appreciated. Management also should make self-development easy by tuition refund plans, by adjusting work shifts to fit class schedules, and by showing interest in each person's progress.

It is part of the training man's function to give educational and vocational guidance that stimulates self-activity. If he feels inadequate, a course or two in guidance procedures at some nearby college or university will enable him to fulfill this responsibility.

428   **If a Man Is Worth His Salt, He Doesn't Need to Be Stimulated to Improve. Why Should We Try to Prod Men in Improvement?**

The statement preceding this question is not true. Many very good men—men who are capable of doing more difficult jobs than they hold and of increasing their service to themselves, their companies, and society—still need stimulation before they will try harder, prepare themselves better, or rid themselves of minor failings that have retarded their progress. The factors underlying their hesitancy may be obscure, complex, or puzzling, but there can be no doubt that men need help in order to overcome them.

A company should interest men in their own development in order to reduce the burden of development and training that rests upon the organization if the men do not undertake part of the task themselves. Stimulation should also be provided because executives, as leaders, have an obligation to get the best possible performance from people under them, so long as the effort to do so does not violate limitations of health and mental equipment. No leader and no business can afford to let men work at tasks with efficiency distinctly below their potential.

This does not mean that we should turn people into over-ambitious climbers, so eager to win a better future that they get no satisfaction from the present. It does require us to bring each man up to the level of performance that is his natural optimum. Both high executives and training men must learn how to recognize both abilities and limitations. Only by doing so can they help subordinates reach their full powers without going too far and so running the risk of becoming frustrated.

429   **There Is No Program for Development in My Company. What Can I Do to Develop Myself?**

You should learn as much as possible about yourself. Sit down some evening and make a few notes about yourself. Include your successes and failures, your strengths and weaknesses, your job preferences and dislikes, the compliments and criticism you have received from your working associates. If your company uses merit ratings, you can add your superior's opinions about you. Think of your health, too, and of your recreational, cultural, and social interests and skills. Review your training and education, your school marks and favorite courses.

Include any psychological evaluations you have had, or better still, go and get an up-to-date one. While you are sizing yourself up, set vocational goals. What are you equipped to do best? Are you in that field, and if not, how can you get there? Specifically, what kind of job do you want, with what company, where? Set long-term as well as immediate vocational goals.

Next, lay out the educational program you will need to reach these progressive goals. This may involve attendance at evening or short daytime classes, correspondence school work, regular university attendance, participation in professional or trade associations, community leadership activities, reading programs, travel, job rotation or job change, on-the-job learning opportunities, etc.

While you are planning your development, read some self-help books.

430   **Isn't Business Invading Privacy and Other Fundamental Rights When It Plans and Directs a Man in His Development? And How Does the Company Know What Is Best for Him?**

The answer here depends upon the degree to which management does the planning and directing. The fact is that few programs succeed where management does all or most of the planning. The best programs are operated cooperatively, with the employee making his own educational and vocational choices based on information provided by his boss, the personnel department, and the training director.

Where management has a part in the planning, it must be careful not to ignore or belittle the employee's interests and welfare. To do so is sure to arouse resentment.

Evaluations and merit ratings enable managers to determine strengths, weaknesses, and needs for training. Psychological tests, and counseling interviews with employees reveal weak spots, native ability and performance. The results of tests and counseling sessions prepare the company to make training suggestions to the promising employee, or at least to discuss with the man his own opinions in regard to his training needs. The Johnson & Johnson management training program includes a two-hour session on self-analysis. This conference aims to help the supervisor or executive to judge his own training needs. Given this stimulation and help, he studies his strengths and weaknesses and is intelligently prepared to discuss his training needs when his superior sits down with him after merit rating.

431   Where Self-Improvement is Encouraged, Isn't the Learner Likely to Develop According to His Own Choice and Not Necessarily in Accord with the Company Needs?

This will happen if the company merely encourages develop-ment but makes no effort to guide it. It is not likely to happen where there are executive audits and counseling between the superior and his subordinates. Audits reveal the man's specific training needs, both personal and job or vocational. Counseling gets him to see his needs and invites him to suggest educational activities to improve himself both as a person and as an employee. Some companies have one or more men in their training depart-ments who have specialized in vocational or educational guidance and can help supervisors with this work.

432   What Responsibility Does an Employee Have for Im-proving Himself?

He has great responsibility, perhaps even full responsibility. It is not enough to say this and let it go at that, however. The prob-lem is to get men to see and act upon this responsibility. Manage-ment cannot be satisfied with developing only those who volun-tarily take responsibility for the job—they are too few in number and not all who press themselves forward into self-development are the best candidates for improving or upgrading. Most devel-opment activities—from employee appraisals and the counseling that follow, on through every development activity that is under-taken—aim to fortify an interest in self-development where it exists and to create it where it is absent. This is motivation. It is one of the most difficult parts of teaching.

433   How Much Development and Training Should Be Self-Initiated, Fully Self-Directed, and Paid for by the Em-ployee?

The man should be free to undertake as much training outside the company and on his own initiative as he chooses. The company should put no limit on this. The man himself should lay out his program on a scale appropriate to his health, available time, the demands of his job, his vocational and educational goals, the type and quality of training available within the company, and his ability to profit from training. Sometimes, of course, a superior must encourage a hesitant man to enlarge his program, or get an overly eager person to see that he cannot do too much.

Most companies today are willing to bear the major responsibility for encouraging learning and for providing the opportunity to learn. They believe, however, that the employee also should play some part in the project. He should devote some of his own time to training classes and self-improvement and possibly pay for some part of it. Improvement of the work force—employees, supervisors and executives—is something from which all parties concerned benefit and for which all share responsibility.

434   Won't a Development Program in the Company Retard the Men's Interest in Their Own Development?

No. The stimulation provided by a company program will be an incentive for some men to undertake self-development. It will show them why there is great interest in adult improvement, arouse the spirit of competition by telling what other companies and other men are doing, and suggest ways and means of achieving improvement. More important still, the company program provides employees with guidance during the discouraging first days which any adult passes through when he becomes a student again.

Chapter 22

HUMAN RELATIONS DEVELOPMENT

435   **How Is the Subject of Human Relations Usually Taught in Industry?**

Industry got its most extensive exposure to human relations training through the Job Relations Training (JRT) given to hundreds of thousands of supervisors during World War II. This was a packaged program, with rigid adherence to a "canned" teacher's outline which provided for a minimum of free discussion. Following JRT or simultaneously with it, many companies offered *conference programs* in leadership. These dealt primarily with human relations and included one or more conferences on such subjects as reprimanding, building morale, handling grievances, supervising women workers, laws of learning, reducing absenteeism, building job enthusiasm, human motivation, discipline, orienting new employees, personnel policies and practices, the meaning of leadership, etc. Following the conference programs or growing out of them came case studies, role playing, and workshops. The JRT program and the conferences sought to instill knowledge about people and how they behave. Case studies and role playing do that, too, but they include learner activities which emphasize participation, self-analysis, practice, and application as means of learning.

Today most plants are in the stage of using conference programs. A small proportion, say five or ten per cent, have progressed to the nondirective techniques.

436   **We Hear of a Great Need for Training in Human Relations. Specifically, What Should Be Taught in Human Relations?**

Malcolm S. Knowles says[1] we must learn to live cooperatively and spells out seven specific training needs to achieve this:

[1] Malcolm S. Knowles, *Informal Adult Education* (New York: Association Press, 1950), pp. 9-10.

ADULTS SHOULD ACQUIRE A MATURE UNDERSTANDING OF THEMSELVES. They should understand their needs, motivations, interests, capacities, and goals. They should be able to look at themselves objectively and maturely. They should accept themselves and respect themselves for what they are, while striving earnestly to become better.

ADULTS SHOULD DEVELOP AN ATTITUDE OF ACCEPTANCE, LOVE AND RESPECT TOWARD OTHERS. This is the attitude on which all human relations depend. Adults must learn to distinguish between people and ideas, and to challenge ideas without threatening people. Ideally, this attitude will go beyond acceptance, love and respect, to empathy and the sincere desire to help others.

ADULTS SHOULD DEVELOP A DYNAMIC ATTITUDE TOWARD LIFE. They should accept the fact of change and should think of themselves as always changing. They should acquire the habit of looking at every experience as an opportunity to learn and should become skillful in learning from it.

ADULTS SHOULD LEARN TO REACT TO THE CAUSES, NOT THE SYMPTOMS, OF BEHAVIOR. Solutions to problems lie in their causes, not in their symptoms.[2] We have learned to apply this lesson in the physical world, but have yet to learn to apply it in human relations.

ADULTS SHOULD ACQUIRE THE SKILLS NECESSARY TO ACHIEVE THE POTENTIALS OF THEIR PERSONALITIES. Every person has capacities that, if realized, will contribute to the well-being of himself and of society. To achieve these potentials requires skills of many kinds—vocational, social, recreational, civic, artistic, and the like. It should be a goal of education to give each individual those skills necessary for him to make full use of his capacities.

ADULTS SHOULD UNDERSTAND THE ESSENTIAL VALUES IN THE CAPITAL OF HUMAN EXPERIENCE. They should be familiar with the heritage of knowledge, the great ideas, the great traditions, of the world in which they live. They should understand and respect the values that bind men together.

ADULTS SHOULD UNDERSTAND THEIR SOCIETY AND SHOULD BE SKILLFUL IN DIRECTING SOCIAL CHANGE. In a democracy the people participate in making decisions that affect the entire social order. It is imperative, therefore, that every factory worker, every salesman, every politician, every housewife, know enough about government, economics, international affairs, and other aspects of the social order to be able to take part in them intelligently.

The content for programs which are to teach human relations should be selected in terms of these needs for greater skill and understanding in social situations.

[2] This is the basis of Guided Experience. See Chapter 5.

437   Are There Any Principles or Assumptions That Should Be Taught in Human Relations?

In the following list of basic assumptions about human behavior, Alexander Leighton provides a good broad statement[3] of some of the things that might well be taught. For teaching purposes, these "principles" may be presented directly, or drawn from case studies and illustrated by role playing.

1. There exist psychological uniformities common to all the tribes, nations, and "races" of human beings.
2. Each psychological uniformity has a range through which it varies; some variants are characteristic of particular groups of people and as such form a part of their culture.
3. All people are disturbed by such general types of stress as threats to life and health, discomfort from pain, heat, cold, dampness, fatigue, poor food, loss of means of subsistence, etc.
4. When these types of stress combine in the following forms, they are by that fact additionally disturbing:
   a. Frustration of expectations, desires, etc.
   b. Dilemma of conflict between mutually incompatible desires and intentions.
   c. Circumstances that create confusion and uncertainty as to what is happening in the present and what can be expected in the future.
5. All people have a "tolerance-for-stress" threshold.
6. Among tribes, nations, and "races" of human beings, individuals vary greatly from one to another in the level of this "tolerance-for-stress" threshold.
7. When the "tolerance-for-stress" threshold is exceeded, all people respond with some combination of psychological patterns.

438   How Can Training Lead Employees to Believe Management's Story?

People cannot believe unless they are told; therefore, management must present its case. But employee understanding, loyalty, and appreciation are not to be secured by hearing facts alone, no matter how true they may be. Appreciation and loyalty result from self-expression in situations in which the employee feels

[3] Alexander H. Leighton, *Human Relations in a Changing World* (New York: E. P. Dutton & Co., Inc., 1949), pp. 76-78.

there is personal sympathy toward him. Training directors must recognize and teach this principle of attitude building to managers.

All subordinates look upon themselves as having inherent personal worth at least as great as that of their superiors. This is true even where they feel their own inferiority in managerial ability or some other trait. They still think, just as you and we do, that because they are individual human beings they have certain values and rights as great as those of anyone else. This sense of personal worth is always offended when people are told and have no opportunity to comment or reply. Even though the telling is well and tactfully done, we do not perform our full obligation merely by telling the truth and telling it often and well. We complete our obligation to each person's human dignity when we allow—or better still, invite—him to express his reactions to what is told, preferably before action is taken. When training men teach this to their management, employee confidence increases.

It may well be that employees will believe management's story to the degree that management is interested in, listens to, and places confidence in its employees' story.

439   How Does Training Persuade the Boss to Throw Away the Club and Put On the Velvet Glove?

Training cannot directly and quickly provide management with new outlooks and techniques. The change asked for here is fundamental—from an authoritarian outlook to a democratic one.

Persuasion alone will not accomplish this change; the boss must come to see his own inadequacy, and teaching can set up situations that cause him to develop insight. Training undertakes this transformation diplomatically and with full knowledge that it will be difficult and time-consuming. Nondirective approaches seem most likely to produce this very important change. Certainly, a variety of programs and methods will be necessary: workshops, syndicates, case studies and role playing, to name some. No one device or course or approach is likely to be enough.

440   What Is the Key Factor in Developing Good Relationship Between Management and Employees?

There is no "key" factor, no formula, no single and simple way to learn to live at peace with others. In varying degrees many factors are involved: one's personality, his family, how he lived as a child and lives as an adult, the influence of the community in which he grew up, the whole pattern of his experiences, his successes, his failures, and his reaction to both, his goals in life, his moral outlook and health, his job and his education—these and many more. The "key factor" in developing good relations with a man who suffers from chronic ill health will be quite different from the key factor in dealing with one who suffers emotionally from frustration and even aggression growing out of the fact that he is part of an unaccepted minority. Every case is a problem in itself and must be studied individually. For some rules useful in understanding what promotes good relations generally, see Questions 436 and 437.

441   What Can a Middle-Aged Man Do Who Has Just Been Given a Staff Job to Develop Better Human Relations in Various Divisions When Many Division Heads Are Old and Set in Their Ways?

Such a person should prepare himself as fully as he can for the position. While doing this he should discover just what the company attitude toward people is. He should collect company writings, speeches, policy manuals, union contracts, and all other materials bearing on his firm's philosophy and policy regarding people and their relationships. When the new staff man has digested these policies he might try his hand at putting them together into a company credo or policy statement. When this has been discussed and approved by all levels of management, it becomes a foundation for action throughout the company and forms ideal subject matter for teaching. The Johnson & Johnson credo, which is quoted on page 320, has been used as teaching matter to help all hands, old and new, understand the company's human relations policies.

If it is possible, use some of the old and experienced supervisors to help prepare the policy statement and to explain or teach it. They will help secure understanding, acceptance, and application of the relationships expected by top management. In preparing a policy statement and in working to secure its general acceptance, they, themselves, learn much.

Our Credo

WE BELIEVE THAT OUR FIRST RESPONSIBILITY IS TO OUR CUSTOMERS
OUR PRODUCTS MUST ALWAYS BE GOOD, AND
WE MUST STRIVE TO MAKE THEM BETTER AT LOWER COSTS.
OUR ORDERS MUST BE PROMPTLY AND ACCURATELY FILLED.
OUR DEALERS MUST MAKE A FAIR PROFIT.

OUR SECOND RESPONSIBILITY IS TO THOSE WHO WORK WITH US—
THE MEN AND WOMEN IN OUR FACTORIES AND OFFICES.
THEY MUST HAVE A SENSE OF SECURITY IN THEIR JOBS.
WAGES MUST BE FAIR AND ADEQUATE.
MANAGEMENT JUST, HOURS SHORT, AND WORKING CONDITIONS CLEAN AND ORDERLY.
WORKERS SHOULD HAVE AN ORGANIZED SYSTEM FOR SUGGESTIONS AND COMPLAINTS.
FOREMEN AND DEPARTMENT HEADS MUST BE QUALIFIED AND FAIR MINDED.
THERE MUST BE OPPORTUNITY FOR ADVANCEMENT — FOR THOSE QUALIFIED
AND EACH PERSON MUST BE CONSIDERED AN INDIVIDUAL
STANDING ON HIS OWN DIGNITY AND MERIT.

OUR THIRD RESPONSIBILITY IS TO OUR MANAGEMENT
OUR EXECUTIVES MUST BE PERSONS OF TALENT, EDUCATION, EXPERIENCE AND ABILITY.
THEY MUST BE PERSONS OF COMMON SENSE AND FULL UNDERSTANDING.

OUR FOURTH RESPONSIBILITY IS TO THE COMMUNITIES IN WHICH WE LIVE.
WE MUST BE GOOD CITIZENS — SUPPORT GOOD WORKS AND CHARITY,
AND BEAR OUR FAIR SHARE OF TAXES.
WE MUST MAINTAIN IN GOOD ORDER THE PROPERTY WE ARE PRIVILEGED TO USE.
WE MUST PARTICIPATE IN PROMOTION OF CIVIC IMPROVEMENT,
HEALTH, EDUCATION AND GOOD GOVERNMENT,
AND ACQUAINT THE COMMUNITY WITH OUR ACTIVITIES.

OUR FIFTH AND LAST RESPONSIBILITY IS TO OUR STOCKHOLDERS.
BUSINESS MUST MAKE A SOUND PROFIT.
RESERVES MUST BE CREATED, RESEARCH MUST BE CARRIED ON,
ADVENTUROUS PROGRAMS DEVELOPED, AND MISTAKES MADE AND PAID FOR.
BAD TIMES MUST BE PROVIDED FOR, HIGH TAXES PAID, NEW MACHINES PURCHASED,
NEW FACTORIES BUILT, NEW PRODUCTS LAUNCHED, AND NEW SALES PLANS DEVELOPED.
WE MUST EXPERIMENT WITH NEW IDEAS.
WHEN THESE THINGS HAVE BEEN DONE THE STOCKHOLDERS
SHOULD RECEIVE A FAIR RETURN.
WE ARE DETERMINED WITH THE HELP OF GOD'S GRACE,
TO FULFILL THESE OBLIGATIONS TO THE BEST OF OUR ABILITY.

442   How Can Training Eliminate Some of the Suspicions, Jealousies, and Mistrust Between Departments?

Charles Lamb, seated in an inn one evening with a friend, pointed to a man at a nearby table and remarked, "See that man over there? Well, I hate him." His friend remonstrated and said, "Why you don't even know him, he's a perfect stranger to you." "That's why I hate him," said Lamb.

It is the unknown which provokes irrational fear, distrust, and dislike.

Orientation training to show the functions and problems of various units of the business usually helps build the understanding among different groups from which cooperation grows. Training programs in which men and women meet together to learn new and better ways of operating or to discuss common problems also help people to know each other better.

Besides training conferences, company papers, parties, recreational programs, teams, visits to other departments, and other group activities will reduce strangeness and distances. Whatever will do this will help to reduce suspicion, friction, and jealousy between departments or individuals.

443   Suppose That Members of Top Level Management Fear That Someone Will Take Over Their Jobs, and so Reject Understudies or Assistants and Refuse to Guide the Experience of Others. How Can Development Take Place Under Such Conditions?

Begin by finding out why these people are suspicious. (See Chapter 5, on the Guided Experience Method.) It may be that they have seen understudies receive opportunities for development which are not available to superiors. This naturally leads the latter to conclude that younger people are being trained to replace them. Sometimes management has sold out too quickly on the ability of its able and experienced men and started replacing them with newcomers, or to train newcomers for the replacement, before trying to train the incumbents. If the company has not offered its senior executives encouragement and opportunities to keep themselves up to date, it should do so, before surrounding them with well-trained assistants and understudies.

There may be a long list of reasons for the condition described in the question. When two or three have been selected as primary, by means of the method outlined in Guided Experience, then group training, more experience or different experience, coaching, or individual counsel can be used to correct the condition.

444   Our Plant Has Been and Is Now Operating with Heavy Losses, Due to Obsolete Methods and Habits Which Management Is Trained In and Refuses to Change. Would You Continue to Suffer Losses While Trying to Change Management Attitudes Through Training, or Would You Change Management?

The answer here depends in part upon the degree of truth in the phrase, "refuse to change." Have these managers been asked to change their methods? Have they been shown the reasons for doing so and given time to learn the new ways? Above all, has management been given regular training in what changes are expected and how they are to be made? When all these conditions are met, a few transfers or retirements of older men may be necessary if some men still stubbornly refuse to learn new methods or cannot do so.

It frequently happens that managements which have tolerated and practiced inefficient methods or who have lived with an outdated management philosophy decide to change overnight. But their change is almost sure to be slow and change is slower still at lower levels. Training can speed this up.

In deciding whether or not to train the old-timers, there is a natural tendency to think that replacing them will be easier than changing their old-fashioned ways. Getting old men out and new ones in their places can be done quickly, but this is only the beginning. The new men must learn their way around, and their associates must be taught to accept them and their ways. Sometimes this is never accomplished and replacement does no good whatever. Even when replacements gain acceptance of themselves and their modern ideas, the shift usually takes a couple of years, at best.

445   Our Executives Do Not Accept Responsibility for Developing Their Subordinates, Nor Will They Allow Members of the Development Staff to Do So. What Should Be Done?

This is not uncommon. Executives must be taught that all men are responsible for developing their subordinates so that good understudies are available for all jobs. In words, this sounds very difficult; actually, the job generally can be done in a one- or two-hour training conference on developing understudies. It also can be done a little less directly in a conference on duties and responsibilities of supervisors and executives. In it, the responsibility for development is emphasized at the same time that the teacher reviews ten or a dozen other responsibilities of leaders. Another way to get at this is through merit rating and the counseling between superior and subordinate which follows. If the superiors at the top of the organization consider development of subordinates a responsibility of supervisors and executives, they should rate those who report to them on the amount and quality of development work that each man has done. This rating is then discussed in the counseling sessions that raters have with their subordinates. Good work is commended; poor work is challenged and help is offered those who need it. When executives see that they are expected to develop subordinates and are to be evaluated upon it, most of them will try to do what is required. Soon this willingness to develop people passes down through the organization.

446   What Should Be Done About the Inability of Supervisors to Recognize the Value of Good Human Relations?

Train them to recognize the values, using one or more of these means:

1. Bring in a sympathetic executive who lectures on the subject, explains the company's attitude, and answers questions. The lecturer should, of course, be one who lives what he says about human relations.

2. Prepare and use data to help prove the values. They will include such examples as the study which showed that 80 per cent of one company's separations in the ranks of management came because of failures in human relations.

3. Use case studies to help. There are many good cases (see the Bibliography) which can serve as examples and lead supervisors to conclude that people and their needs and feelings are important and need as much or more attention than the methods, materials and machines of industry.

4. One personnel director leads a conference in which he asks supervisors to describe briefly all the problems that face them. These he lists on the blackboard; after building a long list he asks which are wholly technical, and which are wholly human relations, and which are both. Usually the human problems outweigh the technical two to one. It is the training director's duty to con-

vince the supervisors in the plant of the importance of human relations, just as it is his duty to develop programs for teaching good relations.

447   Should Personal Enthusiasm for Mental Development and Advancement Be Maintained in an Organization Which Is No Longer Growing?

Yes, to do so may start the company growing again. When teen-agers grow into adults and stop their major physical growth they still need to keep themselves growing mentally and emotionally. So it is with men and women in a stable company. But remember: when any superior is blessed with alert, open-minded, enthusiastic subordinates he is also cursed. He is blessed because they will do his work well, and with constant improvement. He is cursed because they must have active leadership . . . new jobs, new goals, harder and harder challenges, more and more freedom. The good boss finds ways to provide variety, challenge, and opportunity even in a stable organization, but the poor one gives up. He ignores his men and their needs, does not try to find new challenges, and provides no compensation for the static condition of the company. Inevitably, he has trouble!

Highly trained race horses sometimes kick down their stable door if their ability goes unused. Dray horses are more phlegmatic. It is up to the leader to choose which kind of men he will have. Thoroughbreds will do more for him, but will require a higher grade of leadership.

448   What Kind of Training Helps the Personnel Manager to Get Cooperation from the "Bull of the Woods" Who Knows It All?

Broad, general training such as role playing and case studies will help this man to see and accept points of view other than his own. Sometimes the syndicate system helps. It satisfies his excessive need for freedom in learning, and his need for appearing in a position of authority is satisfied when the syndicate committee gives its research report to its associates.

The Guided Experience Method also helps (see Chapter 5). Through GEM the Personnel Director tries to learn the reasons for the supervisor's know-it-all attitude. If these are located, training and coaching are used to remove them. There are other approaches, also. The man may be asked to serve on personnel or training committees in which he will hear different points of view and work with different men with whom he may become sympathetic. Multiple management and auxiliary boards provide the same kind of opportunity for contacts and experience. Meeting with successful men from other departments of the business, hearing their views and working with them frequently does much to tone down the "Bull of the Woods."

449   How Does One Develop a Good Management "Climate"?

This is like asking how to practice law or how to build a bridge. The question is broadly inclusive and complex. First must come knowledge of what constitutes a good management "climate." This leads into a broad study of modern management: its methods, its goals, and the environment under which the goals are most likely to be achieved.

After developing some understanding of what constitutes the ideal climate or relation between superior and subordinate, practice and skill must be used to create that climate. Here case studies, role playing, workshops, and guided experience will help.

450   Can Training Reduce Employee Hostility, Disinterest, and Resistance to Management?

There is no magic in training. It cannot, overnight, remove attitudes that have grown out of long indifference to employee needs or from the unpleasant experiences of workers. Training can, however, teach supervisors to act and think in ways that create understanding and confidence between employees and employers. Moreover, if use is made of training methods that invite free discussion, training can reveal the causes of employee suspicion and ill will. It can draw from both employee and management trainees an understanding and a description of that kind of management behavior which will replace division and conflict with cooperation and teamwork. Training can educate supervisors to handle themselves and their problems of human relations so as to prevent misunderstanding and friction. Training can also show employees their responsibilities in maintaining cooperative relations. It can help employees to meet these responsibilities and improve their own positions because it gives them greater understanding, more skill in their work, and a greater confidence in themselves and their companies.

451   A Clerical Employee Is Apparently Sour on Everything. She Seems to Delight in Antagonizing Other Workers, All of Whom Seem Happy, Satisfied, Etc. What Can Training Do?

Training can first check the assumption that "other employees seem happy." Sometimes what employees seem to be and what they are differ. It may be that this employee is communicating general dissatisfaction with management which others dare not or will not express.

After this check on how other employees feel, training should try to find out why this employee acts as she does. See Chapter 5, on Guided Experience. It may be that the woman's mental or physical health is bad. She may be in the wrong job, have home problems, may be in need of greater recognition from her superiors, may be untrained in her duties and responsibilities, may need training in how to get on with others, etc. Once the cause is found, training may be used in an effort to correct it.

452   What Training Will Contribute Most to Good Relations Between Employees and Management?

In recent years, there has been a concerted drive on the part of management to get employees to learn about economic needs of business. Here and there are attempts to place equal emphasis upon the need for management to learn about production and white collar workers—how they live and think and feel, both as individuals and as groups. Training in sensitivity to oneself as a leader and in how one's actions affect others are fundamental needs.

453   How Can I Be Trained to Improve the Effectiveness of My Personal Contacts?

1. Some of us talk too much. We talk about too many things and too long about each of them. We talk too much about what interests us and not enough about the interests of others. Training in communications and in listening will help correct these faults.

2. Deliberately setting aside certain periods of the day to be with subordinates helps. Walks through the department, chats at

the water fountain, a leisurely coke or coffee with employees in the cafeteria, all facilitate personal contacts and communication.

3. A list of employees' names is helpful, too. Without it a supervisor may unwittingly fail to see and talk with some of his employees for days or weeks at a time. A check list will jostle his memory—and his conscience—so that he seeks out people that might have been neglected.

4. Role playing, case studies, and conferences on human motivation also are valuable.

454   What Conscious Recognition Is Given by Management to the Growing Importance of the Human Element—and What Expression Is Given Through Philosophy or Action?

There are many evidences of the recognition: the establishment of personnel and training departments; the staffing of them with professionally trained workers; training programs in communication, in listening, human motivation, and counseling; the elevation of many personnel and industrial relations directors to vice presidents or board members; the creation of the position of Director of Human Relations in many companies; the employment in industry of psychologists, sociologists, and psychiatrists, and the development of programs aimed at participation, cooperation and teamwork. Last but not least, we mention multiple management plans for bringing lower levels of management into the making of company policy.

455   How Does Training Deal with a Consistently Negative Attitude?

Find out what causes the negativism (see Chapter 5). Then work to remove the causes through *individual* approaches such as job assignments, rotations, change of duties, counseling, and help from the employee's superior. Also use *group* approaches as dictated by the cause—role playing, conferences, case studies, workshops, etc.

Perhaps the cause, when found, will stem from ill-health or from worry over debts, or from disharmonious family or community relations. If the trouble lies outside the work environment, training must be supplemented by other approaches.

456   **How Do You Counsel the Individual Who Wants to Be Boss and Thinks He Should Be Boss?**

In this case, company-wide training in merit rating and counseling with subordinates might get this man's superior to discuss his future with him. In such discussions, the boss would get the man to see his weaknesses, see how they handicap him, and lay out a program for improvement.

Had this man's superior been trained so that he was willing and able to merit-rate or evaluate his subordinate and counsel with him afterwards, it is unlikely that a less useful man would continue to think, over the years, that he should have his superior's job. Such an attitude usually arises where the man is never talked with about his present failings or his future.

Now and then it happens that a man is right in thinking that he has been overlooked. Training in how to evaluate men and how to talk with them afterward[4] sometimes makes a superior see merit in an otherwise neglected man. It also helps the superior to see his responsibility for helping a highly successful subordinate to advance, possibly through rotation or lateral transfer to some department not so adequately staffed at the top.

457   **Two Decades Ago My Superiors Said I Should Learn to Handle My People. Recently They Have Been Saying That "All of Us Should Learn Better to Handle Ourselves in Relation to People." What Do They Mean?**

They mean that people on all levels of management should know themselves and should recognize the existence and persistence of emotions, sentiments, and personal preferences, and perhaps conscious or unconscious biases. All of us must increasingly recognize that much of our behavior, like that of our subordinates, is emotional and non-logical.

Beginning perhaps with the Job Relations Training Program and other conference-type of human relations courses in the 1930's and early 1940's, supervisors and executives were taught to understand and perhaps—at the lowest level—even how to manipulate others. We have passed this stage and training is now teaching men to understand themselves as well as others.[5] In fact, self-

---

[4] See Earl G. Planty and Carlos A. Efferson, "Counseling Executives After Merit Rating or Evaluation," *Personnel*, March, 1951.

[5] See Earl G. Planty and William V. Machaver, "Upward Communications," *Personnel*, January, 1952.

understanding and self-control may be prerequisites to knowing others and leading them.

458　Does Nepotism Tend to Discourage the Ambitious Man from Applying Himself, Since He Feels That Training Is Reserved for the Chosen Few?

Nepotism can do nothing but discourage effort and growth. If men on any level repeatedly see relatives or friends of managing officials being brought in to fill vacancies which apparently had been open to them, they lose confidence in promotion from within and opportunity based on merit. One of the strong factors influencing the birth and growth of labor unions was the need to protect the jobs, if not opportunity for advancement, of working men from the whims and personal preferences of supervisors and owners. Since there are no unions to do this for professional men and line and staff supervisors, management must be particularly careful to (a) Promote and reward only on merit; (b) Determine merit by the most objective and scientific method available, free from personal bias; (c) Establish training to help each man judge the merit of his subordinates and candidates for employment; and (d) Review or follow up on the selections and choices of men for employment and promotion. Discover through this review whose selections succeed and whose fail. Then retrain where retraining is indicated, or shift the responsibility elsewhere.

459　How Can Training Persuade Employees to Give a Fair Day's Work for Their Pay?

Make sure that you, the union, and the employees know what constitutes a fair day's work. Then charge your supervisors with the responsibility for getting it. Next, reward those supervisors who can get a fair day's work without exploitation of labor or development of employee ill will.

Once the above steps are taken, training can help. If some supervisors cannot get the results expected, training may be able to discover why. Perhaps employees are poorly trained. If so, supervisors must be helped to do better job instruction. They may need the JIT program or a refresher in it. Other causes for failure may lie in supervisors who are too weak or too easy, too much centered in the technical aspects of their jobs, or too hard and unbending. If these are the causes, supervisors will need training in leadership, human motivation, building job enthusiasm, communications, and like subjects. Some failures occur where supervisors do not agree that it is their responsibility as supervisors to get a full day's work from employees. Here they will need instruction in duties and responsibilities of men in their position.

General education for employees will help, too. It will build understanding of our economic order which depends upon productivity. It will produce understanding of the company and its problems, and through understanding will come sympathy, respect, and cooperation.

460   How Do You Use Training to Increase the Output of Employees and Still Maintain Good Relations with Them and with Their Unions?

Increased output is the primary responsibility of supervision; to ask how to obtain it is to ask how to supervise. All activities of supervisors which build understanding, cooperation, morale, and teamwork will help maintain employee confidence in their management and help gain acceptance of company goals. Skill training for employees also contributes, for the will to perform at high level must be accompanied by the skill that is necessary to do so.

Most unions, when they are informed of technological change and needs for increased productivity, are cooperative. This is especially true where they are invited to hear company plans and to participate in making them. Training helps supervisors communicate with employees and teaches how to bring them into participation in solving problems.

461   How Can You Train a Man to Think Clearly, Logically, and Without Personal Bias?

Courses in writing, public speaking, communications, and semantics are well-known aids to clear and logical thinking. An employee can often be helped to clear his thinking by individual counseling which exposes the biases, emotions, and frustrations which sometimes overpower rational processes. Counseling may be supplemented by case studies which help men to see their own emotionalism and confusion in thinking. Acting out a job situation in role playing will help, too, since the thinking of the role player will be reviewed and analyzed publicly, and if he has confusion in his thinking, or blind spots and biases, they will be exposed to constructive criticism.

Most of us, of course, need the help implied in this question. It is all too easy to think that managers think logically and that employees reach their conclusions emotionally. Actually, both share the same weaknesses. A recent article in *Fortune*[6] describes how industries like International Business Machines, American Cyanamid, Dresser Industries and others have faced the problem of Training to Think. The article reviews problem-solving methods, case studies, and vertical conference methods used in many companies and schools.

462   How Can We Help the Employee Who Does His Work Well But Does Not Get Along with Other Employees?

1. Study him to learn where he has conflicts and why.

2. Provide him with some human relations training. Get him into conferences devoted to teamwork and cooperation. Use role playing, too.

3. If he is self-centered or shy, try to bring him out of himself. Give him a few responsibilities wherein he will have to work and rely on others.

4. Learn the attitude of his work group toward him. If he is excluded or unaccepted, you may, by tactful suggestion and by subtle sponsorship, help him obtain better group acceptance. This will build warmer feelings in him toward others.

5. Try to get him into the company's recreational and social activities.

6. If he doesn't respond to these measures, perhaps it is best to transfer him to work that removes him from much association with his fellows. He may be the type who will be happy and do very well alone.

463   Our Training Director Believes That a Human Relations Training Program Is Too Academic and Will Not Be Accepted by Plant Management. We Are Ten to Fifteen Years Behind in This Field. How Can This Deficiency Be Overcome?

One must first find out what this man's concept of human relations training is. Perhaps he thinks of it as lectures in social or industrial psychology, with emphasis upon academic terms and theoretical analyses. Perhaps he is justified in his lack of confi-

[6] Perrin Stryker, "Can Executives Be Taught to Think?" *Fortune*, May, 1953.

dence in human relations training, *as he conceives it.* If so, he needs a more adequate point of view.

It may be that his attitudes are influenced by engineering training or experience or by scientific objectivity, to the extent that he considers all intangibles academic. If so, he needs counseling. His superiors will do well to find out how much value he places on smooth-running teamwork and cooperation. It may well be that he has no confidence in any kind of human relations improvement and thinks attention should be devoted to methods, technology, and training in motor skill. If so, he himself needs help.

One phrase in the question, "would not be accepted by plant management," is revealing. Perhaps this training man believes his responsibility is to provide only that training which is recognized as being needed by line operators. Or perhaps he does not know how to proceed when learners do not recognize their needs.

One of the best programs for strengthening a man's relations with associates is the National Training Laboratory in Group Development held each summer at Bethel, Maine, under the sponsorship of the National Training Laboratory in Group Development, Washington, D.C.

464   What Is the Simplest, Most Effective Type of Training Program That Can Improve the Human Relations Between Foremen and Employees in a Small Organization That Has No Training Director?

Role playing, with the conference led by a professionally qualified training man, who is borrowed part-time from some nearby industry or by a professor from a nearby college or university. Good men for this work are usually found in university departments of psychology, education, sociology, industrial relations, management, or human relations. Useful, but not quite so effective, is a series of conferences on human relations. Such programs usually include sessions on morale, leadership, the art of persuasion, communications, training, coaching or counseling, merit rating or evaluation, and the handling of grievances and reprimands.

465   What Is a Good Inducement for Present Executives to Train Their Subordinates in Executive Areas When No Opportunity Exists to Advance the "Trainees" in the Foreseeable Future?

Put the training emphasis upon doing better at the job which is presently held. Careful evaluations almost always show one or more weaknesses in the best of men or in their performance. Shape your training to improve these weaknesses in the men. Minimize promises, or even implications, that training is for promotion.

Train the present crop of executives to see how difficult it is, in such a situation, for their young men to remain patient, but growing understudies. For example, get them to play the roles of their subordinates and thus sense the frustration of able men who are forced to wait over-long for promotion. From this training, superiors may become willing to rotate some of these subordinates, to fatten their present jobs by adding challenging new duties, and even to provide them with training.

This training, as we state, should be primarily to improve the men in their jobs, but without saying it is doing so, it can reach ahead just a little and prepare the men for the distant day when they may be promoted. While training is doing both of these things it will be keeping the men alert, ambitious, and mentally active. It will be a guard against boredom, despair, and frustration.

466   How Do You Implant Drive and Incentive in People, to Give Them the Punch You Think They Ought to Have?

Perhaps the employee has as much "punch" as he desires to have. The boss should make sure his standards are realistic. A fundamental approach will include a study of human motivation. In fact, the questioner might begin by asking why the group shows so little initiative. When he has reasoned out the causes, his solution may be obvious. There is no easy way to "implant" drive. It is a function of the employee's health and constitution, his age, his placement, his training, his economic condition, how he responds to it, and particularly the leadership with which he works and the working climate that is developed for him.

467   How Can Training Be Used to Build Morale?

Alexander Leighton defines morale as "the capacity of a group of people to pull together consistently and persistently in pursuit of a common purpose."[7] The capacity depends upon:

1. The faith of each member of the group in its common purpose;
2. The faith of each member of the group in its leadership;
3. The faith of each member of the group in the other members;
4. The organizational efficiency of the group;
5. The health and balance of emotions in the individuals of the group.

Training is the fundamental tool for making known and understood the common purpose of any industrial or commercial organization. This is done by means of orientation training and other general education programs. Training supervisors and executives in the values and techniques of getting participation puts all levels of industry in a position to know the common purpose by means of sharing in the making of plans and programs.

Training also builds faith in leadership by improving leadership itself. Faith in leadership grows out of good leadership, which training helps to provide. To the degree that training teaches supervisors to unite production workers into teams, it strengthens the tendency of employees to rely upon each other. Training also builds teamwork and efficiency by getting employees in conference programs to share ideas and experiences. By building group spirit and group identity, organizational efficiency improves. Nondirective and informal types of training provide opportunities to be heard, and to participate in activities that reduce strain, frustration, and aggressiveness among individuals in the group. In these ways, training strengthens the capacity to work together toward a common purpose. This capacity is group morale.

[7] Alexander H. Leighton, *Human Relations in a Changing World* (New York: E. P. Dutton & Co., Inc.), 1949.

PART IV

ORGANIZING AND OPERATING DEVELOPMENT

Chapter 23

ORGANIZATION OF TRAINING OR DEVELOPMENT

468   **How Is Training or Development Organized?**

There are five basic plans[1] for organizing training and development:

> Plan One: The supervisor trains without assistance.
> Plan Two: The supervisor's assistant does the training.
> Plan Three: The supervisor does almost all the training, coached by Staff and Training specialists.
> Plan Four: Most of the training is done by staff assistant, at the request of a supervisor.
> Plan Five: The initial training is done by the Training Department before the employee reports to a supervisor.

These five plans differ primarily in their assignment of responsibility for training. At one extreme, in Plan One, line supervision has full responsibility for seeing that training is done and for actually doing it. Plan Five, on the other hand, places much of the responsibility for seeing that training is done, as well as for doing it, upon a staff and service department. The other plans reveal varying divisions of training responsibility between line and staff personnel.

469   **Where There Is a Full-Time Training Director or Development Man, to Whom Should He Report?**

Training programs, like programs for safety, placement, and health, are undertaken by management in order to preserve and improve human resources, and the management of these programs become the responsibility of the personnel department. Since the

---

[1] These plans are detailed in *Training Employees and Managers for Production and Teamwork*, by Earl G. Planty, William S. McCord, and Carlos A. Efferson (New York: The Ronald Press Co., 1948).

organizational principles of homogeneous assignment advises us to group like functions together, development and its director should—like recruitment, interviewing, placement, health, recreation, and safety—report to the personnel director.

Unfortunately, some personnel men and some personnel departments do not enjoy enough prestige within their own companies to enable them to handle the development of executives. This may be the fault of the personnel men themselves, or it may be due to an attitude of management which limits personnel services to wage and low-level salary employees. In either case, until personnel comes of age in these companies, it may be necessary to separate executive development from training and let it report elsewhere.

When the training director's position was first established in industry, he reported to manufacturing or production. Gradually, as personnel departments gained status and skill, the training of employees and managers is increasingly becoming a responsibility of personnel.

470   What About the Long-Standing Opinion That Training and Development Are the Proper Responsibilities and Functions of Line Supervisors?

This opinion is based on one obvious fact: the duty of every line supervisor to see that training is given to people under him. In the days when training was not formally organized, and when it was limited to motor skills, the supervisor could—and generally did—act as his own training "expert." Today, however, supervisors have neither the time nor the specialized interest needed to prepare themselves for the kinds of teaching that are required. Again and again, management finds that training specialists produce better results, at less cost, and in less time. As a result, progressive management is turning training and development over to staff specialists, whose help is invariably welcomed by enlightened line supervisors.

471   How Does the Staff Training Director Assign or Delegate the Actual Work of Training?

He doesn't. Responsibility for seeing that subordinates are trained is inherent in every supervisory or administrative job. The staff training director's functions are (a) to help men realize and accept this responsibility, and (b) to provide whatever assistance is needed in order to fulfill it. The former is accomplished through training classes for executives and supervisors: classes which clarify the functions and duties of executives and supervisors, both in general terms and by preparation of job analyses and job descriptions. If these prove inadequate, individual coaching is used to secure acceptance of responsibility for training, as well as an understanding of how that responsibility can be met.

Once this is accomplished, the executive or supervisor is almost sure to delegate the actual work of training to members of the training department. He also may call upon them to assist him or selected subordinates to carry out training. If he fails to do either of these, the training director must resume the process of education and stimulation which will lead the lagging manager to accept and then exercise his responsibility for training.

472   How Does the Director of Training Convince Operating People He Is a Staff Man?

If the director is a staff man, he acts like one. He stimulates, guides, advises, and assists in training work. He helps others to see needs for training and to establish programs. He helps them to teach and to follow up their activities. Unless a line man asks him to do so, he does not perform this work himself or through his subordinates. He limits himself to seeing that line men recognize the need for training, are prepared to give it, willingly undertake it, and carry it to successful completion.

473   Does the Presence of a Staff Training Department Tend to Discourage Independent Training Activities by Line Supervisors?

No. On the contrary, a strong staff department often leads operating men to analyze and improve long-established methods of production, to realize the contributions which training can make, and to undertake programs of self-improvement.

The authors are familiar with one company which has both a strong staff training department and very active training programs conceived and developed in the line. This organization had many young supervisors who looked forward to advancement, were full of ideas, and were unwilling to remain static. There were also several old-time supervisors who were unable to maintain the pace set by the younger men and were unprepared for the growing responsibilities of their jobs. On the other hand, they were actively cooperative and enthusiastic and willingly formed part of a team under the leadership of a young man who possessed both tact and exceptional ability. With only occasional advice from the training department, this group developed a series of monthly meetings held after work hours, with dinner provided by the company. Among the subjects considered in these meetings were:

1. The current engineering program, the status of construction and equipment projects, and their effects upon present processes, costs and personnel.
2. The need for and value of an employee appraisal program. This led to the appointment of a committee to explore the problem.
3. A proposed internal organization change and its possible further effects on the goals, programs, policies, and relationships of individuals and departments.
4. Problems of supervisory health. This discussion was preceded by a detailed physical examination of all members of the group.
5. The need for and value of a scientific morale survey. The group developed and applied to itself a trial survey before a professional one was made.
6. A review of standard personnel practices, with specific examples of difficulties encountered in interpretation or application. Individuals voluntarily presented problems which they had encountered in applying specific practices.
7. The line and staff relationship, with discussion of areas of responsibility and authority. Here a panel presented conflicting points of view as the meeting opened and then invited discussion.

This entire project—which ran concurrently with an extensive training program conducted by the company's staff training department—was conceived, developed, and presented by supervisors and technical personnel. By invitation of their committee, the staff training director made suggestions and attended the dinner meetings. The discussions were enthusiastic and thought provoking. Better still, cues for action were always followed. The meetings also led to the development of the following programs and many others:

1. An employee training program designed to acquaint a machine operator group with the specific functioning of the machine parts, the manner of making adjustments, problems of raw ma-

terials, quality, cost, and waste, and an explanation of the incentive rate. The growth of the product on which they worked was detailed, and the possibilities of product changes, increased sales and process changes were reviewed. This was an extended and highly rewarding program.

2. An after-hours indoor sports and calisthenics program for supervision, designed to stimulate an interest in health.

3. Review and improvement of an employee induction and orientation program which extended through a fourteen-week period, introducing the employee to his job, his company, his management, his union, fellow workers, department organization, personnel practices, etc.

4. Establishment of a weekly steward-foreman meeting to consider proposed projects and activities, as well as agreements reached on labor problems in one area which would interest others with similar problems.

5. Establishment of a committee to review employee suggestions and recommend awards.

6. Establishment of employee-management committees to review means of improving safety, health, and comfort of employees.

7. A daily newspaper was developed and posted on bulletin boards. It reported engineering changes, sales trends, production problems, personal news, organization changes, and anything else which affected employees in their daily work, or was of newsworthy interest. Writing and editing was done by the entire group of supervisory and technical personnel, who regularly contributed items. This paper has continued since its start three years ago.

474   How Do You Determine When It Is Necessary to Have a Man Assigned Full-Time to Training or Development?

The executive who asks this must first decide what he expects from training. To do this, he may review other companies' programs and study training literature. When he knows what services training can render he is in a position to choose those which he needs. He may conclude that he needs only a little orientation for new employees and a program of skill training for his machine operators. If the plant is small, these limited requirements may be met by the personnel director and line supervisors, without appointment of a full-time training man.

If the executive wishes to go further and provide a little general education, some economic training, a general course in supervisor training, as well as some orientation and technical training, he may still avoid employment of a full-time man. He can accomplish his purpose by assigning to the job a part-time man who will farm out most of the work to teachers from schools and colleges, training specialists from other companies, line and staff teachers within the company, and sometimes to professionally trained consultants.

These, however, are very limited objectives. The executive who studies literature and company programs will find that:

1. Training can seek to improve every employee, at every level, *in the job he now occupies*. It can challenge and stimulate every member of the organization to develop his own skills and abilities to the utmost. It can lead people to want to improve their performance. Having aroused this desire, it can help them to satisfy it.

2. Training can help line executives to develop regular performance evaluations and can show them how to counsel with every employee on his strengths and how to use them, as well as on his weaknesses and how to improve them.

3. Training can lead men and women at all levels to understand themselves better and thereby to gain understanding of others and their motivations.

4. Training can provide a sort of internal public relations program for the company, its management, and its policies and practices. It can make company and department goals known throughout the organization and secure acceptance of them as well as valuable criticism.

5. Training can show management the importance and values of employee participation in decisions and actions at various levels, and can develop means of securing it. Training can also develop the kind of leadership which satisfies the company's needs and meets the wants and needs of employees as well. In this day of broadening democracy, no organization can deal separately with the needs of the company and those of its employee. Training can make this understood and can provide means of satisfactorily dealing with both.

6. Training can both maintain performance standards and improve them.

The executive who decides that he needs these services, or a substantial part of them, will also find that he requires the services of a full-time director of development and training.

475 Is a Program for Developing Leadership Best Handled by a Full-Time Employee of the Company or by an Outside Firm or Individual?

It is best done within the company if size and resources permit assignment of a full-time man to the job. A full-time, internal man can determine the company's specific—and often unique—needs as no outsider can do. From contact and close association, the insider becomes familiar with the personalities of executives and supervisors and learns how to interest these men in development. A full-time, permanent assignment also allows the man to acquire professional skill and training in development if he lacks them when he comes to his job. Though these skills may not exceed those of the consultant, they can be more constantly and effectively employed.

Some companies, however, are not large enough for a full-time specialist in leadership development, and are forced to give a line man responsibility for part-time training work. Such a man will find it almost impossible to become professionally qualified in the complex and difficult field of human development. He therefore must call in outside help, going first to the business schools and departments of education and psychology in nearby universities. When he turns to consultants for help, he should carefully examine their qualifications.

476 Where There Is a Good Professional Training Staff, Should All Classes Be Taught by Its Members?

No. Some skills and understandings will be too complex, or too highly specialized to be mastered by professional training men. Others will come better from some person of greater stature and position in the company. This is usually true of policy explanations where trainees are reassured and made more confident by hearing the policy from a high-level line superior than from a staff training man. However, where exposition or persuasion is required to carry the learners beyond understanding and secure acceptance of what is taught, it may be well to use a staff training man. The question here is whether it is better to teach the content by firm authority or by persuasion and clear explanation and some degree of learner participation. Where there is a good professional training staff, much of the teaching will be done by them. Part of it will be better done by others whom the staff people will prepare for the work.

477   Who Does the Actual Teaching in a Development Program?

There are six good sources of teachers:

1. The man's boss, on a continuous day-to-day basis through coaching, counseling, and guided experiences.
2. Employees of the organization—people at executive, supervisory, and employee levels—who teach formal classes upon request of the director of development or training.
3. Full-time internal training men or instructors who may or may not be professionally trained teachers.
4. Teachers from vocational schools, public high schools, colleges and universities.
5. Outside specialists and highly qualified experts in various fields, drawn from government and other businesses.
6. Training consultants who are professionally prepared as educators.

478   If, as You Say, a Professional Teacher Makes a Better Training Director Than a Practical Man with Successful Staff or Line Experience, Why Aren't There More Professional Men in Training and Development Jobs?

There are several reasons for this. In the days when training was concerned primarily with the development of motor skills, practical men could handle the job. Many practical men who became training directors during that period are still employed in that capacity. Some have realized what a full program of training can be and are now preparing themselves for it. Others still cling to the early, limited concept of development.[2] They are content to offer skill and motor training through JIT, JMT, apprenticeship courses, and possibly a vestibule school. Until these men grow old and retire, professional men can hardly replace them.

Professional teachers with industrial experience are scarce. The supply of capable professionally qualified training men is too small to meet the present demand, so that others must be employed. The field is still developing and the services which training can render have not yet been made clear to the great body of company presidents and other executives. Many of these men, therefore, retain the old motor-skill concept of training. They are

---

[2] The reader will remember that the words "training" and "development" are used synonymously throughout this book.

satisfied with "practical" teachers, since they do not ask for the kind of training that requires the leadership of professional men.

It is well to remember, also, that some of the early professional training directors failed. Neither they nor the schools and colleges that trained them understood the practical, vital needs of industry. Such directors often were slow, academic, and even incompetent as teachers. They were unwilling to learn about industry and adjust their services and their tempos to the fast-moving, dynamic call of practical-minded adults. They tried to offer adult, successful, business leaders the same courses and the same methods they had used for college undergraduates, who did not have to make profits and meet aggressive competition. Better men are now coming out of the schools. Instead of transplanting into industry something that has worked for adolescents on college campuses, they are prepared to develop courses and methods that actually meet industrial needs.

479   In a Medium-Sized Corporation, What Position Does the Training or Development Director Usually Occupy, in the Hierarchy of Management? How Many Levels away from the President?

Training and development are growing in stature. In a few companies, the director reports to the president, to an assistant to the president, or to some confidant of the top executive. In a great many companies, the training director reports to a vice president in charge of industrial and labor relations or production. Where the personnel or labor relations director is on a level with the director of operations, the training man may report to him—a highly satisfactory arrangement. But where training reports to a personnel director who in turn reports to a director of manufacturing or production, the stature of training is reduced to a point where it is difficult to gain executive cooperation.

In most companies, the training director has traditionally occupied a position above that of general foreman and just a little below that of plant superintendent. In companies where it is still assigned routine, detailed jobs, and is directed by a man who lacks professional preparation, the director enjoys less stature and influence, and merits less. In companies where the full values of modern, professionally directed training are recognized, however, the training director may occupy a position as important as that of the director of engineering services, personnel, or research.

480   How Are Over-All Training Policies and Programs Developed?

Committees established to help the training director are most useful for this purpose. The training director, however, must keep himself up to date on policies and programs that are succeeding elsewhere in order to provide the committee with information necessary for its work. To do this he will have to read extensively, visit other organizations, and attend conferences on management, personnel and training subjects.

Committees sometimes attack policy development directly and spell out answers to the following questions even before they arise:

> When production operators, clerical or secretarial help, or first line supervisors are used to teach, how should they be paid?
>
> Shall formal training take place on company time?
>
> Shall specific programs be developed to meet general company-wide needs and given throughout the organization?
>
> Shall completion of training courses be recorded in personnel records and used as a basis for promotions or salary increases?
>
> Shall the company refund tuition paid by employees for useful school and college courses?
>
> Shall universities or outside consultants be used in the program? If so, what criteria must be used in selecting them?

Sometimes the committee does not spell out these policies in advance. Instead, it meets the problems as they arise and establishes policies to meet actual situations.

481   How Is Development Organized Where There Is No Staff or Outside Help?

Any executive or supervisor who sees a need for training in his department or in the company proceeds to meet that need. If it is limited to his own department, he and his subordinates may act as a committee to:

1. Explore and clearly define the need.
2. Discover what combination of teaching and experience will satisfy it.
3. Prepare the necessary teaching materials or set up the job assignments, committee memberships, rotations, etc.

4. Place the man to be developed where he can learn, either in class or on the job.

5. Follow up on the learning.

Where the need for development goes beyond an executive's own department, he proceeds in similar manner except that he invites other executives to join him, constructing a plan that will meet the requirements of all.

482   How Are the Functions of a Training (or Development) Department Organized?

A typical organization is illustrated below.

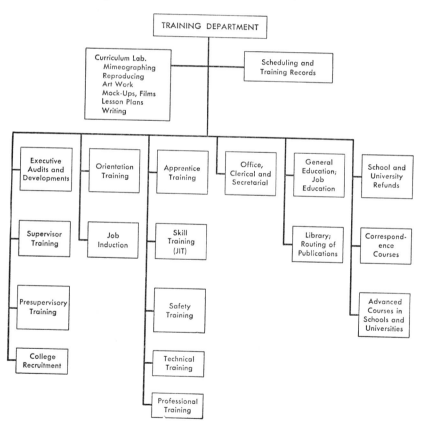

Chapter 24

DETERMINING NEEDS FOR DEVELOPMENT

483 **How Are Development or Training Needs Determined?**

The wise manager will use a variety of approaches, or will see that his training specialists do so. Some of the standard methods of determining what to teach are as follows:

1. Published research reports and magazine articles report widespread needs already discovered by other counselors, training experts, and line executives. Such lists may not fit the individual company or plant, but they provide general background.
2. Questionnaires sent to prospective trainees reveal areas in which they realize their own need for improvement.
3. Outside consultants, personnel directors, in-plant counselors and union stewards frequently hear of organizational or individual weaknesses. Their reports, therefore, may indicate training needs.
4. Training conferences of middle-level executives sometimes reveal inadequacies of other levels, and vice versa.
5. Opinion and attitude surveys are revealing, as are attitudes of the community toward the business and individuals in it.
6. Studies of errors and failures also help: rejections, business losses, grievances, loss of personnel to other companies, inroads of competition, etc.
7. Analysis of the records of men who are promoted and fail in their new jobs show where they need development.
8. Exit interviews provide useful hints, and the medical department can furnish information about emotional problems, work loads, and morale.
9. Statements of the aims and objectives of universities that have had long experience in training managers should be obtained and studied.
10. Job analysis at the executive level is new, but it is bringing results. It reveals the duties of each executive and so provides a basis for individualized and group programs which prepare men to give better and better performance in their jobs.

348

11. Executive and supervisory adults and evaluations undertake to discover and record needs of individuals for improvement. They serve as very fine guides to training needs.
12. Requests for training often come from operating people. Their close association with employees and their performance frequently indicates a need for development.

484   Are Training Needs Specific or General?

Both. Specific needs call for training that will help lick bothersome, costly, immediate problems. Meeting these needs contributes to the immediate momentary success of the operation. It also wins the support and loyalty of practical-minded men whose concern is with day-to-day problems.

Still, training is more than remedial action. It cannot devote all its effort to mending fences and putting out fires. Training must have long-term programs to help anticipate and prevent problems—programs that are preventive, not therapeutic. It is better, easier, and much cheaper to teach executives, supervisors and employees how to operate without causing problems than it is to help solve problems and correct errors once they have developed.

Planned training requires long-term, general objectives. Without them the training director is at the mercy of every operating emergency which arises. His work is purely remedial and his progress over a few years time will be recorded only in a list of specific courses to cure specific ills. The fundamental cause of the problems may never be discovered and attacked systematically through general, preventive training.

This is well illustrated by one company in which turnover was a problem. Supervisors were given a two-hour course in turnover, its cost, and how to reduce it. An analysis of separations seemed to show that methods of reprimanding and poor training techniques were at fault. Stop-gap training in these two areas was given, but the high turnover continued. Another look at the situation brought the company and training a little closer to the real problem. This time it was decided to teach the union contract and grievance handling. Again there was inadequate reduction in turnover. But the training director and his committee began to see the cause of the problem: supervisors resented the union, which had entered the plant a year or two earlier. They thought it reduced their authority and made their work harder. Some of them thought or hoped that it was in the plant only temporarily.

Others cherished an unjustified belief that the company did not want the union and hoped to see it weaken and fail.

When the training man went at the problem in a broad general fashion, he attacked the fundamental attitudes of supervision that were causing the problem. To do this he brought in company executives, outside consultants and supervisors and executives to talk about the place of unionism in American industry today. When these men convinced supervisors that the union had a right to be in the plant, that it was national in character and that the company wanted to cooperate with it, a basis for practical progress was established. By means of role playing, cases, and conferences, the training director then led the men to see what actions increased turnover and what part conduct on their part reduced it. The problem that had resisted piecemeal measures was solved by this broad, general approach.

485   How Are General Development Needs Determined?

1. By reviewing what other companies and the universities and schools are teaching.

2. By comparing the learner's knowledge and skill with that which is known in the field under consideration.

3. By discovering which specific need is found in many divisions of a company. It then becomes a general need.

4. By analyzing jobs and their performance to learn what skills are broadly required—as public speaking and rapid reading for all executives.

5. By careful examination of specific needs. Frequently, questions and analysis reveal that a need which seems to be specific really is only one aspect of a general one.

486   What Training Subjects Generally Attract Attention and Have a Good Chance for Success? In Other Words, What General Needs Are There?

The first general need, of course, is job training in motor and manual skills of all kinds: simple machine and hand operations, elevator operation, carton sealing, stock record procedures, inspection techniques, traffic direction, packaging, motor vehicle operation, loading, dining room practice, making out sales slips, filling out forms, simple maintenance of machines such as cleaning, oiling, etc.

There is also a general need for orientation training at all levels of the business, to enlarge employee knowledge of the company, its product or service, its policies and possible profits.

Furthermore, training in public speaking for all members of management is generally needed, as is training in conference leadership for those who hold or attend many meetings.

487   How Can the Various Levels of Management and the Training Department Cooperate for Maximum Success in Meeting and Dealing with Training Needs?

Probably through training committees. Most companies set up a training committee to guide and assist the training director in determining needs, in developing programs, and in administering them. Represented on this committee are several levels of management and a representative of each function served by the training director. The Goodyear Rubber Corporation has an interesting committee which it calls its Board of Education. Where training committees do not exist, the training director meets with department heads to discuss their training needs and then prepares training programs which meet the most common needs.

Advanced planning also helps. At Johnson & Johnson a yearly plan is issued describing (a) courses definitely to be given, (b) courses requested and being prepared, and (c) courses requested and under investigation. Courses in the first category are those which have been fully planned, prepared, and tried out, and are available to any department which may want them. The second group includes courses definitely decided upon and in such advanced stages of preparation that they probably will be offered during the year. The third category lists courses the need for which is being weighed, along with the training department's ability to teach them. These yearly plans are carefully worked out with training representatives and management. Well circulated at all levels, they inform employees of available training and elicit their opinions before things become final.

488   Does the Director of Development Accept Only Recognized Needs, or Does He Try to Get Acceptance of Needs Which Have Been Overlooked by Others?

He starts by working with needs that are recognized by his associates and trainees. Even during this development however, he may subtly lead learners to perceive educational needs which they have overlooked.

In the long run, of course, the director of development does not ignore fundamental needs merely because others fail to see them. He has an individual training job in getting men to see these weak spots in themselves and others. But he must not force his ideas upon other adults. He will, instead, set situations so that the learners see and accept new learning goals.

489   When There Are Several Needs for Any Person or Groups of Persons, How Does One Determine Which Is Primary?

Where a man has several needs it may be best to start with the one which the learner himself recognizes most clearly and is most eager to meet. Another consideration is whether or not improvement is likely. If a man has more than one major failing, it is best to start with the one which offers the greatest likelihood of improvement. Success here will make easier the task of meeting the other needs.

The cost of the weakness to the man or the company may also determine where to begin. No man should be allowed to slide along with a failing that embarrasses him daily and costs his superior time, money, and unpleasantness.

490   How Do You Get Men to Recognize Their Own Development Needs?

Regular merit rating or evaluation is the best device to reveal men's needs. Direct or indirect suggestion may sometimes help, as in counseling after merit rating. General descriptions of training programs which are posted on company bulletin boards, which appear in company papers, and which are announced in staff meetings, may lead some people to see their needs and seek admission to a program. Attendance in one course may get men to see the need for others. Role playing and case studies also frequently bring about realization of weakness.

Sometimes the problem is not one of recognition but one of permission. The man must be given freedom to determine his own needs instead of accepting some other person's concept of his requirements.

Chapter 25

SECURING ACCEPTANCE FOR TRAINING OR DEVELOPMENT

---

491   **Who Needs to Be Sold on Development and What Selling Is Required?**

Under ideal circumstances, high-level members of management understand development, support it, and welcome it for themselves and for others who need it. Sometimes, however, ignorance or opposition exist at the very top, so that the president and vice presidents must be sold on organized approaches. They need to learn the value of development and what support they will have to give in order to realize those values. Ignorance may exist even where management hires a training or development director and pays his salary and the expenses of his department. In such cases management seems to take development on faith, or as something to be done because others do it. This leaves the training or development department without real backing, since management cannot support development unless it knows what it is, what it has done for other companies, and what it can do for this particular organization.

In most companies, the old, experienced employees at all levels need to be informed and convinced before they can see the values of training. Having grown up in the business, and having learned by the slow and costly process of trial and error, they do not realize the place which development has taken in modern industry or the help it can give them and their subordinates.

Older men and women usually resist a little more than newer employees and occasionally need encouragement to undertake it. No training or development director can assume that people will demand an opportunity to take part in learning activities, without promotional work on his part. Many nonprofessional men in the training field are frustrated by this need to persuade and encour-

353

age people to begin self-development. They see no need for continuous promotion of training and they blame management and individuals for not being enthusiastic about their service. Even when nonprofessional men are willing to promote training, they do not know how to do so. The professional educator or teacher, however, accepts this situation and knows how to meet it. He knows how to arouse and develop interest. He also knows that every lecture, conference, or other learning activity must be planned and conducted so as to motivate the learner, to stimulate or strengthen his desire to improve. By accepting facts for which he is prepared, he feels neither surprise nor resentment, and does not feel frustrated when his first efforts are not welcomed by the people who need his help.

492   How Can Management Be Convinced That Training Is a Desirable Function?

Results are good convincers. If the beginner can get enough support to start instruction, and if the first training results are good, they will be the best means of convincing management. In one division of the Johnson & Johnson companies, for example, a course in reading[1] was offered to help executives who were required to read many reports, surveys, routine memos, and outside magazines and books. Tests given before and after the 17-hour course showed an increase in reading speed of 95 per cent, with a small increase in comprehension. These facts spoke for themselves, and many executives who originally showed no interest in the course later requested it.

In another instance, a group of plant foremen entered a course in public speaking. At its conclusion they organized a speakers' bureau and offered their services to local civic, professional and women's clubs for luncheon and after-dinner speaking. In a year's time, they had filled 170 outside engagements, which is strong proof that they had become proficient. There are now waiting lists of men who want to take public speaking.

If management is to be convinced of the desirability of training where no organized training exists, the best approach is for some one like the questioner to start training activities in his own unit. If his results are good he will be able to extend training to other departments and units of his company.

[1] This is described fully in "A Reading Improvement Program for Industry," by W. V. Machaver and W. A. Borrie, *Personnel*, September, 1951.

493   What Causes Resistance to Development or Training?

The superior hasn't time for individual guidance. He resists the loss of productive time which an employee spends on rotation, guided experience, or other types of learning. The superior believes in learning through unguided experience. Other factors causing resistance to learning are poorly taught classes, unrealistic choice of subjects, lack of management support, fear of failing or of appearing to poor advantage in the classes, poor physical surroundings, classes scheduled at hours when trainees are fatigued, too heavy a teaching load for the instructor, too much telling, and too little participation of trainees in the learning, too little realistic use of training results and records in merit ratings, pay, and selection for promotion. Trainees who are smug or complacent also resist development activities. Before a management or a director of development undertakes to overcome opposition to his activities, he must determine which of these causes are behind resistance, and where he himself is at fault.

494   How Can I Persuade a Long-Established Firm to Introduce Formal Training?

Armed with examples of training programs that have been carried out successfully in other long-established firms, you may ask support for a program in your own unit. You will, of course, have studied your own needs and will show your superiors how the program you plan to establish will help ease your burdens. Once you are in operation, see that heads of other departments have a chance to observe your program, to participate in it, and to follow its results. Participation may involve attending classes as visitor or trainee, teaching certain sections, or serving on committees set up to plan, conduct, or evaluate training.

When constructive results have been obtained, present reports to management which give the full story of how the program has operated, what it has meant in time and cost and effort, and what have been its results in terms of improved performance and better understanding. These reports should be planned carefully for the greatest possible promotional value. Sometimes they will be oral reports at staff or board meetings; sometimes they will be informal oral reports injected into conversations with the proper individuals at the right time and place. At other times the reports will be written and formal. Choosing the proper method of reporting is a delicate task which requires a study of the message conveyed and the personalities and preferences of the men to be informed.

Once you have your own training activities under way or a program or two completed, you will readily assist those who want to undertake similar programs for themselves.

495   Are There Any Case Studies Which Will Help Get Understanding of Management Development and Sell It to Company Executives?

Yes. One case, entitled "George Holmes—Talent Scout," is published by the Executive Program in Business Administration, Graduate School of Business, Columbia University. This case describes a company which had no development program and no men inside the company worthy of promotion. To meet the problem the company hired a talent scout to recruit executives from outside.

Another case, "Robert Harvey," also published by The Executive Program at Columbia, reviews the problems faced by a company with no training or development program when its foremen decided to unionize.

Further help can be secured from references in the bibliography.

496   How Do You Convince Members of Top Management That They Should Spend the Time and Effort to Get Further Training in Techniques of Management?

Expose these skeptics to good management development programs by taking them to visit those in some of our major universities. Let them see the programs in operation, meet the faculty, and discover the stature and competence of some of the trainees who have gone back to school.

Invite teachers and administrators of such programs to company staff meetings or special seminars to describe their programs to company executives.

Tell what other major business executives are doing to develop themselves. Circulate lists of names and titles of top level men who are studying in advanced management schools.

Work intensively with one or two executives who are favorably inclined toward improvement. Once they become active in development work—either in or out of the plant—others are likely to follow.

Discover specific techniques in which resistant executives may be weak, such as upward or horizontal communications, sound investment of reserve capital, or the launching of a new product. Set up one or two meetings on the subject and invite them to attend. Better still, try to get them to help you set up these meetings and conduct them. Find some area of management technique at which the same men are proficient. Get them to teach it as part of a larger program. It often happens that they show an interest in the whole program, once their specialty and their proficiency in it is recognized.

Invite the superiors of these men to talk with them about their need for development and the programs available to help them.

497   How Do I Answer the Very Cooperative Operating Official Who Says, "I Agree with You 100 Per Cent, But I'm Too Busy to Do the Training Myself. You're the Expert and I Depend on You to Relieve Me of This Burden"?

If the official who says he is too busy to do the teaching himself is referring to formal management training classes and not to on-the-job coaching or guided experience, he may be right. Why not take him at his word and relieve him of his burden? It isn't obligatory that he take an active part in the formal training program, especially at the outset. You should be the one to set up the formalized training which his staff needs, in consultation with him or with his men, if that is possible.

When your program is under way, explain to the official why management must take an active interest in training. Then secure his participation gradually. Get him to attend opening meetings of new programs and to make introductory remarks. We have encountered no executive who is too busy either to give a brief introductory talk at the beginning of a new program or to present graduation certificates at the end. As this executive's subordinates grow in ability, through experience and the training they are getting, he can shift some of his activities to them. Thus he will have time to give you substantial help, and even to do some of the teaching.

If the executive thinks he is too busy to provide his men with on-the-job guidance, counsel, and coaching, he is in error, for this work cannot be delegated. Use training and counsel to prove this to him.

498   **How Can I Get Top Management to Support All Development Programs—by Actual Participation as Well as by Spoken Approval?**

Begin with oral support—and then make the most of it. Set up a training meeting or a series of meetings especially for top-level executives. For this first venture find some problem or subject area which they recognize as their responsibility and which has not been adequately treated in other company meetings, outside conferences, or business and professional literature. Likely subjects of a general nature include the dynamics of industrial organization, problems in launching a new product, legal aspects of pricing, the controller's function, new methods of forecasting sales, salary administration, and stockholder or community relations. Research on your part may reveal more specific operating problems of even greater interest to top management.

Approach as many executives as possible while you are planning. Tell them why you chose this particular subject and ask their opinions and help in setting it up. When you are ready to start, invite all members of top management to attend. The attendance may well prove that these people are ready to participate in programs designed especially for them.

Another way to secure support is to persuade as many executives as possible to take part in original planning and even in teaching parts of the training program for their subordinates. At the outset only one or two may be willing to do this, but begin with them and you will find that the prestige and stature which they give to your program will help you attract other executives as teachers. From this start, the alert training man will find or make opportunities to offer training to these executives themselves, and even get them to ask for it. Being active in training their own subordinates, they are not likely to misunderstand or fear activities aimed at their own development.

499   **How Much Support Is Needed from Top Management Successfully to Start a Training Program for Line Supervisors and Department Superintendents?**

The least you must have is top management's approval to start such a program. If this is all you can get at the outset, you must strive to develop such an effective program that it will enlist the actual support of men who at first merely gave approval.

Where management is enthusiastic and strong in its support,

the training supervisor has an excellent chance for success, but no guarantee of it. He will have to develop a sound program, well taught by skillful instructors. Even then he may be required to do some selling and promotion. Adults seldom feel ready-made enthusiasm for their own development. They must be encouraged and stimulated to participate. Whether or not they motivate themselves thereafter depends partly upon their satisfaction with the first exposure.

Chapter 26

GETTING TRAINING OR DEVELOPMENT UNDER WAY

---

500 What Must Be Done to Organize a Development or Training Department?

Once a company decides to establish a training department, it must take four major steps: (1) Define the functions of training—what it is, what it does, who does it, and for whom—and assign authority and responsibility, (2) Place the department in the organization as a whole, deciding where training will report and whom it will serve, (3) Organize training itself by defining the units that go to make up the training service and arrange them into a systematic pattern, and (4) Write job descriptions, staff the department with the training director and his aides.

501 What Are the Early Steps in Establishing a Broad Training Program?

Management should first determine why it needs training programs and what it expects to get from them. It should then ask what the activities will cost in time, money, and participation by learners. When management is thoroughly convinced of the value of training and has appropriated enough money to give the program a three- or four-year trial, the department should be planned and organized.

Planning usually starts with a job description of the training director's position, including his duties and responsibilities. At this point management decides whether the training man will do much of the teaching himself or whether he will concentrate on finding good teachers in the organization, improving their skills, developing good teaching materials for them or helping them to develop teaching aids themselves.

Once these steps have been taken, management is ready to select a training man, introduce him throughout the organization, and patiently explain his function at all levels of the company.

502   What Is the Sequence of Steps in Preparing and Offering Any Training Course?

1. Survey the needs for the particular course. Ask who needs it. Why? How badly is it needed?

2. If the course is needed, survey the demand for it. Is the need for training recognized? Has the training been wanted or requested? Or will the training men have to develop both recognition of the need and a demand for training?

3. Outline on paper the specific training objectives.

4. Survey the resources available for meeting the need. Are course outlines from other companies available for guidance? Are texts, lesson plans, tests, case studies, films, readings or other learning materials available? Who will teach the course? What training and practice will the teachers need? Is the physical equipment available or at hand—projectors, mock-ups, conference or classrooms, recording equipment, public address systems, etc.

5. Estimate the costs, and get necessary approval and support for the program.

6. Prepare the training materials—course outlines, daily lesson plans or conference outlines, work sheets, cases, tests, etc. If these materials are at hand from some other source, revise and adapt them to your own needs.

7. Select and train the instructors. Some training men feel that this should be done before Step six so that the teachers may participate in preparing their own teaching materials.

8. Hold trial or practice sessions to make sure that the teaching is effective.

9. Execute the program.

    a. Create or intensify the demand, as may be necessary.

    b. Schedule the training.

    c. Announce the program.

    d. Teach!—this is the important step. All else is preliminary or subordinate to it.

10. Follow up or evaluate, both while the course is in progress and after its completion.

503   As a Comparatively New Man in the Training Field, How Shall I Start in Order to Give Effective Service?

Begin by preparing yourself for the work ahead. At the same time, get your organization ready for training by taking some such steps as these:

1. Bring in one or two outstanding training men who have established local programs. Let them meet influential executives and supervisors and appear before staff meetings of production or office superintendents. Arrange for the experts to describe their own programs, speak on some timely aspect of training, or discuss some contemplated use of training within your plant. The speakers should, of course, be available to answer questions which executives may ask.

2. Invite a few influential men in the company to observe training programs in nearby plants. Such visits will show what training can do and will stimulate their thinking about its value in their own plant.

3. After these steps, establish an advisory training committee. When the members have been oriented to their responsibilities they should begin to consider the training needs of their plant and start preparing their own program.

504   Where There Has Been No Development Work at All, How Can It Be Determined Which Group Needs Training First: (1) Plant Workers, (2) Foremen, or (3) Executives and Department Heads?

We cannot determine with scientific accuracy which of the three groups mentioned stands in greatest need of training. Even if we could do so, we might find this an unwise group to start with. The wise training director starts where there is both a recognized need and a likelihood that training can be well done and will be enthusiastically received by the trainees.

505   Where Is the Best Place to Begin Formal Training in a Small Company That Has Virtually No Formal Training Program?

Begin with the induction and orientation of new workers. The first steps in orientation are accomplished by the persons who do the hiring. In the employment interview, they give the new worker constructive concepts of the organization. After employment comes formal orientation: a carefully planned meeting in which company information is presented, questions are answered for the newcomer, and positive attitudes toward the company and the job are developed. A second part of the orientation program introduces the new employee in the department where he is to work. For this an outline should be prepared indicating the things that his immediate supervisor should discuss with him during his first day on the job. This orientation procedure may last more than one day; in many plants it does. In any event, orientation makes an ideal starting point for formal training activities.

A second area in which formalized training may be started is on-the-job training. In it supervisors are shown how to prepare job breakdowns for teaching purposes, as well as how to teach.

Experience shows that public speaking, supervisory practices, conference leadership and work simplification all make starting points that offer considerable promise of success.

506   We Have About 200 Employees But No Training Program for Supervisors. How and Where Should We Begin One?

The first step in starting such a program is to assign the responsibility for training to one individual and make it a significant part of his job. The person chosen may well be a line or a staff man who has shown interest in training and development. He should first meet with the supervisors and discuss training needs with them. He should find out what they want to learn and should be prepared to show them what other companies do in the way of supervisor training. Examples of good programs can be obtained from the American Management Association, Metropolitan Life Insurance Company, state or local universities, and from other companies. After studying what is needed in his own company, and after reviewing what other companies have done, he may decide to start with a series of meetings on some one of the following:

Work Simplification	Supervisory Orientation
Quality Control	Conference Leadership
Public Speaking	Communications
Leadership	Operating Budgets
Safety	Job Instruction
Human Relations	

Or, it may be decided that a general course in supervisory practices is needed. Such a course might include meetings on such subjects as the following:

Maintaining Discipline	Giving Orders and Direction
Handling Grievances	Principles of Organization
Getting Participation	Human Wants and Needs

507   **How Can the Controller of a Company Without a Training Director Start a Development Program in His Department?**

He will first prepare his group. In his weekly staff meetings the controller will start referring to training and its values. He will circulate training outlines or programs from nearby companies or from other divisions of his own concern. If anyone in his department shows interest, the controller will invite him to visit nearby plants and offices and to report to the regular staff meeting on the training he observes. The controller may also ask one or two of his group to visit the training sections of conferences or seminars sponsored by the American Management Association, the Society for the Advancement of Management, the National Association of Cost Accountants, or the National Office Management Association. An outside training man or consultant may be brought in to speak to the controller's group on office training. Clear and concise articles on training can be routed through his staff.

When the group seems to understand training and what it can do, he will invite a few of his men to survey the training needs of their departments. Their report may suggest such training needs as Comptometer operation, telephone technique, secretarial etiquette, typing, shorthand, bookkeeping, keypunch operation, elementary economics, orientation to the company or the department, business letter writing, the handling of customer complaints, interpreting budgets, tax law, forecasting, etc.

The course or courses in greatest demand will be decided upon in group discussion. The controller then appoints a small committee to prepare outlines for teaching. The controller will teach the subjects himself, or will seek an instructor elsewhere—either in the company or possibly outside the concern.

Chapter 27

DUTIES AND RESPONSIBILITIES OF THE DIRECTOR OF TRAINING OR DEVELOPMENT

508 What Are the General Functions of the Director of Training or Development?[1]

There are four major functions to be performed by the person in charge of training or development:

1. He determines the needs for training and development, helping decide *who* needs to learn more or different things, and helping decide *what* it is they should learn.

2. He teaches or otherwise provides the required learning opportunites, helping to provide facilities or services, mostly in the nature of on-the-job or off-the-job development activities, that make efficient learning possible. He takes part in the actual work of instruction when that is desirable.

3. He promotes the use of training, encouraging participation in training and helping individuals develop willingness to learn. These actions may take place simultaneously with the preceding ones.

4. He evaluates and follows up on training, helping his staff or line men to review achievements in training and measure its results. He helps instructors and supervisors reshape programs in terms of their findings.

509 What Are the Specific Duties of the Director of Development?

These vary from company to company, but the following specific statements, taken at random from half a dozen job descriptions, indicate that the typical director will:

[1] See "A Survey of Duties and Responsibilities of Training Personnel in Business and Industry," by David F. Reeve, Division of Education and Applied Psychology, Purdue University, June, 1953. This is a 42-page digest of 308 answers to a questionnaire, filled out by development men, which inquired about their duties, age, education, tenure, salary, etc. The pamphlet describes an excellent research.

1. Establish a system of supervisory and executive audits.
2. Set up training and development programs, both formal and informal, based upon needs revealed by audits, opinion surveys, studies of errors, job analysis, and common teaching practices in the industry.
3. Develop and administer the following specific programs:
    a. A program for orientation of new employees and supervisors.
    b. A cadet training program for recent college graduates and other employees of comparable status.
    c. A supervisor training program for group and individual development of established supervisors.
    d. An executive development program for individual and group training of executives.
    e. A program of educational courses offered in collaboration with outside agencies.
    f. A program for vestibule, apprentice, on-the-job, clerical, safety, machine operator, and other types of motor and mechanical training.
    g. A program of general education for wage and salary employees, supervisors and executives.
4. Select prospective teachers and train them in conference leadership, methods of instruction, use and development of teaching aids, curriculum construction and classroom management.
5. Provide refresher training for experienced teachers.
6. Furnish and equip classrooms, and arrange vestibule and production situations for training.
7. Prepare budgets and keep unit cost figures on training.
8. Prepare course outlines, write manuals, job sheets, and flyers for short specialized courses drawn from the broad fields of engineering, industrial management, personnel administration, skilled trades, office practices, sales, vocational psychology, teacher training, public and human relations, etc.
9. Keep records of attendance and course completions.
10. Contact state, federal, and private educational agencies, and obtain their services when they can be useful.
11. Plan and direct company schools, workshops, and conferences established to promote training objectives.
12. Train division and plant personnel to use daily work situations in order to develop their subordinates.
13. Counsel individually with top management on problems that might be solved through training. Participate in management's planning when it involves the development of executives, supervisors, or employees.

14. Help executives and supervisors find and use job assignment, rotations, committee work, and other internal opportunities for promoting the growth of their subordinates.
15. Establish a library, encourage its use, and supervise its growth.
16. Determine how training needs differ at various levels in the company and discover practical group and individual methods of developing presidents and vice presidents at one extreme and semiskilled or unskilled wage earners at the other.
17. Analyze jobs and operations. Make job breakdowns for teaching purposes.
18. Counsel, advise, and teach so as to develop throughout the organization a climate that encourages individual growth and development.
19. Publicize, dramatize, and sell the values of training. Stimulate use of training through bulletin boards and news stories for the company papers. Contact operating departments, supervisors and employees, win their confidence, and offer development services useful to them, at the same time building management and employee attitudes that are receptive to training.
20. Advise management on the promotion, transfer and wider use of persons who are competent and well trained.
21. Offer vocational and educational guidance to those who need it.
22. Develop and administer procedures to evaluate the results accomplished by training activities.

510   When There is a Director of Executive Development, Operating Separately from the Regular Training Program, What Are His Duties?

One multi-company organization with a long history of executive development introduced the position and described its functions in the following memorandum from the Chairman of the Board to all major executives:

Over the years our executive staff has grown to large proportions. This is particularly true when one considers our associate companies operating in this area. We believe that our relations with the employee level have been improved, but we find that no provision has been made in the field of executive relations beyond the fact that many divisions and companies are conducting themselves well in this field. However, due perhaps to our rapid expansion and our concentrated attention upon building plants and staffing them, there seem to be weaknesses in several directions. Hence, we decided that someone should make this field his responsibility. We have called the position Director of Executive Development and have assigned the following responsibilities to it:

1. To improve communications at all executive levels.
2. To inquire into and gain first-hand information from educational institutions, concerning refresher courses and other institutional activities which may be of assistance to our executives, and to encourage executives to take advantage of appropriate adult education.
3. To study and encourage job rotation.
4. To become informed about company executives, and so operate a clearing house for candidates to which an executive in one division or company may go if he wishes to fill an important post and prefers to secure a qualified member of our executive team from some other division or company than his own.
5. To study the administrative and executive procedures of the best-managed companies in the United States and bring to us information and detailed data from such corporations.
6. To arrange executive meetings for the total staff with really well-qualified speakers and teachers.
7. To examine our executive relations on all levels in an attempt to locate and define our weaknesses and make recommendations for their elimination. To discover our best practices and recommend them from plant to plant.
8. To improve our executive community relations.
9. To encourage management to recruit qualified juniors and to aid the growth and development of these juniors through counsel and advice, both with them and their superiors.

Our future as a successful enterprise depends upon our ability to locate, develop, and retain good executives. Our success in doing this will depend upon the strength of our executive relations and our development activities.

This memo illustrates an advanced step in introducing executive development into a company. There were, of course, many preliminary conversations with executives—conversations that clarified needs and brought essential agreement before the position was created and the statement about it prepared.

511   What Personal Qualifications Are Important in the Man Who Directs Development Work?

1. He should be well above average in intelligence.
2. He should have the ability to grasp situations quickly, an ability possessed only by persons with naturally alert and curious minds.
3. He should have a constructive dissatisfaction with inefficient

ways, confusion, mismanagement, and waste of human and material resources. Instead of merely finding fault, he should be ready to help make improvements.

4. He should be willing and able to put himself into other men's places before judging people or systems.

5. He should be able to communicate new ideas and to generate enthusiasm for them, be able to use words effectively and persuasively, and be possessed of a poise that will inspire trust and confidence.

6. He should be willing to work long and hard to achieve what ought to be but too seldom is.

512   Which Is More Desirable in the Leader of a Training or Development Program: Knowledge of Company Personnel, Policies, and Procedures, or Knowledge of Pedagogy?

Knowledge of teaching and learning is paramount. The training director can learn a large part of the necessary company policy and procedure if he is to teach it. In most cases he can learn this subject matter more quickly than the line or staff executive can learn to teach effectively.

If the training director is too heavily involved in planning and organization to teach courses himself, or if he finds it impractical to master certain technical subject matter, he may delegate the work of actual instruction. In such cases his responsibility is to teach others to teach. Above all, therefore, he must be a specialist in the art and science of pedagogy.

In fact, the quality of the teaching is the training director's primary responsibility. He may handle all other functions well and yet fail completely if he provides poor instruction. Too many development programs in industry have surrounded their teaching with so many preliminaries, mechanical gadgets, supports, and follow-ups that the director has no chance to focus his efforts on teaching. His attention is claimed by flyers, give-aways, films, sound systems, demonstrations, packaged programs, "selling," public speaking, attendance records, graduations, prettily colored or expensively bound diplomas, audits, inventories, replacement charts, and so on, while the core of his work is neglected.

Teaching, or as it has been called, "setting the stage for learning," is the heart of development work. Command of its principles and methods is essential to success.

513   Why Can't Any Person Who Thinks and Speaks Logically Do a Good Training Job?

While logical thinking and speaking are important, the primary factors in learning are psychological. Learning is a complex function, especially when attitudes and habits of thought are strongly entrenched. A development program requires professionally trained teachers if learning is to be quick and permanent, and as cheap and painless as possible.

514   What Degrees Are Desirable to One Working in the Development Field?

First come degrees in education and psychology. Closely related areas are personnel administration, sociology, vocational guidance and human relations. If candidates with degrees in one of these fields are not available, broad training in business administration, production management or engineering will suffice, if the man has not become a narrow specialist, and if there is time and opportunity to orient him to teaching.

515   Should Field Training Directors Whose Assignments Are to Run for Only a Few Years Try to Become Professionals?

Yes—within reasonable limits. Such men may outline a program which can be completed soon enough to be used during their brief "stop" in the training field. One suggested program follows:

First Step—Read two or three books on training.

Second Step—Join the American Society of Training Directors and read its publications. Read, also, in the field of human relations and in human growth and development—the basic area in which training operates.

Third Step—Review the program that is to be administered What has been done, what needs to be done? Make the acquaintance of a few local directors of development. Observe their programs in operation.

Fourth Step—Visit a university or college in the region where work is to be done. Meet the professors of engineering, business administration, management, education, psychology, or industrial education who work cooperatively with industry. Find out what services they offer and how they can be used.

Fifth Step—Begin to think about or to plan the changes or improvements you wish to make in the program you are to take over. Be sure to carry on the program as you inherited it until you have prepared people to accept your new ideas. Make changes gradually and slowly—after all, you are a "professional" of only a few weeks' standing.

This kind of preparation will do more than keep the newly assigned training man from making many mistakes. It will give him increased security and confidence during his few years' sojourn in training.

516   We Have Tried Two College Professors in Our Executive Development Teaching, But Neither Did Well. Why, and What Might Have Made Them Successful?

If you read the list of qualifications set forth in Question 508, you will realize that the competent, qualified training director is a rare, or at least an unusual person. The fact that a man is a respected and successful professor does not guarantee his success as a director of training.

Still, the fault may not have lain wholly with those two professors. College teachers who are brought into industry are likely to be regarded as outsiders, or as impractical theorists who know little or nothing of the practical world. When that happens the insiders who "know what's what" are almost sure to resist suggestions and reject or make little use of the service which the teachers are prepared to give.

On the other hand, trouble is almost sure to develop when executives emphasize the need for quick and comprehensive action. The ex-professor who receives and heeds such instructions is almost sure to interpret them in terms of his college experience, in which he dealt with immature persons who accepted his authority. He therefore moves too rapidly, gives orders or advice instead of making tactful suggestions, and thereby arouses opposition instead of cooperation.

The professor who turns training director needs and is entitled to receive a few months in which to study training requirements of the organization, the people whom he is to teach, and those with whom he is to cooperate. Business has hired him because of the knowledge, skills, and understanding which he has developed as a professor. It must realize, however, that conditions in a store, office, or factory are very different[2] from those in a university. The constant search for knowledge, the careful testing, the determination to get all the facts before making a decision—these and other factors which are proper in the university do not and cannot prevail in business. Furthermore, industrial trainees differ from college students in age, maturity, specialization, outlook, and in the time they have available for study. To make things more difficult, they differ greatly among themselves. Finally, although supervisors and executives probably are no more jealous than professors, they must be approached in different ways.

Executives who hire a professor as a training or development director must give him time in which to adjust himself to these new conditions. They also must let him come to *realize*—he already *knows*—that education is not a primary objective in the shop and office. It is only one of many factors that contribute to the major functions of a company. This relationship gives purpose to the training director's work, but it also gives him lower status than he possessed as a professor.

Finally, high executives who select a professor as a training director should leave no doubt that they have confidence in him and are giving him their support. By acts and words—the latter frequently repeated—they will assure skeptics and conservatives that management expects training to succeed, respects the man chosen to head it, and has confidence in him. This attitude on the part of executives is a strong incentive to a training director's success. If they have chosen a man who meets formal requirements, has good judgment, and is adaptable, he probably will succeed.

517   In Looking Through Our Organization to Select a Man Who Can Become a Training or Development Director, What Previous Work Experience Should We Look For?

Look for a record which includes a goodly proportion of these attainments:

1. Business or industrial experience in an administrative or supervisory capacity with *personal* responsibility for such activities as training employees to improve their job performance, interviewing and selecting employees, and independently negotiating with representatives of other organizational units to work

---

[2] This difference is analyzed in detail in Earl G. Planty, William S. McCord, and Carlos A. Efferson, *Training Employees and Managers for Production and Teamwork* (New York: The Ronald Press Co., 1948), Ch. 10.

out solutions to operating problems, developing and writing procedures, and putting them into operation.

2. Experience as a supervisor or consultant in an educational program.

3. Experience in county agricultural extension or home demonstration work.

4. Teaching in a program of vocational, technical, adult, or general education.

5. Teaching in an accredited secondary school.

6. Teaching courses in education, public administration, psychology or business administration on the college level.

7. Experience as a social group worker with responsibility for planning group activities in such organizations as the Y.M.C.A., Y.W.C.A., Federation of Settlement Houses, Boy Scouts of America, etc.

518   You Recommend That Training Positions Be Filled by People Who Have Been Trained for Teaching, But Many a Small Company Cannot Afford a Professional Trainer. What Is It to Do?

A company's personnel records sometimes reveal a secretary, a clerk, a foreman, a promising production worker, or even an executive who has had teacher training and even teaching experience. Failing this, many small companies go to the local schools and secure the part-time services of a vocational or industrial arts teacher who has had adequate experience. Sometimes training directors in larger nearby industries will come in and lend assistance during their off hours. State and private universities very often have extension programs geared to supply programs and even teachers to small industries that cannot justify a full-time man in development work. At any rate, they can always provide valuable guidance and counsel to small plants seeking to undertake developmental work.

Chapter 28

PREPARING THE FULL-TIME DIRECTOR
OF TRAINING OR DEVELOPMENT
AND HIS ASSOCIATES

519 **I Am a Beginning Training Man. How Can I Improve Myself?**

1. Seek criticism of your own teaching—ask it from trainees, business superiors, and other training men.

2. Visit schools, colleges and other industries to observe good teaching. Do this at least once a year.

3. Build yourself a professional library on adult education, industrial training and teaching. Use this library.

4. Go back to some good teachers' college, or to a general college or university every two years and take some course in education, psychology, or business management, thus keeping yourself up to date and increasing your mental equipment.

5. Join and support at least one professional society.

6. Invite other training men into your plant to examine your over-all program and criticize it.

7. Become acquainted with leaders in the training and development field, visit them, correspond with them, learn what they are thinking, and thus keep abreast of changes in this rapidly growing profession.

520 **How Can I Improve My Teaching?**

It is impossible to answer this question briefly or specifically. It is like asking, "How can I become a better lawyer?" A study of the profession of law is the first step: the practice of law under the guidance and direction of experienced lawyers comes next. Then follows a lifetime of experience, self-criticism, and study. So it is with teaching.

There are, however, some starting points for self-improvement among teachers. A few suggestions are listed below:

1. When did I last teach before another training man in order to secure his criticism?
2. How many different training men have I observed in action—that is, in teaching—during the last year?
3. Do I belong to professional organizations and attend meetings of personnel groups, engineering, office management, rubber, textile, paper or other trade groups, groups of teachers or educators—professional, technical or trade groups of any kind?
4. Have I recently *reread* any textbook on training or teaching? Do I have a professional library which I keep up to date? Do I buy and read at least one book a month?
5. Do I read professional magazines in my own field? Do I read books and magazines in the industrial areas represented by my company?
6. Do I keep myself alive, alert and active? Do I help my community, my schools, my training society? Do I fly an airplane, repair old furniture, raise a garden, engage in political activity, or pursue some other hobby or interest with enthusiasm?
7. When did I last revise my course outlines?
8. What new techniques have I used in my teaching (role playing, for example)? What new training aids?
9. Have I encouraged criticism of my courses by those who have taken them. Have I considered their comments?
10. Have I recently visited other development programs, observed some of their sessions, read some of their material?
11. Have I recently taken any courses in education or other fields related to my teaching?
12. Have I added new courses or do I teach the same courses which I installed when I took over? Do I challenge my ability by teaching courses that employees and supervisors need and want or only those that I know I can teach without much effort because I have been teaching them for a long time?
13. Do I evaluate my results and adapt my work in terms of the findings?

521   Where Can a New Development Man Secure the Most Experience in the Shortest Time, at Moderate Cost to His Company?

His best bet is to try to become an apprentice for two or three months in some outstanding, nationally known development program. Here he will observe, study, and perhaps get some opportunities to participate. If he cannot be absent so long or cannot make such a connection, he will do well to rely upon some of the self-help activities outlined in the answers given in this chapter.

522   What Are the Most Helpful Professional Societies for the Training Man?

The one that is best for a specific person is determined by his own background and needs. If he is already an engineer, he probably will not join a society made up largely of engineers, for example. He will, instead, seek broadening in his new specialty.

Some good professional groups are the American Society of Training Directors, The American Management Association, The Society for the Advancement of Management, The National Industrial Conference Board, The Industrial Relations Research Association, The American Psychological Association, and the National Society of Sales Training Executives.

523   What Books Should Comprise a Development Director's Library, for His Own Professional Use?

This, too, depends upon his experience and education. If he is a professional educator, his personal library will already contain materials on learning, teaching, methods, curriculum, etc. He will then need many books to help orient him to business and industry. If, on the other hand, the training director has had considerable experience in industry but only limited contacts with education, his books will emphasize the latter subject.

524   We Are a Small Company Which Up to Now Has Had No Personnel Director. We Have Recently Chosen One of Our Industrial Engineers for the Job. Please Spell Out the Training We Should Give Him.

First, you should find out what he knows by experience and training about the field of personnel. Then define the job clearly in writing and in detail so that both of you know clearly what duties he is being prepared for.

The next step is for both of you to discuss the problem, survey the means for training that are available and agree upon a few. Some of the means that will surely come up for consideration are:

1. A week or two spent in visiting other industries to study personnel programs first-hand.

2. Visits with company executives to find out what services they expect personnel to render.
3. The same kind of informal visits with supervisors and rank and file workers.
4. Taking out a membership in the American Management Association—attending their Personnel Conferences and getting their publications in the field.
5. Outlining a reading course in personnel administration, including a few basic texts.
6. Outlining, step by step, the new man's undertaking; determining whether employment, training, or union relations are primary; deciding where to begin and outlining priorities for the important first jobs.

525   How Do You Develop Training Staff Personnel from Academic Theorists into Practical, Productive Men?

Before this question is answered directly, we would like to comment on the academic theorist *vs.* the practical men. A training man must be academic to a certain degree. He needs to understand human motivation, theories of learning, and the underlying truths of what he's teaching.

Sometimes, because a training man emphasizes principles and philosophy of management, he is criticized as being too academic. Realizing that fundamentals must be taught in order to understand and get practical application, he does teach theory, and in this sense he is academic.

On the other hand, the "practical" training man is often one who directs his training efforts at correcting symptoms rather than fundamental causes. He is considered to be practical, since his subject matter is easily grasped and he attacks readily recognizable problems. As an illustration, consider a plant in which there is too much absenteeism. The "practical" training man will have supervisors give their ideas on the causes and cures, and will outline a course of action. A "practical" training job is done to correct specific causes. The "academic theorist," knowing that absenteeism results from complex, deep-seated attitudes, as well as from concrete, specific causes, will concentrate on fundamentals of human behavior that may explain not only absenteeism but other important problems. This man, too, will evolve a plan of action. But instead of merely "putting out fires," he will attempt to discover and overcome essential causes of unrest, dissatisfaction, and escape mechanisms, of which absenteeism is only one result. In the long run which man is really the more practical?

Overly academic people should not be chosen for jobs in industry, and training men who are chosen from the academic world should be given time and help to orient themselves to the fast tempo of modern business. The over-practical men in industry can learn too. They can learn that haste often makes waste, and that a fundamental attack is better than quick but superficial remedies.

526   We Have a Full-Time Staff of Ten People in Our Training and Development Department. Should We Have a Full-Time, Formal In-Service Teacher Training Program?

Certainly. Training and development men who are busy training others must not fail to keep themselves up to date.

527   What Will a Formal In-Service Teacher Training Program Include?

It will begin with weekly staff meetings of teachers and their supervisors, for upward and downward communications and for horizontal exchange of work experiences. There will be long-time planning for attendance at conventions and conferences. Schedules will be worked out whereby the department members take turns in attending meetings of the American Society of Training Directors, conferences of the Society for the Advancement of Management, seminars of the American Management Association, state and private university sessions, etc. The same kind of planning will select men for attendance at summer schools, training laboratories, and other improvement programs lasting for several weeks.

Rotation plans will enable instructors to exchange teaching assignments and will allow training men to get practical line rotations into operating jobs—for the purpose of observation if actual work experience cannot be provided. Scheduled observation of instructors by other instructors is another helpful activity. Observation is followed by discussion in which the observer helps the teacher by his comments and questions, and at the same time finds new approaches to problems he encounters in his own instruction.

The preceding activities will be supplemented by formal meetings to be held monthly, usually on company time and lasting for about two hours. A committee will determine what the group needs to know, arrange for inside or outside speakers to meet these needs, and will provide necessary facilities. Such a program, developed for a training unit in the Air Force, included monthly meetings devoted to the following subjects:

1. How to Build Attitudes
2. How to Broaden the Engineer and Research Worker
3. A review of Orientation and Indoctrination Training
4. New Concepts in the Psychology of Training and Teaching
5. Current Research on How to Evaluate Men
6. Leadership Today and Yesterday
7. Assumptions Underlying Employee and Supervisory Development
8. Nondirective Techniques in Teaching
9. Evaluation of Training
10. Preparing Training Budgets
11. Conventional Ways of Determining Training Needs *vs.* the Practice of Basing Need on Weaknesses Revealed in Audits
12. Taking Full Advantage of Learning Opportunities in Day-to-Day Operations

Chapter 29

TRAINING AND USING LINE AND STAFF OPERATING MEN IN THE PROGRAM

---

528   **How Does the Development or Training Director Get the Line Men to Do the Training?**

In instances where it seems desirable for line men to do both classroom and on-the-job training, the first requirement is to make sure that these men are interested in teaching. In some men the interest may be already aroused; in others it may need stimulation.

Given the necessary interest, the training man must teach the line men how to teach. This is a long-time, continuous job that includes courses in job instruction (JIT), conference, leadership, and public speaking. It may subsequently be necessary to add training in communications, psychology of learning, role playing, and the case study method. For line supervisors who show exceptional interest and aptitude, private and state colleges can provide courses on teaching methods, curriculum construction, and educational psychology.

When a supervisor lacks interest in developing his men, a variety of actions is possible. First, the supervisor should be led to accept the concept of supervision which makes the leader one who gets work done willingly and well instead of driving or doing it himself. This demands that he rely upon his men, who can meet his requirements only if they are *trained.* The training director also sees to it that training is made a part of the supervisor's job description and that he is evaluated—and rewarded or penalized—according to his willingness and skill in training his subordinates.

---

529   **If We Are to Use a Line or Staff Operating Man to Teach, What Are Some of the Things He Must Learn?**

The new teacher must learn:

To get away from over-specialized, technical terms and concepts.
To give individualized instruction.

To be persuasive, not "bossy."

To realize that telling is not teaching.

To recognize and remove barriers to learning.

To give adequate time to preparation.

To direct attention to his learners and their responses rather than to himself.

To organize content both logically and psychologically.

To invite and secure learner participation.

To realize that some kinds of teaching can have unexpected, negative outcomes.

To understand the importance of making learning meaningful.

To create and maintain student interest in learning.

To preserve for learners the thrill involved in the discovery, adaptation, and use of knowledge, skill, and new viewpoints.

To make teaching practical.

To evaluate his own performance.

To recognize the subtle attitudes that are taught, sometimes unknowingly, along with skills and understandings.

To be enthusiastic about his subject and the teaching job.

To find out why the learner behaves as he does before trying to change his habits.

530   We Have Asked Our Works Manager to Teach Company History to Our Supervisors. He Has Never Had Any Formal Courses in Teaching and Will Accept Only Individual Help. How Should We Train Him?

1. Work out with him, and perhaps with a committee of senior executives, a statement as to what the aims of this teaching are. Let the manager realize clearly why he is teaching, as well as the added knowledge and the change in attitude among students that are expected from his work.

2. Help him think of content, methods, and "illustrations" that will meet the objectives: stories and anecdotes, pictures, interviews with oldest living employees, records, old products, organization charts, exhibits of early documents, etc. Help him arrange or organize this material into some appropriate sequence for presentation.

3. Work with him to decide upon a method, or methods, of presentation—dramatic skit, lecture, illustrated lecture, tableau, and flashback, etc. Have him go through two or three practices followed by analysis and criticism from himself, from you, and from any others you invite to the preview.

If you can get the manager to work through these steps, it will be surprising how much teacher-training you can do, in a realistic, practical way.

531   What Problems Are Involved in Getting Line and Staff Men Within the Company to Do the Formal Group or Classroom Teaching?

1. They are oftentimes too busy to prepare themselves *generally* for teaching. This means study and practice in conference leadership, the laws of learning, the art of persuasion, public speaking, group dynamics, the case study method, principles and practices in teaching, Job Instructor Training, etc.

2. They are often too busy to prepare themselves specifically for the subject they are to teach—this may include reading, visits to other departments or plants, observation, review and analysis of their experience to select appropriate parts for teaching, organization of the material they are to teach, and choice of method to be used.

3. They are often too busy to practice their presentations before making them.

4. Frequently, they are not able to avoid shop talk and technical terms. The result is that the learner, less experienced in the field, is left behind.

5. They may be so much more interested in the subject they are teaching than in the learner that he is lost sight of and does not learn.

6. Many competent men in business and industry are not able to tell what they do. Many of their methods and decisions come from insight, which they do not recognize and cannot pass on to others. In one instance known to the authors, a woman who was highly skilled in a delicate hand operation endeavored to teach others. Very few of them ever learned the operation. When training men taught the successful operator JIT and observed her instruction after this preparation, trainees still had trouble. Eventually a film was taken of the woman's hands at work. It revealed that at a critical stage of the operation she used both small fingers in a lightning fast movement to guide a piece of cotton into place. In a complex series of rapid hand movements, the woman was unaware that she made this particular one. How, then, could she teach it? Comparable unawareness of essential details is found in the fields of social and leadership skills.

7. Operating people seldom place training high on their list

of responsibilities—it is something they will do in spare time or after the day's quotas are met. These prior requirements leave little time, energy, or thought for training.

532   Isn't Development a Part of the Supervisor's Job Which He Cannot Delegate?

This was once accepted without question, but there are differences of opinion about it today. The traditional case for requiring the supervisor to do his own training is well stated by Alex Bavelas:[1]

Experiences in many and varied situations in which training has been attempted led the writer to the conviction that training is an integral part of the management function and cannot easily be delegated. The logical and psychological point at which training can best take place is between an individual and his immediate superior. Any other arrangement necessitates such a close and comprehensive liaison between trainer and line management as is seldom achieved. The proper duties of the training consultant as the staff man to whom the problem of training has been assigned are not the conducting of training courses. This may appear at first to be helpful; actually it is an inefficient procedure and is often deleterious to management in the long run. The training consultant's objective should be to restore and to implement, not to perform the training function for management. He should work to create an awareness at all levels of management of the importance of training. He should make available to management resources for training in the form of materials and methods. He should assist in the diagnosis of training needs and in the development of training programs. He should stimulate and guide the evaluation of training programs both completed and in process. He should, in short, help management to acquire the skills and understandings it needs to do the job for itself.

533   What Arguments Are There Against a Line Supervisor Doing His Own Training?

Some of the major arguments are:

1. The supervisor does not and cannot be expected to teach as well as a specialist in teaching. Because of this, trainees often learn slowly and poorly. Just as supervisors call on engineers, chemists, and accountants to do special work for them, so they must call on educators if habits are to be changed quickly, easily, and at a low cost.

[1] Alex Bavelas, *Role Playing and Management Training*, Massachusetts Institute of Technology, Department of Economics and Social Science, Publications in Social Science, Series 2, No. 21.

2. It takes too long to train supervisors to teach, and some never learn to do it well. Supervisors don't have the time to (a) learn to teach, (b) learn the subject matter or at least organize it for teaching if they already know it, (c) do the actual teaching.

3. Supervisors cannot teach that which they do not know or accept. For example, a supervisor who is basically opposed to unions and the union movement is not competent to teach cooperation in labor management relations.

4. Sometimes it is necessary to teach a company policy or point of view uniformly throughout the company. One or two full-time, professional instructors can do this quickly, clearly, and uniformly. If line teachers are used in each department, however, each may have his own understanding of what the policy is and how it is to be applied. Even when different men agree, they may communicate the ideas in such a way as to produce different impressions. Some of this variation is unconscious, but when some of the men disagree with the policy or are unenthusiastic about it, some differences in presentation or interpretation probably will be deliberate. In either case, dilution, filtering, and personal interpretation occur as information passes through the minds of different men, and are likely to cause confusion and trouble.

534   Why Is There Strong Allegiance to the Rule That the Line Man Should Do All His Own Teaching?

This concept became established long ago when there were few staff departments and much resistance to those that existed. Once accepted, the rule was incorporated into textbooks without serious analysis or criticism, and has stayed there for the same reason. It also appeals to line supervisors who want to "run their own shows."

Generally speaking, line supervisors have resisted costs, engineering, personnel, quality control, production scheduling and other services when these were first offered to them. Some line men do not see their function as that of coordinating many services, some of which do not report directly to them. They have not accepted the staff concept. They want to handle directly all functions involved in their work. Instead of seeing their job growing into a new, challenging and difficult function of coordinating services provided for them, they fear their status is being reduced, their responsibility lessened and their control diluted.

535   How Should We Go About Selling Modern Training Techniques to Our Supervisors Who Are Teaching?

We should train them in use of modern techniques. The supervisor who has been prepared to handle Job Instructor Training for the workshop, to lecture, to lead a conference, to handle role playing, or the case study discussion, becomes pretty well convinced of the value of his repertoire. It is the carpenter whose skill is limited to the use of hammer and saw who resists finer tools and doing better work.

536   What Service Should the Director of Development Render Supervisors and Executives Who Are Doing Good Individual On-the-Job Development of Their Men?

Probably his greatest service is to provide adequate, supplementary formal training. If well done, this training will strengthen what is taught on the job by making it more understandable and integrating it with other knowledge and activities of industrial life. Where on-the-job activities are as adequate as they can be, the director of development will want to know those things that are not being taught in the factory or office and shape his program to cover them.

Good as on-the-job development is, there are limitations upon it. The learner cannot easily be exposed to what the superior does not know. This requires the director of development to know the limitations and weaknesses of each man who is developing subordinates. The director of development is likely to find men who are poor at planning, weak at control, indifferent to human reactions or more interested in words than in action. Obviously, such men cannot teach their subordinates what they do not know. Here is the place where the director of development can render service by offering, either through formal courses or by individual approaches, information which cannot be learned on the job.

Chapter 30

MECHANICS OF TRAINING

---

537   **What Are Some of the Most Common Aids to Training?**

Textbooks, flyers, outlines, lesson plans, study questions, manuals, charts, mock-ups, slides, blackboards, films, projectors, flannel boards, exhibits, tests, recordings, recorders, flip charts, training records, demonstrations, easel pads, photographs, bulletin boards, radio and television models, samples, maps, house organs, oral questions, company letters and memos to men in the field, cartoons, and commercially prepared supervisory or management letters.

538   **Where Can a New Development Director Go for Specific Help in Setting Up Courses?**

A new development director should secure advice and help from some of the following sources:

1. The extention department at his state or municipal university.
2. The industrial relations schools and centers at many of our large state and endowed universities.
3. Nearby teachers' colleges and schools of education.
4. Departments of business administration, industrial psychology, education, or management at any college or university. If one department cannot help, the new director should go to others until he gets what he needs.
5. The American Society of Training Directors, Indianapolis, Indiana.
6. The Training Directors' Society in the state where the new director lives.
7. The U. S. Office of Education and the Department of Education of the state in which the industry is located.
8. Development directors already established in nearby organizations.
10. Business consultants.
11. Major American book publishers.

The new training man may be able to register in regular college credit courses designed to help him, or may attend brief seminars or conferences for the same purpose. Men from some of the agencies listed above also may be available for individual consultation in which they will help him plan for his needs. In still other instances, teachers and complete courses are available for use in the plant program.

539　　What Services Do State Institutions Offer Training Directors?

Through their extension services, some colleges and universities will send skilled training men into industry to help determine training needs, set up classes, and teach them. Many schools also conduct a variety of short seminars and conferences on their own campuses designed to train men and women sent there from industry. Although the quality of these programs varies, some of the work meets very high standards and covers broad fields.

One Midwestern state university recently offered short extension programs under such titles as Industrial Inspection Methods, Advanced Industrial Supervision, Motivation in Modern Industry, Work Simplification, Communications, Office Supervision, Job Evaluation, Salary and Wage Administration, Quality and Waste Control for Plant Superintendents, Contract Negotiations, Interviewing and Counseling, Purchasing, Motion and Time Study, Foremanship, Costs and Budgets, Understanding the Worker, Employee Attitudes, The Supervisor as Trainer, Industrial Organization, Understanding Ourselves and Others, Duties and Responsibilities of a Private Secretary, Marketing and Sales Management.

The school of business administration in another state university, which shapes its offerings to the needs of trade associations, has held conferences in Trade Association Management, Restaurant Management, Advertising, Sales Management, Direct Selling, Life Agency Management, Retail Clothing Store Management, Industrial Personnel, Sales Management for Textbook Publishers, Retail Lumber Yard Management, and Retail Hardware Selling.

As these examples show, these programs vary greatly in content, making it necessary for the development director to shop around until he finds the courses that his people need or, better still, an institution that will provide courses built to his specific needs.

The quality of courses varies. Some are well planned and well taught. Others are poorly handled. The director who buys such services will certainly want to see the teachers in action and will want to check an adequate sample of men from industry who have studied with them.

540   Is There Any Repository for Training Course Outlines and Company Development Programs?

Yes, extensive libraries of industrial training materials are maintained at the School of Industrial and Labor Relations at Cornell University and also at Purdue University. Other good libraries for training materials are those at Massachusetts Institute of Technology, Princeton University, the University of Minnesota, the American Management Association, and the National Industrial Conference Board.

541   Do Trade and Professional Magazines Give Enough Help in Training to Justify Their Cost on a Company-Wide Distribution Basis?

Yes, but some employees and supervisors who are given subscriptions read them, and others don't. After magazines have been provided for a few months and delivered at offices or homes, find out whether the recipient is reading the magazine and wishes to continue receiving it. Also ask what new ones he would like to read. One's money goes further and more learning usually results if six different magazines are bought and routed to six readers than if individual copies of a single magazine are sent to all six men.

542   We Are Not in a Position to Hire Outside Teachers or Use Schools and Universities for Training. What Internal Opportunities Are Open to Us For Training?

There is a great variety of action available, including the following:

1. Use part of the regular staff meetings for training. Encouragement of plant executives to represent the company in service, civic and community welfare groups.
2. Route books and magazines to trainees.
3. Develop an understudy program.
4. Employ job rotations.
5. Appoint acting supervisors whenever the superior is absent.

6. Provide coaching, counseling, guided experience.
7. Employ merit rating and evaluation.
8. Appoint trainees to committees, task forces, multiple management boards, etc.
9. Establish internal supervisors' clubs, etc.
10. Appoint men to "assistant to" positions.
11. Delegate responsibility and authority to subordinates for development purposes where possible.
12. Ask line and staff experts to describe their functions to other supervisors in meetings designed to broaden knowledge of the company.
13. Provide financial aid to employees who take correspondence courses and avail themselves of other educational opportunities.
14. Organize self-study groups, perhaps in evenings, to discuss basic text material or new developments in appropriate areas of specialization.
15. Buy or rent films to meet the training need of such groups.
16. Help line supervisors to develop an orientation program (including employee and supervisor manuals) and on-the-job training programs.
17. Collaborate with local high schools in organizing a program of evening adult education.
18. Use supervisors and other executives as teachers in company training programs.

543 How Extensively Are Films Used in Industry?

Films have had greatly increased use in business and industry since World War II, when their value was proved by training programs in government and the military services. General Motors now publishes a 65-page, colored catalog describing its films, which are used to promote external public relations and to orient employees in such fields as safety, machine operations, motor transportation, the General Motors Institute, mass production, and principles of lubrication. Subjects of more general interest, such as food freezing, also are dealt with in General Motors' films.

The Shell Oil Company, New York City issues a similar catalog, as do:

Aluminum Company of America	Westinghouse Electric Corporation
Bell Telephone Companies	Goodyear Tire & Rubber Company
Esso Standard Oil Company	United States Rubber Company
General Electric Company	United States Steel Corporation
Ford Motor Company	General Mills Company

Films made by these companies are available for loan to other industries, frequently without charge.

544   What Is a Flyer?

A flyer is a handout, a give-away, a release, a teaching aid. It is used before, during, or after a class and has various purposes:

1. It is used to *announce* a training program or a single meeting.

2. It is frequently distributed during class *to stimulate discussion.*

3. It may be distributed after a meeting or a series of meetings in order *to summarize and provide a record* to be used in review or as a guide when the trainee teaches elements of the course or program to his subordinates.

4. The flyer may take the form of a true-false exercise, especially when answers are discussed orally, *to provide practice* in interpreting and applying the material and to measure group performance.

5. Now and then the flyer is used *to illustrate* what has been taught.

6. In many cases it provides a visual stimulus *to reinforce* the auditory one. The fact that someone has taken the time and trouble to prepare the flyer convinces the trainee that its content is important.

Some flyers are colored, illustrated, novel in size or construction; others are very simple and direct. The design should be in keeping with the purpose, which means that the flyer meant to inform need not be as showy as the one designed to attract attention.

545   Can You Give an Illustration of a Discussion Type of Flyer?

The brief extracts given below come from a flyer used by Johnson & Johnson training men to train hospital supervisors in human motivation. It is sometimes used before two hours of lecture and conference on human needs, and sometimes follows the direct teaching on the same subject. The first questions direct the learner but the succeeding ones leave him freedom to explore without direction by the instructor.

DISCUSSION CASES

MANAGEMENT TRAINING

The following cases illustrate good and bad management practice. What do you think about them?

1. An administrator in a hospital in this city phones all supervisors in his unit on their birthdays and invites them to his office. When they arrive he congratulates them and talks with them personally for a while.

    What effect does this have upon morale?

    What basic drives does it help satisfy?

    Are there any objections to this policy?

2. An employee complained to a dietary service supervisor about food. The supervisor promised to start a survey promptly, asking employees their opinions. Next morning, he started the survey; two days later, and before he could do anything about the food, the complaining employee came to him, thanked him for making the survey and for making improvements so quickly. The food, she said, was much better.

    How do you account for such an illogical reaction?

    What might a supervisor think about an employee who makes an excessive number of suggestions?

3. A new chief nurse is hired, the third in four years. She is an excellent woman, strong in all areas. She sees weakness in previous systems and previous supervision of the department. She institutes revised systems and improved supervision. But her subordinates resist her, block her reforms, dislike her and her program.

    What may be some reasons for this?

    What should she and her subordinates do about this condition?

546   How Is a Summary Flyer Made and What Does It Look Like?

The summary flyer may be made by the instructor, by one of the learners, or by a group of them. The flyer illustrated below was made by a committee of trainees to summarize what they had agreed upon at the end of a course in driving fork-lift trucks, given in the Chicago plant of Johnson & Johnson.

RULES FOR DRIVERS OF FORK-LIFT TRUCKS

1. Each day the driver will check his own machine for serious mechanical defects before using it. Mechanically defective trucks will not be operated.

2. No passengers, with the exception of an instructor when necessary, will be permitted to ride on trucks.

3. Only properly authorized and trained personnel will operate the truck. Its key will be removed when a driver leaves his truck.
4. Operators shall not repair their truck. This is to be done by trained and responsible mechanics.
5. Trucks should never be used for greater than maximum loads. The load capacity should be clearly marked on each truck.
6. Stunt driving, horseplay, creeping up on pedestrians, and crowding pedestrians will not be allowed.
7. Drivers must be in good health, and mentally and physically alert.
8. Drivers will always slow down on wet or slippery floors.
9. Any unsafe condition noted on the floor will be called to the attention of the foreman or the safety director at once.
10. No one will be permitted to pass or stand under elevated forks.
11. Operators will slow down when approaching intersections so that the lift will be under control. This also applies in approaching groups of people.
12. Operators shall always look in the direction of travel.
13. Quick starts and stops are to be avoided, as well as quick turns, especially when stacking merchandise.
14. Operators will not follow another lift truck at an unsafe distance (15 feet or less) and shall not pass another truck going in the same direction.
15. Operators will not park in aisles.
16. Operators will not leave lift truck controls in gear.
17. Loads will be carried as low as possible to give operator maximum vision.
18. Horns should be blown when approaching intersections, not once but several times.
19. Trucks must not be left when the lifting mechanism is in operation.

547   What Is a Teaching Outline?

It is a statement of objectives for the unit and of its content, plus suggestions on how to teach. The outline therefore serves as a guide for the teacher, showing where he is to go and what steps he will take to get there. It is most detailed and specific when direct teaching is involved and when factual knowledge and specific skills are to be developed, least so when teaching is to be nondirective and spontaneous.

548   How Is a Teacher's Outline Made?

The outline we have chosen to answer this question represents the fifth session in a Johnson & Johnson training course on Effective Job Organization, designed specifically for Supervisors. The individual conferences or sessions deal with the following topics:

I. Defining the Job
II. Delegating Work
III. Making Decisions
IV. Planning
V. Scheduling and Budgeting Your Time
VI. Personal Efficiency
VII. Office or Shop Efficiency.

The Instructor's Outline for Conference Five is reproduced below:

TEACHING OUTLINE

COURSE IN EFFECTIVE JOB ORGANIZATION
Scheduling and Budgeting Your Time

Tie the subject in with over-all planning. Sound planning for the department (scheduling of work, men, machines, materials, reports) helps the supervisor to budget his own time more effectively. Good planning, in fact, includes a plan for the budgeting of the supervisor's time. The preceding sessions emphasized the supervisor's responsibility for planning, organizing and directing his department. This and the following session ("Personal Efficiency") focus on the supervisor's responsibility for improving his personal efficiency and the performance of his own job.

Draw from the trainees a blackboard list of the jobs they do. It is important to determine what type of work the manager or supervisor is required to do, to budget his time effectively. Most executive and supervisory activity will break down into the four types indicated here. Conference leaders should illustrate each type of work, then lead into a definition of it as indicated, and then return to the job list and have the trainees determine in which category each job should go.

HANDOUT: "Interested in Saving Time?" *Management,* February 29, 1952.

I. OBJECTIVES OF TIME-BUDGETING CONFERENCE

A. To encourage more attention to creative work and less to routine, especially among high-level supervisors.
B. To set up some procedures and principles regarding efficient use of time.
C. To avoid work habits that are confusing, fatiguing, and/or wasteful.
D. To get the learners to make written work plans.

II. TYPES OF WORK

A. The work of a supervisor during an ordinary day may be divided into four types:

1. *Routine Work:* Minor duties performed regularly, such as clock punching, noting absences, signing leave slips, cleaning up, etc.

Note that careful planning, training, and delegation will avert many "emergencies" and they will become "regular work." For example, training, counseling, and good human relations generally will avert many sudden grievances and mistakes. Many supervisors spend so much time on things that are *urgent* that they have none left to spend on those that are *important*.

2. *Regular Work*: The regular daily tasks. This work is the major part of an individual's day.
3. *Special work*: Emergency or "rush" work, or work not ordinarily done in the department.

4. *Creative work* is incentive work. It is developing or putting into practice your own ideas and encouraging employees to submit and try out their creative ideas—different ways to do a job, to cut down time, to increase quality, to furnish more detailed or concise information, to communicate, etc.

Ask for suggestions for dividing the day according to percentages of time spent on each type of work. Put the four types of work on the board and list suggested percentages after each. Build up need for more attention to creative work. Discuss supervisors entangled with details. Ask why this is. Perhaps someone will show how delegation and better planning of routine work will permit more time for essentials. Stress that a supervisor's reputation is built on his ability to do this.

III. DIVISION OF TIME
Routine —10% ⎫
Regular —65% ⎪ approximate
Special —15% ⎬ percentages
Creative—10% ⎭

HANDOUT: "How to Use the 'Rule of Exception'," *Management Information*, December 15, 1952.

HANDOUT: "Questions for Time Budgeteers." These are not principles as much as they are suggestions on how to plan effectively.

IV. PRINCIPLES OF TIME BUDGETING (Draw as many of these as possible from the trainees)

See how turnover was reduced among girls copying names on envelopes from the telephone directory.

A. Schedule enough work to keep you busy, but not so much that you get discouraged.

Except for creative work after hours, the supervisor who takes his work home with him (or works overtime when his department is not doing so) is probably budgeting his time poorly—or has organized his department badly.

QUESTION: Do we control our jobs or do our jobs drive us?

The man who boasts "I always work best under pressure" is probably rationalizing his failure to budget his time wisely or to manage well in general. He is the slave, not the master of time. Perhaps he is also trying to impress someone with his importance.

See rotation of operators and rest periods at some of our plants. Cite the example of laborers weeding sugar-beet fields. Their production was increased 30 per cent by the simple device of putting markers every 100 feet along the rows, thus giving the weeders a series of goals.

See surveys that have been made on wasted movements on farms or kitchens.

B. Group tasks so that specialized work can be done at one sitting. "Do it now" is not always the best advice.

C. Change tasks several times each day to cut down on fatigue and monotony. If that is not practical, at least change the tempo.

D. Alternate hard and easy tasks. One can't constantly be kept at a top pace.

E. Ask what jobs could be delegated. Then delegate them.

F. Ask yourself where your greatest time waste is.

G. Plan to do the difficult or most disliked work first. Get it out of the way.

H. Plan stopping places. While this is most important in routine, repetitive work, it is also important to supervisors on their own jobs. Work is done best when there are definite points to stop so that we can recognize what has been accomplished.

I. Keep on hand short jobs which can be performed during spare moments.

J. Build up habits which save time, such as keeping things where you can find them quickly.

K. Eliminate backtracking.

L. Make decisions on small matters quickly, or eliminate needless details.

M. Don't spend too much time in developing plans—put them to work.

N. Plan your day so that visits and meetings will generally be held during certain hours.

O. Know at what time of day (usually morning) you are best able to do taxing mental work and what time is best for routine work (usually late in day).

Issue HANDOUTS: "Principles of Time Budgeting," "If I Only Had More Time."

Use this discussion as the basis for asking the participants to keep time records of their activities for one or two weeks. Arrange for department head to review these records in conference with each of the supervisors.

Invite trainees to tell how much work planning they do. Do they use daily memory joggers in which they record the jobs they are to do? Do they group these jobs or attack them with any system.

Introduce a few books and articles here. Show how they may be gotten from the plant or local libraries.

P. In learning a new skill, practice it frequently for short periods (not once for a long period).

Q. Up-to-date organization charts and job descriptions will save you time in communicating, making decisions, assignments, etc.

R. Don't lose time waiting for a decision about an important matter. Go after it; follow up until you get it.

S. Spend a few minutes at end of each day to decide where and how your time will be spent the next day.

T. Periodically analyze how you actually spent your time each day for a week—just what you did, where you did it, and how long it took you to do it.

V. WORK SCHEDULE AND PLANS
  A. Get the learners to list the reasons why they should make plans.
  B. Ask how detailed they should be.
  C. Illustrate by showing several individual work schedules kept by supervisors and executives in the plant.

VI. Encourage the men to study and read about the effective use of time.

549   How Do You Inform Participants of the Schedule of Meetings for a Training Course?

Usually supervisors inform their subordinates when they are expected to attend training It is also good practice for the training supervisor to send each enrollee a personal, written invitation which may include a listing of the meetings with the subjects, time, place, and instructors indicated. Even with all these preliminaries, many development men phone the trainee or his superior on the day before the course starts to remind him of it. In addition, at the first meeting of a course, the instructor hands out a course program and reviews the schedule of meetings.

550   What Are the Easiest Methods of Determining Meeting Times for Busy Supervisors?

There is no time when it is easy for busy supervisors to get away for training. The authors have seen the following methods for setting the time of meetings used effectively:

1. The training supervisor picks a time for a meeting through his analysis of supervisors' commitments.
2. The training supervisor contacts a representative number of supervisors and with their help designates a meeting time.
3. The training supervisor consults the supervisor of the men scheduled for meeting and with him decides on a suitable time.

In general, it is best to let the group determine the best time. *Then notify all, in writing, well in advance of meetings.*

551   Is There Any Best Time During the Work Day to Hold Training Meetings?

There are two major considerations in determining the best time to hold training meetings. The first relates to the demands of the jobs which the participants hold. When scheduling training meetings for members of management, they prefer to spend the first hour at their desks, getting their day's work in order, planning assignments, and handling their mail. Likewise, the last hour of the day usually is spent in resolving problems and winding up the day's activities. Other members of the organization such as clerks, typists, and machine operators have little or no aversion to spending the first hour of the day in training class but prefer not to have classes that are held right up to quitting time.

The second major consideration is the best time from a learning point of view. We know that employees are more receptive to learning when they are fresh and alert and not fatigued. Therefore, schedule training classes in the morning, before employees become fatigued from their normal activities.

552   We Are Planning a Ten-Session Training Course for Supervisors. Should Meetings Be Held Daily? Twice a Week? Once a Week? Or How Frequently?

It is difficult to state, flatly, what the interval between training meetings should be. Local conditions such as the pressure of work, urgency of the training, availability of instructors, etc., will have considerable influence on the interval chosen. However, experience in supervisor training conference has shown that most satisfactory results are obtained when the interval between meetings is not less than one week or more than two weeks.

This appears to be true for the following reasons:

1. The conferees need this interval to think through and practice what was taught.
2. This interval also gives them adequate time to prepare for the next meeting.
3. Management is reluctant to allow supervisors to be away from their jobs more frequently.
4. Continuity of meetings can be maintained, since supervisors can recall the previous discussion. If meetings are held less frequently there is danger that the continuity of the teaching will not be maintained and that too much time will have to be devoted to review and reteaching.
5. Training programs for others in the organization can operate at the same time. The training staff does not devote its attention exclusively to one group when other pressing training problems may also need their attention.
6. Generally, supervisors express a desire to attend a regularly scheduled series of meetings held weekly or fortnightly.

553   How Long Should a Training Meeting Last?

There can be no one answer to this question. The length of training meetings will depend on a number of variables. The most important of these are:

1. *The instructor.* Meetings which are led by capable, interesting, experienced instructors can usually be longer than those led by uninteresting, unprepared, and boring instructors.

2. *The subject matter.* When participants feel that the subject matter has a direct and immediate value to them, meetings can be longer, for trainees are interested and involved in the discussion or activity at hand.

3. *The teaching method.* Training meetings that allow the participants to discuss, demonstrate, or participate actively in the training can be longer than those in which participation is limited.

4. *The physical facilities.* When the physical conditions of the training room, such as heat, light, comfortable chairs and so forth are satisfactory, meetings can be longer. The temperature of a training room should be approximately 68 degrees, since higher

temperatures induce lethargy and sleep, and lower temperatures are too cool for comfort. Comfortable chairs with arm rests should be used, rather than folding chairs.

Even when these variables are favorable to training, meetings should rarely extend beyond two hours and should usually last from an hour to an hour and one half.

554   How Important Are the Physical Conditions of the Room Used for Training Classes?

These factors do have a bearing on the success of the program. How significant a role they play cannot be measured. However, we know that learning takes place most easily when these factors are favorable. For example, a training meeting could be held in a dilapidated wooden structure, without heat or proper ventilation, with inadequate lighting and seating accomodations, and where there are loud and distracting noises. Learning could take place, but not easily and quickly. Under these conditions both the instructor and the group work doubly hard in order to accomplish a reasonable amount of learning. When factors are favorable to learning, the learners can concentrate on the lesson more successfully and learning comes more easily. As to favorable physical conditions, see Question 555.

555   What Are the Best Physical Conditions for a Conference —Kind of Room, Time, Seating Arrangements, Etc.

We offer the following suggestions from our own experience:

1. *Temperature*—65° to 68°—not too warm, lest the conferees become dull or uncomfortable. Be sure there is adequate ventilation. Many crowded rooms that seem to be hot merely are excessively humid, with accompanying odors of breath and perspiration.

2. *Room*—free from distracting noises (production machines, traffic, etc.), easily accessible, clean and as comfortable as possible, with adequate lighting.

3. *Tables and chairs*—no glass-topped tables because of reflections, which are disturbing and often uncomfortable. Plenty of foot room under tables. The chairs should have padded seats, and arm rests.

4. *Seating*—seat conferees around tables so that they face each other. Face-to-face discussion promotes mutual understanding,

for communication is more than the use of words. Gestures, bodily movements, and facial expressions are important elements in it.

5. *Time*—morning meetings are the best. The conferees are fresher and more willing to enter into discussion in the morning than in the afternoon.

6. *Identification*—use name cards for each conferee, showing in large letters the man's name and position. This information is helpful to both leader and conferees.

556   What Would You Consider Standard Equipment for a Training Department?

Certain pieces of equipment should be available for use by a training department. These are used to assist the instructors in preparing or presenting instructional material and to help them clarify and vitalize their teaching. The following are considered standard equipment: easel, blank flip charts, movable projection screen, sound projector (16 mm.), strip film and slide projector with sound attachment, blackboard, duplicating machine, movie camera (16 mm.), recording machine, overhead projector, flannel board, opaque projector.

557   Do You Have Any Suggestions About the Seating of Participants in a Training Meeting?

Training meetings in industry usually involve discussion by the trainees. Sitting around a table so that participants enjoy a face-to-face relationship is best. Frequently, individual place cards made of folded cardboard, with the name printed in large letters on both sides, are used to identify the participants and facilitate easy recognition.

Sometimes participants pick up their place cards from the leader and sit any place they desire. On the other hand, some leaders plan where each participant will sit and place the identifying cards. Either method is satisfactory; the latter is used most frequently when participants are from different departments and have no preferences as to their neighbors in the meeting. Also, it is used to disperse talkative, attention-seeking participants who may form a clique and make it hard for the leader to obtain a balanced discussion.

If special seating arrangements are desired, the leader must make them before or during the first meeting. The seating arrangement takes care of itself from then on, since participants will usually continue to take the seat they chose in the first meeting. Subsequent changes in seating arrangements may cause wonderment and even embarrassment for some trainees.

558   Should Attendance at Training Classes Be Compulsory?

No. Learning should be undertaken willingly. It cannot be forced. In fact, compulsion may bring resistance to the whole idea of training and set up a permanent barrier in the minds of those who are coerced.

Training should be made attractive and useful. It should then be publicized and promoted respectably to the end that men seeing its purpose and value to them, undertake it voluntarily, possibly enthusiastically.

559   Should Employees Be Paid While Attending Training Classes?

In general, training classes held during working hours are designed and offered to employees for the purposes of decreasing costs and increasing profits through improved operating efficiency. Although employees may profit personally from such training through increased earnings and promotion, this is a secondary consideration for offering the training. An organization must be willing to invest in training in order to achieve its profit objectives. Therefore, employees should be compensated for the time spent in training classes during regular working hours.

Some organizations offer voluntary courses, after working hours, which are not directly related to an employee's job. In such cases the employees are not compensated for time spent in class. Moreover, they even may be asked to share the expense of the course.

560   There Seems to Be Disagreement on Having the Superiors of Men in the Same Training Class with Them. What Do You Think About This?

Some say that having various levels represented in a training meeting, including some bosses and their subordinates, has the following advantages:

1. The superiors enliven the discussion by drawing upon their more extensive experience. They raise the level of discussion.

2. The superiors are a stabilizing and serious influence which encourages others to participate earnestly and seriously.

3. The superiors have an opportunity to evaluate the thinking of their men and can identify weaknesses which they can help correct on the job.

4. Both upward and downward communications are encouraged. Barriers between levels are lessened.

The disadvantages are as follows:

1. Contributions from lower-level employees are stifled because of their fear of being wrong and making a bad impression on higher level employees. Also lower-level employees are reluctant to offer ideas that differ from those presented by higher level employees.

2. For best learning, discussion should be geared to the need of those who are the least capable. This pace is usually too slow for higher level employees and they become impatient and disinterested in the training. If the level of the discussion is raised it is over the heads of many in the group.

3. Higher-level employees tend to monopolize the discussion.

We would recommend organizing training groups that are as nearly homogeneous as possible. We believe that learning takes place most easily when the training is planned to meet the needs of a given employee level in the organization.

561   Should Participants in Industrial Training Classes Receive Marks?

Training men, in general, feel that traditional grading systems as used in public schools are impractical for participants in most industrial training programs. These programs are designed to meet the immediate needs of the trainees and the measure of effectiveness of the training comes from the analysis of the improvement the trainee shows in his daily work, not from an artificial grade or mark given by the instructor. Tests, term papers, and other written assignments which form the basis of grades in public schools are not used frequently in industrial training. Formal grading is used only in such programs as a course in speed reading, apprenticeship training, on-the-job training for semiskilled workers and pre-supervisory training where measurable skills are taught or where the training is to contribute to selection. Narrative reports (see Question 562) describing the behavior of participants during training are used more frequently than grades or marks.

562   Please Cite a Sample Narrative Report Which Gives the Instructor's Evaluation of a Participant in a Pre-supervisory Training Course.

CLASS PARTICIPATION

Jones was one of the most active members of the group. He sparked many discussions with comments and questions that were often incisive and challenging. At times he was inclined to be negative and would continue a discussion to the point of stubbornness. On the whole, however, his critical approach was a stimulant to group discussions. He had a tendency to resist what he appeared to believe were idealistic concepts of human relations with the argument that people simply don't behave that way. His behavior was in no sense obstructive. He seemed to be genuinely trying to modify a skepticism based on bitter past experience. He was earnestly seeking solutions and, in a stubborn kind of way, was learning to assimilate the leadership role of the modern supervisor. His interest throughout the course was high.

TEST RESULTS

Jones did extremely well in the four written tests given at intervals during the course. He had an average ranking of second in the group of sixteen.

ASSIGNED READINGS

Jones did capable work on the assigned readings, although he failed to complete the last three assignments. His standing in this part of the work was twelfth in the group.

ON-THE-JOB ASSIGNMENTS

Jones completed satisfactorily three of the four projects related to his job.

GROUP EVALUATION

On the whole, Jones was highly regarded by the other participants in the course. His final ranking, made by the group, was fifth. The other fifteen group members were particularly impressed by his decisiveness, his analytical ability, and his powers of expression. Significantly, they ranked him very low in "sensitivity quotient." This rather confirms the observations recorded under class participation.

563   How Much Should Industry Spend per Worker for Development?

To this question there is no answer which can be applied universally. Many conditions determine the amount of money to be spent: the worker's age, length of time with company, his record of achievement, his need for training to do the rudiments of the job, whether or not the training is for immediate job improvement or for long-term individual development, the profit position of the company, the present and future need in the company for the man and his contribution, and the trainee's ability to learn and the company's interest in development.

The sum spent per person for development work ranges widely, so widely as to be almost useless for general comparisons. Averaging the cost training for all employees of a company produces figures in some cases as low as ten dollars per year and in other cases as high as several hundred dollars. These cost figures include time of learner and teacher, heat, light, books, stationery, visual aids, charge for classroom and office space, plus travel and maintenance if the trainees are away from home.

564   In General, What Should Be the Ratio Between the Total Working Force Employed by an Organization and the Number of Full-Time Training People?

It varies greatly, depending upon training need and management's recognition of the need. The senior author was once part of a development staff of 450 instructors established to serve a work force of 20,000, almost all of whom were new at their jobs. This is a ratio of one training man to forty-five employees. Most plants of 1,000 employees today need a full-time training man. There are an increasing number of organizations of 500 employees, too, that find use for a full-time specialist. In smaller organizations, the personnel director usually handles development, at least until it is well enough established to make it a full-time job for someone.

565　　How Can You Best Defend the Cost of Training Programs for Older Employees?

Let us say a man is 55 years old and lacks ten years of being retired. Assume that he earns $5,000 a year. His total salary will be $50,000 for the next ten years. The money spent on providing him with working tools—machinery, desk, phone, travel expenses, files or other equipment—will add an additional sum to this figure. The money involved in possible decisions made by the man may run into hundreds of thousands of dollars, but let us limit our thinking to his $50,000 salary. How much would anyone expect to spend yearly on the care and upkeep of a $50,000 investment— say a house, a car, or a business property? In the case of an automobile, for example, we keep it insured and have ours overhauled —oiled, greased, and the motor tuned up. In fact, the older the automobile, the more we spend on it. In the light of this example, a few hundred dollars spent yearly on training employees with long service seems reasonable, especially since older employees need certain kinds of brush-up training more than do younger hands recently out of school and therefore more flexible in mind.

566　　Is It Cheaper to Use Line and Staff Men to Do the Formal Group Teaching or to Use Full-Time Professional Training Men?

If each group achieved the same results from the training, then the answer would depend upon the salaries paid the two types of teacher and on the amount of time which they require for preparation. Salaries for line and staff executives probably run higher than for professional teachers. In most cases the line and staff insiders come higher by the hour. However, the second important factor is also involved—the time spent in preparation and practice, preliminary to the teaching. It is quite certain that a professionally prepared teacher can prepare a lesson plan, a case study, or a test in about a third of the time required by the nonprofessional man, and his requirement for practice is less, too.

Assuming that inside line and staff men taught just as well as specialists and got just as many changes in habits as the professional teachers, the latter would still cost less. It is questionable, however, whether operating men teach as well as specialists. Many believe that trained teachers surpass line and staff operating men in getting understanding, acceptance, and practice of what is taught.

567   **Is It Customary to Include Man Hours Spent in Training in Computing Training Costs?**

Yes. A good example of this is to be found on pages 81-85 of a "Report to the California State Senate on In-service Training in the California State Service," March, 1952, prepared by the California Department of Public Works. It reads:

Cost of Training

Estimated cost of 1951 formal in-service training in terms of man-hours of attendance and estimated trainee salary cost is as follows:

Program	Course hours	Persons attending	Man-hours attendance	Estimated trainee salary costs	Other costs reported
Orientation					
(a) Water Resources	3	140	420	$ 684.94	$
Specialized					
Division of Highways					
(a) Accident prevention..	1¼	1,500	2,000	4,147.20	7,000
(b) Right of way.......	24	171	4,104	11,391.00	650
(c) Aerial surveying	84	20	1,680	5,969.00	3,100
(d) Soil properties	6	250	3,000	––	100
(e) Highway problems ..	24	90	2,160	7,674.91	1,500
(f) Bridge design	6	175	1,050	4,309.00	2,500
(g) Letter writing, etc...varies		71	852	1,389.00	
Water Resources					
(a) Letter writing, etc...varies		60	1,680	2,739.74	
Supervision					
Division of Highways					
(a) Elements of supervision	20	9	180	355.75	
Water Resources					
(a) Elements of supervision	20	2	40	79.00	
			17,166	$38,739.54	$14,850
TOTAL:				$52,589.54	

PART V

EVALUATION

Chapter 31

EVALUATING DEVELOPMENT ACTIVITIES

568   Is Evaluation of Training or Development Worth While?

While truly scientific evaluation may not always be possible or even desirable, some kind of evaluation—even if it is no more than recorded opinion—should be required at the completion of every training program. This evaluation will help to determine what the company has or has not secured from training and will indicate the review and repetition needed by trainees who have not reached predetermined goals. Evaluation will also point out opportunities for advanced training where goals have been achieved.

569   Where Does One Start Evaluating Training or Development?

The start is with specific objectives, written down for reference. Without them progress cannot be measured and failure cannot be determined. With clearly phrased, recorded objectives, work can be accurately directed and measurement attempted. If there is no clear target for a rifleman there is no way to tell what his accomplishments are. So it is with training.

570   How Can Training Results Be Related to Dollars Saved?

Training courses in reduction of errors, breakage, waste, complaints, and learning time are easily related to money values. It takes a little more time and imagination to translate the results of training designed to increase quality, speed, productivity or output of services into direct savings. But both kinds of training can be related to savings.

A good illustration is found in training employees on new jobs. In this case, statistics are kept showing the time taken to learn the new job and the amount of wasted materials, both with and without systematic training. In one case where new workers had been taking three weeks to learn a machine operation without systematic training, other new employees reduced their learning period to two weeks and cut their scrap 50 per cent after formal training was installed. This saving, of course, can be translated into dollars and cents.

571   Does All Evaluation of Training Mean Measuring Results in Dollars and Cents?

No. As was said in the answer to Question 570, limited courses that deal with such problems as breakage, waste, and speed of learning can be evaluated in money. So also, in a general way, can courses devoted to productivity and speed. But broad training, such as that given under the Sloan Fellowships at the Massachusetts Institute of Technology, cannot be reduced to dollars and cents saved and earned. This is equally true of the courses in communications given in many industries.

Methods of evaluation must fit the training to be evaluated. If its accomplishments can be expressed in hours, pieces, tons, or money, that method should be used. If this is impossible, other methods must be employed. In many fields, evaluation can be based only upon a record of all available evidence which shows the degree to which training objectives were or were not realized, the improvements effected, and their effect upon the company. From this evidence, training men and executives will decide whether the degree of success justifies the expenditure of time, energy and money. Such an evaluation will be subjective and may be far from scientific, but it will be the only one possible. It also will be vastly better and more informative than a dollars-and-cents evaluation in which values are hypothetical.

Some readers will object to the subjective nature of this measurement, claiming that evaluation must be wholly objective and always capable of being translated into dollars and cents. This is a happy wish, but not one likely to be fulfilled in an area dealing with social skills. To demand and expect in the social fields the same kind of measurement that is possible in the physical sciences is impractical and visionary, indeed.

572   Should All Development Be Evaluated in Terms of Results?

Yes. But when results cannot be seen or measured directly, some values may be determined by examining techniques or methods. There are established laws of learning and principles of teaching which, if successfully applied, are almost sure to lead to the desired results. The skill with which this is done can be told by watching how a teacher motivates his learners, whether he gets them to take responsibility for their own learning, whether self-expression takes place among them, and whether the experiences that are arranged have meaning and value for the participants. An educator worthy of the name should be able to judge from observing a teacher at work whether or not adequate learning is taking place and the desired results are being achieved.

573   What Are the Common Methods of Evaluating Training?

There are six primary methods, as follows:

1. Measurement, or at least enumeration, of improvements that appear after training.
2. Recording the regularity of attendance at training classes and the number and insistence of requests for more training.
3. Tabulation and analysis of opinions—given either by trainees or by their superiors—through questionnaires, interviews or informal discussions.
4. Tests—paper and pencil tests or actual on-the-job tryouts.
5. Measurement or observation of the degree to which the teaching follows the laws and conditions of learning.[1]
6. Determination of the amount of training accomplished in terms of hours in class and ground covered.

574   What Is "Before and After" Evaluation of Training or Development?

Before and *after* evaluation involves observation and measurement of some performance before planned development work takes place and measurement of the same operation after training. A comparison of the results reveals the effect of training.

575   What Would Constitute an Example of a Truly Scientific Evaluation of Training Results?

The executives of a company, having expressed a desire for a course in rapid reading, are tested to determine their initial read-

[1] Earl G. Planty, "New Methods for Evaluating Supervisor Training," *Personnel,* January, 1945

ing speed. They are then divided into two groups. As nearly as possible, these groups contain members which are equal in age, intelligence, kind of position held, salary, and initial reading speeds.

One group is then given training in reading while the other group receives no instruction, all other conditions being held as constant as possible. At the end of the training, both groups are tested again. If the trained group has improved in reading speed, the gain may be properly accepted as a measure of the progress achieved by training.

576   What Kinds of Training Are Most Easily Evaluated?

All kinds of training should be evaluated, regardless of the difficulty. It is easiest, of course, to measure the results of programs that involve motor skills or knowledge. The results of training in typing, carton sealing, simple machine operations, keeping stock records, and other motor activities can be measured quickly and reliably in terms of increased productivity, in reduction of errors, and in rejects after training. Knowledge of company policy, distribution of the sales dollar, or provisions of the union contract can also be measured readily through paper and pencil tests. Complex skills, however, such as handling grievances and making decisions, or deeper knowledge and understandings such as timing the launching of a product or understanding the causes of inflation are more difficult to measure. Most difficult of all to evaluate are training programs designed to develop wholesome, constructive *attitudes*. Any appraisal of success in these fields is bound to be highly subjective and dependent on circumstances which are seldom fully understood.

577   How Should I Evaluate One Method of Training in Comparison with Another?

To do this scientifically, two groups of trainees are organized. Groups are matched as nearly as possible in ability, experience, and motivation for learning. Both are instructed in the same subject matter, but by a different method. One group studying how to lift, for example, may be exposed to twenty minutes of lecture, a twenty-minute film, and then an hour of directed practice. The other group may get no lecture and no film, and spends the whole time in directed practice.

Paper and pencil tests may be used to get a partial evaluation and the results may then be combined with a year's record of back strains or injuries for both groups. If there is a significant difference between the two groups in back injuries or in sprains, cuts, and broken bones from lifting, the training method used for the superior group may be accepted as the better one in this field.

578   How Useful Are Testimonials as an Evaluation of Training?

The use of testimonials attempts to record the attitudes of the learners toward their training. It assumes that the trainees are able and willing to report honestly on the value of instruction, and that a favorable attitude guarantees both acquisition of new knowledge and the will to apply it.

In the early days of training, testimonial letters from graduates were very popular. Anxiety to receive such testimonials, however, has led some training directors to adopt any halfway program or ineffectual method that will bring commendation. Too often, testimonials are written by trainees who have no real understanding of the objectives sought.

One of the authors had occasion to send out a half dozen teachers to instruct supervisors in sub-installations of a government agency. At the completion of the training, many complimentary letters came back to headquarters. One instructor, who was no better than the rest, received especially commendatory letters from almost every station he visited. Being questioned upon his return, he had no reason to give for the unusual number of letters of commendation which followed. However, it was learned that he had always arranged to take the training officer out to dinner and upon leaving had always presented him with a quart of whiskey, which apparently did the trick. Magazines and advertisers have so overdone "big name" testimonial letters that the latter have lost all semblance of reliability and much of their effect on the public.

579   Is Visitation of the Trainee and Observation of Him at Work Useful in Evaluation?

Yes. A few training directors have developed this practical approach to the evaluation of supervisor training. They schedule instructors to visit supervisors while the latter are performing their daily functions. These visits begin when the training is about half completed and continue with decreasing frequency for six months thereafter. Instructors make appointments, spend from thirty minutes to two hours with each supervisor, and discuss and observe the ways in which he applies his training.

In most cases, the work habits of supervisors reveal concrete evidence of changes in their methods of management as a result of training. The first time the senior author tried this kind of evaluation, a woman trainer was scheduled to visit ten supervisors who were currently attending her classes. She found many evidences of the application of training and returned with two efficiency rating scales developed and put into use by class members, a booklet of job breakdowns for instructional purposes, a case study showing how a supervisor had traced a wage complaint to jealousy of another worker's clothing, and a set of departmental organization charts drawn up where none had existed before. Samples of more than a hundred similar supervisory tools and an equal number of case studies showing the handling of personnel problems were collected through this sort of evaluation of a single supervisory program.

These visits helped also to locate those supervisors who had not applied their training. Once found, these men could be given encouragement, help, and even individual guidance by members of the training department. In this way the visits served to evaluate, helping the instructor locate persons who have either not learned or had not been motivated to apply their learning.

580   How Are Specific Objectives Used in Evaluation of Training and Development?

Let us answer this by an example from the field of economic education for executives. One company spelled out three major objectives for such a course. One was "to increase interest in the economic affairs of this business, this community, and our nation." While evaluation of the attainment of this aim could only be objective, it was decided to watch the following actions as indicators of increased interest:

1. Better attendance at an already established bi-monthly economic conference open, on a voluntary basis, to all executives in the company.
2. More penetrating economic analyses of projects when appropriations for them were requested.
3. More and better discussion of economic problems in regular board and staff meetings.

4. More withdrawals of economic texts and requests for others from the company library.
5. More and better analyses of alternatives when capital investments are being considered.
6. More volunteer attendance at National Industrial Conference Board and American Management Association conferences on economic and financial subjects.
7. More reading and more lunch-time discussion of magazine articles from *Fortune, Harvard Business Review, Business Week, Dun's Review,* and other business publications.
8. More willingness on the part of executives to participate in local and national committees and governing bodies dealing with economics.
9. More intelligent support and defense of economic opinions, expressed during day-to-day operations and in casual conversations.

Informal observation of these indications convinced company officials that the course had actually promoted interest in economic affairs. Had more accuracy been desired, executives might have made notes of their observations, bringing them together in some more or less formal statement six months after the training had closed. From this collection of evidence, any executive with sound judgment could have given a well-supported opinion about the value of the training.

Any program of training which starts with a specific statement of aims can be evaluated in this way. Although training experts and executives have talked much about the need for evaluation, most of them have avoided the detailed work which accurate appraisals require.

581   How Are Home Study Courses Evaluated?

Again we may answer with an example. The Home Study Department of the University of Chicago evaluated one of its courses on Human Relations in Industry by means of a written questionnaire. The course included thirty lessons and used textbook readings and case studies. The questions, which are reproduced below, may suggest leads for industrial development men who wish to try out written evaluations.

1. What did you expect to get out of this course?
2. How did the course stack up in terms of what you expected? In what ways did it live up to your expectations? In what ways did it *fail* to meet your expectations?

3. Did you find things in the course that you hadn't expected? What were they and how do you feel about them?

4. What would you say was the best thing about the course? (Please explain.)

5. What would you say was the worst thing about the course? (Please explain.)

6. What changes do you recommend be made in it?

7. Have you found opportunities to apply what you have learned? Would you give an example?

8. Would you recommend the course to others? To anyone or just to certain people? (Please explain the reason for your answer.)

9. If you were unable to complete the course, what would you say was the main reason?

582   Should Directors of Training and Development Keep a Yearly Record of Different Methods and Types of Programs They Use?

Yes, variety of approach makes training attractive to adults and appropriate to their needs and interests. Good programs organize learning so as to attract busy adults of varying needs, abilities, and interests. Many different approaches are necessary if the training and development activities are to get the participation of most of the men and women in the shop or office. Yearly records will indicate whether or not the program itself is growing in diversity of method.

In one research study involving 530 programs it was found that those using the widest variety of approaches interested the greatest number of learners. Since stimulation of interest is one of the major problems of development directors, this research is significant.

583   How Can a Good, or Successful, Program of Executive Development Be Recognized or Evaluated?

The ideal way to answer this question would be to list a series of standards by which any program of executive development could be evaluated. But a standard is a criterion of excellence that is accepted by common consent, and in that sense there are no real standards in the field of development. Until training men agree upon what is good and what is not, we must rely upon criteria which really are not much more than opinions. The following are the opinions held by the authors:

1. Any good program of executive development must have as its primary objective the growth and improvement of human beings. This means that at least half the effort, and preferably more, must be devoted to such fundamental learning activities as workshops, case studies, role playing, guided experience, conferences, rotation, counseling, lectures, etc. Inventories, evaluations, and plotting of futures, which dominate some management development programs, are aspects of executive *auditing*. Although useful and even necessary, they do not constitute executive *development*.

2. Executive development involves the education and improvement of capable, experienced adults, many of whom are mature, eminently successful, and fixed in their ways of thinking and doing. This work therefore is difficult, complex, and time consuming, and demands the services of qualified specialists. As a result, any successful program requires the full-time service, within the organization, of at least one educator, psychologist, or line executive who has specialized in the field of development and knows how to get results.

3. Any good, successful program encourages and helps executives to broaden their understandings and increase their skills, and in doing so leads them to assume increasing responsibility for their own improvement. This leads them to rely less and less upon the director of development and his planned programs, and more upon their own understanding of their needs and abilities. At the same time, they may demand more service. This comes in the form of requests for the staff training man to develop programs for them and give advice and counsel on plans and programs which they develop for themselves.

4. Executive development, if it is successful, leads to promotions from within. Once a program passes the experimental stage, therefore, management should find less and less need to go outside for supervisory, executive, technical, and even professional people, and should fill more and more important positions by advancing people who have followed programs of development.

5. Successful development cultivates open-mindedness toward change and a willingness to examine and try out new and possibly better methods. This does not mean that new things are accepted just because they are novel and old ones rejected because they are old. Rather, there is a wholesome balance between respect for stability and willingness to give it up for new and demonstrably better things.

6. Development succeeds only when it enables executives to meet today's requirements and also prepares them for the future.

Meeting present-day requirements means that each person masters the best ideas and procedures that prevail in his department and firm while the course of development is in progress. Preparation for the future goes further—it brings into the company good thought and practice not already there. To do this, development seeks to broaden vision, increase understanding, and add to information, on the premise that modern management is always interested in improving or replacing what is now good in preparation for a better tomorrow.

7. A good program of executive development results, not merely in the progress of a few men, but in sound growth and increasing success of the entire business. In other words, it enables the management team to meet the profit requirements of the owners, the social and citizenship requirements of the community and the individual needs of all its employees.

In our opinion, any program of executive development may be called successful if it meets these seven requirements. We doubt, however, whether rules can be given for a more precise evaluation.

Can we, for example, say that a program which gives 75 per cent of its time and effort to fundamentals is necessarily one fourth better than one that gives 60 per cent? Are all programs conducted by one full-time specialist to be rated as equal, and are those with two specialists necessarily better than programs that get along with one? Unless such questions can be answered with *yes*—and they can't be—it is obvious that evaluations must be relative and subjective, and can apply only to individual programs in individual companies.

584   Suppose a Course Is Well Planned and Excellently Taught But Results in Changed Behavior Do Not Follow. What Should Be Done?

Such a condition cannot exist. To be "excellently taught" means to have excellent results—in this case, changes in behavior. This questioner does not know what constitutes excellent teaching. He probably mistakes presentation, showmanship or teacher control and domination of the situation for good instruction, though they really are quite different. If any course or program of development fails to produce changes in behavior, we may safely assume that teaching is poor. The remedy is to learn what is wrong and then institute improvements.

585   Aren't Supervisory and Executive Audits a Device to Evaluate Training?

In a general way, yes. Where they take place annually or more often they should reveal regular improvement in men who have been trained.

586   When Are Written Tests Used in Evaluating Training?

They are used most often when specific information has been taught and when knowledge of facts is important. Thus written tests may indicate progress made in the study of such subjects as the annual report or the company policy on retirement or vacations. Tests also measure the success of courses in shop mathematics or in letter writing for executive secretaries, to give only a few examples. On the other hand, there are serious objectives to the use of written tests, as we find in the answer to the next question.

587   Are Written Tests Welcome or Objectionable? Why?

No one objects to written tests when they are used only as learning devices or as guides and incentives to discussion. On the other hand, training departments, trainees, and many executives doubt that they should be widely used as means of evaluation, especially while training is in progress. The principal objections are:

1. Even the best written tests measure knowledge, but give no indication of whether and how well it will be used.
2. Tests often reveal innate ability, but do not measure or evaluate new learnings and attitudes.
3. There is no acceptable standardized test of superiority or executive ability, though several have been attempted. There is little chance that any single training department can produce tests that have much value.
4. Tests sometimes block or inhibit free expression. Persons who do badly in a few written tests may withdraw from discussions, lest they reveal their weakness.
5. Tests often shake the confidence of those who receive low marks, sending them back to the job fearful and uncertain.
6. Persons who receive low marks often feel resentment and project it to the training instructor or department. As a result, they resist its efforts, question its judgment, and doubt or deny the value of its work.

7. Tests given during training arouse a suspicion among trainees that they are being rated. If the grades are sent on to management, that suspicion is justified. Even though the training department treats grades as provisional indicators of progress, management is likely to accept them as reliable and unchangeable ratings.

In general, the main objective of training should be to develop the innate abilities of people who already have been placed on jobs. Selection of certain persons for advancement and others for demotion should be done by other departments. If written tests lead to a violation of this rule, their use should be curtailed or avoided.

588   Does the Number of Hours Spent in Development Help in Evaluating the Program?

Time spent cannot measure quality of teaching, nor does it reveal the trainees' response. Both must be judged by qualitative —not quantitative—standards. On the other hand, hours do provide a useful measure of the effort expended on development. A record of hours spent in training measures how much has been done, quantity-wise. Coupled with some measure of quality, hours spent in training give an adequate measure of training and development activity.

589   What Is a Satisfactory Way of Computing the Amount of Formal Activity in Training and Development?

A very simple formula, and the one most frequently employed, is this:

Number of class meetings x Hours per class x Number of employees per class = Total man-hours of training

Since the gross figure thus arrived at is obviously weighted in favor of the large organization, a further refinement of the formula is suggested: to include the factor of company size. When this is done, the formula would read:

Number of class meetings $\times$ Hours per class $\times$ Number of employees per class $\div$ Total number of employees = Per capita man-hours of training[2]

[2] Earl G. Planty, William S. McCord, and Carlos A. Efferson, *Training Employees and Managers for Production and Teamwork* (New York: The Ronald Press Co., 1948), p. 103.

This formula must be employed with recognition of its limitation as a measure of training values. In spite of this, it may be used to compare the training carried out by separate plants or by units within a single company, to compare the many units in a government agency, or the companies within one type or class or industry. Whenever there is need for a concise, standardized statement of the amount of training being done in any organization, this formula may be applied.

590   How Soon After the Conclusion of the Course Should It Be Evaluated?

Evaluation should be made immediately, before there are significant losses or accretions from other sources. If retention of habits or knowledge is to be measured, however, subsequent evaluations must be made. Planning for evaluation should begin when the development activities are planned, should continue throughout learning, and should culminate as the course or program draws to an end.

591   Does Evaluation Provide Guidance for the Men Doing the Training and Development or for High Executives?

It serves both. Training and development men can improve their performance only by learning where they have succeeded and where—and why—they have failed. Research in learning has proved that betterment comes most rapidly when one knows where he stands and how he is progressing. This rule applies to the director of development and training as much as it does to his students.

The goals of training—better morale, increased productivity, lower costs, and greater job satisfaction among all levels of employees—are of great importance to every employer. Top management must know whether or not these goals are being achieved in order to measure its performance and correct its direction if it is off the course. Not to know is to fly blind among many dangerous hazards.

Top management also must be informed about the results of training if it is to maintain the interest and confidence shown when the program was established. Any activity that drops out of sight is likely to be forgotten; if inquiry reveals lack of success, work may be summarily stopped. On the other hand, if training encounters obstacles and reports them frankly, top management may willingly help analyze the problem and correct whatever is wrong.

592 Are Not Some Evaluations of Training Bound to Be Approximate and Subjective?

Most of the goals sought in executive training are essentially qualitative; we seek to *improve* human beings, their thoughts and actions, not to increase units of production or cut down units of waste. Suppose, for example, that an executive learns to be more flexible, more persuasive, more judicious, or more far-sighted than he was before embarking on a program of development. We can tell that this or that change takes place, and can tell whether the degree of change is great, moderate, or slight by making an anecdotal case study and by psychological evaluation. But we cannot translate results into dollars and cents or percentages.

593 Why Are Many Training Men Reluctant to Evaluate Their Programs?

There seem to be two principal reasons. The demand for evaluation of training comes largely from production, engineering, and scientific management groups, made up of people who like to deal in figures. But training can seldom be evaluated precisely. Training men, therefore, are unwilling to attempt the impossible, and are reluctant to bring forth approximate, subjective evaluations which will be rejected as "unscientific" or used with blind faith.

We must also remember that training is one kind of education, and that educators in general have not been called upon to prove the exact value of their wares. No one questions the value of reading, writing, and arithmetic; no one asks for evaluations to prove the value of ability to think well, speak clearly and forcefully, or reason soundly. Similarly, no one doubts that schooling educates more effectively than does hit-or-miss, unorganized learning. If we accept all these things on faith, as part of the wisdom derived from human experience, the training man sees no reason why he should have to prove the value of his particular methods and accomplishments.

594 Have Attitude Surveys Been Used to Evaluate Development? If So, What Did They Show?

A training executive of Koppers Company, Inc., tells the authors about the use of attitude surveys as follows:

We administered attitude surveys to employees at some locations before the management development programs were undertaken and also after they had been in effect for a year or more. In these cases, we can point to definite improvement in practically every area of management activity as indicated by the employees' response. While we cannot accredit this entirely to the Management Development Program, we feel that it has been a definite influence.

In one fairly large plant in which there had been no management development activity of any kind, our "before" survey showed that 68% of the non-supervisors felt that their company was a good place to work; 78% liked the job they had at the time; 36% felt free to discuss complaints with their supervisor. At the end of 14 months, during which a full-scale and intensive management development program, ranging from appraisal, counseling and coaching, through both group and individual training programs, had been implemented, there was a 16% increase in liking toward the company, 5% increase in job satisfaction, 10% increase in the feeling that they were kept informed about company matters, and other significant increases almost straight down the line.

In another department, under the same conditions, we have had as much as 32% increase in liking for the company, 22% increase in job satisfaction, 28% increase in satisfaction with communications, and 27% improvement in the feeling that the supervisor handled people well. We feel that a good part of this is attributable to the Management Development program.

595   How Do We Answer the Question "Does Training of Supervisors and Junior Executives Pay Off?" In Other Words, How Can We Convince Doubters That Training Really Is Worth While?

Suppose we answer this question by telling what *could* be done, what *can* be done, and what we actually *do*.

With a lot of time and money, freedom to set up control groups, and skill in research, we could study the results of training and doubtless establish its value. In doing this we would analyze promotions from within before and after training, to show whether training provides so many capable men that need to go outside is reduced. We would set up control groups and study speed of learning with and without training. We would tabulate the reduction of grievances, of errors and mistakes, of waste and rejects. We would set up morale surveys and examine attitudes with and without, or before and after, training. We would keep before-and-after records, endeavoring to show an increase in the number of competent men who applied to us for employment, and would use tests or other scientific devices to support our opinions that opportunities for training attracted increasingly able men. We also would study turnover figures to show how much training improved our retention of employees.

We *could*, and perhaps *would*, do these things if we had almost limitless resources. Since we haven't, we *can* take only those steps mentioned in the answers to Questions 571 and 572. But since we, as training men, are educators, we actually fall back upon the attitude set forth in answers to Question 593. Americans somehow know or believe that education is worth while without demanding actual proof of its material value. We turn to the colleges for trained chemists, engineers, and accountants without objective proof of the material value of their education. Why should the education of employees, supervisors and executives be an exception to this rule?

596   How Does One Appraise the Development of Executives?

Probably the most realistic method is to observe and evaluate their performance over the years. A review of merit ratings taken over a span of years is helpful, as well as psychological evaluations taken a few years apart. An increasing number of management positions in the company which are filled from within is another measure of progress.

597   Are Outsiders of Much Help in Evaluating Training and Development?

A specialist in General Adult Education of the Adult Education Association answers this questions as follows:[3]

Self-appraisal usually is better than appraisal by outsiders. The benefits of evaluation accrue chiefly to the persons who go through the process of analytic appraisal. A thoughtful examination of the details of a program will suggest many points for improvement and stimulate the imagination. Mechanical checking may yield a score, but in itself assures little growth; it may even stimulate complacency.

It is often better to build your own evaluative instruments than to use ready-made ones. An instrument is useful if it stimulates improvement and if it measures objectives accepted by those involved in the program. Developing instruments and applying them to one's own program is a self-appraisal activity of a creative sort.

[3] Committee on Evaluation, Adult Education Association, "Program Evaluation in Adult Education" (Washington, D.C.: The Association, 1952).

Comparison with self leads to more growth than comparison with others. Experience indicates that program objectives and circumstances vary so widely that inter-program comparisons are often invalid and even dangerous. Measurement of growth cannot be made against the objectives of some other program. What is desired is achievement of one's own objectives rather than comparison with others.

Evaluation offers greatest potential benefit if it is a long-time, continuous, and built-in part of the total educational process.

598   Should Trainees Evaluate Themselves and Their Growth?

Yes. We do too little of this in business and industry. In the workshops at Wayne University, learners are given two self-evaluation sheets—one when the course is about a third over and the other when it is nearly done. The self-evaluation questionnaire asks questions like the following—"What role am I playing in these meetings?" "Is it satisfying to me, to my associates?" "What is my attitude toward this workshop now?" "Do I understand what is being attempted?" "How could I help the workshop to succeed better?" "What am I getting out of it?" "What are the blocks to my progress?"

The first questionnaire aims to encourage the learner to evaluate his own goals and progress; the second asks similar questions. At the end of the course both evaluations are returned to the learner. They frequently surprise the trainee by showing, in his own writing, his growth in attitudes toward himself and the program.

599   Does the Available Number of Trained Understudies in a Company Help to Evaluate Its Program of Training and Development?

Yes, especially where formal evaluations and audits are part of the development program. Here is an answer to this question based on seven years of experience Esso Standard Oil has had with a formal development program:[4]

In 1952 we made a statistical comparison of our Program from the standpoint of job replacements as compared to 1946, as follows:

[4] William H. McGaughey, "Measuring Results of Management Development Activities," Nash Kelvinator Corporation, December, 1952.

Year	No. of Jobs in Program	Jobs with 2 or more Replacements		Jobs with 1 Replacement		Jobs Without Replacements		Total Employees in Program
		No.	%	No.	%	No.	%	
1946	695	450	65%	157	23%	88	13%	1040
1952	822	644	78%	155	19%	23	3%	1602
Difference ..	+127	+194	+20%	−2	−8%	−65	−77%	+562

The above statistics reveal that the number of jobs with two or more replacements increased from 65% in 1946, to 78% in 1952, and the jobs with only one replacement decreased in number from 23% in 1946, to 19% in 1952, and lastly the jobs without any replacements decreased from 13% to 3% between the same two dates.

Our Management Development Program has grown over a period of seven years to a point where management now knows a great deal more about management people and their potential ability than it ever knew before. . . . Our inventory indicates that we now have good men available as replacements in the right place and at the right time. While we may have some weak replacement situations, we know where they exist and are working on the necessary steps to correct them.

600   How Is One to Judge the Value of Training in Overcoming the Traditional Negative Reactions to Management?

Many will object to the word "traditional" in this question. Ignoring this point, however, the first step is to find out why management evokes these negative reactions, for we cannot prevent an action or an attitude unless we understand its cause. Perhaps management has been too much concerned with methods, machines, and systems to win the confidence of its people. Perhaps, for example, people suspect that the company considers waste of material more important than waste of human resources. Perhaps the company still considers its people as an economic commodity, to be bought and sold, soullessly. Management may not listen to its people as they tell of their needs, or it may listen and ignore what it hears. Perhaps the rank and file see the company officials rarely, and so regard them impersonally and resentfully. Perhaps pay rates, company philosophy, physical conditions of the workplace, poor supervision, or antagonistic union leadership contributes to the problem.

Since the causes for hostility of workers toward management vary, training must vary to meet them. It will, however, follow the same practices that are recommended for other training. In doing so, it will avoid the popular fallacy that training can easily and effectively cancel out long-standing attitudes caused by acts of management to which workers have objected. The most that training can do is to teach management to detect actions that cause negative attitudes and how to avoid such actions. Management itself then must decide what changes it wishes to make.

BIBLIOGRAPHY

A Note to the Reader: This bibliography groups together and numbers the references that will be found helpful in working out the training or development problems discussed in the book. For your convenience, the numbers of the books and articles which are especially relevant to particular chapters are listed below.

Selected References by Chapters

Chapter 1—Definitions and Values, 19, 24, 40, 45, 65, 82, 84, 94

Chapter 2—Learning and Teaching, 4, 16, 17, 24, 30, 48, 49, 60, 64

Chapter 3—Leadership, 5, 7, 11, 13, 18, 23, 27, 36, 38, 42, 43, 51, 54, 85, 88

Chapter 4—The Management Audit, 25, 26, 53, 62, 65, 69, 80, 84

Chapter 5—The Guided Experience Method, 62, 81

Chapter 6—The Conference Method, 2, 9, 15, 21, 39, 57, 90, 98, 99, 102

Chapter 7—Job Rotation, 12, 25, 62, 84

Chapter 8—Multiple Management, 8, 14, 58, 76, 95

Chapter 9—Role Playing, 6, 22, 29, 55, 57, 63, 64, 68, 70, 77, 96, 103

Chapter 10—The Case Study Method, 3, 4, 10, 28, 35, 47, 61, 75, 87, 91, 92

Chapter 11—Staff Meetings for Development, 34, 84, 90, 98

Chapter 12—Miscellaneous Development Methods and Programs, 8, 14, 25, 39, 40, 57, 58, 62, 66, 74, 81, 84

Chapter 13—Executive Development, 5, 7, 8, 12, 23, 25, 35, 54, 61, 62, 64, 75, 84, 89

Chapter 14—Supervisory Development, 9, 10, 12, 17, 25, 40, 54, 61, 62, 64, 75, 78, 84, 92, 99, 104

Chapter 15—Management Trainee Programs, 25, 40, 42, 78, 84, 97

Chapter 16—General Education, 20, 32, 52, 55, 66, 71, 82, 93, 94

Chapter 17—Orientation Training, 40, 66, 71, 82, 93

Chapter 18—Training for Breadth and Change, 31, 81, 82, 93

Chapter 19—Skill Training, 1, 40, 65, 82, 93

Chapter 20—Development for Research, Scientific, and Technical Personnel, 72, 73, 82

Chapter 21—Promoting Self-Development, 50, 69, 86, 89

Chapter 22—Human Relations Development, 4, 10, 19, 22, 28, 31, 44, 47, 56, 64, 67, 78, 79, 83, 100, 101

Chapter 23—Organization of Training or Development, 40, 46, 59, 82

Chapter 24—Determining Needs for Development, 25, 37, 45, 82

Chapter 25—Securing Acceptance for Training or Development, 82

Chapter 26—Getting Training or Development Under Way, 45, 82, 84

Chapter 27—Duties and Responsibilities of the Director of Training or Development, 40, 82, 84

Chapter 28—Preparing the Full-Time Director of Training or Development and His Associates, 12, 25, 40, 45, 46, 53, 62, 65, 74, 82, 84, 93, 94

Chapter 29—Training and Using Line and Staff Operating Men in the Program, 39, 82

Chapter 30—Mechanics of Training, 40, 46, 57, 82

Chapter 31—Evaluating Development Activities, 25, 33, 37, 41, 57

SELECTED REFERENCES

1. ALLGOOD, MARY BROWN. *Demonstration Techniques*. New York: Prentice-Hall, Inc., 1947.
2. AMERICAN MANAGEMENT ASSOCIATION. *A Guide to Successful Conference Leadership*. New York, 1948.
3. ANDREWS, KENNETH R. (ed.). *The Case Method of Teaching*. Cambridge: Harvard University Press, 1953.
4. ———. *Human Relations and Administration*. Cambridge: Harvard University Press, 1953.
5. ARGYRIS, CHRIS. *Executive Leadership*. New York: Harper & Bros., 1953.
6. ———. *Role Playing in Action*. Ithaca, New York: New York State School of Industrial Relations, Bulletin No. 16, April, 1952.
7. BARNARD, CHESTER I. *The Nature of Leadership*. Cambridge: Harvard University Press, 1940.
8. BECHTOLD, A. S. "Multiple Management—The New Approach to Executive Development," *Proceedings of the Louisiana Personnel Management Conference*, Louisiana State University, Baton Rouge, La., 1952.
9. BECKMAN, R. O. *How to Train Supervisors*. New York: Harper & Bros., 1944, revised 1952.
10. BERRIEN, FRED K. *Comments and Cases on Human Relations*. New York: Harper & Bros., 1951.
11. BOWER, MARVIN (ed.). *The Development of Executive Leadership*. Cambridge: Harvard University Press, 1949.
12. BRADSHAW, T. F. *Developing Men for Controllership*. Cambridge: Harvard University Press, 1950.
13. BROWNE, C. G. "Study of Executive Leadership in Business—Social Group Patterns," *Journal of Applied Psychology*, February, 1950.
14. BUCKLEY, J. L., JR. "Seventeen Years of Multiple Management," *NACA Bulletin*, December, 1949.
15. BUSCH, HENRY M. *Conference Methods in Industry*. New York: Harper & Bros., 1949.
16. CANTOR, NATHANIEL. *Dynamics of Learning*. Buffalo: Foster & Stewart Publishing Corp., 1947.
17. ———. *Learning Through Discussion*. Buffalo: Human Relations for Industry, 1951.
18. CARTER, LAUNOR, and NIXON, MARY. "Ability, Perceptual, Personality, and Interest Factors Associated With Different Criteria of Leadership," *Journal of Psychology*, April, 1949.
19. CHASE, STUART. *Roads to Agreement*. New York: Harper & Bros., 1951.
20. CONANT, JAMES BRYANT. *Education in a Divided World*. Cambridge: Harvard University Press, 1948.
21. *Conference Leadership*. Esso Standard Oil Co., Esso Training Center Publication, 1947.
22. COOK, LLOYD ALLEN (ed.). "Intergroup Relations—The Educator's Role," in *Toward Better Human Relations*. Detroit: Wayne University Press, 1952.
23. COPELAND, MELVIN T. *The Executive at Work*. Cambridge: Harvard University Press, 1951.
24. DEWEY, RICHARD, and HUMBER, W. J. *The Development of Human Behavior*. New York: The Macmillan Co., 1951.
25. DOOHER, M. JOSEPH (ed.). *The Development of Executive Talent*. New York: American Management Association, 1952.

26. DOOHER, M. JOSEPH, and MARGUIS, VIVIENNE (eds.). *Rating Employee and and Supervisory Performance.* New York: American Management Association, 1950.

27. DORIOT, G. F. *How to Pick Men.* Boston: Harvard University, Graduate School of Business Administration, 1952.

28. DUBIN, ROBERT. *Human Relations in Administration.* New York: Prentice-Hall, Inc., 1951.

29. FRENCH, J. R. P., JR. "Role Playing as a Method of Training Foremen," in S. D. Hoslett (ed.), *Human Factors in Management.* New York: Harper & Bros., 1946.

30. FRYER, DOUGLAS H., and HENRY, EDWIN R. *Handbook of Applied Psychology.* New York: Rinehart & Co., Inc., 1950.

31. GARDNER, BURLEIGH B., and MOORE, DAVID G. *Human Relations in Industry.* Homewood, Ill.: Richard D. Irwin, Inc., 1945, revised 1950.

32. *General Education in a Free Society.* Cambridge: Harvard University Press, 1945.

33. GHISELLI, EDWIN H., and BROWN, CLARENCE W. *Personnel and Industrial Psychology.* New York: McGraw-Hill Book Co., Inc., 1948.

34. GLASS, JOSEPH G. *How to Plan Meetings and Be a Successful Chairman.* New York: Merlin Press, Inc., 1951.

35. GLOVER, J. D., and HOWER, R. M. *The Administrator.* Homewood, Ill.: Richard D. Irwin, Inc., 1949.

36. GOULDNER, ALVIN W. (ed.). *Studies in Leadership; Leadership and Democratic Action.* New York: Harper & Bros., 1950.

37. GRACE, ALONZO G. *Educational Lessons from Wartime Training.* Washington, D. C.: American Council on Education, 1948.

38. GUETZKOW, HAROLD S. (ed.). *Groups, Leadership, and Men.* Pittsburgh: Carnegie Press, 1951.

39. HAAS, KENNETH B., and EWING, CLAUDE H. *Tested Training Techniques.* New York: Prentice-Hall, Inc., 1950.

40. HALSEY, GEORGE D. *Training Employees.* New York: Harper & Bros., 1949.

41. HARRELL, THOMAS WILLARD. *Industrial Psychology.* New York: Rinehart & Co., Inc., 1949.

42. HENRY, WILLIAM. *Executive Personality and Job Success.* American Management Association, Personnel Series No. 120. New York, 1948.

43. ———. *Identifying the Potentially Successful Executive.* American Management Association, Personnel Series No. 127. New York, 1949.

44. HOSLETT, SCHUYLER D. *Human Factors in Management.* New York: Harper & Bros., 1946, revised 1951.

45. *Industrial Training Abstracts.* Published quarterly, by the School of Business Administration, Wayne University.

46. *The Journal of Industrial Training.* Published bi-monthly, by the American Society of Training Directors.

47. JUCIUS, MICHAEL J. *Personnel Management.* Homewood, Ill.: Richard D. Irwin, Inc., 1949.

48. KELLEY, EARL C. *The Workshop Way of Learning.* New York: Harper & Bros., 1951.

49. KELLEY, EARL C., and RASEY, MARIE I. *Education and the Nature of Man.* New York: Harper & Bros., 1952.

50. KIENSLE, G. J., and DARE, E. H. *Climbing the Executive Ladder.* New York: McGraw-Hill Book Co., Inc., 1950.

51. KNICKERBOCKER, IRVING. "Leadership: A Conception and Some Implications," *The Journal of Social Issues,* Summer, 1948.

52. KNOWLES, MALCOLM S. *Informal Adult Education.* New York: Association Press, 1950.

53. LAIRD, DONALD A., and LAIRD, ELEANOR C. *Sizing Up People.* New York: McGraw-Hill Book Co., Inc., 1951.

54. LEARNED, E. P., ULRICH, D. N., and BOOZ, D. R. *Executive Action.* Boston: Harvard University, Graduate School of Business Administration, 1951.

55. LERNER, HARRY H., and KELMAN, HERBERT C. (eds.). "Group Methods in Psychotherapy, Social Work, and Adult Education," *The Journal of Social Issues,* Vol. VIII, No. 2, 1952.

56. LINDGREN, HENRY CLAY. *The Art of Human Relations.* New York: Hermitage House, Inc., 1953.

57. LIVERIGHT, A. A. *Union Leadership Training.* New York: Harper & Bros., 1951.

58. McCORMICK, C. P. *The Power of People: Multiple Management Up to Date.* New York: Harper & Bros., 1949.

59. McGEHEE, WILLIAM. "Training in Industry," in WAYNE DENNIS (ed.), *Current Trends in Industrial Psychology.* Pittsburgh: University of Pittsburgh Press, 1949.

60. McGEOCH, J. A., and IRION, A. L. *The Psychology of Human Learning.* New York: Longmans, Green & Co., 1952.

61. McLARNEY, WILLIAM J. *Management Training: Cases and Principles.* Homewood, Ill.: Richard D. Irwin, Inc., 1952.

62. MACE, MYLES L. *The Growth and Development of Executives.* Boston: Harvard University, Graduate School of Business Administration, 1950.

63. MACHAVER, WILLIAM V., and FISCHER, FRANK E. "The Leader's Role in Role Playing," *The Journal of Industrial Training,* January-February, 1953.

64. MAIER, NORMAN R. F. *Principles of Human Relations.* New York: John Wiley & Sons, Inc., 1952.

65. MEE, JOHN F. (ed.). *Personnel Handbook.* New York: The Ronald Press Co., 1951.

66. METROPOLITAN LIFE INSURANCE COMPANY. "The Information Rack in the Employee Communications Program." New York, 1952.

67. MILLER, DELBERT C., and FORM, WILLIAM H. *Industrial Sociology.* New York: Harper & Bros., 1951.

68. MOODY, K. A. "Role Playing Can Be Effective," *Journal of Industrial Training,* September-October, 1950.

69. MOORE, ROBERT F. *How Am I Doing? Self-Appraisal for the Aspiring Executive.* New York: B. C. Forbes & Sons Pub. Co., Inc., 1952.

70. MORENO, J. L. *Psychodrama.* New York: Beacon House, 1946.

71. NATIONAL INDUSTRIAL CONFERENCE BOARD, INC. *Employee Education.* Studies in Personnel Policy, No. 119. New York, 1951.

72. NATIONAL MANPOWER COUNCIL. *A Policy for Scientific and Professional Manpower.* New York: Columbia University Press, 1953.

73. NATIONAL SOCIETY OF PROFESSIONAL ENGINEERS. *How to Improve the Utilization of Engineering Manpower.* Washington, D. C., 1952.

74. NATIONAL SOCIETY OF SALES TRAINING EXECUTIVES. *Handbook of Sales Training.* New York: Prentice-Hall, Inc., 1949.

75. NEWMAN, W. H. *Administrative Action.* New York: Prentice-Hall, Inc., 1951.

76. NICHOLS, J. S., JR. *An Adventure in Multiple Management.* New Brunswick: Permacel Tape Corporation, 1950.

77. O'DONNELL, W. G. "Role Playing as a Practical Training Technique," *Personnel,* November, 1952.

78. PFIFFNER, JOHN M. *The Supervision of Personnel.* New York: Prentice-Hall, Inc., 1951.

79. PIGORS, PAUL, and MYERS, CHARLES A. *Personnel Administration.* New York: McGraw-Hill Book Co., Inc., 1951.

80. PLANTY, EARL G., and EFFERSON, CARLOS A. "Counseling Executives After Merit Rating or Evaluation," *Personnel,* March, 1951.

81. ———. "Developing Leadership for Tomorrow's Tasks," *Dun's Review,* January and February, 1952.

82. PLANTY, EARL G., McCORD, WILLIAM S., and EFFERSON, CARLOS A. *Training Employees and Managers for Production and Teamwork.* New York: The Ronald Press Co., 1948.

83. REILLY, WILLIAM J. *Successful Human Relations.* New York: Harper & Bros., 1952.

84. RIEGEL, JOHN W. *Executive Development.* Ann Arbor: University of Michigan Press, 1952.

85. ROETHLISBERGER, F. J. *Management and Morale.* Cambridge: Harvard University Press, 1950.

86. SIMMONS, HARRY. *How to Get Ahead in Modern Business.* New York: Prentice-Hall, Inc., 1953.

87. SMITH, G. A. *Policy Formulation and Administration.* Homewood, Ill.: Richard D. Irwin, Inc., 1951.

88. STAGDILL, RALPH M. "Personal Factors Associated with Leadership," *Journal of Psychology,* January, 1948.

89. STARCH, DANIEL. *How to Develop Your Executive Ability.* New York: Harper & Bros., 1943.

90. STRAUSS, BERT, and STRAUSS, FRANCES. *New Ways to Better Meetings.* New York: The Viking Press, 1951.

91. TERRY, G. R. *Case Problems in Business and Industrial Management.* Dubuque, Iowa: William C. Brown Co., 1949.

92. THOMASON, CALVIN C. *Human Relations in Action.* New York: Prentice-Hall, Inc., 1947.

93. THOMSON, DAVID CLEGHORN (ed.). *Training Worker Citizens.* London: Macdonald & Evans, 1949.

94. TICKNER, F. J. *Modern Staff Training.* London: University of London Press, Ltd., 1952.

95. TOYNE, J. R. "The Junior Board," *Bacie Journal* (British Association for Commercial & Industrial Education), June, 1953.

96. TYLER, A. H. "A Case Study of Role Playing," *Personnel,* September, 1948.

97. UHRBROCK, RICHARD S. *Recruiting the College Graduate: A Guide for Company Interviewers.* New York: American Management Association, 1953.

98. UTTERBACK, WILLIAM E. *Committees and Conferences, How to Lead Them.* New York: Rinehart & Co., Inc., 1950.

99. WAGNER, RUSSELL H., and ARNOLD, CARROLL C. *Handbook of Group Discussion.* Boston: Houghton Mifflin Co., 1950.

100. WAITE, WILLIAM W. *Personnel Administration.* New York: The Ronald Press Co., 1952.

101. WALKER, CHARLES R., and GUEST, ROBERT H. *The Man on the Assembly Line.* Cambridge: Harvard University Press, 1952.

102. WALSER, FRANK. *The Art of Conference.* New York: Harper & Bros., 1948.

103. WYN-JONES, I. "The Significance of Role Playing," *Bacie Journal,* January-February, 1952.

104. ZALENZNIK, A. *Foreman Training in a Growing Enterprise.* Boston: Harvard University, Graduate School of Business Administration, 1951.

INDEX

References are to Question Numbers

Accounting, training college recruits in, 326

Administration, developing interest in, among technical men, 391

Adults
acceptance of idea of continuing education by, 30
learning ability of, 26

Advancement
danger of preparing executives for faster than opportunities arise, 253
frustration as result of waiting for, 254

Advisory training committee, establishment of, 503

Aids, training, 538
value of, 25

Antagonistic workers, handling, 451

Appraisal, executive
as a line responsibility, 64
day-to-day operation, 69
defined, 58
individual's knowledge of his own appraisal, 70
role of personnel director in, 64

Apprentice training, advantages of program for, 414

Attitudes
developing good, 21
negative, how training deals with, 455

Attitude surveys, use in evaluation, 594

Audit, executive
defined, 45
frequency of, 50
limitations of plans and practices in, 51
procedure, 48
responsibility for, 46
review of organizational structure prior to, 49
values of, 47
who makes it, 46

Audits, as device to evaluate training, 585

Authority, teaching management to assign, 264

Bias, personal, training to overcome, 461

Books, for director of development, 523

"Buddy" system (orientation), 200

Carrier Cabinet, defined, 210

Case studies
advantages, 155, 157
evaluating discussion, 175
that help get understanding of management development, 495
incident process, 220-222
internal or outside cases, 160
limitations, 155
preparation for leading discussion of, 158
purpose of, 166, 167, 171
questions in, 163
results of, 32
selecting cases, 159
for selling development, 495
size of group, 170
solutions in, 164, 165
starting discussion, 161, 172, 173
subjects for, 166
uses of, 156

Case study method
defined, 154
groups used with successfully, 167
leader in, 162, 164, 165, 169, 174
obtaining cases for supervisory development, 286
overcoming frustration of participants, 168
preference for, over other methods, 171
purpose of, 167
special advantages of, 157
use of written questions to stimulate discussion, 173

Check lists
usefulness in determining potential for leadership, 38
use in orientation, 383

Classes; see also Orientation
attendance at, 558
grading systems, 561
importance of physical conditions of rooms used for, 554
levels represented in, 560
pay while attending, 559

Classes (*Continued*)
taught by others than professional training staff, 476
College recruits
competition among, 330
establishing and operating training program for, 325, 326
problem in developing, 323
problem of leaving company after training, 331
reason for special training of, 322
training program for, 321
who teaches, 333
Committee assignments
limitations, 202
use of, in development, 201, 202
Conference group
determining makeup of, for training purposes, 89
Conference leaders
handling men who won't talk, 98
handling silent groups, 98
handling wise guys, 98
need not be an authority on subject being discussed, 92
selection of, 91
use of criticism of conference members' superiors by, 95
Conference leadership training
course content, 97, 99
defined, 97
selling to management, 96
values, 97
Conference method
advantages, 94
limitations, 94
of organizing and carrying out a training program, 86
as pooling of experience, 88
of teaching, and its use in training, 85
use of criticism of the conference members' superiors by leader, 95
vs. lecture method in training salespeople, 217
when to use, 93
Conference program, typical, for supervisors, 87
Conferences
best physical conditions for, 555
handling men who won't talk, 98
handling select groups, 98
handling wise guys, 98
sales, training director's aid in, 223
supervisor training, frequency of, 100
who should lead supervisor training, 90

Controller, how he can start development program in his department, 507
Cooperation
achieving, 448, 462, 497, 498
capacity for, 467
Correspondence courses for supervisory development, 288, 289
Costs, development
defending, for older people, 565
inclusion of man hours spent in training in computing, 567
per person, 563
of professional vs. line training men, 566
Counseling
after evaluation, 70, 75
evaluation of, 213
following executive evaluation, 75
how used in development, 194
limitations, 195
values of, 195
Courses, 262, 266, 269; *see also* Subjects
cooperative, given by General Motors Institute, 197
correspondence, 288, 289
evaluation of, time for, 590
failure of, to produce behavior changes, 584
general educational, 346
informing participants of schedule of meetings of, 549
repositories for outlines of, 540
supervisory development, 276, 277, 293, 318
university development, 249

Development; *see also* Training
case studies that help get understanding of, 495
convincing management it is a desirable function, 492
cost per worker, 563
courses, 4
danger in stating a man's potential for, 71
determining need for assigning a man full time to, 474
determining needs for, 483, 485, 486
director; *see* Director of development
distinction between training and, 1
enthusiasm for, in company no longer growing, 447
evaluation of
approximate and subjective nature of, 592
attitude surveys used in, 594

available number of trained under-studies as aid in, 599

"before and after," 574

computing amount of formal activity in, 589

guidance resulting from, 591

meaning of, 571

methods, 573

need for, 568

outsiders' help in, 597

reluctance of training men to, 593

scientific, 575

self-evaluation of trainees, 598

starting point, 569

in terms of results, 572

testimonials as, 578

time for, 590

use of specific objectives in, 580

use of trainee visitation and observation in, 579

written tests used in, 586, 587

executive

appraisal of, 596

areas of need for, 244, 245

"assistant to" positions, 251

assumptions underlying, 231, 232

best type, 247

busy executives and, 235

contrast of methods, 250

courses offered by universities and professional management societies, 262

danger of frustration following, 254

danger of preparing men for advancement faster than opportunities arise, 253

defined, 226

director of, 240, 248, 259

evaluation of, 583

example of full and complete program, 269

individualized, 271

inducing management to cooperate in programs, 237

initial steps, 243

line executives role in, 261

methods, 246, 252

need for, 227, 239

outsiders' aid in, 260

overcoming resistance to, 235, 445

place of, in relation to personnel and training program, 229

responsibility for, 230

selecting trainees for, 233, 234

selling programs, 237, 238

small company program, 263

starting the program, 232, 241, 242, 243

timeliness of, in rapidly expanding companies, 228

flat organizational structure and, 214

future of, 14

geographic separation and, 290

guided experience method of

defined, 76

help needed by line executives to conduct, 81

how steps are worked out, 78

limitations of, 80

persuading managers to devote time to, 83

psychological supports for, 84

response of groups to, 82

steps in applying, 77

strengths of, 79

hours spent in, use in evaluation, 588

human relations; see Human relations development

methods most often used in, 7

needs

determining primary, 489

getting men to recognize their own, 490

newly discovered fundamentals of, 17

organization of department for, 481, 500

organization where there is no staff or outside help, 482

plans for organizing, 468

primary educational problem in, 16

program

defined, 2

getting top management to support, 498, 499

rate of, 31

reason for stressing participation in, 28

reasons for increased interest in supervisory, 13

resistance to, causes of, 493

role of, 19

role of line supervisors in, 470

selling required, 491

serves both employees and employer, 12

steps in selling program for, to top management, 206

syndicate system of

advantages, 205

defined, 204

limitations, 205

use of committee assignments in, 201

References are to Question Numbers

Development (*Continued*)
  use of counseling by staff specialists
    or outside consultants in, 194
  who does actual teaching, 477
  who needs to be sold on, 491
Director of development; *see also*
    Training, director
  acceptance of training needs by, 488
  as a staff man, 472
  assigning work of training, 471
  books for, 523
  characteristics, 259
  degrees desirable, 514
  full-time, determining need for, 474
  functions and duties of, 508, 509, 510
  getting line men to do the training,
    528
  how to secure most experience in
    shortest time, 521
  human relations training, 463
  place in organization, 240, 469, 479
  professionals as, 515, 516
  professional societies for, 522
  qualifications, 511, 512, 513
  self-improvement, 519, 520
  service rendered to others doing on-
    the-job training, 536
  services offered by state institutions,
    539
  in small companies, 518
  sources of, 518
  sources of help in setting up courses,
    538, 539, 540
  to whom he should report, 469
  work experience needed by, 517
Drive, implanting, 466

Economics program for teaching col-
    lege trainees business economics,
    332
Education, general; *see* General educa-
    tion
Employee handbooks, use in orienta-
    tion, 373
Employees
  antagonizing of other workers by,
    451
  developing good relations between
    management and, 440
  helping those who work well but
    don't get along with other em-
    ployees, 462
  training
    to achieve good relations between
      management and, 452
    to believe management's story, 438
    to improve relations between fore-

men and, 464
  to increase output of, 460
Engineers
  developing interest of, in administra-
    tion and leadership, 391
  development activities for, 417
  training
    to fill executive positions in export
      territories, 419
    for job of personnel director, 524
Evaluation
  approximate and subjective nature of,
    592
  attitude surveys used in, 594
  available number of trained under-
    studies as aid in, 599
  before and after training, 574
  executive
    counseling following, 75
    form for, 73
    precautions in, 67
    training in rating for the evaluators,
      74
    uses for, 59
  of executive development program,
    583
  of home-study courses, 581
  kinds of training most easily eval-
    uated, 576
  meaning of, 571
  methods, 573
  need for, 568
  outsiders' help in, 597
  reluctance of training men to, 593
  scientific, 575
  self-evaluation of trainees, 598
  starting point, 569
  in terms of results, 572
  of training methods, 577
  use of specific objectives in, 580
  use of trainee visitation and observa-
    tion in, 579
  written tests used in, 586
Executive appraisal
  as a line responsibility, 64
  day-to-day operation, 69
  defined, 58
  individual's knowledge of his own
    appraisal, 70
  role of personnel director, 64
Executive audit
  defined, 45
  frequency of, 50
  limitations of plans and practices, 51
  procedure, 48
  responsibility for, 46

review of organization structure prior
to, 49
values of, 47
Executive development
appraisal of, 596
areas of need for, 244, 245
"assistant to" positions, 251
assumptions underlying, 231, 232
best type, 247
busy executives and, 235
contrast of methods, 250
courses offered by universities and
professional management societies,
262
danger of frustration following, 254
danger of preparing men for advancement faster than opportunities
arise, 253
definition, 226
director of, 240, 248, 259
evaluation of, 583
example of full and complete program, 269
individualized, 271
inducing management to cooperate
in programs, 237
initial steps, 243
line executives' role in, 261
methods, 246, 252
need for, 227, 239
outsiders' aid in, 260
overcoming resistance to, 235, 445
place of, in relation to personnel and
training program, 229
responsibility for, 230
selecting trainees, 233, 234
selling programs, 237, 238
small company program, 263
starting the program, 232, 241, 242,
243
timeliness of, in rapidly expanding
companies, 228
Executive evaluations
counseling following, 75
form for, 73
precautions in, 67
training in rating for the evaluators,
74
uses for, 59
Executive inventory
defined, 56
Executives; see also Leadership; Management
amount of time spent in a training
course, 270
appraisal of, by immediate superiors,
63

building from within vs. acquiring
from outside, 272
cause of failure following promotion,
257
characteristics or traits essential to,
42
continuous training of, 255
definition of, 225
demoted, development of, 258
determining number of, needed in
the future, 55
developing interest in, in training
subordinates, 266
getting them to accept responsibility
for developing subordinates, 445
getting them to learn and try new
things, 390
group-appraisal method of evaluation
advantages, 62
defined, 61
disadvantages, 62
handling executives with no potential
for promotion, 256
junior, overcoming fears of, 582
limitations placed upon teachers and
teaching methods by, 22
line and staff as teachers, 15
merits of college graduate recruitment of, 320
orientation of, 357
precautions in evaluating, 67
reasons why formal appraisal is necessary, 60
replacement chart, 52
responsibility for improving themselves, 268
sales, where to send for training, 216
selecting for development, 233, 234
service rendered by development director to those doing on-the-job
training, 536
time that should be spent in evaluating subordinates, 65
training subordinates when no opportunity exists to advance, 465
traits found in unsuccessful, 36
Exhibition of products, orientation and,
370
Experience
conference method as pooling of, 88
as substitute for training, 8
Export territories, training engineers to
fill executive positions in, 419

Failures, handling, to get most development from experience, 267
Fellowships, Sloan, 215

References are to Question Numbers

Films
 how extensively used, 543
 use in orientation, 372, 386
Flat organizational structure, bearing on development, 213
Flyers
 definition, 544
 illustration, 545
 summary, description of, 546
 use in orientation class, 367
Foremen; see also Supervisors
 getting old-line foremen to attend classes, 315
 help in solving problems of, 281
 training to improve relations between employees and, 464
 use of in plant foremen clubs in developing supervisors, 283
Fork lift truck driver training, 396

General education
 committee
  functions, 342
  operation, 343
  size, 343
 defined, 336
 information racks, 348, 349, 350
 program
  committees, 341
  participants in, 337
  starting, 339
  subjects, 338, 340
  time for, 347
 publicizing courses in, 346
General manager, training of, 265
General Motors Institute, cooperative courses given by, 197
Grading systems, use of, 561
Group appraisal method of evaluation (executives)
 advantages, 62
 defined, 61
 disadvantages, 62
Guided experience method (development)
 defined, 76
 help needed by line executives to conduct, 81
 how steps are worked out, 78
 limitations of, 80
 persuading managers to devote time to, 83
 psychological supports for, 84
 response of groups to, 82
 steps in applying, 77
 strengths of, 79

Handbooks, employee, relation to orientation, 373
High school students, orientation of, 380
Home office training, defined, 198
Home-study courses, evaluation of, 581
Humanities, improving one's self in areas of, 345
Human relations development
 assumptions to be taught in, 437
 changing fixed attitudes, 439, 441
 changing negative attitude of training director toward, 463
 eliminating suspicions, jealousies and mistrust, 442
 how taught in industry, 435
 principles to be taught in, 437
 types of, 464
 what should be taught in, 436
Human relations, inability of supervisors to recognize value of good, 446

Improvement, rate of, 31
Incentive, implanting, 466
Incident process of case analysis
 definition, 220
 how it works, 221
 values, 222
Induction
 definition of, 351
 difference between orientation and, 351
 by supervisor, procedure for, 387
Industrial training
 differences between instruction in schools and colleges and, 27
 distinction between development and, 1
 methods most often used in, 7
Information racks
 administration of, 350
 defined, 348
 use, 349
In-plant foremen clubs, values of, 283
Inventory, executive, defined, 56

J.I.T., 199, 400
J.M.T., defined, 199
J.R.T., defined, 199
Jealousies, reduction of, 442
Job breakdown
 defined, 401
 procedure for preparing, 401
 sample, 401
Job instructor training, 199, 400
Job method training, 199

Job relations training, 199, 435
Job rotation
  advantages, 103
  complex types, 105
  cost of, 126
  definition, 101
  easiest kind, 104
  examples of, 130
  frequency of, 131
  individual needs in, 116
  lateral, 120
  length of, 115, 121
  limitations, 103, 128
  loss through, 117
  number of men involved, 122
  pay during, 125
  planning, 109, 110, 116
  preparing employees for rotation of
    their superior, 113, 114
  problems in, 128
  promotion and, 127
  purpose, 107
  reaction to, 118, 129
  reserving spots for, 112, 123
  resistance to, 119
  starting, 106, 111
  superior during, 124
  vacancies created by, 123
  where most often practiced, 102
  who is rotated, 108
Joint consultation, defined, 208
Junior boards; *see also* Multiple man-
    agement
  conditions necessary for success of,
    134
  establishment of, 135
  functions, 133, 135
  kind of prospects undertaken by, 137
  purpose, 133
  turnover among members, 138

Labor unions, role of, in orientation,
    374
Leaders
  case studies, 162, 164, 165, 169, 174
  conference
    handling men who won't talk, 98
    handling of silent groups, 98
    handling wise guys, 98
    need not be authority on subject
      being discussed, 92
    selection of, 91
    selling conference leadership train-
      ing to management, 96
    use of criticism of conference
      members' superiors by, 95
  traits found in unsuccessful, 36

Leadership; *see also* Executives; Man-
    agement
  characteristics of, 44
  defined, 33
  developing interest in, among tech-
    nical men, 391
  individual qualifications for, 41
  influence of attitudes toward leader-
    ship roles on one's behavior as a
    leader, 44
  group dynamic theory and, 43
  importance of quality of, in obtain-
    ing high productivity and em-
    ployee satisfaction, 37
  person to handle program for de-
    veloping, 475
  sales, kind of training for, that can
    be offered inside company, 218
  traits of, 35, 40
  types of, 44
  usefulness of check lists and rating
    scales in determining potential for,
    38
  use of general abilities and skills of,
    in all kinds and levels of administra-
    tration, 39
  use of role-playing in training for,
    147
  what research has revealed about
    qualities of, 34
Learners, breaking down personal de-
    fenses of, 18
Learning
  ability of adults, 26
  developing interest in, 20
  establishing desired atmosphere for,
    24
  from example of superior, 292
  psychological preliminaries, 23
  readiness for, 23
Lecture method, vs. conference method
    in training salespeople, 217
Libraries, for director of development,
    523, 540
Line and staff operating men
  getting them to do the training, 528
  problems in getting them to teach,
    531
  reasons for doing own teaching, 534
  training to teach, 530
  what they must learn before teach-
    ing, 529
Loop training, defined, 203

Magazines, trade and professional, help
    of vs. cost, 541

References are to Question Numbers

Management; *see also* Executives
  change from authoritarian outlook to
    democratic one, 439
  convincing that training is a desirable
    function of, 492
  convincing to get further training in
    techniques, 496
  cooperation in meeting training needs,
    487
  developing a good management "cli-
    mate," 449
  developing good relations between
    employees and, 440
  getting top management to support
    all development programs, 498, 499
  multiple; *see also* Junior boards
    advantages, 136
    definition, 132
    limitations, 136
    results, 139
  negative reaction to, training tech-
    niques in overcoming, 600
  recognition of importance of human
    element by, 454
  reducing employee hostility, disin-
    terest and resistance to, 450
  reluctance of, to change methods, 444
  selling conference leadership train-
    ing to, 96
  steps in selling an executive develop-
    ment program to, 206
  teaching to assign authority and re-
    sponsibility, 264
  training employees to believe story
    of, 438
  training to achieve good relations be-
    tween employees and, 452
Management trainee programs
  business economics, 332
  content, 321
  establishing, 325
  guidance needed in, 323
  keeping men satisfied while waiting
    for advancement, 329
  length of, 334
  need for, 322
  preliminary to general management
    development program, 335
  problems in, 323, 327
  programs for, 324, 326, 335
  selecting trainees, 328
  starting, 324
  teachers for, 333
  work assignments, 326
Man specification
  defined, 57

  illustration of, 57
  preparation of, 57
Maps, use in orientation, 371
Marks, for trainees, 561
Massachusetts Institute of Technology,
  Sloan Fellowships, 215
Meetings; *see also* Staff meetings
  determining time for, 550, 551
  frequency of, 552
  informing participants of schedule of,
    549
  length of, 553
  seating arrangements for, 557
"Memory joggers," defined, 212
Mistrust, eliminating, 422
Morale, training used to build, 467
Multiple management; *see also* Junior
  boards
  advantages, 136
  definition, 132
  limitations, 136
  results, 139

Negative attitudes, how training deals
  with, 455
Nepotism, effect of, 458

Observational assignment, meaning of,
  211
Old people, development programs and,
  388, 389, 441
On-the-job training
  bonus for instructor, 403
  coordination in small company, 404
  cost, 411
  difficulties faced by employees, 406
  establishing program for, 396, 397
  evaluation of instructor's work, 402
  function of training department in,
    405
  learning period, 398
  length of, 398
  need for, 394, 395, 396
  objections by supervisors to, 408
  overcoming specific obstacles or faults
    of learners, 410
  preparation needed by instructor for,
    399
  procedure, 400
  teaching long and difficult operations
    to an employee, 409
  treatment of employees during and
    after training compared, 407
  to whom it applies, 393
Open-mindedness, factor in executive
  success, 356

Organizational structure, review of, prior to an executive audit, 49

Orientation
"buddy" system of, 200
check list, 383
content of groups, 375
definition, 351
difference between induction and, 351
employee hostility and, 450
executive, 357
exhibition of products, 370
films, 372, 386
flyers for, 367
follow-up, 376
getting new employees to attend classes, 363
handbooks, 373
high school students, 380
how program for production workers differs from that for supervisors, 355
importance of participation in class, 366
informing employees of procedure for, 360
informing line supervisors about, 382
long-service employees' need for, 381
maps and, 371
number of meetings for, 364
pay for attending, 384
plant tours and, 368, 369
poor workers and, 379
preliminaries to, 359
proper time for, 362
purposes, 354
reasons for program of, 353
size of group, 365
sponsor system of, 377
starting, 358
supervisors and, 385, 387
teachers for, 361
time for meeting department head and plant manager, 378
union's part in, 374

Outline, teacher's
defined, 547
how made, 548

Participants, informing of scheduled meetings for course, 549
Pay, while attending classes, 559
Personal contacts, improving effectiveness of, 453
Personnel Director
role of, in executive appraisal, 64

training engineer for job as, 524
"Phillips 66" method of training, defined, 209
Plant tours, orientation and, 368, 369
Presidents, getting them to learn and try new things, 390
Pre-supervisory training
report on evaluation of participant in, 562
steps in establishing program, 310
Products, exhibition and story of, as part of orientation, 370
Professional societies, for the training man, 522
Promotion
cause of failure of executives following, 257
danger in stating a man's potential for, 71
handling executives with no potential for, 256

Quiz programs, role of, in development and training, 19

Rating forms, use in evaluating supervisors, 72
Rating scales, usefulness in determining potential for leadership, 38
Recruitment of college graduates with executive talent, 320
Recruits, college
competition among, 330
establishing and operating training program for, 325, 326
problem in developing, 323
problem of learning company after training, 331
reason for special training of, 322
training program for, 321
who teaches, 333
Refresher training
advisability of using, 291
defined, 196
Replacement chart
defined, 52
illustration of, 53
Replacement table
defined, 54
illustration of, 54
Research personnel
cautions to be observed in setting up development work for, 422
development activities for, 417
different from other businessmen, 420
need for training, 424

References are to Question Numbers

Research personnel (*Continued*)
problems of, as supervisors or administrators, 423
training to see problems of management, 418
what should be taught and how, 421
Role playing
advantages, 144
definition, 140
disadvantages, 145
line executives use of, in training supervisors, 152
observer methods in, 149
observer values, 148
obtaining problems for, 150
problem designing, 142
procedure in, 141
role reversal, 153
selling supervisors on, 143, 151
use in leadership training, 147
use of sound-recorder in, 146
variation in, 141

Sales conferences, training director's aid in, 223
Sales executives, where to send for training, 216
Sales leadership, kind of training that can be offered for, inside company, 218
Salespeople, conference method vs. lecture method in training, 217
Sales training
college programs, 216
starting, 219
Self-control, need for, 457
Self-development
arousing interest in, 427, 428
company development program vs., 434
company's role in, 430, 431
evidence of interest in, 426
pay for, 433
responsibility for, 432
self-initiation and, 425, 433
steps in, 429
training directors, 519
Self-initiated development, 425, 433
Self-understanding, need for, 457
Skill training: *see* Apprentice training; On-the-job training; Trade training; Vestibule training
Skits, role of, in development and training, 19
Sloan Fellowship, defined, 215
Sponsor system of orientation, 377

Staff man, role of, when executive is appraising his men, 66
Staff meetings
climate for, 180
frequency of, 185
leading, 181, 182
length of, 184
minutes of, 191
participants in, 178, 192
participation in, 182
preparation for, 181
principles for, 193
purposes of, 176, 177, 185, 190
relationship to training program, 188
rotating chairmanship of, 189
subject matter, 179
values of, 183, 186, 187
who should attend, 178
Staff Training Department, independent training activities by line supervisors and, 473
Subjects; *see also* Courses
that attract attention, 486
supervisory training, 277
Superintendents, department, support needed from management to start training program for, 499
Superiors
learning acquired from example set by, 292
selling ideas to, 392
willingness to go on record with comments on their men, 68
Supervisors; *see also* Foremen
cautions to be observed in training, 277
determining meeting times for, 550
encouraging new to think as management does, 312
failure of, 307
failure to practice what they learn, 295, 316
formal training desirable for, 276
getting them to attend classes, 316
inability to recognize good business relations, 446
knowledge needed by new, 279
line
role in training, 470
support needed for management to start training program for, 499
media for training when they are at widely separated points, 290
objections raised by, to on-the-job training, 408
orientation by, 385

overcoming resistance of, to training, 274, 314
pre-training, 408
procedure for induction by, 387
research personnel as, problems of, 423
in retail stores, training requirements of, 224
selection of, 305, 306, 307, 309
selling modern training techniques to, 535
service rendered by development director to, 536
stimulating to prepare for advancement, 296
training by
  arguments against, 533
  delegation of, 532
training conferences, frequency of, 100
typical conference program for, 87
union organizations and, 282
use of rating forms in evaluating, 72
use of supervisory clubs in developing, 283
value of monthly meetings to discuss current topics, 299
what to teach when they go into a new department, 311
where and how to start training program for, 506
Supervisory clubs
  problems of, 285
  programs of, 284
  values of, 283, 299
Supervisory development
  acceptance of, 274, 316, 317
  cases for, 286
  cases to sell, 495
  cautions in, 278
  characteristics of, 319
  composition of groups for, 298, 304, 313
  correspondence courses in, 288, 289
  courses in, 276, 277, 293, 318
  determining what training to give, 301
  failure in, 307
  long-range plans for, 293
  management trainees and, 335
  methods, 287, 300
  nurses and, 545
  objectives, 275
  reason for increased interest in, 13
  resistance to, 274, 314
  selling to top management, 317
  subjects in, 277

top management's role in, 280
types of, 294, 318
use of company time for, 297
value of repeating or reviewing programs, 291
when to start, 302, 303
who should receive, 273
Surveys, attitude, use in evaluation, 594
Suspicions, eliminating, 442, 443
Syndicate system of development
  advantages, 205
  definition, 204
  limitations, 205

Task force
  characteristics of, 207
  defined, 207
  purposes, 207
Teachers
  limitations placed upon, by executives, 22
  line and staff executives as, 15
  line or staff operating men as, what they must learn, 529
  for management trainee programs, 333
  for orientation, 361
  reason for lack of professionals as training directors, 478
  sources of, 477
Teacher's outline
  defined, 547
  how made, 548
Teacher training program
  content of, 527
  need for, 526
Teaching
  conference method, 85
  methods, limitations placed upon by executives, 22
  outcomes of nondirective technique differ from outcomes of directed teaching, 32
  self-improvement in, 520
Technical men, developing interest of, in administration and leadership, 391
Testimonials, use in evaluation of training, 578
Think, training to, 461
Trade training
  defined, 412
  sources of help in setting up program, 413
Trainees, self-evaluation, 598
Training; see also Development
  aids, 25, 538

References are to Question Numbers

Training (*Continued*)
  beginnings of, 11
  case studies that help get under-
    standing of, 495
  completion of, 29
  conference leadership
    course content, 99
    defined, 97
    selling to management, 96
    values, 97
  convincing doubters of value of, 595
  convincing executives of personal
    need of, 236
  convincing management it is a de-
    sirable function, 492
  costs, 566, 567
    defending, 565
    per worker, 563
  courses, 4
  determining makeup of conference
    group for purposes of, 89
  determining need for assigning a
    man full time to, 474
  determining which group needs it
    first, 504
  developing over-all policies and pro-
    grams, 480
  differences between industrial train-
    ing and instruction in schools and
    colleges, 27
  director, 259
    acceptance of training needs by,
      488
    as a staff man, 472
    assigning work of training, 471
    books for, 423
    degrees desirable, 514
    development of demoted execu-
      tives by, 258
    duties of, 509, 510
    functions of, 508
    getting line men to do training,
      528
    how to secure most experience in
      shortest time, 521
    place of, in organization, 240, 469,
      479
    professionals as, 515, 516
    professional societies for, 522
    qualifications, 511, 512, 513
    self-improvement, 519, 520
    services offered by state institutions,
      539
    sources of, 518
    to whom he should report, 469
    work experience needed by, 517

  distinction between development and,
    1
  evaluation of
    approximate and subjective nature
      of, 592
    attitude surveys used in, 594
    available number of trained under-
      studies as an aid in, 599
    "before and after," 574
    computing amount of formal ac-
      tivity in, 589
    guidance resulting from, 591
    meaning of, 571
    methods, 573
    need for, 568
    outsiders' help in, 597
    reluctance of training men to, 593
    scientific, 575
    self-evaluation of trainees, 598
    starting point, 569
    in terms of results, 572
    testimonials as, 578
    time for, 590
    use of specific objectives in, 580
    use of trainee visitation and ob-
      servation in, 579
    written tests in, 586, 587
  executive, best type of, 247
  experience as substitute for, 8
  formal, place to begin, 505
  home office, defined, 198
  how new men in field of training
    should start, 503
  individuals who want to be and think
    they should be boss, 456
  internal opportunities for, 542
  kinds most easily evaluated, 576
  leadership, use of role-playing in, 147
  loop, 203
  methods
    evaluation of, 577
    most often used, 7
  needs
    cooperation in meeting and dealing
      with, 487
    determining, 483, 485, 486, 489
    getting men to recognize their
      own, 490
    specific and general, 484
  newly discovered fundamentals of
    17
  organization chart, 482
  orientation; *see* Orientation
  persuading long-established firm to
    introduce, 494
  "Phillips 66" method of, 209
  plans for organizing, 468

primary educational problem in, 16
program
  conference method of organizing
    and carrying out, 86
  defined, 2
  steps in establishing, 501
purposes of, 5
reason for stressing participation in,
  28
reasons for, 6
reasons for further training of employees already trained for their
  jobs, 10
reasons for present-day interest in,
  9
refresher
  advisability of using, 291
  defined, 196
resistance to, causes of, 493
results related to dollars saved, 570
role of, 19
role of line supervisors in, 470
selling required, 491
steps in preparing and offering
  courses, 502
types of, 3
where to send sales executives for,
  216
who needs to be sold on, 491
for whom intended, 5

Training department
  cooperation in meeting training needs,
    487
  organizing, 500
  standard equipment for, 556
Training staff
  developing academic theorists into
    practical productive men, 525
  ratio between total working force
    and number of, 564

Unions, part in orientation, 374
University development courses, ad-
  vantages of, 249
Unpromotables, handling, 308

Vestibule training
  advantages, 416
  defined, 415
  disadvantages, 416
  when used, 415
Vice presidents, getting them to learn
  and try new things, 390

Work, how training persuades employees to give fair day's work for
  their pay, 459
Written tests, use in evaluation, 586,
  587

References are to Question Numbers

EARL G. PLANTY has won wide recognition in the field of personnel development for the training methods he has established at Johnson & Johnson, makers of surgical dressings. As Training Director, and now as Executive Counselor in charge of executive development, he has lectured at many universities and has spoken to dozens of groups of executives and management personnel, all over the country. He has taken part in many management and training conferences, including the chairmanship of the executive development section of the Tenth International Management Conference at Sao Paulo, Brazil.

J. THOMAS FREESTON has spent twelve years in the field of education, in business and industry. He was a civilian training specialist for the U. S. Army Air Force prior to his becoming Training Director at the Chicago plant of Johnson & Johnson. From this position he moved to New Brunswick, as Assistant Training Director at the main Johnson & Johnson plant. He is now Personnel Director for Ethicon, Inc., and lectures on management at the Institute of Management and Labor Relations at Rutgers University.